THE RIGHTS INTERNATIONAL COMPANION TO CRIMINAL LAW & PROCEDURE

THE RIGHTS INTERNATIONAL COMPANION TO CRIMINAL LAW & PROCEDURE

An International Human Rights and Humanitarian Law Supplement

Francisco Forrest Martin
President
Rights International,
The Center for International Human Rights Law, Inc.

Richard J. Wilson
Professor and Director
International Human Rights Law Clinic
Washington College of Law
American University

Published under the auspices of

Rights International
THE CENTER FOR INTERNATIONAL HUMAN RIGHTS LAW INC

KLUWER LAW INTERNATIONAL
The Hague • London • Boston

Published by Kluwer Law International,
P.O. Box 85889, 2508 CN The Hague, The Netherlands.

Sold and distributed in the U.S.A. and Canada
by Kluwer Law International,
675 Massachusetts Avenue, Cambridge, MA 02139, U.S.A.

In all other countries, sold and distributed
by Kluwer Law International,
P.O. Box 85889, 2508 CN The Hague, The Netherlands.

ISBN 9041193324

THE RIGHTS INTERNATIONAL COMPANION SERIES

This book is part of the RIGHTS INTERNATIONAL COMPANION SERIES ON CONSTITUTIONAL LAW, PROPERTY, AND CRIMINAL LAW & PROCEDURE. This Companion is designed for use as an international human rights and humanitarian law supplement to criminal law and criminal procedure casebooks. To assist the professor, cross references to other leading  criminal law and criminal procedure casebooks will be posted on the Rights International website.

The RIGHTS INTERNATIONAL COMPANION SERIES is published under the auspices of Rights International, The Center for International Human Rights Law, Inc. Rights International is a not-for-profit organization devoted to protecting and furthering the rights recognized in the Universal Bill of Human Rights and other human rights instruments. It seeks to accomplish this mission in two ways.

First, Rights International provides legal assistance to victims of human rights violations before international human rights tribunals, including those established by the UN, the Council of Europe, the Organization of African Unity, and the Organization of American States.

Second, Rights International trains lawyers and law students in international human rights law and practice. As part of its training program, Rights International has published INTERNATIONAL HUMAN RIGHTS LAW & PRACTICE: CASES, TREATIES AND MATERIALS (The Hague: Kluwer Law International, 1997) and this COMPANION SERIES.

If you are interested in learning more about Rights International or working on one of our international cases, please visit our website for information about the following programs:

Cooperating Attorney/Firm Program
Frank C. Newman Internship Program
Law School Consortium Program

www.rightsinternational.org

We dedicate this book to . . .

Paul Chevigny, Geronimo ji Jaga Pratt & Stuart Hanlon, Stanley & Jane Teitler

We also wish to acknowledge and thank the following persons and institutions . . .

Stephen J. Schnably   Frederic Kirgis
Jonathan Simon   Robert Levy
Ronald Slye   Catherine Albisa
Edward Koren   Ana Vallejo
Christine Gould   John Berger
Anne Heindel   Timothy Schulz

University of Miami School of Law Library

Note regarding editing

To facilitate reading, some footnotes and citations have been removed from or placed within brackets in the case excerpts. The editors also have changed citation styles within case excerpts from the European Court of Human Rights for purposes of consistency, clarity, and brevity. Footnote numbering contained in this book may not reflect the original numbering in excerpts. Finally, the editors' comments generally are enclosed in brackets.

TABLE OF CONTENTS

PART ONE: AN OVERVIEW OF INTERNATIONAL CRIMINAL LAW
AND
ITS ENFORCEMENT MECHANISMS

PART TWO: PRINCIPLES OF STATE LIABILITY
AND INDIVIDUAL CULPABILITY

PART FIVE: PUNISHMENT

PART ONE: AN OVERVIEW OF INTERNATIONAL CRIMINAL LAW AND ITS ENFORCEMENT MECHANISMS

Introduction

The question is "Why do lawyers and law students need to know international human rights and humanitarian law for understanding and practicing criminal law?" There are several answers to this question. First, international law is constitutional law in many countries. International human rights law has provided the initial and continuing visions of different constitutions -- national and state. Some countries have adopted wholesale international human rights protections that address criminal law.[1]

In the case of the United States, international law is part of the "supreme Law of the Land." The U.S. Constitution states that "all Treaties made, or which shall be made, under the Authority of the United States, shall be the supreme Law of the Land."[2] The U.S. Constitution also states that Congress "shall have Power . . . To define and Punish Piracies and Felonies committed on the high Seas, and Offences against the Law of Nations."[3]

Accordingly, international law is binding on U.S. courts. International law was part of the common law received from England.[4] Much of early U.S. constitutional law clearly was informed by international law.[5] Indeed, at its birth the U.S. had not concluded any treaties, and, therefore, international law was wholly "customary international law" for the U.S. (We will return to this very important source of international law below.) Furthermore, international law governs relations between states except as modified by the U.S. Constitution.[6]

---

[1] 48 REVUE INTERNATIONALE DE DROIT PENAL nos. 3 & 4, at 219 (1977) (18 nations incorporating Universal Declaration of Human Rights into constitutions).

[2] U.S. CONST. art. VI, § 2.

[3] U.S. CONST. art. I, § 8.

[4] *Talbot v. Jansen*, 3 U.S. (3 Dall.) 133, 161 (1795) (Iredell, J.); *see generally* Sprout, *Theories as to the Applicability of International Law in the Federal Courts of the United States*, 26 AM. J. INT'L L. 280 (1932); Louis Henkin, *International Law as the Law of the United States*, 88 MICH. L. REV. 155 (1984); Louis Henkin, *The Chinese Exclusion Case and Its Progeny*, 100 HARV. L. REV. 853 (1987).

[5] On the flip side, constitutional law has served to provide some of the initial and continuing visions of international human rights law. One of the earliest recognitions of individual rights appeared in the U.S. Constitution -- specifically in the Bill of Rights. Louis Henkin, THE AGE OF RIGHTS 1 (1990).

[6] *See, e.g., Kansas v. Colorado*, 185 U.S. 125 (1901) (using international law to determine states' water rights); *Sinclair Pipe Line Co. v. State Com'n of Revenue and Tax*, 184 Kan. 713, 718, 339 P.2d 341, 346 (1959) (international law governed tax status of Delaware corporation doing business in Kansas); *State v. Miller*, 157 Ariz. 129, 755 P.2d 434 (App. 1988) (applying international law to determine jurisdiction over extraterritorial acts in Colorado and Nevada).

Another reason why learning international criminal law is important is that such an approach allows a deeper understanding of issues frequently coming before domestic courts. International law jurists have approached the same substantive issues differently from domestic courts interpreting their country's criminal law. International tribunals have reached different outcomes in similar cases before domestic courts. For example, U.S. law is less protective of defendants' rights than international law in the areas governing the right to presumption of innocence[7] and the death penalty.[8] On the other hand, there also is some U.S. law that is more protective. The U.S. law governing arrest[9] and prosecutorial discretion[10] is generally more protective of a suspect's rights than international law. Given these differences, students and lawyers need to know how and when international criminal law is binding on domestic courts. Familiarity with international criminal law allows the practitioner to provide a different perspective to a court and guidance as to an appropriate outcome when domestic criminal law is silent or ambiguous on an issue.

Finally, changing world conditions have produced a globalization of legal accountability. The world is getting smaller. National boundaries and sovereignty are eroding. The reasons for these changes include the fall of the Soviet Union, the growing power and influence of intergovernmental organizations (*e.g.,* the UN, World Bank) and non-state actors (*e.g.,* corporations, non-governmental charitable organizations, private individuals), and the telecommunications revolution. The end of the Cold War enabled intergovernmental organizations (NGOs) to grow in power by filling the power vacuum left by the demise of the Soviet Union. Intergovernmental organizations were able to more effectively meet their mandates in human rights protection, conflict resolution, and development. Non-governmental organizations and private individuals also acquired power and influence on the international level. The internet has connected NGOs and individuals around the world and made national borders almost irrelevant for the transmission of information. These developments have produced a globalization of legal accountability.

---

[7] Compare *Allenet de Ribemont v. France*, 308 Eur. Ct. H.R. (ser. A) (1995), with U.S. prosecutorial immunity for false statements made to the press.

[8] Compare *Pinkerton and Roach v. United States*, Resolution No. 3/87, Case No. 9647, Inter-Am. Cm. H.R., ANNUAL REPORT OF THE INTER-AMERICAN COMMISSION ON HUMAN RIGHTS 1986-1987, OEA/Ser.L/V/II/71, doc. 9 rev. 1, 147 (1987), with *Stanford v. Kentucky*, 492 U.S. 361 (1989), addressing the execution of persons who committed a capital offense under the age of 18.

[9] Compare *Murray v. United Kingdom*, 300-A Eur. Ct. H.R. (ser. A) (1994), with *Spinelli v. United States*, 393 U.S. 410 (1969), addressing whether "reasonable suspicion" versus "probable cause" is necessary for arrest.

[10] Compare the private person's international right to compel state authorities to investigate, prosecute, and punish perpetrators of gross human rights violations with the customary exclusive power of state prosecutors under US federal and state law. *See Velásquez Rodríquez v. Honduras*, Inter-Am. Ct. H.R., Judgment of 29 July 1988, Ser. C, No. 4; *X. and Y. v. The Netherlands*, 91 Eur. Ct. H.R. (ser. A) (1985).

Lawyers practicing domestic criminal law cannot afford to be unfamiliar with international criminal law. Governments increasingly are seeking the extradition of persons who allegedly have committed international crimes. Spain's attempt to extradite Gen. Augusto Pinochet has put numerous other former dictators on notice that immunity for their crimes is questionable. Domestic courts are using international law to prosecute persons committing international crimes.[11] International law is no longer "soft" law. International criminal tribunals are effecting arrests, convicting, and imprisoning numerous persons. National governments almost always comply with the orders of other international courts and tribunals. Only in extremely rare cases does a government either delay or refuse to obey.[12]

Because of the effectiveness of these international courts, there has been a litigation explosion over the last ten years in turn resulting in the creation of a considerable corpus of international criminal law, as seen in the following chapters. Although the following caselaw may be interpreting treaties to which a particular country may not be a party, these treaties and caselaw create customary international law and *jus cogens* which are binding on *all* countries (which will be discussed below). The result is the globalization of legal accountability.

We now turn to the sources and principles of international law.

---

[11] For example, Klaus Barbie (the Gestapo chief in Vichy France), Paul Touvier (the intelligence chief of a Vichy Government-sponsored militia), and Erich Priebke (an officer in Italy) have been prosecuted by the French and Italian governments, respectively.

[12] Among the thousands of international court decisions, only a handful of court orders have not been complied with by governments. One infamous example is the US' failure to comply with the International Court of Justice's decision in *Case Concerning Military and Paramilitary Activities In and Against Nicaragua (Nicaragua v. US)*, [1984] I.C.J. Rep. 392. In the criminal law area, some of the new governments in the former Yugoslavia initially failed to turn over war crimes suspects to the International Criminal Tribunal.

Chapter 1.   The Sources and Principles of International Law

There are three important sources of international law: treaties, customary international law, and *jus cogens*.[1] The first source, treaties, sometimes are called "conventions," "covenants," "pacts," or "protocols." A treaty is an "international agreement concluded between States in written form and governed by international law."[2] Under U.S. constitutional law, treaties are international agreements that have received the "advice and consent" of two-thirds of the Senate and that have been ratified by the President.[3] Some of the leading international human rights treaties dealing with criminal law and procedure include the International Covenant on Civil and Political Rights[4] (ICCPR), the American Convention on Human Rights[5] (ACHR), the European Convention on Human Rights[6] (ECHR), and the African Charter on Human and Peoples' Rights[7] (Banjul Charter). Some of the leading international humanitarian treaties are the Hague and Geneva Conventions.

When one thinks of international law, s/he usually thinks of treaties first -- not caselaw. Historically, nation-states organized the relations among themselves through agreements, *i.e.*, treaties, in the absence of supernational authoritative institutions, such as a United Nations or an International Court of Justice, although certainly war, commerce restrictions, and religio-moral[8] imperatives also served as supernational restraints on behavior perceived by nation-states as unacceptable. Projects aimed at rationalizing treaties produced both naturalist and positivist theories. Grotius' famous naturalist maxim, "*pacta sunt servanda*" ("promises given must be kept"), clearly focussed on agreements to do something -- *i.e.*, treaties. Positivism's focus on the nation-state's supremacy placed emphasis on treaties as evidence of the nation-state's will. Finally, those scholars who provided the initial rationalization of international law were trained in civil law, and civil law focuses on statutory-type instruments -- such as treaties -- not caselaw. Therefore, treaties historically have had primacy in the conceptualization and development of international law.

---

[1] Other sources are "the general principles of law recognized by civilized countries" and "judicial decisions and the teachings of the most highly qualified publicists of the various nations, as subsidiary means for the determination of rules of law." Art. 38 (b) and (c), Statute of the International Court of Justice, 26 June 1945, 59 Stat. 1005, T.S. 993.

[2] Art. 2.1(a), Vienna Convention on the Law of Treaties, adopted 23 May 1969 (entered into force 27 January 1980), U.N. Doc. A/CONF. 39/27 (1969), 63 A.J.I.L. 875 (1969), 8 I.L.M. 679 (1969).

[3] U.S. CONST. art. II, § 2.

[4] G.A. Res. 2200A (XXI), U.N. Doc. A/6316 (1966), adopted 16 December 1966 (entered into force 23 March 1976).

[5] Signed 22 November 1969 (entered into force 17 July 1978), OEA/Ser.L/V/II, doc. 21, rev. 6 (1979).

[6] Signed 4 November 1950 (entered into force 3 February 1953), 213 U.N.T.S. 221.

[7] Adopted 27 June 1981(entered into force 21 October 1986), O.A.U. Doc. CAB/LEG/67/3 Rev. 5.

[8] *See, e.g.*, St. Augustine, CITY OF GOD (discussing concept of just war).

The second source of international law is customary international law. It consists of two elements: (i) *opinio juris* (*i.e.*, a sense of legal obligation) and (ii) a general practice. Customary international law can supersede a treaty. However, if a state has been a persistent objector to a customary international law, the state is considered to be exempt from an obligation to observe this law.[9] This is known as the "persistent objector rule."

Customary international law can be established in a number of ways. For example, a global or multilateral treaty with a high number of state parties,[10] or a UN General Assembly resolution can reflect customary international law. The International Covenant on Civil and Political Rights is an example of both a global and widely accepted multilateral treaty containing customary international law rights. The Universal Declaration of Human Rights is an example of a UN General Assembly resolution that has the status of customary international law. Customary international law can be reflected in different treaties employing similar language concerning rights or duties. For example, the right to humane treatment is recognized as customary international law.[11] This right is guaranteed in nearly identical language in all the major multilateral human rights treaties.[12] Also, customary international law can be reflected in the uniformity of domestic law.

Most importantly, customary international law can be reflected in the decisions of international tribunals interpreting widely accepted treaties or different treaties using similar language.[13] When the Statute of the International Court of Justice was adopted in 1945, its drafters probably did not foresee the future enormous growth of international caselaw -- especially those cases addressing human rights. Over the last twenty years, both global and regional human rights tribunals have interpreted a wide variety of domestic and international legal sources, thereby creating an enormous body of international law. And, because international judges are interpreting similar -- if not nearly identical -- language from different human rights and humanitarian treaties, this caselaw is serving to establish a highly authoritative source of customary international human rights and humanitarian law. Indeed, it is likely that this international caselaw may be the clearest expression of customary international law because it is law that is being applied *in concreto*, law that is taking into account competing arguments by parties, law that is addressing diverse socio-political issues, and law that is being articulated by the

---

[9] *See* I. BROWNLIE, PRINCIPLES OF PUBLIC INTERNATIONAL LAW 10 (4th ed. 1990) (discussing persistent objector rule).

[10] RESTATEMENT (THIRD) OF FOREIGN RELATIONS LAW OF THE UNITED STATES (hereafter, Restatement) § 102(3) (1987).

[11] Restatement § 702(d).

[12] *See* Art. 7, ICCPR ("No one shall be subjected to torture or to cruel, inhuman or degrading treatment or punishment."); Art. 5, ACHR ("No one shall be subjected to torture or to cruel, inhuman, or degrading punishment or treatment."); Art. 3, ECHR ("No one shal be subjected to torture or to inhuman or degrading treatment or punishment."); Art. 5, ACHPR ("All forms of exploitation and degradation of man particularly . . . torture, cruel, inhuman or degrading punishment and treatment shall be prohibited.").

[13] Restatement § 103(2).

world's leading jurists. One may say that much of this customary international law is not merely *inter*national but *super*national because this body law transcends particular relations between states and binds all states.

The RESTATEMENT (THIRD) OF FOREIGN RELATIONS LAW OF THE UNITED STATES lists specific acts that violate customary international law. Among these acts are international crimes such as genocide, slavery, and causing the disappearance of individuals.[14] But most importantly, what clearly has emerged with the growth of international human rights caselaw is also an enormous growth of specific customary international law norms.

The third source of international law is the highest source of international law. It is called *jus cogens* (peremptory norms).[15] *Jus cogens* is defined as law that prohibits behavior that "shocks the conscience of humankind;" one can never justify behavior contrary to these peremptory norms. Therefore, *jus cogens* is non-derogable law, even during periods of war when other rights can be suspended. Most importantly, *jus cogens* trumps all treaty law.[16] Examples of *jus cogens* include the prohibition of aggressive war, slavery, and crimes against humanity.[17] Note that this highest source of international law addresses criminal acts.

Finally, it is important to note that as it is to be expected with the development of international caselaw, international judges have created tests and standards in order to fill the logical lacunae of legal sources and provide coherence to international law. These judicially-created tests and standards bear a striking resemblance to those created by U.S. courts addressing constitutional challenges of state laws and practices. This is not too

---

[14] Restatement § 702.

[15] Some commentators have argued that *jus cogens* is part of customary international law. *See, e.g.*, Restatement § 102, Reporters' n. 6 (*jus cogens* "is now widely accepted . . . as a principle of customary law (albeit of higher status)"); I. BROWNLIE, PRINCIPLES OF PUBLIC INTERNATIONAL LAW 513 (3d ed. 1979) (*jus cogens* as rules of customary law). However, given the role of the persistent objector rule for determining the binding character of customary international law on particular states, it is difficult to see how *jus cogens* is part of customary international law unless an exception to the rule is made in the case of *jus cogens*. Furthermore, the Inter-American Commission on Human Rights has noted that a *jus cogens* norm may be recognized even though it is not customary international law. *See Pinkerton and Roach v. United States*, Resolution No. 3/87, Case No. 9647, Inter-Am. Cm. H.R., ANNUAL REPORT OF THE INTER-AMERICAN COMMISSION ON HUMAN RIGHTS 1986-1987, OEA/Ser.L/V/II/71, doc. 9 rev. 1, 147 (1987) at § § 56, 60. A reasonable solution may be that a particular *jus cogens* norm can be customary international law if a sufficient number of states have adopted it as a practice. On the other hand, a *jus cogens* norm may not be part of customary international law because an insufficient number of states have adopted it in practice. But, most importantly, what distinguishes a *jus cogens* norm is that it is non-derogable regardless of its status as being part of customary international law.

[16] Restatement § 702 comment n.

[17] Ian Brownlie, PRINCIPLES OF PUBLIC INTERNATIONAL LAW 513 (1979).

surprising given the fact that constitutional law is similar to international human rights law in two ways: constitutional law often deals with individual rights, and constitutional law trumps state law like international law can trump domestic law. Furthermore, U.S. courts have been dealing with human rights issues long before international human rights tribunals were even established.

A very important example of such judicially-created tests and standards are governmental deference tests. The European Court of Human Rights refers to them as "margin of appreciation" tests. Basically, international judges will articulate how much deference should be given to a state in its reasons for limiting a particular right. For example, in European Court of Human Rights decisions, if very little deference is given, the state is said to "enjoy a narrow margin of appreciation," analogous to using the U.S. constitutional "strict scrutiny test." If the state-party enjoys considerable deference, the state-party has a "wide margin of appreciation." Sometimes no deference is allowed because the treaty does not allow any derogation or limitation of the right. These absolute rights usually are peremptory norms, discussed above, and give rise to what U.S. courts would call *per se* violations of the U.S. Constitution.

Chapter 2. How International Human Rights, Humanitarian, and Criminal Law Is Binding on U.S. and Other Domestic Courts.

International law is binding on domestic courts if it has been incorporated into domestic law. There are a number of ways that international law can be incorporated. These methods include treaties, customary international law, domestic legislation, and domestic tribunal decisions.

Treaties

International law can be incorporated through ratified treaties. Some countries[1] -- including the U.S.[2] -- distinguish between those treaties that are "self-executing" and those

---

[1] These countries include Argentina, Austria, Belgium, Cyprus, Egypt, France, Greece, Italy, Japan, Luxembourg, Malta, Mexico, the Netherlands, Spain, Switzerland, and Turkey. Richard Lillich, *Invoking International Human Rights Law in Domestic Courts*, 54 CINN. L. REV. 367, 373 n. 31 (1987).

[2] In the U.S., many commentators have taken issue with the doctrine of self-execution. The distinction between self-executing and non-self-executing treaties was first drawn by the Supreme Court in *Foster v. Neilson*, 27 U.S. (2 Pet.) 253 (1829). At that time, the intent of the parties to the treaty, as indicated by the language of the treaty, controlled the treaty's designation as self-executing or non-self-executing. More recently, the Senate has declared a number of multilateral human rights treaties to be non-self-executing, appearing to focus on the intent of the U.S. or the Senate itself, not all the parties to the treaty. L. HENKIN, ET AL., INTERNATIONAL LAW, CASES AND MATERIALS 218-19 (3rd ed. 1993). Since the U.S. Constitution simply states that all treaties are part of the "supreme law of the land," the designation of self- or non-self-executing is a judicially-created distinction. Provisions of the U.S. Constitution, such as the due process guarantee in the 14th Amendment, are often drafted in general terms. Nevertheless, these provisions are enforced in the courts without enabling legislation. Congress is allowed to enforce constitutional provisions through legislation (such as 42 U.S.C. § 1983), but this measure is not necessary to render the U.S. Constitution effective. The Framers may have had a similar procedure in mind for treaties, in which the rights and duties assigned in the treaty would be enforced by the courts, and Congress would have the power to enact further legislation to guide enforcement.

The constitutional authority of the Senate to make a declaration limiting the ability of the federal courts to enforce treaty rights has been challenged by leading scholars. Since the U.S. Constitution gave treaty making power to the President with the Senate, to the exclusion of the House or Congress, allowing a Congressional or Senate resolution to render a treaty inapplicable domestically contradicts the provisions of the Constitution. Commentators question whether this practice "is contrary to both the letter and spirit of the Constitution, and to the distribution of power between the Senate and the House intended by the Framers." *Id.* at 219; Lori Fisler Damrosch, *The Role of the United States*

(continued...)

that are "non-self-executing." Self-executing treaties are those that are intended to be judicially enforceable domestic law without implementing legislation. Hence, self-executing treaties are binding on domestic courts. An example of a self-executing treaty in U.S. law is the Vienna Convention on Consular Relations.[3] An example of a non-self-executing treaty under U.S. law is the Convention Relating to the Status of Refugees. However, most countries do not distinguish between self-executing and non-self-executing treaties. The important issue is whether the country considers that the treaty supersedes domestic law in order that one knows which is a controlling legal authority.

In the U.S., the U.S. Constitution trumps treaty obligations.[4] Furthermore, U.S. federal statutes will trump treaty obligations if the statute was enacted after the ratification of the treaty. This is known as the "last-in-time rule."[5] It is only when Congress explicitly

---

[2](...continued)
Senate Concerning "Self-Executing" and "Non-Self-Executing" Treaties, 67 Chi.-Kent. L. Rev. 515, 526 (1991) ("[a] Senate declaration purporting to negate the legal effect of otherwise self-executing treaty provisions is constitutionally questionable as a derogation from the ordinary application of Article VI of the Constitution . . . ."); Jordan J. Paust, *Self-Executing Treaties,* 82 Am. J. Int'l L. 760, 775 & 766 n.41 (1988) ("[i]t is the judiciary, not Congress, that has been granted the power . . . under Article III of the Constitution to apply treaty law in cases or controversies otherwise properly before the courts"; and citing *Owings v. Norwood's Lessee,* 9 U.S. (5 Cranch) at 348-349 (1809) for the declaration that the "reason for inserting that clause [Art. III, 2, cl. 1]...was, that all persons who have real claims under a treaty should have their causes decided.").

[3] Adopted 24 April 1963 (entered into force 19 March 1967), 21 U.S.T. 77, T.I.A.S No. 6820, 596 U.N.T.S. 261.

[4] *Reid v. Covert,* 354 U.S. 16-17 (1957).

[5] It should be noted that the application of the last-in-time rule to treaties has been criticized for a number of reasons. Firstly, the aetiology of the last-in-time rule undermines the rule's validity. The U.S. Supreme Court adopted the rule in the nineteenth century in a series of cases upholding anti-immigrant and racist federal statutes. *See, e.g., Stephens v. Cherokee,* 174 U.S. 445 (1899) (breaking treaty with Cherokee nation by taking land); *Thomas v. Gay,* 169 U.S. 264 (1898) (breaking treaty with Cherokee nation by denying self-government); *The Chinese Exclusion Case,* 130 U.S. 581 (1889) (breaking treaty with China by excluding Chinese immigrants); *Whitney v. Robinson,* 124 U.S. 190 (1888); *Head-Money Cases,* 112 U.S. 580 (1884) (breaking friendship treaties by charging head tax on all aliens entering US); *Cherokee Tobacco,* 78 U.S. (11 Wall.) 616 (1871) (breaking treaty with Cherokee nation by charging tax on tobacco); *see also* Howard Tolley, *The Domestic Applicability of International Treaties in the United States,* 17 REV. JUR. U.I.P.R 403 (1983) (criticizing development of rule).

Secondly, the rule was developed in the nineteenth century when international treaty law consisted mostly of bilateral treaties. The multilateral treaty was not the customary
(continued...)

and clearly states in the statute or its legislative history that it intends to override a prior treaty that the last-in-time rule can apply.[6] Although a treaty can trump a federal statute if the treaty was ratified after the enactment of the federal statute, the U.S. Supreme Court has held that whenever possible a statute and a treaty should be interpreted to give meaning to both.[7]

However, it is arguable whether the last-in-time rule can apply to multilateral human rights/humanitarian treaties. Because of their status both as being multilateral and addressing fundamental human rights, such treaties have a greater authority than other non-human rights/humanitarian or bilateral treaties.[8] If treaties have the same legal status as federal statutes, then the rule that multilateral human rights/humanitarian treaties are considered superior to non-human rights/humanitarian or non-bilateral treaties suggests that multilateral human rights/humanitarian treaties are superior to federal statutes.

---

[5](...continued)
international agreement. With a bilateral treaty, the parties clearly establish a date when their obligations come into force. Under the last-in-time rule, Congress subsequently can enact legislation to supercede these treaty obligations because there is a clear date. This is not the case with multilateral human rights treaties. Multilateral human rights treaties almost always have clauses allowing interstate complaints. *E.g.*, Art. 41, ICCPR; Art. 45, ACHR; Art. 25, ECHR; Art. 47, ACHPR. As different states adopt a multilateral treaty over time, new rights and obligations are created for the U.S. with those new state-parties. (It should be noted that the U.S. ratified Article 41, ICCPR, that addresses interstate complaints without reservations.) Therefore, for the purposes of establishing a date by which the last-in-time rule can operate in regard to treaties, multilateral human rights treaties make the last-in-time rule increasingly less applicable.

[6] *United States v. Dion*, 476 U.S. 734 (1986).

[7] *Asakura v. City of Seattle*, 265 U.S. 332, 342 (1924).

[8] A reason for this argument is that multilateral human rights treaties recognize rights that transcend *inter*-national relations. These rights are *super*-national. Multilateral human rights treaties do not primarily address *inter*-national relations. These treaties primarily address the rights of individuals – not nation-states. *Soering v. United Kingdom*, 161 Eur. Ct. H.R. (ser. A) (1989) (European Convention on Human Rights supercedes U.K.-U.S. Extradition Agreement of 1972); *Aloeboetoe et al. v. Suriname*, Inter-Am. Ct. H.R., Judgment of 10 September 1993, Inter-Am. Ct. H.R. (Ser. C) No. 15 (1994) (holding Dutch-Surinamese slavery treaty violative of *jus cogens*); *see also* Dugard & Van den Wyngaert, *Reconciling Extradition with Human Rights*, 92 AM. J. INT'L. L. 187, 194-95 (1998) (supremacy of human rights norms stems from recognition in multilateral treaties or from notions of fundamental rights or *jus cogens*).

Finally, it is important to note that treaties trump state law in the U.S.[9] (This includes both self-executing and non-self-executing treaties.[10]) Consequently, the last-in-time rule does not apply to state law.

Customary International Law

The second way that international law can be incorporated into domestic law is through customary international law. For example, the U.S. Supreme Court in *The Paquete Habana*, declared that international law, including customary international law, "is part of our law, and must be ascertained and administered by the courts of justice . . . ." 175 U.S. 677, 700 (1900). Also, as noted above, customary international law is also part of the "supreme Law of the Land."[11] Interestingly enough, the U.S. Supreme Court has yet to declare that the U.S. Constitution trumps customary international law.[12]

---

[9] *Asakura v. Seattle*, 265 U.S. 332 (1924); Restatement § 115 comment e.

[10] *Gordon v. Kerr*, 10 F. Cas. 801, 802 (C.C.D. Pa. 1806) (No. 5,611) (apparently non-self-executing treaty "is supreme" over state constitution); 6 Op. Att'y Gen. 291, 293 (1854) (opining all treaties are supreme law over state law, even treaties requiring "enactment of a statute to regulate the details"); Restatement § 115 comment e (any treaty -- including non-self-executing one -- "may sometimes be held to be federal policy superseding State law or policy"). So, for example, if the U.S. Senate passes a resolution stating that a treaty is non-self-executing (as it did with the ICCPR), it probably has overreached its authority because although the Senate may have the power to decide the proper role of federal courts, it does not have such authority over state courts. States retain "a residuary and inviolable sovereignty."*Printz v. United States*, 521 U.S. 898, 934 (1997) (quoting THE FEDERALIST NO. 39, at 245 (J. Madison)). This residuary sovereignty probably includes a state court's general jurisdiction.

[11] Restatement § 111 comment d.

[12] As one commentator has observed,

Arguably, the fact that treaties are subject to constitutional limitations does not conclude the issue with respect to customary law. Customary law is general law binding on all nations, and no country should be able to derogate from it because of that country's particular constitutional dispositions. The law of nations antedated the Constitution, and the framers evinced no disposition to subordinate that law to the new Constitution. Nevertheless, it is unlikely that the Court would subordinate the Constitution to the law of nations and give effect to a principle of international law without regard to constitutional restraints.

Louis Henkin, *The Constitution and United States Sovereignty: A Century of Chinese Exclusion and Its Progeny*, 100 HARV. L. REV. 853, 869-70 (1987) (footnotes omitted).

11

As to U.S. federal statutes, the U.S. Supreme Court has not yet ruled on whether the customary international law can trump federal statutes. Presently, there is a conflict among U.S. Circuit Courts of Appeal on this issue.[13] In regard to the law of the sea, President Reagan effectively accepted that customary international law modified earlier treaties as well as federal statutes.[14]

The argument that customary international law cannot trump statutes is based on dictum in *The Paquete Habana*:

> International law is part of our law, and must be ascertained and administered by the courts of justice of appropriate jurisdiction, as often as questions of right depending upon it are duly presented for their determination. For this purpose, *where there is no treaty, and no controlling executive or legislative act or judicial decision, resort must be had to the customs and usages of civilized nations...*

175 U.S. 677, 700 (emphasis provided). However, the dictum's language does not exclude the possibility of customary international law being used in conjunction with treaties, statutes, or executive acts. The dictum's language also does not exclude the possibility of customary international law trumping treaties, statutes, or executive acts. Therefore, the conclusion that customary international law cannot trump federal statutes is overreaching.

Furthermore, this conclusion is inconsistent with the international law doctrine that customary international law trumps treaties.[15] It also mis-characterizes customary

---

[13] *United States v. Javino*, 960 F. 2d 1137 (2d Cir.) (customary international law may override federal statute) (dictum), *cert. denied*, 113 S.Ct. 447 (1992); *Rodriquez-Fernandez v. Wilkinson*, 654 F.2d 1382 (10th Cir. 1981) (noting fundamental international law principle against arbitrary detention), *aff'g*, 505 F.Supp. 878 (D.Kan. 1980) (indefinite detention of excludable alien violative of customary international law and trumps executive order); *contra Galo-Garcia v. Immigration & Naturalization Serv.*, 86 F.3d 916 (9th Cir. 1996) (where there is extensive legislative scheme, customary international law is inapplicable and cannot confer jurisdiction); *Committee of United States Citizens in Nicaragua v. Reagan*, 859 F. 2d 929 (D.C.Cir. 1988) (federal statute overrides customary international law); *United States v. Merkt*, 794 F.2d 950, 964 n. 16 (5th Cir. 1986) (Congress not bound by "custom" of international law), *cert. denied*, 480 U.S. 946 (1987); *Garcia-Mir v. Meese,* 788 F.2d 1446 (11th Cir) (executive and legislative acts override customary international law), *cert. denied* 479 U.S. 889 (1986); *United States v. Howard-Arias*, 679 F.2d 363 (4th Cir.) (federal statute overrides customary international law), *cert. denied*, 459 U.S. 874 (1982).

[14] L. HENKIN ET AL., INTERNATIONAL LAW: CASES AND MATERIALS 1234 (3d ed. 1993); Restatement § 115 comment d.

[15] Restatement § 115 comment d.

international law as common law, which can be superceded by statute.[16] And finally, this conclusion is inconsistent with the U.S. president's foreign affairs authority and domestic duty to enforce international law as U.S. law.[17]

Assuming that customary international law can trump U.S. federal statutes, the last-in-time rule, however, is problematic for customary international law. There are a number of reasons for this. First, the rule conflicts with the persistent objector rule.[18] Secondly,

---

[16] Louis Henkin, *The Constitution and United States Sovereignty: A Century of Chinese Exclusion and Its Progeny*, 100 HARV. L. REV. 853 (1987).

[17] To interpret the dictum in *The Paquete Habana* to mean that *any* executive act can supercede customary international law probably should be considered unconstitutional. Only acts of the President, and *only* acts taken in the role of Commander-in-Chief concerning foreign affairs, can be Executive acts controlling over international law. L. HENKIN, FOREIGN AFFAIRS AND THE UNITED STATES CONSTITUTION 245 (2nd ed. 1996) (hereinafter Henkin, Foreign Affairs). Presidential authority must not extend to violations of customary law that recognize rights for individuals, such as human rights. Louis Henkin, *International Law as Law in the United States*, 82 MICH. L. REV. 1555 n. 44 (1984). These laws "do not directly implicate the State's foreign relations," and thus fall outside the President's authority. *Id.*

However, a U.S. Court of Appeals has allowed any executive act to supercede customary international law with horrible results. In *Garcia-Mir*, 788 F.2d 1446 (11th Cir. 1986), *cert. denied*, 479 U.S. 889 (1986), a U.S. Court of Appeals for the Eleventh Circuit held that the US Attorney General could order the indefinite detention of Cuban nationals who could not be deported back to Cuba or another country -- even though the court recognized that this constituted arbitrary detention in violation of customary international law. The court's decision has been severely criticized by leading scholars. *See, e.g.,* Jordan J. Paust, *Customary International Law in the United States*, 40 GERMAN Y.B. INT'L L. 78, 98 (1998); Henkin, Foreign Affairs at 244-45; Frederic Kirgis, *Federal Statutes, Executive Orders and "Self-Executing Custom,"* 81 AM. J. INT'L L. 371 (1987).

[18] The last-in-time rule directly conflicts with the persistent objector rule. Whereas the persistent objector rule is responsive to the dynamics of emerging customary international law, the last-in-time rule is not. By allowing a non-persistent objector to object after the customary international law norm has emerged, the last-in-time rule offends and undermines the authority of customary international law because the rule can allow *any* nation to enact legislation at *any* time to thwart *any* of its obligations that up to the date of the superceding legislation had been a legal obligation under customary international law. The last-in-time rule can arbitrarily decimate the authority of customary international law.

the application of the last-in-time rule would create the absurd situation of allowing the U.S. President to use his/her foreign policy power to overturn Congressional action. The President in his/her foreign policy role could bind the U.S. to a customary international law rule by simply stating that the U.S. is bound by the norm -- regardless of whether Congress had earlier enacted a statute overriding the pre-existing rule. Thirdly, the rule's underlying purpose of protecting national sovereignty is not served in the context of fundamental human rights.[19] Furthermore, the actual application of this principle presents difficulties because customary international law is either very frequently emerging or

---

[19] In the case of customary international *human rights/humanitarian* law, the last-in-time rule probably should not be applied because the rule's purpose is not served in the context of an individual's fundamental human rights. The rule's purpose is to ensure the U.S.' national sovereignty *vis-a-vis* other countries. However, in the case of the domestic legal protection of an individual's fundamental human rights, the U.S.' sovereignty *vis-a-vis* other countries is not at issue. *Cf. Kovacevic Case*, Case No. IT-97-24-AR73, Int. Crim. Trib.-Yugo, Appeals Chamber (29 May 1998 (drawing distinction between customary international law principle governing relations between states and customary international law principle governing arrangements with ICT-Y as supernational body) at § 37.

Any lawful authority that the last-in-time rule may possess as a judicially-created test rests on the particular facts in those cases (using the rule) that gave rise to the issue of national sovereignty because this issue was not explicitly addressed by the Supremacy Clause (hence, the need for a judicially-created rule). In those cases using the rule to exempt the U.S. from its customary international law obligations, the facts involved interests outside the U.S. and implicating its relations with other countries. *See, e.g., Committee of United States Citizens in Nicaragua v. Reagan*, 859 F. 2d 929 (D.C.Cir. 1988) (U.S.-supported paramilitary operations in Nicaragua); *Garcia-Mir v. Meese*, 788 F.2d 1446 (11th Cir. 1986) (Cuban national detainees); *United States v. Howard-Arias*, 679 F.2d 363 (4th Cir. 1982) (prosecution for possession of illegal drugs on high seas); *Tag v. Rogers*, 267 F.2d 664 (D.C.Cir. 1959) (seizure of property owned by German enemy alien). If facts in a different case do not raise these issues, the test should not be applicable. In other words, the case can be distinguished from those cases using the rule. The rule's application in such a case only serves to violate the U.S.' government's constitutional obligation to comply with customary international human rights/humanitarian law.

continuously present.[20]   Therefore, the last-in-time rule's application to customary international law is suspect.

Finally, like treaties, customary international law in principle trumps state law in the U.S.[21] Also, customary international human rights norms may not need implementing legislation, as is sometimes asserted to be the case with non-self-executing treaties.[22]

Domestic Legislation

Thirdly, international law can be incorporated through domestic legislation. For example, the U.S. has incorporated its obligations as a state party to the Convention

---

[20] Some commentators have argued that recognition of a customary international law norm always will be the most recent act because judicial decisions and the practice of nations continuously "reenact" the customary international law norm. Karen Parker & Lyn Beth Neylon, *Jus Cogens: Compelling the Law of Human Rights*, 12 HASTINGS INT'L & COMP. L.R. 411, 451(1989); Jordan Paust, *Rediscovering the Relationship between Congressional Power and International Law: Exceptions to the Last in Time Rule an the Primacy of Custom*, 28 VA. J. INT'L L. 393, 418 (1988). Most -- if not all -- international human rights/humanitarian treaties are multilateral. Because these multilateral human rights/humanitarian treaties employ almost identical language, the rights and duties recognized in those treaties often establish customary international law. As different states adopt these treaties over time, the customary international law norm is continually established, thereby making a date by which the last-in-time rule can operate, repeatedly irrelevant.

Also, there are over a dozen international human rights/humanitarian tribunals. These tribunals continually are creating customary international law norms.   Hundreds of decisions addressing an array of fundamental human rights are issued by these tribunals each year. Again, the date by which the last-in-time rule can operate effectively, becomes repeatedly and frequently irrelevant for customary international law.

Most importantly, other national governments continuously observe many of these customary international law norms through both overt acts or extant protections in their domestic legal systems. Therefore, the date by which the last-in-time rule can operate, becomes irrelevant for customary international law.

[21]*Kansas v. Colorado*, 206 U.S. 46 (1906) (using international law principle of coequality of sovereigns to trump state law); *People v. Liebowitz*, 140 Misc. 2d 820 (N.Y. Co. Ct. 1988) (international law doctrine of specialty trumps state law in extradition case); *Peters v. McKay*, 238 P.2d 225 (Or. 1951) (*en banc*) (international law trumps state statute of limitations); Restatement § 115 comment e.

[22] Frederic Kirgis, *Federal Statutes, Executive Orders and "Self-Executing Custom,"* 81 AM. J. INT'L L. 371, 372 (1987).

Relating to the Status of Refugees[23] and Protocol I[24] by enacting the Refugee Act, 8 U.S.C. § 1101 *et seq.* Although the text of the domestic statute is the applicable law, the treaty can be used as an interpretive aid.[25]

Domestic Tribunal Decisions

Finally, international law can be incorporated through domestic tribunal decisions. A good example of such incorporation is *Pratt v. Attorney General of Jamaica*[26] in which the Law Lords in the United Kingdom adopted the European Court of Human Rights' decision in *Soering v. United Kingdom.*[27] That decision found certain death row conditions presumptively violative of the right against inhuman treatment.

Through these different methods of incorporation, international law can legally bind U.S. and other domestic courts. However, there are practical concerns about using international law in domestic courts. For example, in U.S. federal courts, there is a tendency for federal judges' eyes to "glaze over" when briefed by litigants on international law.[28] There is a tendency for federal judges to see federal law as a "closed system" in which international law is foreign and distracting. For this reason, some U.S. Supreme Court justices have been very hostile to international law in death penalty and extradition

---

[23] Signed 28 July 1951 (entered into force 22 April 1954), 189 U.N.T.S. 150.

[24] Opened for signature 31 January 1967 (entered into force 4 October 1967), 660 U.N.T.S. 195.

[25] *See, e.g., Haitian Refugee Center v. Smith,* 676 F. 2d 1023 (5th Cir. 1982) (using Protocol I Relating to the Status of Refugees as interpretive aid for domestic legislation); *contra Stanford v. Kentucky,* 492 U.S. 361 (1989) (Scalia, J. dissenting) (international standards should not be used to interpret US Constitution).

[26] [1994] 2 AC 1, [1993] 4 All ER 769, [1993] 3 WLR 995, 143 NLJ 1639.

[27] 161 Eur. Ct. H.R. (ser. A) (1989).

[28] For example, Prof. Paul Hoffman describes the difficulty facing litigators briefing judges on customary international law as "the blank stare phenomenon." Prof. Hoffman gives a concrete example of the phenomenon:

> ... [The judge] was gracious enough to allow me to talk for about an hour [about the application of international law in the case, involving a claim of "sanctuary," or temporary refuge as a humanitarian norm], during which he asked me some questions. Yet, when we spoke about customary law, there was that stare. That blank stare. It was as if the concepts we had so meticulously briefed bore no resemblance to law in the eyes of [the judge]. The same phenomenon has occurred in other courtrooms. This judicial skepticism is one of the largest obstacles for a lawyer trying to use customary law in domestic litigation.

Paul L. Hoffman, *The "Blank Stare Phenomenon": Proving Customary International Law in U.S. Courts,* 25 GA. J. INT'L & COMP. L. 181, 182 (1995-96).

cases.[29] Interestingly enough, however, state judges may be more receptive to international law because their courts have general jurisdiction, unlike federal courts. Another concern is that international law generally has been considered "soft" law – not a controlling or authoritative source of law. As discussed above, this certainly is no longer a correct view. Another concern is that many judges in the U.S. and other countries are just not familiar with international law. Nevertheless, if the rule of law and logic have any sway over judges and the forces producing global legal accountability continue to gather, it is inevitable that U.S. and other domestic courts increasingly will be looking to international law.

---

[29] *See, e.g.*, *Alvarez-Machain v. United States*, 504 U.S. 655 (1992) (extradition); *Sanford v. Kentucky*, 492 U.S. 361 (1989) (death penalty).

Chapter 3.   The History and Operations of International Human Rights, Humanitarian, and Criminal Tribunals

We will be examining the treaties and their interpretive caselaw from five major international adjudicative systems: (i) the International Military Tribunal (also known as the Nuremberg War Crimes Tribunal), (ii) the International Criminal Tribunals for the Former Yugoslavia and Rwanda, (iii) the European Court of Human Rights, (iv) the Inter-American Commission and Court of Human Rights, and (v) the International Criminal Court. In lesser degree, we also will look at cases from the International Military Tribunal for the Far East (also known as the Tokyo War Crimes Tribunal), Control Council No. 10 Law Proceedings, International Court of Justice, the UN Human Rights Committee and other UN organs, the Human Rights Commission for Bosnia and Herzegovina, and the African Commission on Human and Peoples' Rights.

A. Historical Background

Because international law historically concerned only interstate relations, international *crimes* have been intrinsically linked with interstate conditions giving rise to crimes. Such precipitating conditions usually have been wars. Therefore, international criminal tribunals historically have addressed war crimes.

Although the concept of war crimes goes back as far as the fifth-century with St. Augustine's discussion of a just war in his treatise, CITY OF GOD, it was not until 1268 that someone was tried and executed for beginning an unjust war.[1] Two hundred years later in 1474, twenty-seven judges of the Holy Roman Empire tried and condemned Peter von Haganbach for crimes his troops committed against civilians.

In the late 1800s, we begin seeing attempts at establishing international humanitarian law. In 1898, Czar Nicholas II called for a peace conference to discuss the codification of laws of war. In the following years, several conferences were held producing a series of treaties collectively known as The Hague Conventions, which limited the use of force in war.

In the aftermath of World War I, the Treaty of Versailles of 1919 addressed German violations of the laws of war. The treaty provided for the establishment of *ad hoc* tribunals for the prosecution of war criminals. However, no such *ad hoc* tribunals were established. Through an arrangement with the Allies, Germany was permitted to try its own officials in Leipzig before the Supreme Court of Germany.[2] Only a tiny minority of the accused violators were ever brought to trial; an even smaller number were convicted. The Treaty of Sevres of 1920, which was the peace treaty between the Allies and the Ottoman Empire, provided for Turkey's surrender of persons responsible for the murder of an estimated 600,000 Armenians in 1915; however, this provision was never implemented because of a subsequent treaty.

---

[1] Christopher L. Blakesley, *Report on the Obstacles to the Creation of a Permanent War Crimes Tribunal*, 18 FLETCHER FORUM OF WORLD AFFAIRS 77 (No. 2, 1994).

[2] *See, e.g., Case of Lieutenants Dithmar and Boldt Hospital Ship "Llandovery Castle"*, Supreme Court of Germany (1921), 16 AMER. J. INT'L L. 708 (1922) (sinking of unarmed hospital ship by German U-Boat).

Between the World Wars, other humanitarian treaties were adopted. The Geneva Convention of 1929 governed the conduct of war, and the Kellog-Briand Pact outlawed war of aggression. In 1937, the League of Nations adopted a Convention Against Terrorism, and an optional protocol provided for the establishment of a special international criminal court to prosecute crimes of terrorism, although the Convention never came into force.[3]

B. Nuremberg, Tokyo, and Other War Crimes Tribunals

During World War II many and various gross human rights and humanitarian law violations were perpetrated by both the Allies and Axis powers. However, many atrocities were not covered by the laws of war. These atrocities included discrimination against and mass murder of Jews, as well as the Romani, homosexuals, and communists, by Nazi Germany. The U.S. government interned Japanese-Americans in concentration camps, an action upheld by the Supreme Court in *Korematsu v. United States*, 323 U.S. 214 (1944). These human rights violations were not covered by the laws of war insofar as they constituted a state's mistreatment of its own citizens, persons believed by many at the time not to be covered by international legal protection.

In the summer of 1945, Allied leaders met in London to discuss the establishment of a war crimes tribunal. Consequently, the Allies signed the London Agreement and Charter[4] that provided for establishing an *ad hoc* tribunal for prosecution of German war criminals. This tribunal was called the International Military Tribunal (IMT) or Nuremberg War Crimes Tribunal.

Prior to this agreement, alternative fora were entrusted with the responsibility of trying war criminals. These tribunals were not displaced by the IMT. These trials took place before, during, and after the time of the Nuremberg trials. The most significant of these were the "Subsequent Proceedings" authorized by Control Council Law No. 10 that took place in the U.S. Zone of Occupied Germany. During these proceedings, about 200 Nazi doctors, lawyers, SS leaders, generals and diplomats were tried. There were other courts that tried Nazi war criminals as well: local courts throughout Germany, or elsewhere in Europe, and military courts martial, both British and American.

The Allies thought, however, that the IMT was necessary for the prosecution of other Nazi war criminals because the Allies feared that these criminals would escape punishment under domestic law. For example, some of the crimes were committed in a number of European jurisdictions, and it was unclear which country had a better claim to jurisdiction. The IMT's international jurisdiction mooted such jurisdictional issues. Also, many of the courts of the occupied nations used domestic law that allowed an affirmative defense of obedience to superior orders. However, under the London Charter, the IMT disallowed the defense of obeying orders.

---

[3] C. Oliver, THE INTERNATIONAL LEGAL SYSTEM 910 (4th ed. 1995).

[4] (U.S., U.S.S.R., Britain, France) Agreement signed at London August 8, 1945, 59 Stat. 1544, E.A.S. No. 472 [hereinafter London Charter].

In addition to charging defendants with violations of the laws of war, the IMT punished new categories of offenses. The London Charter established other crimes than those identified in The Hague Conventions. These were crimes against peace, conspiracy to commit crimes against peace, and crimes against humanity. The assertion that a person could be held criminally liable under international law for conspiracy was controversial because there was no analogous criminal liability in the civil law traditions of two members of the Allied Powers — France and the USSR. The last of these crimes, crimes against humanity, had some grounding in The Hague Conventions. In the London Charter, they were defined as:

> "murder, extermination, enslavement, deportation and other inhumane acts committed against any civilian population, before or during the war . . . whether or not in violation of the domestic law of the country where perpetrated."[5]

However, as in the case of crimes against peace, this was to be the first instance of the imposition of international criminal liability for such offenses.

The Nuremberg trial lasted eleven months. The IMT tried twenty-two individuals and six organizations. Of those tried, the IMT sentenced twelve individuals (including Fritz Sauckel, Arthur Seyss-Inquart, Martin Bormann, Julius Streicher, and Herman Goering) to death by hanging and imprisoned seven others at the Allies' Spandau Prison outside Berlin. Three of the six Nazi and German governmental organizations were found guilty as well.

A year after the IMT was established, Gen. Douglas MacArthur, Supreme Allied Commander for the Pacific Theater, established an equivalent tribunal in Tokyo by military order. This tribunal was called the International Military Tribunal for the Far East (IMT-FE). The IMT-FE was very similar to its counterpart in Nuremberg regarding subject matter jurisdiction. As with the IMT, the IMT-FE had jurisdiction over crimes against humanity, crimes against peace, conspiracy, and other war crimes.[6]

---

[5] *Id.* at Art. 6(c)

[6] Besides these tribunals, there were other military commissions responsible for prosecuting violations of the law of war. *See, e.g., In re Yamashita*, 327 U.S. 1, 347 (1946) (recognizing "command responsibility" for failure of Japanese general to stop war atrocities committed by his troops). Following World War II, there have been some important domestic cases addressing humanitarian law. The foremost case was *Attorney-General of Israel v. Eichmann*, 36 INT'L L. REP. 5 (1968) (District Ct. of Jerusalem, 1961), in which the former Nazi leader in charge of the "Final Solution" was prosecuted under Israeli law. Another notable case was *United States v. Calley*, 48 C.M.R. 19 (US Ct. of Military App., 1973), 48 C.M.R. 19 (US Ct. of Military App., 1973), in which a US soldier was convicted of murdering civilians in the My Lai Village during the Vietnam War. And in *Matter of Demjanjuk*, 603 F. Supp. 1468 (N.D. Ohio 1985), an alleged Treblinka concentration camp guard was extradited to Israel to stand trial; however, he subsequently was found not guilty by an Israeli court and ordered to be allowed to return to the U.S.

C. United Nations Courts and Tribunals

The United Nations (UN) has created a number of courts and quasi-tribunals for protecting human rights and punishing international crimes. These courts and tribunals are either treaty-based or UN Charter-based. The most prominent UN Charter-based court is the International Court of Justice in The Hague. It only considers cases between states, or between states and intergovermental organizations. It has decided a few cases dealing with human rights.

International Criminal Tribunals and Court

In response to genocidal practices in the former Yugoslavia and Rwanda in the early 1990s, the UN Security Council established the International Criminal Tribunal for the Former Yugoslavia (ICT-Y) in 1993 and the International Criminal Tribunal for Rwanda (ICT-R) in 1994. Both are *ad hoc* tribunals whose life spans are linked to the restoration and maintenance of peace and security in the territories of the former Yugoslavia and Rwanda. Both cover crimes committed in a specific time span.

For each Tribunal, there are six Trial Chamber judges (two Chambers with three judges each). However, both Tribunals share the five judges sitting in the Appeals Chamber. They also share the same Chief Prosecutor. There are no juries. The seat of the ICT-Y is in The Hague, the ICT-R in Arusha, Tanzania. The Appeals Chamber for both tribunals sits in The Hague.

The ICT-Y's jurisdiction is limited to the former Yugoslavia. The ICT-Y has jurisdiction over grave breaches of the Geneva Conventions, violations of the laws and customs of war, genocide, and crimes against humanity. The ICT-Y does not have jurisdiction over crimes against peace.

The ICT-R's jurisdiction extends to Rwanda and neighboring countries. The ICT-R has jurisdiction over grave breaches of the Geneva Conventions, violations of the laws and customs of war, genocide, and crimes against humanity. Furthermore, the ICT-R can apply certain protocols and articles of the Geneva Conventions, including those relating to non-international conflicts.[7] Also, unlike the ICT-Y Statute, the ICT-R Statute does not require that crimes against humanity be committed in the context of armed conflict.

As of Winter 1999, the ICT-Y has indicted, arrested, and convicted numerous individuals. The ICT-R has arrested numerous persons and convicted a few people.

In July 1998, the Statute of the International Criminal Court (ICC) was adopted in Rome as a multilateral treaty. The ICC will be established upon the ICC Treaty coming into force. The ICC has jurisdiction over the crimes of genocide, crimes against humanity, war crimes, and the crime of aggression.[8] The UN Conference that established the ICC declined to give the ICC jurisdiction over crimes of terrorism or illegal drug trafficking.

The UN Security Council or a state party to the ICC Statute can refer a case to the ICC Prosecutor for investigation. The Prosecutor also can initiate an investigation *propio*

---

[7] Statute of the International Tribunal for Rwanda, art. 4, U.N. Doc. S/Res/955, Annex (1994) [hereinafter ICT-R Statute].

[8] Art. 5(1), Statute of the International Criminal Court, U.N. Doc. A/CONF.183/9 (17 July 1998).

motu. Upon the information gathered by the Prosecutor, the ICC's Pre-Trial Chamber makes a decision as to admissibility. There is also an Appeal Chamber.

Treaty-Based Committees and Working Group on Arbitrary Detention

The UN also has adopted a number of human rights treaties that establish various quasi-tribunals. The most prominent is the UN Human Rights Committee, which was established by the International Covenant on Civil and Political Rights (ICCPR) in 1976. The Optional Protocol to the ICCPR allows the UN Human Rights Committee to examine complaints (called "communications") from individuals against state parties to the ICCPR, make factual and legal findings, and make non-binding recommendations to the state party. The Committee is not a criminal tribunal. However, the Committee can recommend to a state party that it investigate, prosecute, and punish persons responsible for gross human rights violations.

The procedure of the Committee is as follows. The Committee first will decide if the communication is admissible, examining whether domestic remedies have been exhausted and whether the case is pending before another international proceeding. If the petition is found admissible, the Committee will examine the merits and make a finding.

Two other quasi-tribunals that produce criminal law-related decisions are the UN Committee Against Torture and the Working Group on Arbitrary Detention. The UN Committee Against Torture was established by the Convention Against Torture and Other Cruel, Inhuman, or Degrading Treatment[9] in 1987. Like the UN Human Rights Committee, this committee also examines communications from individuals alleging violations of the respective treaties by state parties. The Committee makes factual and legal findings as well as recommendations.

The UN Working Group on Arbitrary Detention is a UN Charter-based organ under the UN Sub-Commission on Prevention of Discrimination and Protection of Minorities. The Working Group has adopted a quasi-judicial character. It receives communications, investigates cases, and issues reasoned decisions.

D. European Court of Human Rights

In 1950, the Council of Europe adopted the European Convention for the Protection of Human Rights and Fundamental Freedoms (ECHR). As of 1999, there are forty states-parties to the ECHR. The ECHR established the European Commission and Court of Human Rights. The European Commission and Court can consider cases both between states, and between legal persons (*e.g.*, private individuals, corporations) and states. (The Commission and Court are not criminal tribunals.) Under Protocol No. 11to the ECHR, which came into force in November 1998, the European Commission of Human Rights

---

[9] Adopted 10 December 1984 (entered into force 26 June 1987), G.A. Res. 39/46, 39 UN GAOR Supp. (No. 51), U.N.Doc. A/39/51 at 197 (1984).

will no longer consider new cases.[10] The Commission will be eliminated. Parties will submit cases directly to the European Court of Human Rights.

The typical procedure is for individuals to file a case (called an "application") alleging some violation of the ECHR. The Court (or Commission if before November 1998) will first make a finding as to whether the application is admissible, examining issues such as whether domestic remedies have been exhausted, whether the application was filed within six months of exhaustion, and whether the case is pending before another international tribunal. If the application is admissible, the Court will seek a settlement between the parties. If no settlement is reached, the European Court will make a decision on the merits. If the Court finds a violation of the ECHR, the state party must obey the decision of the Court. To date, every state party has done so. These decisions can include compensation and attorney's fees and costs awards. In the area of injunctive relief, the European Court has left it to the state party's discretion as how to best remedy a violation.

E. Human Rights Commission for Bosnia and Herzegovina

The Dayton Agreement ending the conflict in Bosnia and Herzegovina provided for the establishment of the Human Rights Commission for Bosnia and Herzegovina, whose headquarters are in Sarajevo. The Commission consists of two parts: an Office of Human Rights Ombudsman and the Human Rights Chamber. The Commission is competent to examine and adjudicate cases (called applications) submitted by individuals, state-parties, groups, or NGOs alleging human rights violations as defined by the European Convention on Human Rights committed by any of the states-parties. It also is competent to examine and adjudicate cases alleging human rights violations arising from discrimination in the enjoyment of rights guaranteed by several other global and regional human rights treaties addressing genocide, torture, inhuman treatment, refugees, and war crimes.[11] (The Commission is not a criminal tribunal.)

The typical procedure is for the Ombudsman to investigate a case submitted by an applicant and to make findings, conclusions, and recommendations. The state-party is allowed to submit an explanation of the Ombudsman's finding of a violation. If the state party does not comply with the Ombudsman's recommendations, the Ombudsman publishes a public report disclosing the failure of the state-party to comply. The Ombudsman also can refer the case to the Chamber for adjudication.

If the Ombudsman refers the case to the Chamber, the Chamber first examines whether the application is admissible, examining issues such as whether domestic remedies have been exhausted, whether the application was filed within six months of exhaustion, and whether the case is pending before another international tribunal. During

---

[10] The Commission will consider the remaining cases of its docket over the following year.

[11] Dayton Agreement, The General Framework Agreement for Peace in Bosnia and Herzegovina, initialed 21 November 1995 (entered into force 14 December 1995), Annex Six.

any stage of the proceedings, the Chamber may seek a settlement between the parties. If no settlement is reached, the Chamber will make a decision on admissibility and the merits. The Chamber's decision is binding. Its decision can include injunctive relief, compensation and costs awards.

F. Inter-American Commission and Court of Human Rights

In the Americas, there are two major international human rights tribunals established by the Organization of American States (OAS). In 1948, the OAS adopted the American Declaration on the Rights and Duties of Man.[12] In 1959, the Inter-American Commission on Human Rights was established in Washington, D.C. In 1965, the Commission was given authority to accept complaints from individuals and others against OAS states. It could request information from governments regarding these complaints and make recommendations. Under the authority of the American Declaration, the Inter-American Commission has competence to examine complaints against all states in the Americas -- including the U.S.[13] The Inter-American Commission first will decide if the petition is admissible, examining whether domestic remedies have been exhausted, whether the petition was filed within six months of exhaustion, and whether the case is pending before another international proceeding. If the petition is found admissible, the Commission will examine the merits and make a finding. The Commission can undertake investigations. It also seeks a friendly resolution between the parties. The Commission can only recommend -- not order -- countries to comply with their international legal obligations under the American Declaration as OAS members.[14] Unfortunately, while many countries comply with the Commission's recommendations, some countries -- including the U.S. -- have failed to comply. However, the Commission can publish its findings of violations, thereby embarrassing the state party.

In 1969, the OAS adopted the American Convention on Human Rights (ACHR) that authorized the creation of the Inter-American Court of Human Rights, which eventually was established in 1978 in Costa Rica. Under the ACHR, once the Inter-American Commission finds a state party in violation of the ACHR, the Commission transmits its report to the state party. If the state party fails to comply with the Commission's recommendations, the Commission transmits its report to the OAS Secretary General and can release the report to the public. Most importantly, the Commission can refer the case

---

[12] Signed 2 May 1948, OAS Res. XXX, adopted by the Ninth International Conference of American States (1948), *reprinted in* BASIC DOCUMENTS PERTAINING TO HUMAN RIGHTS IN THE INTER-AMERICAN SYSTEM, OEA/SER.L.V/II.82 doc. 6 rev. 1 at 17 (1992).

[13] Although Cuba was ejected from membership in the OAS, the Commission still has competence to examine complaints against Cuba.

[14] *Interpretation of the American Declaration of the Rights and Duties of Man Within the Framework of Article 64 of the American Convention on Human Rights,* Inter-Am. Ct. H.R., Advisory Opinion OC-10/89 of 14 July 1989, Inter-Am. Ct. H.R. (Ser. A) No. 10 (1989).

to the Inter-American Court if the state party has accepted the Court's jurisdiction. If the Court also finds a state party in violation, the state party must comply with the orders of the Court. Over two dozen countries are state parties to the ACHR, and over a dozen have accepted the jurisdiction of the Court. The Inter-American Court can order compensation and injunctive relief as well as award legal fees and costs.[15] The Court does not convict persons, but it can order a state party to investigate, prosecute, and punish persons responsible for gross human rights violations.

G. African Commission on Human and Peoples' Rights

In Africa, the Organisation of African Unity (OAU) established the African Commission of Human and Peoples' Rights when it adopted the African Charter on Human and Peoples' Rights (the "Banjul Charter") in 1981. The African Commission can receive complaints from both individuals and state parties. It does not prosecute persons for criminal violations. Its procedures are similar to the Inter-American and European Commissions. Because the African Commission only can make recommendations and its decisions have lacked rigorous legal analysis, the Commission has not been very successful; however, the OAU may establish an African Court of Human and Peoples' Rights in the near future with greater power and authority.

Let us now turn to the international human rights treaties and caselaw.

---

[15] The Inter-American Court for the first time recently awarded legal fees and costs. *See Suarez Rosero v. Ecuador*, Decision on Reparations of 20 January 1999; *Loayza Tamayo v. Peru*, Decision on Reparations of 27 November 1998.

PART TWO: PRINCIPLES OF STATE LIABILITY AND INDIVIDUAL CULPABILITY

Treaties

International Covenant on Civil and Political Rights

Article 2

1. Each State Party to the present Covenant undertakes to respect and to ensure to all individuals within its territory and subject to its jurisdiction the rights recognized in the present Covenant, without distinction of any kind, such as race, colour, sex, language, religion, political or other opinion, national or social origin, property, birth or other status.

2. Where not already provided for by existing legislative or other measures, each State Party to the present Covenant undertakes to take the necessary steps, in accordance with its constitutional processes and with the provisions of the present Covenant, to adopt such legislative or other measures as may be necessary to give effect to the rights recognized in the present Covenant.

3. Each State Party to the present Covenant undertakes:

(a) To ensure that any person whose rights or freedoms as herein recognized are violated shall have an effective remedy, notwithstanding that the violation has been committed by persons acting in an official capacity;

(b) To ensure that any person claiming such a remedy shall have his right thereto determined by competent judicial, administrative or legislative authorities, or by any other competent authority provided for by the legal system of the State, and to develop the possibilities of judicial remedy;

(c) To ensure that the competent authorities shall enforce such remedies when granted.

American Convention on Human Rights

Article 1. OBLIGATION TO RESPECT RIGHTS.

1. The States Parties to this Convention undertake to respect the rights and freedoms recognized herein and to ensure to all persons subject to their jurisdiction the free and full exercise of those rights and freedoms, without any discrimination for reasons of race. color, sex, language, religion, political or other opinion, national or social origin, economic status, birth, or any other social condition.

2. For the purposes of this Convention, "person" means every human being.

Article 2. DOMESTIC LEGAL EFFECTS.

Where the exercise of any of the rights or freedoms referred to in Article I is not already ensured by legislative or other provisions, the States Parties undertake to adopt, in accordance with their constitutional processes and the provisions of this Convention, such legislative or other measures as may be necessary to give effect to those rights or freedoms.

Article 25. RIGHT TO JUDICIAL PROTECTION.

1. Everyone has the right to simple and prompt recourse, or any other effective recourse, to a competent court or tribunal for protection against acts that violate his fundamental rights recognized by the constitution or laws of the state concerned or by this Convention, even though such violation may have been committed by persons acting in the course of their official duties.

2. The States Parties undertake:

    a. To ensure that any person claiming such remedy shall have his rights determined by the competent authority provided for by the legal system of the state;
    b. To develop the possibilities of judicial remedy; and
    c. To ensure that the competent authorities shall enforce such remedies when granted.

European Convention on Human Rights

ARTICLE 1

The High Contracting Parties shall secure to everyone within their jurisdiction the rights and freedoms defined in Section I of this Convention.

ARTICLE 13

Everyone whose rights and freedoms as set forth in this Convention are violated shall have an effective remedy before a national authority notwithstanding that the violation has been committed by persons acting in an official capacity.

African Charter on Human and Peoples' Rights

Article 1

The Member States of the Organization of African Unity parties to the present Charter shall recognize the rights, duties and freedoms enshrined in this Chapter and shall undertake to adopt legislative or other measures to give effect to them.

Convention Against Torture and Other Cruel,
Inhuman or Degrading Treatment of Punishment

Article 2

1. Each State Party shall take effective legislative, administrative, judicial or other measures to prevent acts of torture in any territory under its jurisdiction.

2. No exceptional circumstances whatsoever, whether a state of war or a threat or war, internal political instability or any other public emergency, may be invoked as a justification of torture.

3. An order from a superior officer or a public authority may not be invoked as a justification of torture.

Article 4

1. Each State Party shall ensure that all acts of torture are offences under its criminal law. The same shall apply to an attempt to commit torture and to an act by any person which constitutes complicity or participation in torture.

2. Each State Party shall make these offences punishable by appropriate penalties which take into account their grave nature.

Article 5

1. Each State Party shall take such measures as may be necessary to establish its jurisdiction over the offences referred to in article 4 in the following cases:

   (a) When the offences are committed in any territory under its jurisdiction or on board a ship or aircraft registered in that State;

   (b) When the alleged offender is a national of that State;

   (c) When the victim is a national of that State if that State considers it appropriate.

2. Each State Party shall likewise take such measures as may be necessary to establish its jurisdiction over such offences in cases where the alleged offender is present in any territory under its jurisdiction and it does not extradite him pursuant to article 8 to any of the States mentioned in Paragraph 1 of this article.

3. This Convention does not exclude any criminal jurisdiction exercised in accordance with internal law.

Article 6

1. Upon being satisfied, after an examination of information available to it, that the circumstances so warrant, any State Party in whose territory a person alleged to have committed any offence referred to in article 4 is present, shall take him into custody or take other legal measures to ensure his presence. The custody and other legal measures shall be as provided in the law of that State but may be continued only for such time as is necessary to enable any criminal or extradition proceedings to be instituted.

2. Such State shall immediately make a preliminary inquiry into the facts.

3. Any person in custody pursuant to paragraph 1 of this article shall be assisted in communicating immediately with the nearest appropriate representative of the State of which he is a national, or, if he is a stateless person, to the representative of the State where he usually resides.

4. When a State, pursuant to this article, has taken a person into custody, it shall immediately notify the States referred to in article 5, paragraph 1, of the fact that such person is in custody and of the circumstances which warrant his detention. The State which makes the preliminary inquiry contemplated in paragraph 2 of this article shall promptly report its findings to the said State and shall indicate whether it intends to exercise jurisdiction.

Article 12

Each State Party shall ensure that its competent authorities proceed to a prompt and impartial investigation, wherever there is reasonable ground to believe that an act of torture has been committed in any territory under its jurisdiction.

Inter-American Convention to Prevent and Punish Torture

Article 4

The fact of having acted under orders of a superior shall not provide exemption from the corresponding criminal liability.

Article 6

In accordance with the terms of Article 1, the States Parties shall take effective measures to prevent and punish torture within their jurisdiction.

The States Parties shall ensure that all acts of torture and attempts to commit torture are offenses under their criminal law and shall make such acts punishable by severe penalties that take into account their serious nature.

The States Parties likewise shall take effective measures to prevent and punish other cruel, inhuman, or degrading treatment or punishment within their jurisdiction.

Inter-American Convention on the Forced Disappearance of Persons

ARTICLE IV

The acts constituting the forced disappearance of persons shall be considered offenses in every State Party. Consequently, each State Party shall take measures to establish its jurisdiction over such cases in the following instances:

a. When the forced disappearance of persons or any act constituting such offense was committed within its jurisdiction;

b. When the accused is a national of that state;

c. When the victim is a national of that state and that state sees fit to do so.

Every State Party shall, moreover, take the necessary measures to establish its jurisdiction over the crime described in this Convention when the alleged criminal is within its territory and it does not proceed to extradite him.

This Convention does not authorize any State Party to undertake, in the territory of another State Party, the exercise of jurisdiction or the performance of functions that are placed within the exclusive purview of the authorities of that other Party by its domestic law.

ARTICLE VIII

The defense of due obedience to superior orders or instructions that stipulate, authorize, or encourage forced disappearance shall not be admitted. All persons who receive such orders have the right and duty not to obey them.

The States Parties shall ensure that the training of public law-enforcement personnel or officials includes the necessary education on the offense of forced disappearance of persons.

ARTICLE IX

Persons alleged to be responsible for the acts constituting the offense of forced disappearance of persons may be tried only in the competent jurisdictions of ordinary law in each state, to the exclusion of all other special jurisdictions, particularly military jurisdictions.

The acts constituting forced disappearance shall not be deemed to have been committed in the course of military duties.

Privileges, immunities, or special dispensations shall not be admitted in such trials, without prejudice to the provisions set forth in the Vienna Convention on Diplomatic Relations.

Inter-American Convention on the Prevention, Punishment, and Eradication of Violence Against Women

CHAPTER III
DUTIES OF THE STATES

Article 7

The States Parties condemn all forms of violence against women and agree to pursue, by all appropriate means and without delay, policies to prevent, punish and eradicate such violence and undertake to:

a. refrain from engaging in any act or practice of violence against women and to ensure that their authorities, officials, personnel, agents, and institutions act in conformity with this obligation;

b. apply due diligence to prevent, investigate and impose penalties for violence against women;

c. include in their domestic legislation penal, civil, administrative and any other type of provisions that may be needed to prevent, punish and eradicate violence against women and to adopt appropriate administrative measures where necessary;

d. adopt legal measures to require the perpetrator to refrain from harassing, intimidating or threatening the woman or using any method that harms or endangers her life or integrity, or damages her property;

e. take all appropriate measures, including legislative measures, to amend or repeal existing laws and regulations or to modify legal or customary practices which sustain the persistence and tolerance of violence against women;

f. establish fair and effective legal procedures for women who have been subjected to violence which include, among others, protective measures, a timely hearing and effective access to such procedures;

g. establish the necessary legal and administrative mechanisms to ensure that women subjected to violence have effective access to restitution, reparations or other just and effective remedies; and

h. adopt such legislative or other measures as may be necessary to give effect to this Convention.

Convention on the Prevention and Punishment of Genocide

Article I

The Contracting Parties confirm that genocide, whether committed in time of peace or in time of war, is a crime under international law which they undertake to prevent and to punish.

Article IV

Persons committing genocide or any of the other acts enumerated in Article III shall be punished, whether they are constitutionally responsible rulers, public officials or private individuals.

Article V

The Contracting Parties undertake to enact, in accordance with their respective Constitutions, the necessary legislation to give effect to the provisions of the present Convention and, in particular, to provide effective penalties for persons guilty of genocide or any of the other acts enumerated in Article III.

Article VI

Persons charged with genocide or any of the other acts enumerated in Article III shall be tried by a competent tribunal of the State in the territory of which the act was committed, or by such international penal tribunal as may have jurisdiction with respect to those Contracting Parties which shall have accepted its jurisdiction.

Charter of the International Military Tribunal

Article 6.

The Tribunal established . . . for the trial and punishment of the major war criminals of the European Axis countries shall have the power to try and punish persons who, acting in the interests of the European Axis countries, whether as individuals or as members of organizations, committed any of the following crimes. [Crimes Against Peace, War Crimes, Crimes Against Humanity]

Leaders, organizers, instigators and accomplices participating in the formulation or execution of a common plan or conspiracy to commit any of the foregoing crimes are responsible for all acts performed by any persons in execution of such plan.

Article 7.

The official position of defendants, whether as Heads of State or responsible officials in Government Departments, shall not be considered as freeing them from responsibility or mitigating punishment.

Article 8.

The fact that the Defendant acted pursuant to order of his Government or of a superior shall not free him from responsibility, but may be considered in mitigation of punishment if the Tribunal determines that justice so requires.

Article 9.

At the trial of any individual member of any group or organization the Tribunal may declare (in connection with any act of which the individual may be convicted) that the group or organization of which the individual was a member was a criminal organization.

After the receipt of the Indictment the Tribunal shall give such notice as it thinks fit that the prosecution intends to ask the Tribunal to make such declaration and any member of the organization will be entitled to apply to the Tribunal for leave to be heard by the Tribunal upon the question of the criminal character of the organization. The Tribunal shall have power to allow or reject the application. If the application is allowed, the Tribunal may direct in what manner the applicants shall be represented and heard.

Article 10.

In cases where a group or organization is declared criminal by the Tribunal, the competent national authority of any Signatory shall have the right to bring individual to trial for membership therein before national, military or occupation courts. In any such case the criminal nature of the group or organization is considered proved and shall not be questioned.

Article 11.

Any person convicted by the Tribunal may be charged before a national, military or occupation court, referred to in Article 10 of this Charter, with a crime other than of membership in a criminal group or organization and such court may, after convicting him, impose upon him punishment independent of and additional to the punishment imposed by the Tribunal for participation in the criminal activities of such group or organization.

Statute of the International Criminal Tribunal [for the Former Yugoslavia]

Article 6
Personal jurisdiction

The International Tribunal shall have jurisdiction over natural persons pursuant to the provisions of the present Statute.

Article 7
Individual criminal responsibility

1. A person who planned, instigated, ordered, committed or otherwise aided and abetted in the planning, preparation or execution of a crime referred to in articles 2 to 5 of the present Statute, shall be individually responsible for the crime.

2. The official position of any accused person, whether as Head of State or Government or as a responsible Government official, shall not relieve such person of criminal responsibility nor mitigate punishment.

3. The fact that any of the acts referred to in articles 2 to 5 of the present Statute was committed by a subordinate does not relieve his superior of criminal responsibility if he knew or had reason to know that the subordinate was about to commit such acts or had done so and the superior failed to take the necessary and reasonable measures to prevent such acts or to punish the perpetrators thereof.

4. The fact that an accused person acted pursuant to an order of a Government or of a superior shall not relieve him of criminal responsibility, but may be considered in mitigation of punishment if the International Tribunal determines that justice so requires.

Article 8
Territorial and temporal jurisdiction

The territorial jurisdiction of the International Tribunal shall extend to the territory of the former Socialist Federal Republic of Yugoslavia, including its land surface, airspace and territorial waters. The temporal jurisdiction of the International Tribunal shall extend to a period beginning on 1 January 1991.

Statute of the International Criminal Tribunal for Rwanda

Article 5
Personal jurisdiction

The International Tribunal for Rwanda shall have jurisdiction over natural persons pursuant to the provisions of the present Statute.

Article 6
Individual criminal responsibility

1. A person who planned, instigated, ordered, committed or otherwise aided and abetted in the planning, preparation or execution of a crime referred to in articles 2 to 4 of the present Statute, shall be individually responsible for the crime.

2. The official position of any accused person, whether as Head of State or Government or as a responsible Government official, shall not relieve such person of criminal responsibility nor mitigate punishment.

3. The fact that any of the acts referred to in articles 2 to 4 of the present Statute was committed by a subordinate does not relieve his or her superior of criminal responsibility if he or she knew or had reason to know that the subordinate was about to commit such acts or had done so and the superior failed to take the necessary and reasonable measures to prevent such acts or to punish the perpetrators thereof.

4. The fact that an accused person acted pursuant to an order of a Government or of a superior shall not relieve him or her of criminal responsibility, but may be considered

in mitigation of punishment if the International Tribunal for Rwanda determines that justice so requires.

Article 7
Territorial and temporal jurisdiction

The territorial jurisdiction of the International Tribunal for Rwanda shall extend to the territory of Rwanda including its land surface and airspace as well as to the territory of neighbouring States in respect of serious violations of international humanitarian law committed by Rwandan citizens. The temporal jurisdiction of the International Tribunal for Rwanda shall extend to a period beginning on 1 January 1994 and ending on 31 December 1994.

Statute of the International Criminal Court

Article 23
Nulla poena sine lege

A person convicted by the Court may be punished only in accordance with this Statute.

Article 25
Individual criminal responsibility

1. The Court shall have jurisdiction over natural persons pursuant to this Statute.

2. A person who commits a crime within the jurisdiction of the Court shall be individually responsible and liable for punishment in accordance with this Statute.

3. In accordance with this Statute, a person shall be criminally responsible and liable for punishment for a crime within the jurisdiction of the Court if that person:

(a) Commits such a crime, whether as an individual, jointly with another or through another person, regardless of whether that other person is criminally responsible;
(b) Orders, solicits or induces the commission of such a crime which in fact occurs or is attempted;
(c) For the purpose of facilitating the commission of such a crime, aids, abets or otherwise assists in its commission or its attempted commission, including providing the means for its commission;
(d) In any other way contributes to the commission or attempted commission of such a crime by a group of persons acting with a common purpose. Such contribution shall be intentional and shall either:

(i) Be made with the aim of furthering the criminal activity or criminal purpose of the group, where such activity or purpose involves the commission of a crime within the jurisdiction of the Court; or
(ii) Be made in the knowledge of the intention of the group to commit the crime;

(e) In respect of the crime of genocide, directly and publicly incites others to commit genocide;

(f) Attempts to commit such a crime by taking action that commences its execution by means of a substantial step, but the crime does not occur because of circumstances independent of the person's intentions. However, a person who abandons the effort to commit the crime or otherwise prevents the completion of the crime shall not be liable for punishment under this Statute for the attempt to commit that crime if that person completely and voluntarily gave up the criminal purpose.

4. No provision in this Statute relating to individual criminal responsibility shall affect the responsibility of States under international law.

Article 26
Exclusion of jurisdiction over persons under eighteen

The Court shall have no jurisdiction over any person who was under the age of 18 at the time of the alleged commission of a crime.

Article 27
Irrelevance of official capacity

1. This Statute shall apply equally to all persons without any distinction based on official capacity. In particular, official capacity as a Head of State or Government, a member of a Government or parliament, an elected representative or a government official shall in no case exempt a person from criminal responsibility under this Statute, nor shall it, in and of itself, constitute a ground for reduction of sentence.

2. Immunities or special procedural rules which may attach to the official capacity of a person, whether under national or international law, shall not bar the Court from exercising its jurisdiction over such a person.

Article 28
Responsibility of commanders and other superiors

In addition to other grounds of criminal responsibility under this Statute for crimes within the jurisdiction of the Court:

1. A military commander or person effectively acting as a military commander shall be criminally responsible for crimes within the jurisdiction of the Court committed by forces under his or her effective command and control, or effective authority and control as the case may be, as a result of his or her failure to exercise control properly over such forces, where:

(a) That military commander or person either knew or, owing to the circumstances at the time, should have known that the forces were committing or about to commit such crimes; and

(b) That military commander or person failed to take all necessary and reasonable measures within his or her power to prevent or repress their commission or to submit the matter to the competent authorities for investigation and prosecution.

2. With respect to superior and subordinate relationships not described in paragraph 1, a superior shall be criminally responsible for crimes within the jurisdiction of the Court committed by subordinates under his or her effective authority and control, as a result of his or her failure to exercise control properly over such subordinates, where:

(a) The superior either knew, or consciously disregarded information which clearly indicated, that the subordinates were committing or about to commit such crimes;
(b) The crimes concerned activities that were within the effective responsibility and control of the superior; and
(c) The superior failed to take all necessary and reasonable measures within his or her power to prevent or repress their commission or to submit the matter to the competent authorities for investigation and prosecution.

Article 30
Mental element

1. Unless otherwise provided, a person shall be criminally responsible and liable for punishment for a crime within the jurisdiction of the Court only if the material elements are committed with intent and knowledge.

2. For the purposes of this article, a person has intent where:

(a) In relation to conduct, that person means to engage in the conduct;
(b) In relation to a consequence, that person means to cause that consequence or is aware that it will occur in the ordinary course of events.

3. For the purposes of this article, "knowledge" means awareness that a circumstance exists or a consequence will occur in the ordinary course of events. "Know" and "knowingly" shall be construed accordingly.

Article 31
Grounds for excluding criminal responsibility

1. In addition to other grounds for excluding criminal responsibility provided for in this Statute, a person shall not be criminally responsible if, at the time of that person's conduct:

(a) The person suffers from a mental disease or defect that destroys that person's capacity to appreciate the unlawfulness or nature of his or her conduct, or capacity to control his or her conduct to conform to the requirements of law;
(b) The person is in a state of intoxication that destroys that person's capacity to appreciate the unlawfulness or nature of his or her conduct, or capacity to control his or her conduct to conform to the requirements of law, unless the person has become

voluntarily intoxicated under such circumstances that the person knew, or disregarded the risk, that, as a result of the intoxication, he or she was likely to engage in conduct constituting a crime within the jurisdiction of the Court;

(c) The person acts reasonably to defend himself or herself or another person or, in the case of war crimes, property which is essential for the survival of the person or another person or property which is essential for accomplishing a military mission, against an imminent and unlawful use of force in a manner proportionate to the degree of danger to the person or the other person or property protected. The fact that the person was involved in a defensive operation conducted by forces shall not in itself constitute a ground for excluding criminal responsibility under this subparagraph;

(d) The conduct which is alleged to constitute a crime within the jurisdiction of the Court has been caused by duress resulting from a threat of imminent death or of continuing or imminent serious bodily harm against that person or another person, and the person acts necessarily and reasonably to avoid this threat, provided that the person does not intend to cause a greater harm than the one sought to be avoided. Such a threat may either be:

(i) Made by other persons; or
(ii) Constituted by other circumstances beyond that person's control.

2. The Court shall determine the applicability of the grounds for excluding criminal responsibility provided for in this Statute to the case before it.

3. At trial, the Court may consider a ground for excluding criminal responsibility other than those referred to in paragraph 1 where such a ground is derived from applicable law as set forth in article 21. The procedures relating to the consideration of such a ground shall be provided for in the Rules of Procedure and Evidence.

Article 33
Superior orders and prescription of law

1. The fact that a crime within the jurisdiction of the Court has been committed by a person pursuant to an order of a Government or of a superior, whether military or civilian, shall not relieve that person of criminal responsibility unless:

(a) The person was under a legal obligation to obey orders of the Government or the superior in question;
(b) The person did not know that the order was unlawful; and
(c) The order was not manifestly unlawful.

2. For the purposes of this article, orders to commit genocide or crimes against humanity are manifestly unlawful.

Chapter 4. State Liability for Failure to Investigate, Prosecute, and Punish Gross Human Rights Violations and International Crimes

Velásquez Rodríguez v. Honduras
Inter-American Court of Human Rights
Judgment of July 29, 1988, Ser. C No. 4

. . . .

147. The Court now turns to the relevant facts that it finds to have been proven. They are as follows:

a. During the period 1981 to 1984, 100 to 150 persons disappeared in the Republic of Honduras, and many were never heard from again . . . .

b. Those disappearances followed a similar pattern, beginning with the kidnapping of the victims by force, often in broad daylight and in public places, by armed men in civilian clothes and disguises, who acted with apparent impunity and who used vehicles without any official identification, with tinted windows and with false license plates or no plates . . . .

c. It was public and notorious knowledge in Honduras that the kidnappings were carried out by military personnel or the police, or persons acting under their orders . . . .

d. The disappearances were carried out in a systematic manner, regarding which the Court considers the following circumstances particularly relevant:

i. The victims were usually persons whom Honduran officials considered dangerous to State security . . . . In addition, the victims had usually been under surveillance for long periods of time . . . ;

ii. The arms employed were reserved for the official use of the military and police, and the vehicles used had tinted glass, which requires special official authorization. In some cases, Government agents carried out the detentions openly and without any pretense or disguise; in others, government agents had cleared the areas where the kidnappings were to take place and, on at least one occasion, when government agents stopped the kidnappers they were allowed to continue freely on their way after showing their identification . . . ;

iii. The kidnappers blindfolded the victims, took them to secret, unofficial detention centers and moved them from one center to another. They interrogated the victims and subjected them to cruel and humiliating treatment and torture. Some were ultimately murdered and their bodies were buried in clandestine cemeteries . . . ;

iv. When queried by relatives, lawyers and persons or entities interested in the protection of human rights, or by judges charged with executing writs of habeas corpus, the authorities systematically denied any knowledge of the detentions or the whereabouts or fate of the victims. That attitude was seen even in the cases of persons who later reappeared in the hands of the same authorities who had systematically denied holding them or knowing their fate . . . ;

v. Military and police officials as well as those from the Executive and Judicial Branches either denied the disappearances or were incapable of preventing or investigating them, punishing those responsible, or helping those interested discover the whereabouts and fate of the victims or the location of their remains. The investigative committees created by the Government and the Armed Forces did not produce any results. The judicial proceedings brought were processed slowly with a clear lack of interest and some were ultimately dismissed . . . ;

e. On September 12, 1981, between 4:30 and 5:00 p.m., several heavily-armed men in civilian clothes driving a white Ford without license plates kidnapped Manfredo Velásquez from a parking lot in downtown Tegucigalpa. Today, nearly seven years later, he remains disappeared, which creates a reasonable presumption that he is dead . . . .

f. Persons connected with the Armed Forces or under its direction carried out that kidnapping . . . .

g. The kidnapping and disappearance of Manfredo Velásquez falls within the systematic practice of disappearances referred to by the facts deemed proved in paragraphs a-d. To wit:

i. Manfredo Velásquez was a student who was involved in activities the authorities considered "dangerous" to national security . . . .

ii. The kidnapping of Manfredo Velásquez was carried out in broad daylight by men in civilian clothes who used a vehicle without license plates.

iii. In the case of Manfredo Velásquez, there were the same type of denials by his captors and the Armed Forces, the same omissions of the latter and of the Government in investigating and revealing his whereabouts, and the same ineffectiveness of the courts where three writs of habeas corpus and two criminal complaints were brought . . . .

h. There is no evidence in the record that Manfredo Velásquez had disappeared in order to join subversive groups, other than a letter from the Mayor of Langue, which contained rumors to that effect. The letter itself shows that the Government associated him with activities it considered a threat to national security. However, the Government did not corroborate the view expressed in the letter with any other evidence. Nor is there any evidence that he was kidnapped by common criminals or other persons unrelated to the practice of disappearances existing at that time.

148. Based upon the above, the Court finds that the following facts have been proven in this proceeding: (1) a practice of disappearances carried out or tolerated by Honduran officials existed between 1981 and 1984; (2) Manfredo Velásquez disappeared at the hands of or with the acquiescence of those officials within the framework of that practice; and (3) the Government of Honduras failed to guarantee the human rights affected by that practice.

X

. . . .

153. International practice and doctrine have often categorized disappearances as a crime against humanity . . . .

154. Without question, the State has the right and duty to guarantee its security. It is also indisputable that all societies suffer some deficiencies in their legal orders. However, regardless of the seriousness of certain actions and the culpability of the perpetrators of certain crimes, the power of the State is not unlimited, nor may the State resort to any

means to attain its ends. The State is subject to law and morality. Disrespect for human dignity cannot serve as the basis for any State action.

155. The forced disappearance of human beings is a multiple and continuous violation of many rights under the Convention that the States Parties are obligated to respect and guarantee. [The Court found that disappearances violate Articles 7 (right to personal liberty), 5 (right to humane treatment), and 4 (right to life).] . . .

158. The practice of disappearances, in addition to directly violating many provisions of the Convention, such as those noted above, constitutes a radical breach of the treaty in that it shows a crass abandonment of the values which emanate from the concept of human dignity and of the most basic principles of the inter-American system and the Convention. The existence of this practice, moreover, evinces a disregard of the duty to organize the State in such a manner as to guarantee the rights recognized in the Convention, as set out below.

XI

. . . .
161. Article 1(1) of the Convention provides:

Article 1. Obligation to Respect Rights

1. The States Parties to this Convention undertake to respect the rights and freedoms recognized herein and to ensure to all persons subject to their jurisdiction the free and full exercise of those rights and freedoms, without any discrimination for reasons of race, color, sex, language, religion, political or other opinion, national or social origin, economic status, birth, or any other social condition.

162. This article specifies the obligation assumed by the States Parties in relation to each of the rights protected. Each claim alleging that one of those rights has been infringed necessarily implies that Article 1(1) of the Convention has also been violated.

. . . .
164. Article 1(1) is essential in determining whether a violation of the human rights recognized by the Convention can be imputed to a State Party. In effect, that article charges the States Parties with the fundamental duty to respect and guarantee the rights recognized in the Convention. Any impairment of those rights which can be attributed under the rules of international law to the action or omission of any public authority constitutes an act imputable to the State, which assumes responsibility in the terms provided by the Convention.

165. The first obligation assumed by the States Parties under Article 1(1) is "to respect the rights and freedoms" recognized by the Convention. The exercise of public authority has certain limits which derive from the fact that human rights are inherent attributes of human dignity and are, therefore, superior to the power of the State. . . .

166. The second obligation of the States Parties is to "ensure" the free and full exercise of the rights recognized by the Convention to every person subject to its jurisdiction. This obligation implies the duty of the States Parties to organize the

governmental apparatus and, in general, all the structures through which public power is exercised, so that they are capable of juridically ensuring the free and full enjoyment of human rights. As a consequence of this obligation, the States must prevent, investigate and punish any violation of the rights recognized by the Convention and, moreover, if possible attempt to restore the right violated and provide compensation as warranted for damages resulting from the violation.

167. The obligation to ensure the free and full exercise of human rights is not fulfilled by the existence of a legal system designed to make it possible to comply with this obligation — it also requires the government to conduct itself so as to effectively ensure the free and full exercise of human rights.

168. The obligation of the States is, thus, much more direct than that contained in Article 2, which reads:

Article 2. Domestic Legal Effects

Where the exercise of any of the rights or freedoms referred to in Article 1 is not already ensured by legislative or other provisions, the States Parties undertake to adopt, in accordance with their constitutional processes and the provisions of this Convention, such legislative or other measures as may be necessary to give effect to those rights or freedoms.

169. According to Article 1(1), any exercise of public power that violates the rights recognized by the Convention is illegal. Whenever a State organ, official or public entity violates one of those rights, this constitutes a failure of the duty to respect the rights and freedoms set forth in the Convention.

170. This conclusion is independent of whether the organ or official has contravened provisions of internal law or overstepped the limits of his authority: under international law a State is responsible for the acts of its agents undertaken in their official capacity and for their omissions, even when those agents act outside the sphere of their authority or violate internal law. . . .

172. Thus, in principle, any violation of rights recognized by the Convention carried out by an act of public authority or by persons who use their position of authority is imputable to the State. However, this does not define all the circumstances in which a State is obligated to prevent, investigate and punish human rights violations, nor all the cases in which the State might be found responsible for an infringement of those rights. An illegal act which violates human rights and which is initially not directly imputable to a State (for example, because it is the act of a private person or because the person responsible has not been identified) can lead to international responsibility of the State, not because of the act itself, but because of the lack of due diligence to prevent the violation or to respond to it as required by the Convention.

173. Violations of the Convention cannot be founded upon rules that take psychological factors into account in establishing individual culpability. For the purposes of analysis, the intent or motivation of the agent who has violated the rights recognized by the Convention is irrelevant - the violation can be established even if the identity of the individual perpetrator is unknown. What is decisive is whether a violation of the rights recognized by the Convention has occurred with the support or the acquiescence of the

government, or whether the State has allowed the act to take place without taking measures to prevent it or to punish those responsible. Thus, the Court's task is to determine whether the violation is the result of a State's failure to fulfill its duty to respect and guarantee those rights, as required by Article 1(1) of the Convention.

174. The State has a legal duty to take reasonable steps to prevent human rights violations and to use the means at its disposal to carry out a serious investigation of violations committed within its jurisdiction, to identify those responsible, to impose the appropriate punishment and to ensure the victim adequate compensation.

175. This duty to prevent includes all those means of a legal, political, administrative and cultural nature that promote the protection of human rights and ensure that any violations are considered and treated as illegal acts, which, as such, may lead to the punishment of those responsible and the obligation to indemnify the victims for damages. It is not possible to make a detailed list of all such measures, since they vary with the law and the conditions of each State Party. Of course, while the State is obligated to prevent human rights abuses, the existence of a particular violation does not, in itself, prove the failure to take preventive measures. On the other hand, subjecting a person to official, repressive bodies that practice torture and assassination with impunity is itself a breach of the duty to prevent violations of the rights to life and physical integrity of the person, even if that particular person is not tortured or assassinated, or if those facts cannot be proven in a concrete case.

176. The State is obligated to investigate every situation involving a violation of the rights protected by the Convention. If the State apparatus acts in such a way that the violation goes unpunished and the victim's full enjoyment of such rights is not restored as soon as possible, the State has failed to comply with its duty to ensure the free and full exercise of those rights to the persons within its jurisdiction. The same is true when the State allows private persons or groups to act freely and with impunity to the detriment of the rights recognized by the Convention.

177. In certain circumstances, it may be difficult to investigate acts that violate an individual's rights. The duty to investigate, like the duty to prevent, is not breached merely because the investigation does not produce a satisfactory result. Nevertheless, it must be undertaken in a serious manner and not as a mere formality preordained to be ineffective. An investigation must have an objective and be assumed by the State as its own legal duty, not as a step taken by private interests that depends upon the initiative of the victim or his family or upon their offer of proof, without an effective search for the truth by the government. This is true regardless of what agent is eventually found responsible for the violation. Where the acts of private parties that violate the Convention are not seriously investigated, those parties are aided in a sense by the government, thereby making the State responsible on the international plane.

178. In the instant case, the evidence shows a complete inability of the procedures of the State of Honduras, which were theoretically adequate, to carry out an investigation into the disappearance of Manfredo Velásquez, and of the fulfillment of its duties to pay compensation and punish those responsible, as set out in Article 1(1) of the Convention.

179. As the Court has verified above, the failure of the judicial system to act upon the writs brought before various tribunals in the instant case has been proven. Not one writ

of habeas corpus was processed. No judge had access to the places where Manfredo Velásquez might have been detained. The criminal complaint was dismissed.

180. Nor did the organs of the Executive Branch carry out a serious investigation to establish the fate of Manfredo Velásquez. There was no investigation of public allegations of a practice of disappearances nor a determination of whether Manfredo Velásquez had been a victim of that practice. . . . The offer of an investigation in accord with Resolution 30/83 of the Commission resulted in an investigation by the Armed Forces, the same body accused of direct responsibility for the disappearances. This raises grave questions regarding the seriousness of the investigation. The Government often resorted to asking relatives of the victims to present conclusive proof of their allegations even though those allegations, because they involved crimes against the person, should have been investigated on the Government's own initiative in fulfillment of the State's duty to ensure public order. This is especially true when the allegations refer to a practice carried out within the Armed Forces, which, because of its nature, is not subject to private investigations. No proceeding was initiated to establish responsibility for the disappearance of Manfredo Velásquez and apply punishment under internal law. All of the above leads to the conclusion that the Honduran authorities did not take effective action to ensure respect for human rights within the jurisdiction of that State as required by Article 1(1) of the Convention.

181. The duty to investigate facts of this type continues as long as there is uncertainty about the fate of the person who has disappeared. Even in the hypothetical case that those individually responsible for crimes of this type cannot be legally punished under certain circumstances, the State is obligated to use the means at its disposal to inform the relatives of the fate of the victims and, if they have been killed, the location of their remains.

182. The Court is convinced, and has so found, that the disappearance of Manfredo Velásquez was carried out by agents who acted under cover of public authority. However, even had that fact not been proven, the failure of the State apparatus to act, which is clearly proven, is a failure on the part of Honduras to fulfill the duties it assumed under Article 1(1) of the Convention, which obligated it to ensure Manfredo Velásquez the free and full exercise of his human rights.

183. The Court notes that the legal order of Honduras does not authorize such acts and that internal law defines them as crimes. The Court also recognizes that not all levels of the Government of Honduras were necessarily aware of those acts, nor is there any evidence that such acts were the result of official orders. Nevertheless, those circumstances are irrelevant for the purposes of establishing whether Honduras is responsible under international law for the violations of human rights perpetrated within the practice of disappearances.

. . . .

185. The Court, therefore, concludes that the facts found in this proceeding show that the State of Honduras is responsible for the involuntary disappearance of Angel Manfredo Velásquez Rodríguez. Thus, Honduras has violated Articles 7, 5 and 4 of the Convention.

. . . .

[The Court also held that there had been a violation of the duty under Article 1(1) to protect the rights under each of those articles. Finally, it ordered Honduras "to pay fair compensation to the next-of-kin of the victim."]

❖ ❖ ❖

Chapter 4. State Liability for Failure to Investigate, Prosecute, & Punish Gross Human Rights Violations and International Crimes

Questions & Comments

(1) The central holding in *Velásquez Rodríguez* — that a state has a duty to investigate and prosecute disappearances — has been reiterated in subsequent cases. *See, e.g., Godínez Cruz*, Inter-Am. Ct. H.R., Ser. C, No. 4 (Judgment of January 20, 1989); *Neira Alegría v. Peru*, 20 Inter-Am. Ct. H.R, Ser. C (Judgment of January 1, 1995). Prior to the *Velásquez Rodríguez* case, the Inter-American Commission had previously done so on a number of occasions.

The UN Human Rights Committee similarly has recognized a duty to investigate and prosecute. In *Ana Rosario Celis Laureano v. Peru*, views adopted 25 March 1996, U.N. Doc. CCPR/C/56/D/540/1993 (1996), the Committee addressed a case involving a 16-year-old who had been kidnaped by the Shining Path and escaped, then detained by the military, released by a judge, and finally abducted by paramilitary forces acting together with the military: The Committee stated:

> 8.3 In respect of the alleged violation of article 6, paragraph 1, the Committee recalls its General Comment 6 [16] on article 6 which states, *inter alia,* that States parties should take measures not only to prevent and punish deprivation of life by criminal acts, but also to prevent arbitrary killing by their own security forces. States parties should also take specific and effective measures to prevent the disappearance of individuals and establish effective facilities and procedures to investigate thoroughly, by an appropriate and impartial body, cases of missing and disappeared persons in circumstances which may involve a violation of the right to life.
>
> . . . .
>
> 9. The Human Rights Committee, acting under article 5, paragraph 4 of the Optional Protocol to the International Covenant on Civil and Political Rights, is of the view that the facts before the Committee reveal violations of articles 6, paragraph 1; 7; and 9, paragraph 1, *all juncto* article 2, paragraph 1; and of article 24, paragraph 1, of the Covenant.
>
> 10. Under article 2, paragraph 3, of the Covenant, the State party is under an obligation to provide the victim and the author with an effective remedy. The Committee urges the State party to open a proper investigation into the disappearance of Ana Rosario Celis Laureano and her fate, to provide for appropriate compensation to the victim and her family, and to bring to justice those responsible for her disappearance notwithstanding any domestic amnesty legislation to the contrary.

The UN Human Rights Committee also has found a state affirmative duty to investigate a wounding allegedly perpetrated by police. *García Fuenzalida v. Ecuador*, Communication No. 480/1991, views adopted 12 July 1996, U.N. Doc. CCPR/C/57/D/480/1991 (1996)

(2) The *Velásquez Rodríguez* Court speaks sweepingly of "the duty to organize the State in such a manner as to guarantee the rights recognized in the Convention." What

limitations can reasonably be put on the Court's holding? What role should the dichotomy between private *vs.* governmental duties play in this context?

(3) A state might incur international responsibility where it carries out or is otherwise complicit in the disappearance. Suppose it takes no part in the disappearance. What does *Velásquez Rodríguez* say about the state's responsibility in that situation? On this issue, see *X. & Y. v. The Netherlands*, 91 Eur. Ct. H.R. (ser. A) (1985), reproduced below.

(4) What precise measures must a state take to fulfill its obligation to secure the protection of human rights in the disappearances context? What specific factors made Honduras' investigation inadequate, in the view of the Court?

(5) What measures are adequate to satisfy the state's duty to respond to disappearances? Would it be enough, for example, to dismiss members of the military who took part in disappearing someone? Why or why not? Consider *Bautista de Arellana v. Colombia*, views adopted 27 October 1995, U.N. Doc. CCPR/C/55/D/1993 (1995). The victim, a member of Colombia's M-19 guerrilla movement, was abducted in 1987 by armed men dressed as civilians, tortured, mutilated, and buried. When her body was later identified in 1990, disciplinary proceedings were begun against some members of the military, and then dropped. In 1993, her relatives filed a petition with the UN Human Rights Committee. In 1994, formal proceedings were instituted before the National Delegate for Human Rights, a Colombian official. In July 1995, the Delegate issued a decision holding Col. Velandia Hurtado and Sgt. Ortega Araque responsible for the disappearance, and requesting their summary dismissal from the Armed Forces. Following the Delegate's findings, the Administrative Tribunal of Cundinamarca awarded the victim's family damages, and the President dismissed Col. Velandia Hurtado from the armed forces (although the order was subject to appeal). The criminal investigation was still pending as of 1995. The Committee noted:

> 8.2 In its submission of 14 July 1995, the State party indicates that Resolution 13 of 5 July 1995 pronounced disciplinary sanctions against Messrs. Velandia Hurtado and Ortega Araque, and that the 'judgment of the Administrative Tribunal of Cundinamarca of 22 June 1995 granted the claim for compensation filed by the family of Nydia Bautista. The State party equally reiterates its desire to guarantee fully the exercise of human rights and fundamental freedoms. These observations would appear to indicate that, in the State party's opinion, the above-mentioned decisions constitute an effective remedy for the family of Nydia Bautista. The Committee does not share this view, because purely disciplinary and administrative remedies cannot be deemed to constitute adequate and effective remedies within the meaning of article 2, paragraph 30 of the Covenant, in the event of particularly serious violations of human rights, notably in the event of an alleged violation of the right to life.

(6) Suppose the state undertakes an investigation that is not on its face inadequate, but the victim's whereabouts remain undiscovered and no one is punished. In *Caballero-Delgado v. Colombia* Series C, No. 17 (Judgment of December 8, 1995), the Inter-

American Court found that the Colombian army and its collaborators had disappeared Isidro Caballero-Delgado and María del Carmen Santana six years earlier; they had never been seen again. At the time of the disappearance, a judge denied a writ of habeas corpus, apparently after detention centers denied having detained Caballero-Delgado. Three members of the army were detained for alleged involvement in the crime, but released by the court for insufficient evidence. One of those three was later discharged from the military for disappearing other individuals in a nearby region. The criminal investigation was re-opened twice, but at the time of the Inter-American Court's decision no one had been convicted. The Court found that Colombia had violated Articles 7 and 4 in conjunction with Article 1(1), as well as Article 5, and then held:

> 57. In the instant case, Colombia has undertaken a prolonged judicial investigation, not free of defects, to find and sanction those responsible for the detention and disappearance of Isidro Caballero-Delgado and María del Carmen Santana, and those proceedings have not been closed. . . .
> 58. . . . Nevertheless, to fully ensure the rights recognized in the Convention, it is not sufficient that the Government undertake an investigation and try to sanction those guilty; rather it is also necessary that all this Government activity culminate in the reparation of the injured party, which in this case has not occurred.
> 59. Therefore, as Colombia has not remedied the consequences of the violations carried out by its agents, it has failed to comply with the duties that the above-cited Article 1(1) of the Convention imposes on it. . . .
> 69. In the instant case, reparations should consist of the continuation of the judicial proceedings inquiring into the disappearance of Isidro Caballero-Delgado and María del Carmen Santana and punishment of those responsible in conformance with Colombian domestic law.

Dissenting, Judge Nieto-Navia accused the majority of applying, in effect, a strict liability standard:

> It is not enough that there be a violation to say that the State failed to prevent it. To interpret the Convention in this manner obviously goes farther than what the States accepted on subscribing to it, because it would imply that it is sufficient that the act of State which violates a protected right be present for the State to have to answer for it. . . .
> The record of this case does not prove that "reasonable" steps to prevent acts of this nature, do not exist, or if they do exist, that they have not been taken. . . .
> One cannot attribute to the Republic of Colombia negligence or indolence in the investigation. Moreover, the fact that those implicated have been absolved in the first proceeding does not signify that there is "collusion" between them and the Public Power given that the rules that criminal judges must apply require that doubts be resolved in favor of the accused. Nor has it been demonstrated that the judges were not independent.

Similarly, in *Bautista de Arellana v. Colombia* (discussed above), the Human Rights Committee noted:

8.6 The author has finally claimed a violation of article 14, paragraph 3(c), on account of the unreasonable delays in the criminal proceedings instituted against those responsible for the death of Nydia Bautista. As the Committee has repeatedly held, the Covenant does not provide a right for individuals to require that the State criminally prosecute another person.[1] The Committee nevertheless considers that the State party is under a duty to investigate thoroughly alleged violations of human rights, and in particular forced disappearances of persons and violations of the right to life, and to prosecute criminally, try and punish those held responsible for such violations. This duty applies *a fortiori* in cases in which the perpetrators of such violations have been identified.

Should it be acceptable for the state to close a disappearance case without having found the victim's body? Convicted anyone? Does it depend on whether there is simply an allegation of a disappearance, or a finding by the Court that the state has disappeared someone?

(7) Compare the discretion that the Prosecutor of the International Criminal Court has under its Statute.

Article 13
Exercise of jurisdiction

The Court may exercise its jurisdiction with respect to a crime referred to in article 5 in accordance with the provisions of this Statute if:

(a) A situation in which one or more of such crimes appears to have been committed is referred to the Prosecutor by a State Party in accordance with article 14;

(b) A situation in which one or more of such crimes appears to have been committed is referred to the Prosecutor by the Security Council acting under Chapter VII of the Charter of the United Nations; or

(c) The Prosecutor has initiated an investigation in respect of such a crime in accordance with article 15.

---

[1] See the decisions on cases No. 213/1986 (*H.C.M.A. v. the Netherlands*), adopted 30 March 1989, paragraph 11.6; No. 275/1988, (*S.E. v. Argentina*), adopted 26 March 1990, paragraph 5.5; Nos. 343-345/1988 (*R.A., V.N. et al. v. Argentina*)., adopted 26 March 1990, paragraph 5.5.

Chapter 4. State Liability for Failure to Investigate, Prosecute, & Punish
Gross Human Rights Violations and International Crimes

Article 14
Referral of a situation by a State Party

1. A State Party may refer to the Prosecutor a situation in which one or more crimes within the jurisdiction of the Court appear to have been committed requesting the Prosecutor to investigate the situation for the purpose of determining whether one or more specific persons should be charged with the commission of such crimes.

2. As far as possible, a referral shall specify the relevant circumstances and be accompanied by such supporting documentation as is available to the State referring the situation.

Article 15
Prosecutor

1. The Prosecutor may initiate investigations *proprio motu* on the basis of information on crimes within the jurisdiction of the Court.

2. The Prosecutor shall analyse the seriousness of the information received. For this purpose, he or she may seek additional information from States, organs of the United Nations, intergovernmental or non-governmental organizations, or other reliable sources that he or she deems appropriate, and may receive written or oral testimony at the seat of the Court.

3. If the Prosecutor concludes that there is a reasonable basis to proceed with an investigation, he or she shall submit to the Pre-Trial Chamber a request for authorization of an investigation, together with any supporting material collected. Victims may make representations to the Pre-Trial Chamber, in accordance with the Rules of Procedure and Evidence.

How does the ICC Statute comport with the international human rights law that establishes state liability for failure to investigate, prosecute, and punish gross human rights violations? Should the Prosecutor be held liable for failure to investigate gross human rights violations? Should inter-governmental bodies be held liable as states are?

(8) Under the ICC Statute, ICC can exercise jurisdiction over cases in which the domestic courts have been unwilling and/or incompetent to prosecute (Art.17). In such a case and assuming that the state is a party to the ACHR or ECHR, how much weight should be given to the ICC's admissibility decision in a case on the merits before the Inter-American or European Courts of Human Rights? What kind of factors should the Inter-American or European Courts consider in transposing an admissibility decision in a criminal matter to a decision on the merits in a quasi-civil matter?

X. and Y. v. The Netherlands
European Court of Human Rights
91 Eur. Ct. H.R. (ser. A) (1985)
8 E.H.R.R. 235 (1986)

[In this case, the European Court of Human Rights reviewed a state's response to a claim of sexual violence. A sixteen-year-old Dutch girl with mental disabilities had been allegedly raped by an acquaintance. Being incompetent under the law, the police concluded that the girl could not file a complaint, instead directing that her father file on her behalf. The prosecutor's office declined to file charges against the alleged rapist on the condition that the latter not commit a similar offence within the next two years. The father appealed this decision, and asked the court to direct that the prosecutor institute proceedings against the suspect. The Dutch court refused, and raised questions about whether a charge of rape could be proved in this case. The Dutch court also noted that the father was not legally empowered to file a complaint since his daughter was over the age of sixteen (complaints involving individuals over sixteen could only be filed by the victim under Dutch law), and thus there was no official complaint upon which the prosecutor could act.]

. . . .

21. According to the applicants, the impossibility of having criminal proceedings instituted against Mr B violated Article 8 of the Convention, which reads:

1. Everyone has the right to respect for his private and family life, his home and his correspondence.

2. There shall be no interference by a public authority with the exercise of this right except such as is in accordance with the law and is necessary in a democratic society in the interests of national security, public safety or the economic well-being of the country, for the prevention of disorder or crime, for the protection of health or morals, or for the protection of the rights and freedoms of others.

The Government contested this claim; the Commission, on the other hand, agreed with it in its essentials.

22. There was no dispute as to the applicability of Article 8: the facts underlying the application to the Commission concern a matter of 'private life', a concept which covers the physical and moral integrity of the person, including his or her sexual life.

23. The Court recalls that although the object of Article 8 is essentially that of protecting the individual against arbitrary interference by the public authorities, it does not merely compel the State to abstain from such interference: in addition to this primarily negative undertaking, there may be positive obligations inherent in an effective respect for private or family life. (*Airey v. Ireland*, § 32.) These obligations may involve the adoption of measures designed to secure respect for private life even in the sphere of the relations of individuals between themselves.

Chapter 4. State Liability for Failure to Investigate, Prosecute, & Punish Gross Human Rights Violations and International Crimes

1. Necessity for criminal-law provisions

24. The applicants argued that, for a young girl like Miss Y, the requisite degree of protection against the wrongdoing in question would have been provided only by means of the criminal law. In the Government's view, the Convention left it to each State to decide upon the means to be utilised and did not prevent it from opting for civil-law provisions.

The Court, which on this point agrees in substance with the opinion of the Commission, observes that the choice of the means calculated to secure compliance with Article 8 in the sphere of the relations of individuals between themselves is in principle a matter that falls within the Contracting States' margin of appreciation. In this connection, there are different ways of ensuring 'respect for private life', and the nature of the State's obligation will depend on the particular aspect of private life that is at issue. Recourse to the criminal law is not necessarily the only answer.

25. . . . .

The Government stated that under Article 1401 of the Civil Code, taken together with Article 1407, it would have been possible to bring before or file with the Netherlands courts, on behalf of Miss Y:

-- an action for damages against Mr B for pecuniary or non-pecuniary damage;

-- an application for an injunction against Mr B, to prevent repetition of the offence;

-- a similar action or application against the directress of the children's home.

The applicants considered that these civil-law remedies were unsuitable. They submitted that, amongst other things, the absence of any criminal investigation made it harder to furnish evidence on the four matters that had to be established under Article 1401, namely a wrongful act, fault, damage and a causal link between the act and the damage. Furthermore, such proceedings were lengthy and involved difficulties of an emotional nature for the victim, since he or she had to play an active part therein.

. . .

27. The Court finds that the protection afforded by the civil law in the case of wrongdoing of the kind inflicted on Miss Y is insufficient. This is a case where fundamental values and essential aspects of private life are at stake. Effective deterrence is indispensable in this area and it can be achieved only by criminal-law provisions; indeed, it is by such provisions that the matter is normally regulated.

Moreover, as was pointed out by the Commission, this is in fact an area in which the Netherlands has generally opted for a system of protection based on the criminal law. The only gap, so far as the Commission and the Court have been made aware, is as regards persons in the situation of Miss Y; in such cases, this system meets a procedural obstacle which the Dutch legislature had apparently not foreseen.

. . . .

III. Alleged Violation of Article 3, taken alone or in conjunction with Article 14, as regards Miss Y

33. According to the applicants, Miss Y suffered at the hands of Mr B 'inhuman and degrading treatment' contrary to Article 3 of the Convention. They maintained that, for the purposes of this provision, the State was in certain circumstances responsible for the acts of third parties and that the chronic psychological trauma caused to Miss Y had attained such a level as to fall within the ambit of that Article.

34. According to the Commission, Article 3 had not been violated since there was no close and direct link between the gap in the Dutch law and 'the field of protection covered' by the Article.

At the hearings, the Government adopted this opinion and submitted that they were not answerable for the treatment inflicted on Miss Y.

Having found that Article 8 was violated, the Court does not consider that it has also to examine the case under Article 3, taken alone or in conjunction with Article 14.

. . . .

VI. Article 50

38. Under Article 50 of the Convention,

> If the Court finds that a decision or a measure taken by a legal authority or any other authority of a High Contracting Party is completely or partially in conflict with the obligations arising from the . . . Convention, and if the internal law of the said Party allows only partial reparation to be made for the consequences of this decision or measure, the decision of the Court shall, if necessary, afford just satisfaction to the injured party.

In her letter of 27 August 1984, Ms van Westerlaak explained that 'approximately seven years after the event, the girl in question is still experiencing daily the consequences of the indecent assault of which she was the victim' and that 'this is the source of much tension within the family'. Ms van Westerlaak stated at the hearings that non-pecuniary damage was still being suffered.

The Commission did not comment on these allegations.

The Government also did not challenge the allegations as such, but they argued that the suffering was the result of the act committed by Mr B and not of the violation of the Convention. Accordingly, there was no reason to afford just satisfaction.

39. The Court notes that the claim is confined to non-pecuniary damage and does not relate to the costs of the proceedings.

40. No one contests that Miss Y suffered damage. In addition, it is hardly deniable that the Dutch authorities have a degree of responsibility resulting from the deficiency in the legislation which gave rise to the violation of Article 8.

The applicants left it to the Court's discretion to determine a standard for compensation.

The damage in question does not lend itself even to an approximate process of calculation. Assessing it on an equitable basis, as is required by Article 50, the Court considers that Miss Y should be afforded just satisfaction which it fixes at 3,000 Dutch guilders.

For these reasons, THE COURT unanimously

1. Holds that there has been a violation of Article 8 as regards Miss Y;
2. Holds that it is not necessary to give a separate decision:

   (a) on her other complaints;
   (b) on the complaints of Mr X;

3. Holds that the respondent State is to pay to Miss Y three thousand (3,000) Dutch guilders under Article 50.

❖ ❖ ❖

Questions & Comments

(1) Note that the European Court of Human Rights did not order the Dutch Government to investigate, prosecute, and punish the alleged rapist in *X. & Y. v. The Netherlands* unlike the Inter-American Court of Human Rights has done repeatedly in disappearance cases. Instead, the European Court limits its forms of relief to money damages and declaratory relief. However, as part of its declaratory relief, the European Court often does declare that certain measures if undertaken by the state-party would bring the government into conformity with its obligations under the ECHR.

(2) The European Court of Human Rights has declared that state-parties have affirmative duties in other criminal law contexts. *See, e.g., Assenov v. Bulgaria*, -- Eur. Ct. H.R. (ser. A) (1998) (state duty to investigate police brutality); *Ergi v. Turkey*, -- Eur. Ct. H.R. (ser. A) (1998) (duty to investigate circumstances of applicant's death during security force operation); *Güleç v. Turkey*, – Eur. Ct. H.R. (ser. A) (1998) (duty to investigate applicant's death during clash with police during demonstration).

(3) As seen in the above decisions from the Inter-American Court, UN Human Rights Committee, and European Court of Human Rights, states incur liability for failing to investigate, prosecute, and/or punish perpetrators of gross human rights violations. In light of these cases, how would you argue a customary international law claim in U.S. courts that the failure of the government to investigate, prosecute, and punish perpetrators of gross international human rights violations makes the government civilly liable? What relevance is there that victims of war crimes can sue war criminals in both federal and state courts. Jordan J. Paust, *Suing Saddam: Private Remedies for War Crimes and Hostage-Taking*, 31 VA. J. INT'L L. 351 (1991)?

(4) In *REINICIAR v. Colombia*, the Inter-American Commission held the following:

the State has the nonderogable and nondelegable duty to prosecute public action crimes ("delitos de acción pública"), crimes for which the State has exclusive power to prosecute, in order to preserve public order and ensure the right to justice.

Report No. 5/97, Case 11.227, ANNUAL REPORT OF THE INTER-AMERICAN COMMISSION ON HUMAN RIGHTS 1996 99, OEA/Ser.L/V/II.95, Doc. 7 rev. (14 March 1997) at 113 n.30.

Chapter 5.   Conspiracy and Corporate Responsibility

Judgment for the Trial of German Major War Criminals
International Military Tribunal
1946

[The Law as to the Common Plan or Conspiracy]

. . . .

In the previous recital of the facts relating to aggressive war, it is clear that planning and preparation had been carried out in the most systematic way at every stage of the history.

Planning and preparation are essential to the making of war. In the opinion of the Tribunal aggressive war is a crime under international law. The [London] Charter defines this offence as planning, preparation, initiation or waging of a war of aggression " or participation in a common plan or conspiracy for the accomplishment . . . of the foregoing." The Indictment follows this distinction. Count One charges the common plan or conspiracy. Count Two charges the planning and waging of war. The same evidence has been introduced to support both counts. We shall therefore discuss both counts together, as they are in substance the same. The defendants have been charged under both counts, and their guilt under each count must be determined.

The "common plan or conspiracy" charged in the Indictment covers twenty-five years, from the formation of the Nazi party in 1919 to the end of the war in 1945. The party is spoken of as "the instrument of cohesion among the defendants" for carrying out the purposes of the conspiracy the overthrowing of the Treaty of Versailles, acquiring territory lost by Germany in the last war and "lebensraum"[1] in Europe, by the use, if necessary, of armed force, of aggressive war. The seizure of power "by the Nazis, the use of terror, the destruction of trade unions, the attack on Christian teaching and on churches, the persecution of the Jews, the regimentation of youth -- all these are said to be steps deliberately taken to carry out the common plan. It found expression, so it is alleged, in secret rearmament, the withdrawal by Germany from the Disarmament Conference and the League of Nations, universal military service, and seizure of the Rhineland. Finally, according to the Indictment, aggressive action was planned and carried out against Austria and Czechoslovakia in 1936-1938, followed by the planning and waging of war against Poland; and, successively, against ten other countries.

The Prosecution says, in effect, that any significant participation in the affairs of the Nazi Party or Government is evidence of a participation in a conspiracy that is in itself criminal. Conspiracy is not defined in the Charter. But in the opinion of the Tribunal the conspiracy must be clearly outlined in its criminal purpose. It must not be too far removed from the time of decision and of action. The planning, to be criminal, must not rest merely on the declarations of a party programme, such as are found in the twenty five points of the Nazi Party, announced in 1920, or the political affirmations expressed in "Mein Kampf" in later years. The Tribunal must examine whether a concrete plan to wage war existed, and determine the participants in that concrete plan.

It is not necessary to decide whether a single master conspiracy between the defendants has been established by the evidence. The seizure of power by the Nazi Party,

---

[1] "Living space." Ed's. Note.

and the subsequent domination by the Nazi State of all spheres of economic and social life must of course be remembered when the later plans for waging war are examined. That plans were made to wage wars, as early as 5th November, 1937, and probably before that, is apparent. And thereafter, such preparations continued in many directions, and against the peace of many countries. Indeed the threat of war -- and war itself if necessary -- was an integral part of the Nazi policy. But the evidence establishes with certainty the existence of many separate plans rather than a single conspiracy embracing them all. That Germany was rapidly moving to complete dictatorship from the moment that the Nazis seized power, and progressively in the direction of war, has been overwhelmingly shown in the ordered sequence of aggressive acts and wars already set out in this Judgment.

In the opinion of the Tribunal, the evidence establishes the common planning to prepare and wage war by certain of the defendants. It is immaterial to consider whether a single conspiracy to the extent and over the time set out in the Indictment has been conclusively proved. Continued planning, with aggressive war as the objective, has been established beyond doubt. The truth of the situation was well stated by Paul Schmidt, official interpreter of the German Foreign Office, as follows:

> The general objectives of the Nazi leadership were apparent from the start, namely the domination of the European Continent to be achieved first by the incorporation of all German speaking groups in the Reich, and secondly, by territorial expansion under the slogan 'Lebensraum.' The execution of these basic objectives, how ever, seemed to be characterised by improvisation. Each succeeding step was apparently carried out as each new situation arose, but all consistent with the ultimate objectives mentioned above.

The argument that such common planning cannot exist where there is complete dictatorship is unsound. A plan in the execution of which a number of persons participate is still a plan, even though conceived by only one of them; and those who execute the plan do not avoid responsibility by showing that they acted under the direction of the man who conceived it. Hitler could not make aggressive war by himself. He had to have the co-operation of statesmen, military leaders, diplomats, and business men. When they, with knowledge of his aims, gave him their co-operation, they made themselves parties to the plan he had initiated. They are not to be deemed innocent because Hitler made use of them, if they knew what they were doing. That they were assigned to their tasks by a dictator does not absolve them from responsibility for their acts. The relation of leader and follower does not preclude responsibility here any more than it does in the comparable tyranny of organised domestic crime.

Count One, however, charges not only the conspiracy to commit aggressive war, but also to commit war crimes and crimes against humanity. But the Charter does not define as a separate crime any conspiracy except the one to commit acts of aggressive war. Article 6 of the Charter provides:

> Leaders, organisers, instigators and accomplices participating in the formulation or execution of a common plan or conspiracy to commit any of the foregoing crimes are responsible for all acts performed by any persons in execution of such plan.

56

In the opinion of the Tribunal these words do not add a new and separate crime to those already listed. The words are designed to establish the responsibility of persons participating in a common plan. The Tribunal will therefore disregard the charges in Count One that the defendants conspired to commit war crimes and crimes against humanity, and will consider only the common plan to prepare, initiate and wage aggressive war.

. . . .

Article 9 of the Charter provides:

> At the trial of any individual member of any group or organisation the Tribunal may declare (in connection with any act of which the individual may be convicted) that the group or organisation of which the individual was a member was a criminal organisation.

> After receipt of the Indictment the Tribunal shall give such notice as it thinks fit that the prosecution intends to ask the Tribunal to make such declaration and any member of the organisation will be entitled to apply to the Tribunal for leave to be heard by the Tribunal upon the question of the criminal character of the organisation. The Tribunal shall have power to allow or reject the application. If the application is allowed, the Tribunal may direct in what manner the applicants shall be represented and heard.

Article 10 of the Charter makes clear that the declaration of criminality against an accused organisation is final, and cannot be challenged in any subsequent criminal proceeding against a member of that organisation. Article 10 is as follows:

> In cases where a group or organisation is declared criminal by the Tribunal, the competent national authority of any Signatory shall have the right to bring individuals to trial for membership therein before national, military or occupation courts. In any such case the criminal nature of the group or organisation is considered proved and shall not be questioned.

The effect of the declaration of criminality by the Tribunal is well illustrated by Law Number 10 of the Control Council of Germany passed on the 20th day of December, 1945, which provides:

> Each of the following acts is recognised as a crime:

> (d) Membership in categories of a criminal group or organisation declared criminal by the International Military Tribunal.

> . . . .

In effect, therefore, a member of an organisation which the Tribunal has declared to be criminal may be subsequently convicted of the crime of membership . . . . This is not to assume that international or military courts which will try these individuals will not exercise appropriate standards of justice. This is a far-reaching and novel procedure. Its application, unless properly safeguarded, may produce great injustice.

Article 9, it should be noted, uses the words "The Tribunal may declare" so that the Tribunal is vested with discretion as to whether it will declare any organisation criminal. This discretion is a judicial one and does not permit arbitrary action, but should be exercised in accordance with well settled legal principles one of the most important of which is that criminal guilt is personal, and that mass punishments should be avoided. If satisfied of the criminal guilt of any organisation or group this Tribunal should not hesitate to declare it to be criminal because the theory of "group criminality" is new, or because it might be unjustly applied by some subsequent tribunals. On the other hand, the Tribunal should make such declaration of criminality so far as possible in a manner to insure that innocent persons will not be punished.

A criminal organisation is analogous to a criminal conspiracy in that the essence of both is cooperation for criminal purposes. There must be a group bound together and organised for a common purpose. The group must be formed or used in connection with the commission of crimes denounced by the Charter. Since the declaration with respect to the organisations and groups will, as has been pointed out, fix the criminality of its members, that definition should exclude persons who had no knowledge of the criminal purposes or acts of the organisation and those who were drafted by the State for membership, unless they were personally implicated in the commission of acts declared criminal by Article 6 of the Charter as members of the organisation. Membership alone is not enough to come within the scope of these declarations.

Since declarations of criminality which the Tribunal makes will be used by other courts in the trial of persons on account of their membership in the organisations found to be criminal, the Tribunal feels it appropriate to make the following recommendations:

1. That so far as possible throughout the four zones of occupation in Germany the classifications, sanctions and penalties be standardised. Uniformity of treatment so far as practical should be a basic principle. This does not, of course, mean that discretion in sentencing should not be vested in the court; but the discretion should be within fixed limits appropriate to the nature of the crime.

2. Law No. 10, to which reference has already been made, leaves punishment entirely in the discretion of the trial court even to the extent of inflicting the death penalty.

The De-Nazification Law of 5th March, 1946, however, passed for Bavaria, Greater-Hesse and Wuerttemberg-Baden, provides definite sentences for punishment in each type of offence. The Tribunal recommends that in no case should punishment imposed under Law No. 10 upon any members of an organisation or group declared by the Tribunal to be criminal exceed the punishment fixed by the De-Nazification Law. No person should be punished under both laws.

3. The Tribunal recommends to the Control Council that Law No. 10 be amended to proscribe limitations on the punishment which may be imposed for membership in a criminal group or organisation so that such punishment shall not exceed the punishment prescribed by the De-Nazifiction Law.

The Indictment asks that the Tribunal declare to be criminal the following organisations: The Leadership Corps of the Nazi Party; . . . and The General Staff and High Command of the German Armed Forces.

THE LEADERSHIP CORPS OF THE NAZI PARTY

Structure and Component Parts: The Indictment has named the Leadership Corps of the Nazi Party as a group or organisation which should be declared criminal. The Leadership Corps of the Nazi Party consisted, in effect, of the official organisation of the Nazi Party, with Hitler as Fuehrer at its head. The actual work of running the Leadership Corps was carried out by the Chief of the Party Chancellery (Hess, succeeded by Bormann) assisted by the Party Reich Directorate, or Reichsleitung, which was composed of the Reichleiters, the heads of the functional organisations of the Party, as well as of the heads of the various main departments and offices which were attached to the Party Reich Directorate. Under the Chief of the Party Chancellery were the Gauleiters, with territorial jurisdiction over the main administrative regions of the Party, the Gaus. The Gauleiters were assisted by a Party Gau Directorate or Gauleitung, similar in composition and in function to the Party Reich Directorate. Under the Gauleiters in the Party hierarchy were the Kreisleiters with territorial jurisdiction over a Kreis, usually consisting of a single county, and assisted by a Party of Kreis Directorate, or Kreisleitung. The Kreisleiters were the lowest members of the Party hierarchy who were full time paid employees. Directly under the Kreisleiters were the Ortsgruppenleiters, then the Zellenleiters and then the Blockleiters. Directives and instructions were received from the Party Reich Directorate. The Gauleiters had the function of interpreting such orders and issuing them to lower formations. The Kreisleiters had a certain discretion in interpreting orders, but the Ortsgruppenleiters had not, but acted under definite instructions. Instructions were only issued in writing down as far as the Ortsgruppenleiters. The Block and Zellenleiters usually received instructions orally. Membership in the Leadership Corps at all levels was voluntary.

On 28th February, 1946, the Prosecution excluded from the declaration all members of the staffs of the Ortsgruppenleiters and all assistants of the Zellenleiters and Blockleiters. The declaration sought against the Leadership Corps of the Nazi Party thus includes the Fuehrer, the Reichsleitung, the Gauleiters and their staff officers, the Kreisleiters and their staff officers, the Ortsgruppenleiters, the Zellenleiters and the Blockleiters, a group estimated to contain at least 600,000 people.

Aims and Activities: The primary purposes of the Leadership Corps from its beginning was to assist the Nazis in obtaining and, after 30th January, 1933, in retaining, control of the German State. The machinery of the Leadership Corps was used for the widespread dissemination of Nazi propaganda and to keep a detailed check on the political attitudes of the German people. In this activity the lower Political Leaders played a particularly important role. The Blockleiters were instructed by the Party Manual to report to the Ortsgruppenleiters, all persons circulating damaging rumours or criticism of the regime. The Ortsgruppenleiters, on the basis of information supplied them by the Blockleiters and Zellenleiters, kept a card index of the people within their Ortsgruppe which recorded the factors which would be used in forming a judgment as to their political reliability. The Leadership Corps was particularly active during plebiscites. All members of the Leadership Corps were active in getting out the vote and insuring the highest possible proportion of "yes" votes. Ortsgruppenleiters and Political Leaders of higher ranks often collaborated with the Gestapo[2] and SD[3] in taking steps to determine those who refused to vote or who voted "no", and in taking steps against them which went as far as arrest and detention in a concentration camp.

Criminal Activity: These steps, which relate merely to the consolidation of control of the Nazi Party, are not criminal under the view of the conspiracy to wage aggressive war which has previously been set forth, But the Leadership Corps was also used for similar steps in Austria and those parts of Czechoslovakia, Lithuania, Poland, France, Belgium, Luxembourg and Yugoslavia which were incorporated into the Reich and within the Gaus of the Nazi Party. In those territories the machinery of the Leadership Corps was used for their Germanisation through the elimination of local customs and the detection and arrest of persons who opposed German occupation. This was criminal under Article 6 (b) of the Charter in those areas governed by the Hague Rules of Land Warfare and criminal under Article 6 (c) of the Charter as to the remainder.

The Leadership Corps played its part in the persecution of the Jews. It was involved in the economic and political discrimination against the Jews, which was put into effect shortly after the Nazis came into power. The Gestapo and SD were instructed to co-ordinate with the Gauleiters and Kreisleiters the measures taken in the pogroms of the 9th and 10th November in the year 1938. The Leadership Corps was also used to prevent German public opinion from reacting against the measures taken against the Jews in the East. On the 9th October, 1942, a confidential information bulletin was sent to all Gauleiters and Kreisleiters entitled "Preparatory Measures for the Final Solution of the Jewish Question in Europe. Rumours concerning the Conditions of the Jews in the East." This bulletin stated that rumours were being started by returning soldiers concerning the conditions of Jews in the East which some Germans might not understand, and outlined in detail the official explanation to be given. This bulletin contained no explicit statement that the Jews were being exterminated, but it did indicate they were going to labour camps, and spoke of their complete segregation and elimination and the necessity of ruthless severity. Thus, even at its face value, it indicated the utilisation of the machinery of the Leadership Corps to keep German public opinion from rebelling at a programme which was stated to involve condemning the Jews of Europe to a lifetime of slavery. This information continued to be available to the Leadership Corps. The August, 1944, edition of "Die Lage", a publication which was circulated among the Political Leaders, described the deportation of 430,000 Jews from Hungary.

The Leadership Corps played an important part in the administration of the Slave Labour Programme. A Sauckel decree dated 6th April 1942, appointed the Gauleiters as Plenipotentiary for Labour Mobilisation for their Gaus with authority to co-ordinate all agencies dealing with labour questions in their Gaus, with specific authority over the employment of foreign workers, including their conditions of work, feeding and housing. Under this authority the Gauleiters assumed control over the allocation of labour in their

---

[2] "*Die Geheime Staatspolizei*" or state police. Ed's. Note.

[3] "*Die Sicherheitsdienst des Reichsfuehrer SS*," the intelligence agency for security police. Ed's. Note.

Gaus, including the forced labourers from foreign countries. In carrying out this task the Gauleiters used many Party offices within their Gaus, including subordinate Political Leaders. For example, Sauckel's decree of the 8th September, 1942, relating to the allocation for household labour of 400,000 women labourers brought in from the East, established a procedure under which applications filed for such workers should be passed on by the Kreisleiters, whose judgment was final.

Under Sauckel's directive the Leadership Corps was directly concerned with the treatment given foreign workers, and the Gauleiters were specifically instructed to prevent "politically inept factory heads " from giving too much consideration to the care of Eastern workers. The type of question which was considered in their treatment included reports by the Kreisleiters on pregnancies among the female slave labourers, which would result in an abortion if the child's parentage would not meet the racial standards laid down by the SS[4] and usually detention in a concentration camp for the female slave labourer. The evidence has established that under the supervision of the Leadership Corps, the industrial workers were housed in camps under atrocious sanitary conditions, worked long hours and were inadequately fed. Under similar supervision, the agricultural workers, who were somewhat better treated were prohibited transportation, entertainment and religious worship, and were worked without any time limit on their working hours and under regulations which gave the employer the right to inflict corporal punishment. The Political Leaders, at least down to the Ortsgruppenleiters, were responsible for this supervision. On the 5th May, 1943. a memorandum of Bormann instructing that mistreatment of slave labourers cease was distributed down to the Ortsgruppenleiters. Similarly on the 10th November, 1944, a Speer circular transmitted a Himmler directive which provided that all members of the Nazi Party, in accordance with instructions from the Kreisleiter, would be warned by the Ortsgruppenleiters of their duty to keep foreign workers under careful observation.

The Leadership Corps was directly concerned with the treatment of prisoners of war. On 5th November, 1941, Bormann transmitted a directive down to the level of Kreisleiter instructing them to insure compliance by the Army with the recent directives of the Department of the Interior ordering that dead Russian prisoners of war should be buried wrapped in tar paper in a remote place without any ceremony or any decorations of their graves. On 25th November, 1943, Bormann sent a circular instructing the Gauleiters to report any lenient treatment of prisoners of war. On 13th September, 1944, Bormann sent a directive down to the level of Kreisleiter ordering that liaison be established between the Kreisleiters and the guards of the prisoners of war in order "to better assimilate the commitment of the prisoners of war to the political and economic demands". On 17th October, 1944, an OKW[5] directive instructed the officer in charge of the prisoners of war to confer with the Kreisleiters on questions of the productivity of labour. The use of prisoners of war, particularly those from the East, was accompanied by a widespread violation of the rules of land warfare. This evidence establishes that the Leadership Corps down to the level of Kreisleiter was a participant in this illegal treatment.

---

[4] "*Die Schutzstaffeln Der Nationalsocialistischen Deutschen Arbeiterpartei*," the internal security police of the Nazi Party. Ed's.Note.

[5] German acronym for High Command. Ed's. Note.

The machinery of the Leadership Corps was also utilised in attempts made to deprive Allied airmen of the protection to which they were entitled under the Geneva Convention. On 13th March, 1940, a directive of Hess transmitted instructions through the Leadership Corps down to the Blockleiter for the guidance of the civilian population in case of the landing of enemy planes or parachutists, which stated that enemy parachutists were to be immediately arrested or "made harmless". On 30th May, 1944, Bormann sent a circular letter to all Gau and Kreisleiters "reporting instances of lynchings of Allied low level fliers in which no police action was taken. It was requested that Ortsgruppenleiters be informed orally of the contents of this letter. This letter accompanied a propaganda drive which had been instituted by Goebbels to induce such lynchings, and clearly amounted to instructions to induce such lynchings or at least to violate the Geneva Convention by withdrawing any police protection. Some lynchings were carried out pursuant to this programme, but it does not appear that they were carried out throughout all of Germany. Nevertheless, the existence of this circular letter shows that the heads of the Leadership Corps were utilising it for a purpose which was patently illegal and which involved the use of the machinery of the Leadership Corps at least through the Ortsgruppenleiter.

Conclusion

The Leadership Corps was used for purposes which were criminal under the Charter and involved the Germanisation of incorporated territory, the persecution of the Jews, the administration of the slave labour programme, and the mistreatment of prisoners of war. The defendants Bormann and Sauckel, who were members of this organisation, were among those who used it for these purposes. The Gauleiters, the Kreisleiters, and the Ortsgruppenleiters participated, to one degree or another, in these criminal programmes. The Reichsleitung as the staff organisation of the Party is also responsible for these criminal programmes as well as the heads of the various staff organisations of the Gauleiters and Kreisleiters. The decision of the Tribunal on these staff organisations includes only the Amtsleiters who were heads of offices on the staffs of the Reichsleitung, Gauleitung and Kreisleitung. With respect to other staff officers and party organisations attached to the Leadership Corps other than the Amtsleiters referred to above, the Tribunal will follow the suggestion of the Prosecution in excluding them from the declaration.

The Tribunal declares to be criminal within the meaning of the Charter the group composed of those members of the Leadership Corps holding the positions enumerated in the preceding paragraph who became or remained members of the organisation with knowledge that it was being used for the commission of acts declared criminal by Article 6 of the Charter, or who were personally implicated as members of the organisation in the commission of such crimes. The basis of this finding is the participation of the organisation in war crimes and crimes against humanity connected with the war, the group declared criminal cannot include therefore, persons who had ceased to hold the positions enumerated in the preceding paragraph prior to 1st September, 1939.

. . . .

GENERAL STAFF AND HIGH COMMAND

The prosecution has also asked that the General Staff and High Command of the German Armed Forces be declared a criminal organisation. The Tribunal believes that no declaration of criminality should be made with respect to the General Staff and High Command. The number of persons charged . . . is . . . so small that individual trials of these officers would accomplish the purpose here sought better than a declaration such as is requested. But a more compelling reason is that in the opinion of the Tribunal the General Staff and High Command is neither an "organisation" nor a "group" within the meaning of those terms as used in Article 9 of the Charter.

Some comment on the nature of this alleged group is requisite. According to the Indictment and evidence before the Tribunal, it consists of approximately 130 officers, living and dead, who at any time during the period from February, 1938, when Hitler reorganised the Armed Forces, and May, 1945, when Germany surrendered, held certain positions in the military hierarchy. These men were high-ranking officers in the three armed services: OKH-Army, OKM-Navy, and OKL-Air Force. Above them was the over-all armed forces authority, OKW-High Command of the German Armed Forces with Hitler as the Supreme Commander.[6] The Officers in the OKW, including defendant Keitel as Chief of the High Command were in a sense Hitler's personal staff. In the larger sense they co-ordinated and directed the three services, with particular emphasis on the functions of planning and operations.

The individual officers in this alleged group were, at one time or another, in one of four categories: (1) Commanders-in-Chief of one of the three services; (2) Chief of Staff of one of the three services; (3) "Oberbefehlshabers", the field commanders-in-chief of one of the three services, which of course comprised ,by far the largest number of these persons; or (4) an OKW officer, of which there were three, defendants Keitel and Jodl, and the latter's Deputy Chief, Warlimont. This is the meaning of the Indictment in its use of the term "General Staff and High Command".

The Prosecution has here drawn the line. The Prosecution does not indict the next level of the military hierarchy consisting of commanders of army corps, and equivalent ranks in the Navy and Air Force, nor the level below, the division commanders or their equivalent in the other branches. And the staff officers of the four staff commands of OKW, OKH, OKM, and OKL are not included, nor are the trained specialists who were customarily called General Staff officers.

In effect, then, those indicted as members are military leaders of the Reich of the highest rank. No serious effort was made to assert that they composed an "organisation" in the sense of Article 9. The assertion is rather that they were a "group", which is a wider and more embracing term than "organisation".

The Tribunal does not so find. According to the evidence, their planning at staff level, the constant conferences between staff officers and field commanders, their operational technique in the field and at headquarters was much the same as that of the armies, navies and air forces of all other countries. The over-all effort of OKW at co-ordination and direction could be matched by a similar, though not identical form of organisation in other military forces, such as the Anglo-American Combined Chiefs of Staff.

To derive from this pattern of their activities the existence of an association or group does not, in the opinion of the Tribunal, logically follow. On such a theory the top

---

[6] OKW, OKH, OKM, and OKL are German acronyms for the their respective military branches. Ed's. Note.

commanders of every other nation are just such an association rather than what they actually are, an aggregation of military men, a number of individuals who happen at a given period of time to hold the high-ranking military positions.

Much of the evidence and the argument has centred around the question of whether membership in these organisations was or was not voluntary; in this case, it seems to the Tribunal to be quite beside the point. For this alleged criminal organisation has one characteristic, a controlling one, which sharply distinguishes it from the other five indicted. When an individual became a member of the SS for instance, he did so, voluntarily or otherwise, but certainly with the knowledge that he was joining something. In the case of the General Staff and High Command, however, he could not know he was joining a group or organisation, for such organisation did not exist except in the charge of the Indictment. He knew only that he had achieved a certain high rank in one of the three services, and could not be conscious of the fact that he was becoming a member of anything so tangible as a "group," as that word is commonly used. His relations with his brother officers in his own branch of the service and his association with those of the other two branches were, in general, like those of other services all over the world.

The Tribunal therefore does not declare the General Staff and High Command to be a criminal organisation.

Although the Tribunal is of the opinion that the term "group" in Article 9 must mean something more than this collection of military officers, it has heard much evidence as to the participation of these officers in planning and waging aggressive war, and in committing war crimes and crimes against humanity. This evidence is, as to many of them, clear and convincing.

They have been responsible in large measure for the miseries and suffering that have fallen on millions of men, women and children. They have been a disgrace to the honourable profession of arms. Without their military guidance the aggressive ambitions of Hitler and his fellow Nazis would have been academic and sterile. Although they were not a group falling within the words of the Charter they were certainly a ruthless military caste. The contemporary German militarism flourished briefly with its recent ally, National Socialism, as well as or better than it had in the generations of the past.

Many of these men have made a mockery of the soldier's oath of obedience to military orders. When it suits their defence they say they had to obey; when confronted with Hitler's brutal crimes, which are shown to have been within their general knowledge, they say they disobeyed. The truth is they actively participated in all these crimes, or sat silent and acquiescent, witnessing the commission of crimes on a scale larger and more shocking than the world has ever had the misfortune to know. This must be said.

Where the facts warrant it, these men should be brought to trial so that those among them who are guilty of these crimes should not escape punishment.

. . . .

❖   ❖   ❖

Questions & Comments

(1)   In U.S. federal law, the Racketeer Influenced Corrupt Organizations (RICO) Act establishes both criminal and civil sanctions for enterprises involved in a variety of criminal acts. Enterprises can include partnerships, corporations, associations, unions, or

group of individuals associated in fact although not a legal entity. 28 U.S.C. § 1961(4). Would either the Nazi Party Leadership Corp or the General Staff and High Command in the above *Judgment for the Trial of German Major War Criminals* have met the enterprise definition in the RICO Act?

(2) Is there a need under international criminal law to define an organization as criminal? The ICT-Y, ICT-R, and ICC have jurisdiction only over natural persons. Art. 6, ICT-Y Statute; Art. 5, ICT-R Statute; Art. 25(1), ICC Statute. They do not have authority to declare an organization criminal.

How important is such authority for seizing the assets of a criminal organization? Both Article 24 of the ICT-Y Statute and Article 23 of the ICT-R Statute allow their respective tribunals to order the return of any property and proceeds acquired by criminal conduct. The ICC Statute goes farther:

2. In addition to imprisonment, the Court may order:

(a) A fine under the criteria provided for in the Rules of Procedure and Evidence;

(b) A forfeiture of proceeds, property and assets derived directly or indirectly from that crime, without prejudice to the rights of bona fide third parties.

Art. 77(2), ICC Statute. Should the ICT-Y, ICT-R, and ICC have the authority to declare an organization criminal? How would you argue that there is a customary international law norm allowing the seizure of assets from criminal organizations?

(3) Given the fact that conspiracy law was a foreign notion to many of the Allied countries, how would you have argued in 1940 that there was a customary international law norm allowing criminal liability for conspiracy?

(4) The following chapter discusses command responsibility and obedience to orders defense. In reading the following memorial *amicus curiae*, keep in mind how these two issues compare with the conspiratorial and organizational culpability discussed in the above *Judgment for the Trial of German Major War Criminals*.

Chapter 6. Individual Culpability and Defenses

A. State Actors

Benavides Cevallos v. Ecuador
Inter-American Court of Human Rights
Memorial *Amicus Curiae* **submitted by Rights International (1998)**

INTRODUCTION

In December 1985, Ecuadorean state agents illegally detained, arrested, tortured, and murdered Prof. Consuelo Benavides. Subsequent to Prof. Benavides' disappearance, state agents engaged in extensive efforts to cover up the commission of the crimes committed against her. Ten years after the commission of the crimes, the Ecuadorean Supreme Court convicted two state agents for the illegal and arbitrary detention of Consuelo Benavides and one state agent as an accomplice to the torture and assassination of Consuelo Benavides. At least fourteen state agents have been implicated in the crimes committed against Consuelo Benavides through investigations conducted by the Ecuadorean Government. Yet, no one has been convicted as the material authors of her torture or murder. Furthermore, no was has been tried or convicted as the intellectual authors of any of the crimes.

Amicus curiae will establish that the Republic of Ecuador has a duty as a state-party to the American Convention on Human Rights [hereinafter "ACHR"] under Article 1 to fully investigate the crimes committed against Consuelo Benavides, prosecute the intellectual authors of the crimes, and punish those parties found responsible. Most importantly, *Amicus* will establish that under the customary international law principle of command responsibility, individual criminal responsibility extends not only to the material authors of the crimes but also to the intellectual authors. *Amicus* will conclude this memorial by urging the Court to order the Republic of Ecuador to reinstitute an investigation of the circumstances leading to the death of Consuelo Benavides in order to determine the intellectual and material authors of the crimes, to prosecute these persons, and impose the appropriate criminal punishment for those persons found responsible.

STATEMENT OF THE FACTS

On December 4, 1985 eight armed members of the Ecuadorean Naval Infantry arrived at the home of Serapio Ordoñez where they detained Mr. Ordoñez and Prof. Benavides. After questioning both of the detainees about a group of individuals suspected of subversive activities, the Marines arrested them both and forced them to travel by foot to Chicube, where they arrived on December 5th. Mr. Ordoñez and Prof. Benavides were then transported to a Naval Base in Esmeraldas where they were hooded and interrogated. On December 6th both of the detainees were transported to yet another location. The testimony of Mr. Ordoñez revealed that the two detainees were then put into separate rooms where they were both tortured. Application of the Inter-Am. Comm'n on Human Rights Before the Inter-Am. Ct. of Human Rights in the Case of Consuelo Benavides (10.476) Against the State of Ecuador (March 20, 1996) 3-4. Mr. Ordoñez stated that he was "suspended from cords tied to his thumbs and feet, . . . severely beaten . . . and interrogated about subversive activities in the area of [of his home]." *Id*. at 4. Mr.

Ordoñez knew that Prof. Benavides also was being tortured because he heard her cries of pain and when he later saw her she was "bleeding heavily". Mr. Ordoñez was released and escorted home on or about December 6, 1985. The situation of Prof. Benavides remained unknown for three years until a body which had been previously found on December 13, 1985 and subsequently buried, was exhumed in 1988 and identified as the body of Prof. Benavides. The autopsy revealed that Prof. Benavides died from seven gun shot wounds into her head and neck. *Id.* at 4, 9-10.

After numerous pleas by the family of Consuelo Benavides, the Ecuadorean Government commenced investigations into the occurrences leading to the death of Prof. Benavides. In August 1988 the Ecuadorean National Congress created a Multiparty Commission to initiate investigations into the disappearance of Consuelo Benavides. After conducting six hearings on the matter, the Multiparty Commission concluded that Consuelo Benavides had been illegally and arbitrarily detained, tortured and murdered. *Id.* at 7-10. The Commission found that the crimes were part of a "repressive policy of human rights violations" "designed and implemented" by high ranking governmental officials and that "Governmental authorities were well aware of abuses being committed by the police and armed forces as part of a policy to repress subversion." *Id.* at 10. The Commission determined that government officials were "directly implicated in the violations, and in the further offenses of falsification of documents and perjury" as part of efforts to cover-up governmental knowledge and involvement in the crimes against Prof. Benavides. *Id.* The Commission concluded its report by naming specific state agents as material authors, intellectual authors, accomplices and parties involved in the cover-up. The Multiparty Commission's role, however, was limited to fact-finding. The Commission therefore referred the judgment of criminal responsibility to the Ecuadorean judiciary. *Id.* at 11.

Five years after the military court system commenced proceedings addressing the crimes committed against Prof. Benavides, the Ecuadorean Supreme Court assumed jurisdiction over the case in 1992. Over three years later, the Supreme Court convicted two state agents as material authors for the illegal and arbitrary detention of Prof. Benavides and convicted only one state agent as an accomplice to the torture and assassination of Prof. Benavides. *Id.* at 14, 19-20.

ARGUMENT

I. THE STATE OF ECUADOR HAS NOT FULFILLED ITS AFFIRMATIVE DUTIES UNDER ARTICLE 1(1) OF THE AMERICAN CONVENTION TO ADEQUATELY INVESTIGATE THE HUMAN RIGHTS VIOLATIONS COMMITTED AGAINST CONSUELO BENAVIDES, PROSECUTE THE AUTHORS OF THE CRIMES, AND PUNISH THE RESPONSIBLE PERSONS.

Article 1(1) of the ACHR requires Ecuador, as a party to the Convention, "to respect the rights and freedoms recognized [in the convention] and to ensure to all persons subject to their jurisdiction the free and full exercise of those rights and freedoms. . ." This Court provided concise guidance on what these obligations require in *Velásquez Rodríguez v. Honduras*. In *Velásquez Rodríguez*, a student was violently detained without an arrest warrant by state agents, accused of political crimes, and subjected to harsh interrogation and cruel torture. *Velásquez Rodríguez Case*, Judgment of 29 July 1988, 1988 INTER-AM. Y.B. ON H.R. (Inter-Am. Ct. H.R.) 914 at §§ 3, 10. This Court recognized that Article 1(1) places upon state parties "the fundamental duty to respect and guarantee the rights recognized in the Convention" and any impairment of those rights which can be attributed to the action or omission of any public authority is imputable to the state. *Id.* at § 164.

Implicit in the language of Article 1(1) is the duty of the state to organize its government to juridicially ensure the "free and full enjoyment of human rights." *Id.* at § 166. Consequently, Ecuador has a duty, *inter alia*, to take reasonable steps to prevent human rights violations, to conduct serious investigations of violations, and to take appropriate measures to punish the authors of the violations. *Id.* at §§ 166, 174. It is not sufficient that the government is *designed* to comply with these duties, the government must operate sufficiently effective to *ensure* the "free and full exercise of human rights," and if violations go unpunished, the state has failed to comply with its duty. *Id.* at §§ 167, 176.

Once it is settled that the state has failed to comply with its duty to investigate, prosecute and punish human rights violations, it is a role of the international tribunal reviewing the case to compel the state to fulfill its obligations under international law and take the necessary steps to properly investigate the violations, prosecute the authors of the violations, and punish the responsible parties.

In *Caballero-Delgado v. Colombia*, for example, this Court reviewed evidence concerning the detention and disappearance of Isidro Caballero-Delgado and María del Carmen Santana. This Court noted that the petitioners' detention and disappearances were carried out by state agents, that six years had passed since their disappearances, and therefore concluded that both petitioners were dead. Consequently, this Court ordered injunctive relief requiring the State of Colombia to continue judicial proceedings inquiring into the disappearances of petitioners and punishment of those responsible. Judgment of December 8, 1995, Inter-Am. Ct. of H.R., *reprinted in* 17 HUM. RTS. L.J. 24 (1996).

As part of their customary international law obligations, governments are required to impose criminal sanctions -- not merely administrative or disciplinary ones. In *Nydia Erika Bautista de Arellana v. Colombia*, the U.N. Human Rights Committee examined the torture, mutilation, and assassination of Nydia Bautista. The victim, a member of Colombia's M-19 guerrilla movement, was abducted in 1987 by armed men dressed as civilians. She was subsequently tortured, mutilated, and buried. When her body was later identified in 1990, disciplinary proceedings were commenced against some members of the military, and then dropped. In 1994, formal proceedings were instituted before the Colombian National Delegate for Human Rights. In July 1995, the Delegate issued a decision holding Col. Velandia Hurtado and Sgt. Ortega Araque responsible for the disappearance, and requested their summary dismissal from the Armed Forces. Following the Delegate's findings, the Administrative Tribunal of Cundinamarca awarded the victim's family damages, and Col. Velandia Hurtado was dismissed from the armed forces. The U.N. Human Rights Committee concluded that ". . . the State party is under a duty to investigate thoroughly alleged violations of human rights, and in particular forced disappearances of persons and violations of the right to life, and to prosecute *criminally*, try and punish those held responsible for such violations." U.N. Hum Rts. Comm., U.N. Doc. CCPR/C/55/D/1993, (October 27, 1995) (emphasis added).

Chapter 6. Individual Culpability & Defenses

In the *Order of the Inter-American Court of Human Rights of 15 January 1988*, this Court adopted a provisional measure to protect witnesses in the *Velásquez Rodríguez, Fairén Garbi and Solís Corrales*, and *Godínz Cruz* cases. This Court found that witnesses in all three of those cases had been assassinated. In addition to ordering the Honduran Government to immediately adopt measures to prevent human rights violations against any other persons who had appeared before the Court, this Court also ordered the Honduran Government to employ all means within its power to investigate the crimes committed against witnesses in the cases, identify the perpetrators, and impose the appropriate punishment. 1988 INTER-AM. Y.B. ON H.R. (Inter-Am. Ct. H.R.) 1006.

As all three of the aforementioned cases illustrate, it is a well founded general principle of law, appropriately utilized by this Court in two of those cases, that if a State fails to fulfill its duty to investigate, prosecute and punish human rights violations, then one of the functions of the international tribunal reviewing the case is to order the State to fulfill its obligations and go back and properly investigate, prosecute, and punish the violations.

In the instant case, the Inter-American Commission on Human Rights found that the State of Ecuador violated a multitude of rights protected by the ACHR.[1] Article 2 of the ACHR places a legal duty upon Ecuador to give domestic legal effect to the rights and freedoms protected by the Convention.[2] Consequently, Ecuador has a duty to complete a thorough and sufficiently effective investigation of the abduction, torture and subsequent murder of Consuelo Benavides, as well as a duty to prosecute the responsible parties and impose adequate punishment against those parties found responsible.

Ecuador has failed to comply with these duties. The investigations conducted by the Ecuadorean Government were vitiated with perjury by state agents and were thus incapable of producing the results required under the ACHR. The record reflects that falsified information was provided to both the Multiparty Commission and the judiciary in a "deliberate and largely successful effort to obstruct justice." Application of the Inter-Am. Comm'n on Human Rights (March 20, 1996) at 39. Investigations and judicial proceedings were conducted by military organs, the very same branch of government that is implicated in the crimes against Consuelo Benavides, thus removing any chance of independent review and impartiality. *Id.* at 40. While Ecuador's Supreme Court did convict three individuals, none of the convictions were for the torture or murder of Consuelo Benavides. Furthermore, at least eleven additional state agents have been

---

[1] The Application of the Inter-American Commission on Human Rights Before the Inter-American Court of Human Rights in the Case of Consuelo Benavides (10.476) Against the State of Ecuador (March 20, 1996), established that state agents violated Articles 4.1, 5.1, 5.2, 7.1-3, 7.5-6, and 25 of the ACHR for illegally and arbitrarily arresting and detaining Consuelo Benavides, as well as holding her incommunicado, failing to bring her before a judicial officer, torturing her and finally murdering Consuelo Benavides.

[2] Art. 2, ACHR; *see The Velásquez Rodríguez Case* 1988 INTER-AM. Y.B. ON H.R. (Inter-Am. Ct. H.R.) at §§ 168-80 for an extensive discussion of a state's duty to comply with the rights and freedoms guaranteed by the ACHR.

implicated in the crimes perpetrated against Consuelo Benavides, and have all gone unpunished. *Id.* at 10. Finally, the State of Ecuador has made no efforts to prosecute anyone in connection with the deliberate efforts by state agents to cover up the crimes and obstruct justice.

II.   THE STATE OF ECUADOR HAS VIOLATED CUSTOMARY INTERNATIONAL LAW BY FAILING TO PROSECUTE THOSE PERSONS CRIMINALLY LIABLE UNDER THE PRINCIPLE OF COMMAND RESPONSIBILITY FOR VIOLATING CONSUELO BENAVIDES' HUMAN RIGHTS.

Aside from its failure to fulfill its affirmative obligations under Article 1(1), ACHR, the State of Ecuador also has violated customary international law that imposes individual criminal liability under a command responsibility model, for its failure to prosecute both the material and intellectual authors of the human rights violations committed against Prof. Benavides.

A.   Customary International Law Employs the Principle of Command Responsibility for the Illegal Acts of a Superior's Subordinates Which Were Ordered or Tolerated by the Superior Officer.

It is a well-established principle of international law that individuals who violate international criminal law may be held individually responsible. As the Appeals Chamber of the International Criminal Tribunal for the Former Yugoslavia has noted "[c]rimes against international law are committed by men, not by abstract entities, and only by punishing individuals who commit such crimes can the provisions of international law be enforced." *Prosecutor v. DuŠko Tadic*, Appeals Chamber Decision on the Defence Motion for Interlocutory Appeal on Jurisdiction (Int'l Criminal Tribunal for the Former Yugo.) at 68 (2 Oct. 1995) (citing *The Trial of Major War Criminals: Proceedings of the Int'l Military Tribunal Sitting at Nuremberg Germany*, Part 22, at 447 (1950)) . Often such crimes are committed by state agents under direct orders from the offender's commanding officer or are committed with the knowledge and/or consent of the offender's superiors. In such a context, customary international law requires that if the superior officer had knowledge of and control over the illegal acts of his subordinates, the superior officer also may be held criminally liable for the subordinate's criminal acts.

Most significantly, the recently enacted Statutes of the International Tribunals for the Former Yugoslavia and Rwanda impose command responsibility[3] for international crimes

---

[3] The UN Security Council's establishment of the International Tribunal for Yugoslavia authorized only the use of *already existing* international humanitarian law, including the command responsibility doctrine. As the UN Secretary General in his accompanying report to the Statute of the International Tribunal for Yugoslovia noted,

> the Security Council would not be creating or purporting to 'legislate'
> [international humanitarian] law.   Rather, the International Tribunal
> (continued...)

of the same kind perpetrated in the instant case. Under the Statute of the International Criminal Tribunal for Yugoslavia [hereinafter, ICT-Y Statute], these crimes include "wilful killing," "torture or inhuman treatment," "wilfully causing great suffering or serious injury to body," and "wilfully depriving . . . a civilian of the rights of fair and regular trial". *Report of Secretary General Pursuant to Paragraph 2 of Security Council Resolution 808 (1993)*, U.N. Doc. S/25704 (3 May 1993), Annex, Art. 2 (Grave Breaches of Geneva Conventions of 1949). Under the Statute of the International Criminal Tribunal for Rwanda [hereinafter, ICT-R Statute], these crimes include murder and extra-judicial executions. S/Res/955 (1994) (8 Nov. 1994), Annex, Articles 3 (murder) and 4 (extra-judicial executions). Article 7 of the ICT-Y Statute stipulates that:

1. A person who planned, instigated, *ordered*, committed *or otherwise aided and abetted* in the planning, preparation or execution of a crime referred to in article 2 . . . *shall be individually responsible* for the crime.

2. The official position of any accused person . . . shall not relieve such person of criminal responsibility nor mitigate punishment.

3. *The fact that any of the acts referred to in article[ ] 2 . . . was committed by a subordinate does not relieve his superior of criminal responsibility if he knew or had reason to know that the subordinate was about to commit such acts or had done so and the superior failed to take the necessary and reasonable measures to prevent such acts or to punish the perpetrators thereof . . .*

Art. ICT-Y Statute (emphases added). Article 6 of the ICT-R Statute uses nearly identical language.[4]

---

[3](...continued)
would have the task of applying existing international humanitarian law.

Report of Secretary General Pursuant to Paragraph 2 of Security Council Resolution 808 (1993), U.N. Doc. S/25704 (3 May 1993), ¶ 29.

[4] Article 6 states in relevant part:

1. A person who planned, instigated, ordered, committed or otherwise aided and abetted in the planning, preparation or execution of a crime referred to in articles 2 to 4 of the present Statute, shall be individually responsible for the crime.

2. The official position of any accused person, whether as Head of State or Government or as a responsible Government official, shall not relieve such person of criminal responsibility nor mitigate punishment.

(continued...)

The general principle of law that commanders are individually criminally responsible for the violations committed by their subordinates had its beginnings as early as 1474 when Peter von Hagenbach was convicted and executed for atrocities committed under his command in Breisach, Austria. Timothy L.H. McCormack, *From Sun Tzu to the Sixth Comm.: The Evolution of an Int'l Criminal Law Regime, in* THE LAW OF WAR CRIMES: NATIONAL AND INTERNATIONAL APPROACHES (Timothy L.H. McCormack & Gerry J. Simpson eds, 1997). . . . Several centuries later, the American Colonies adopted a similar approach in the Articles of War which required:

> Every Officer Commanding . . . shall keep good order, and to the utmost of his power, redress all such abuses or disorders which may be committed by any Officer or Soldier under his command; if upon complaint made to him of Officers or Soldiers beating or otherwise ill-treating any person . . . the said commander, who shall refuse or omit to see justice done to this offender . . . [shall] be punished . . . in such manner as if he himself had committed the crimes or disorders complained of.

American Articles of War, Article XII, June 30, 1775 (cited in William H. Parks, *Command Responsibility*, 62 MIL. L. REV. 1, 5 (1973)). This principle was first employed by the United States in the 1800s. *See, e.g.*, *The Trial of Captain Henry Wirz*, 8 Amer. State Trials 666 (1865) (commandant of prisoner-of-war camp convicted and executed for ordering torture, maltreatment and execution of war prisoners in his custody).

The Treaty of Versailles was the first international instrument to articulate in express terms the legal requirement of prosecuting commanders for the illegal acts of his subordinates. Articles 227 and 228 of the Treaty of Versailles created a tribunal to prosecute high ranking German officials for violations the law and customs of war during

---

[4](...continued)

3. The fact that any of the acts referred to in articles 2 to 4 of the present Statute was committed by a subordinate does not relieve his or her superior of criminal responsibility if he or she knew or had reason to know that the subordinate was about to commit such acts or had done so and the superior failed to take the necessary and reasonable measures to prevent such acts or to punish the perpetrators thereof.

Art. 6, ICT-R Statute.

World War I.[5] In response to those provisions, the Germans agreed to administer war crime trials under German law.[6]

Subsequently during World War II in reaction to mistreatment of prisoners of war, a number of national and international laws were enacted establishing command responsibility. Article 3 of the Law of August 2, 1947 of the Grand Duchy of Luxembourg, on the Suppression of War Crimes imposed responsibility on "superiors in rank who have tolerated the criminal activities of their subordinates. . . ." United Nations War Crimes Comm'n, IV LAW REPORTS OF TRIALS OF WAR CRIMINALS 87 (hereinafter cited as "--L.R.T.W.C.--") (1948). Article 4 of the French Ordinance of August 28, 1944 required that when a subordinate was prosecuted as the actual perpetrator of a war crime,

---

[5] As a signatory to the Treaty of Versailles, Ecuador has adopted the international law principle of command responsibility. Treaty of Peace Between the Allied and Associated Powers and Germany, signed at Versailles, Mar. 28, 1919, *reproduced in* THE TREATY OF VERSAILLES AND AFTER: ANNOTATIONS OF THE TEXT OF THE TREATY (1947). Therefore, Ecuador is not a persistent objector for purposes of opting out of the formation of a customary international norm. *see*, Ian Brownlie, PRINCIPLES OF PUBLIC INTERNATIONAL LAW 10 (4th ed. 1990).

[6] The German Supreme Court of Leipzig held that "if the execution of an order in the ordinary course of duty involves such a violation of the law as is punishable, the superior officer issuing such order is alone responsible." *The Dover Castle Case*, cited in 1 THE LAW OF WAR, *supra* note 3, at 868, 881. While the German Court did limit criminal responsibility to the superior officer *alone*, in a subsequent case, the *Llandovery Castle Case*, the same German court did not recognize such a limitation. *Llandovery Castle Case*, S.Ct. Liepzig, Judgement of 16 July 1921, 16 AM. J. INT'L LAW 708, 722 (1922). Indeed, international law does not either. International principles that deal with criminal responsibility mandate as a general principle of law that if an individual commits an act which is recognized as a crime under international law, even if the actor's commander is criminally responsible, the subordinate may also be held criminally accountable. *See* Principles of the Nuremberg Charter and Judgment Formulated by the Int'l Law Comm'n, and adopted by G.A. Res. 177 (II)(a), 5 U.N. GAOR, Supp. No. 12, at 11-14, para. 99, U.N. Doc. A/1316 (principle I states that "Any person who commits an act which constitutes a crime under international law is responsible therefor and liable to punishment . . . ." This principle was adopted by the United Nations General Assembly and is recognized as customary international law. JORDAN J. PAUST, INTERNATIONAL CRIMINAL LAW 1043-44 (1996)); *see also* article 7 of the Statute of the International Tribunal for the Former Yugoslavia ("[a] person who . . . committed . . . a crime referred to in articles 2 to 5 of the present statute, shall be individually responsible for the crime . . . [and] the fact that an accused person acted pursuant to an order of a . . . superior shall not relieve him of criminal responsibility. . ."). Article 7, 32 I.L.M. 1192 (1993); M. Cherif Bassiouni, THE LAW OF THE INTERNATIONAL CRIMINAL TRIBUNAL FOR THE FORMER YUGOSLAVIA 381 n. 103 (1997) (absolute defense of obedience to superior orders no longer "carr[ies] much weight").

his superiors also would be considered as accomplices insofar as they had tolerated the criminal acts of their subordinates. III L.R.T.W.C. 94. Article II(2) of Law No. 10 of the Allied Control Council provided that "[a]ny person . . . is deemed to have committed a crime . . . if he . . . ordered or abetted the [crime] . . . ." I TRIALS OF WAR CRIMINALS BEFORE THE NUREMBERG MILITARY TRIBUNALS UNDER CONTROL COUNCIL NO. 10 (hereinafter cited as "--T.W.C.--") XVI (1948).

After World War II, the Allies conducted trials in Germany and Japan which convicted and sentenced commanding officers from World War II under the principle of command responsibility. In the *High Command Case* of the Trials of War Criminals Before the Nuremberg Military Tribunals under Control Council Law No. 10, the tribunal defined the standard by which command responsibility should be found. "For a defendant to be held criminally responsible, there must be a breach of some moral obligation fixed in international law, a personal act voluntarily done with knowledge of its inherent criminality under international law." XI T.W.C. 510. The tribunal specified that for a order to be "inherently criminal" it must be "one that is criminal on its face, or which [the commander] is shown to have known was criminal." *Id.* at 510-11.

In the International Japanese War Crimes Trial Before the International Military Tribunal for the Far East, twenty-two former Japanese leaders were charged with violating crimes against peace, murder, conspiracy to commit murder, war crimes, and crimes against humanity during World War II and were tried on the basis of command responsibility. In defining command responsibility, the tribunal stated that:

> [T]he principle of command responsibility to be that, if this accused knew, or should by the exercise of ordinary diligence have learned, of the commission by his subordinates . . . of the atrocities . . . or of the existence of a routine which would countenance such, and, by his failure to take any action to punish the perpetrators, permitted the atrocities to continue, he has failed in his performance of his duty as a commander and must be punished.

William H. Parks, *Command Responsibility*, 62 MIL. L. REV. 1, 72 (1973) (citing 19 *United States v. Soemu Toyoda* 5005-06 [Official Transcript of Record of Trial]).

In a case adjudicated in the United States, a United States Military Commission found Japanese General Tomoyuki Yamashita individually criminally responsible for atrocities committed under his command during World War II in the Philippines. In reviewing the case, the United States Supreme Court found that under international law there exists a duty of a military commander to "to take such appropriate measures as are within his power to control the troops under his command for the prevention of [criminal] acts." *In re Yamashita*, 327 U.S. 1, 15 (1946).[7] The Court noted that this duty does not just extend to prisoners of war, but to civilian populations as well. *Id.* at 16.

In 1976, the United Nations International Convention on the Suppression and Punishment of the Crime of Apartheid entered into force. This convention places criminal

---

[7] It should be noted that the *Yamashita Case* has been criticized that the facts did not support Gen. Yamashita's conviction; however, the principle of command responsibility has not been criticized.

responsibility on individuals and their superiors for the crime of apartheid.[8] This convention, which has been ratified by Ecuador, was the first international document to recognize the principle of command responsibility regardless of whether the crime was committed within the context of war or not. This is a significant development since it illustrates that command responsibility is not limited to international war crimes but to other international crimes as well.

"The doctrine of 'command responsibility' now clearly exists in conventional and customary international law." M. Cherif Bassiouni, CRIMES AGAINST HUMANITY IN INTERNATIONAL LAW 389 (1992). It is a principle that is now at least five centuries old. Recent developments such as the International Tribunals for Yugoslavia and Rwanda and the Apartheid Convention have provided guidance on just how far-reaching command responsibility extends and further reinforce its status as a general principle of international humanitarian law as well as human rights law.[9]

B. The State of Ecuador Failed to Fulfill Its Duty Under Customary International Law to Prosecute and Punish Those Persons Who Ordered Their Subordinates to Violate Consuelo Benavides' Human Rights, Those Persons Who Obeyed Such Orders, and Those Persons Who Tolerated Such Violations By Persons Under Their Command.

Customary international law recognizes the principle that if a superior officer ordered a subordinate to commit a violation of international human rights or humanitarian law, or knew of the commission of a violation by his subordinate, and failed to prevent its commission or take action to punish its commission, the superior officer is individually

---

[8] As a prerequisite to command responsibility in the Apartheid Convention, however, the illegal act must be in response to an order. Mere knowledge of the act would not be sufficient. Article 3 of the Convention states in relevant part:

International criminal responsibility shall apply . . . to individuals, members of organizations . . . and representatives of the state . . . whenever they:

Commit, participate in, *directly incite or conspire* in the commission of [acts of apartheid] . . .

Directly abet, *encourage* or co-operate in the commission of the crime of apartheid."

G.A. Res. 3068, U.N. GAOR, art. 3 (1973) (emphases added).

[9] As the Preamble of the Inter-American Convention on the Forced Disappearances of Persons recognizes, "the systematic practice of the forced disappearance of persons constitutes a crime against humanity", and, thereby, a violation of humanitarian law. Here, the distinction between international humanitarian law and international human rights law disappears.

criminally responsible. *See generally* § II(a), *supra*. *Amicus* asserts that in the instant case, the actions and omissions by high ranking Ecuadorean governmental officials rise to this standard of command responsibility.

In the instant case, Ecuador's Multiparty Commission and Supreme Court, as well as the Inter-American Commission on Human Rights, found that state agents committed the crimes of torture and murder against Consuelo Benavides.[10] Application of the Inter-Am. Comm'n on Human Rights Before the Inter-Am. Ct. of Human Rights in the Case of Consuelo Benavides (10.476) Against the State of Ecuador (March 20, 1996) 7-10, 19, 20, 33. The Multiparty Commission also found that the crimes against Consuelo Benavides were part of a repressive state policy of human rights violations. *Id.* at 10. The Commission's report confirms that this "repressive policy" was "designed and implemented" by commanding officials of the Government, armed forces, and National Police.[11] *Id.*

---

[10] The crimes of torture and murder are fundamental violations of the inherent dignity of a human person and are recognized in customary international law as facially criminal and subject to severe punishment. *See* Application of the Inter-Am. Comm'n on Human Rights (March 20, 1996) at 31-34 (establishing both torture and murder as contrary to international law and the American Convention); *see also* the Statute of the International Tribunal for the Former Yugoslavia, Article 2, 32 I.L.M. 1192 (1993) (identifying both "wilfull killing" and "torture or inhuman treatment" as crimes under the Geneva Conventions of 12 August 1949 and international law); Convention Against Torture and Other Cruel, Inhuman or Degrading Treatment or Punishment, Article 4, Annex G.A. Res. 46 (XXXIX 1984), 23 I.L.M. 1027 (1984), as modified, 24 I.L.M. 535 (1985) (torture as crime).

[11] While *amicus* acknowledges that command responsibility has traditionally been imposed within the context of war, its application in the instant case is a necessary extension of the legal principle of command responsibility. The recent adoptions of the Apartheid Convention and the ICT-Y and ICT-R Statutes justify such an expansion of this principle. These three authorities all adopt the command responsibility rule in the context of non-international conflicts. Furthermore, the Appeals Chamber of the International Tribunal for Yugoslavia distinguished how customary international law does not limit individual criminal responsibility to *international* armed conflicts, and held that it applies to *internal* armed conflicts as well. *Prosecutor v. Duško Tadic*, Appeals Chamber Decision on the Defence Motion for Interlocutory Appeal on Jurisdiction (Int'l Criminal Tribunal for the Former Yugo.) at 68-71 (2 Oct. 1995).

In the instant case, there is an ongoing internal conflict between the Ecuadorean Government and an armed guerrilla group known as *Alfaro Vive, Carajo*. AMNESTY INTERNATIONAL, AMNESTY INTERNATIONAL REPORT, 1991 80-81 (1991). In fact, Consuelo Benavides was arrested in 1984 and accused of having ties to that very same group. Application of the Inter-Am. Comm'n on Human Rights (March 20, 1996) at 3-4 n.2. Furthermore, Amnesty International has consistently reported a high number of cases of

(continued...)

[11](...continued)

torture by the National Police in Ecuador, with the allegations going largely unanswered by the government. *See e.g.* AMNESTY INTERNATIONAL, AMNESTY INTERNATIONAL REPORT, 1987 157-60 (1987); AMNESTY INTERNATIONAL, AMNESTY INTERNATIONAL REPORT, 1991 80-81 (1991); AMNESTY INTERNATIONAL, AMNESTY INTERNATIONAL REPORT, 1993 116-118 (1993); AMNESTY INTERNATIONAL, AMNESTY INTERNATIONAL REPORT, 1996 138-40 (1996). Moreover, these findings are further supported by the 51st Session of the United Nations Human Rights Commission which reported a minimum of seventeen reported disappearances in Ecuador during the period of 1985 to 1992, the majority of which concerned people arrested by the National Police. U.N. GAOR, Hum. Rts. Comm'n, 51st Sess., U.N. Doc. E/CN.4/1995/36 (30 December 1994).

Amicus also recognizes that while command responsibility has historically been applied solely to military officials, the circumstances in this case justify the extension of command responsibility to the non-military command structure, including the Minister of Government and the National Police. Every international and national instrument that provides for command responsibility does *not* specify as a requirement that the command structure must be a *military* command structure. *See* § IV, *supra*. It is a historical accident that its application has taken place within the context of war. Therefore, the extension of individual criminal responsibility to civilian commanders is not inconsistent with the principle of command responsibility or customary international law.

Additionally, the crimes committed against Prof. Benavides were part of a joint operation between the military and the National Police. To extend command responsibility to state agents within the military and not the National Police would be an egregious obstruction of justice. Joint operations between the National Police and military forces in Ecuador is a common occurrence, and to limit the imposition of criminal responsibility to military command structures in Ecuador would only be providing the Ecuadorean Government an incentive to conduct future human rights violations under the auspices of civilian command to avoid criminal command responsibility. *See e.g.* U.S. DEPT. OF STATE, ECUADOR COUNTRY REPORT ON HUMAN RIGHTS PRACTICES FOR 1996 (Released by the Bureau of Democracy, Human Rights, and Labor, Jan. 30, 1997). This is particularly relevant since reports of human rights violations in Ecuador evidence that the human rights violations are predominantly committed by the National Police. *Id.*; AMNESTY INTERNATIONAL, AMNESTY INTERNATIONAL REPORT, 1987 157-60 (1987); AMNESTY INTERNATIONAL, AMNESTY INTERNATIONAL REPORT, 1991 80-81 (1991); AMNESTY INTERNATIONAL, AMNESTY INTERNATIONAL REPORT, 1993 116-118 (1993); AMNESTY INTERNATIONAL, AMNESTY INTERNATIONAL REPORT, 1996 138-40 (1996).

Finally, the National Police share a command structure similar to most militaries and the role of the National Police and the armed forces in Ecuador are used interchangeably. *See e.g.* U.S. DEPT. OF STATE, ECUADOR COUNTRY REPORT ON HUMAN RIGHTS PRACTICES FOR 1993 426, 427 (armed forces and then the National Police both conducted anticrime sweeps); U.S. DEPT. OF STATE, ECUADOR COUNTRY REPORT ON HUMAN RIGHTS PRACTICES

(continued...)

Furthermore, the Commission named specific high ranking state agents as intellectual authors of the policy. *Id.* This policy demonstrates that the crimes committed against Consuelo Benavides were in fact ordered by high ranking governmental authorities either directly, or indirectly through instituting such a policy which resulted in the torture and execution of Consuelo Benavides. This conclusion is supported by the Multiparty Commission's findings that numerous high ranking Ecuadorean governmental officials were "well aware of abuses being committed by the police and armed forces as part of a policy to repress subversion," yet these officials did nothing to prevent these crimes or punish their offenders. *Id* at 10 n.5. Therefore, these high ranking state agents must be prosecuted by the State of Ecuador for establishing a policy which contravenes the rights and freedoms protected by the ACHR which led to the death of Consuelo Benavides, as well as failing to prevent the commission of the crimes. Art. 1, ACHR.

Additionally, the high ranking state agents must be prosecuted by the State for failing to take action to punish those parties who committed the crimes against Prof. Benavides. Consuelo Benavides disappeared in December 1985. It took two years before the government took any action at all to investigate the crimes. Even when attempts were made to investigate the crimes, high ranking government officials not only did not take any action to punish the perpetrators of the crimes, but they were involved in efforts to cover up the crimes and their involvement in Prof. Benavides's disappearance. Their attempts to cover up the commission of the crimes against Prof. Benavides is not merely a negative act of tolerance, but a positive act to conceal the truth and avoid responsibility, all in contravention of international law. *See generally* § II(B), *supra.*

It has now been over eleven years since Ecuadorean state agents tortured and murdered Prof. Benavides, yet *no one* has been tried as material or intellectual authors for these crimes. The Ecuadorean Government has had more than a sufficient amount of time to investigate the crimes against Prof. Benavides and prosecute the authors of the crimes. Only three individuals have been punished at all for the crimes committed against Prof. Benavides, while at least fourteen state agents have been implicated in the crimes and the subsequent cover-up. *Amicus* urges this court to compel that State of Ecuador to comply with its international obligations and fully investigate the crimes committed by state agents against Consuelo Benavides, identify the intellectual authors of the crimes and repressive policy of human rights violations, submit the intellectual authors to prosecution, and impose the appropriate criminal punishment for their involvement in the commission of said crimes.

---

[11](...continued)
FOR 1996 (reporting the publication of a book by a former policeman which declared that police units were involved in the execution of suspected leftist guerrillas). To impose criminal liability upon one state agent for a crime and not upon another state agent for the same crime would violate equal protection of the law.

CONCLUSION

Under the ACHR, as informed by customary international law, Ecuador has violated article 1 and 2 of the Convention for not upholding and giving domestic legal effect to the rights and freedoms protected by the ACHR. *Amicus* urges the Court to order the Republic of Ecuador to remedy the violations committed against Consuelo Benavides by properly investigating the crimes, prosecuting the intellectual authors of the crimes, and punishing those parties found responsible under the customary international law requirements imposed by command responsibility.

❖ ❖ ❖

Questions & Comments

(1) On 19 June 1998, in a hearing before the Inter-American Court of Human Rights, the parties in *Benavides v. Ecuador* reached a friendly settlement. Among other aspects of the judgment, the Court required that Ecuador "continue the investigations to sanction all of those persons responsible for violations of human rights" discussed in the decision. The family received $1million in damages – the largest settlement in the Court's history. *Benavides v. Ecuador*, Inter-Am. Ct. H.R., Judgment of 19 June 1998, at 15.

(2) Consider *The Prosecutor v. Delalic and Delic (The Celebici Case)*, Case No. IT-96-21-T, Int'l Crim. Trib.-Yugo., Judgment (16 November 1998). The Trial Chamber recognized that the doctrine of command responsibility encompasses "not only military commanders, but also civilians holding positions of authority (...)" and "not only persons in de jure positions but also those in such position de facto (...)".

(3) In *The Prosecutor v. Jean-Paul Akayesu*, Case No. ICTR-96-4-T, Int'l Crim Trib.-Rwanda, Judgment (2 September 1998), the Trial Chamber examined the *mens rea* requirement for command responsibility. It held that in cases where the commander failed to stop (as opposed to ordered) his/her troops committing humanitarian law violations, there must be " malicious intent, or, at least, . . . negligence . . . so serious as to be tantamount to acquiescence or even malicious intent."

(4) Related to the command responsibility rule is the defense of superior orders, also known as "the Nuremberg defense," in which the offender claims that s/he was just following orders and, thereby, is excused. This defense was rejected by the IMT in *Matter of Von Leeb and Others (German High Command Trial)*. 15 I.L.R. 376 (1949), 11 Trials of War Criminals (1950). However, this defense may be viable in certain circumstances. For example, the defense of duress may provide a partial defense "only by way of mitigation" in cases where the defendant faced a real risk that s/he would face execution had s/he disobeyed an order. *The Prosecutor v. Erdemovic*, Int'l Crim. Trib.-Yugo., Appeals Chamber (5 March 1998), *reported in* Int'l Crim. Trib.-Yugo. 20 *Bulletin* 2 (20 March 1998).

(5) Historically, other defenses have been argued unsuccessfully. They include the defense of *tu quoque* ("you also"), double jeopardy between two sovereigns, and head of

state or official immunity. The *tu quoque* defense refers to the prosecution of offenders by persons/states that also have committed the same crimes. The IMT held that this defense was not valid in *Matter of Von Leeb*. The defense of double jeopardy between two sovereigns refers to the prosecution of the same crime by different sovereigns. For further discussion on the issue of double jeopardy, see Chapter 12(C).

Finally, the defense of head of state or official immunity recently has received much attention in the UK extradition hearings of Gen. Augusto Pinochet. Such immunity is not available as a matter of international law. In cases of gross human rights/humanitarian law violations, this immunity is not available because such violations far exceed ordinary domestic crimes. *See, e.g.,* Art. 31, Vienna Convention on Diplomatic Relations, 500 U.N.T.S. 95, adopted 18 April 1961 (entered into force 24 April 1964). Most importantly, these violations violate both customary international law and *jus cogens*. Accordingly, any domestic law or treaty providing such immunity would be invalid.

(6)   Consider the following quotation:

> Kill one person, they call you a murderer.
> Kill a dozen people, they call you serial killer.
> Kill a thousand people, and they invite you to a peace conference.

> -- attributed to Haris Silajdzic

(7) Amnesty laws have posed an obstacle to punishment and/or accountability -- although amnesty laws have been justified by some commentators as necessary for preventing *further* human rights violations. Some have argued that such a consideration is a legitimate and lawful concern for determining punishment or accountability. Many countries[12] have used amnesty laws to induce repressive regimes and rebel groups to achieve political stability and stop committing human rights violations, but amnesty laws violate states' international law obligations by preventing individuals from exercising their right to a remedy that includes the investigation and prosecution of persons responsible for human rights violations. All of the major human rights treaties require states to "respect and ensure" against violations of protected rights[13] and require states to provide

---

[12] States that have enacted such amnesty laws include Argentina, Brazil, Chile, Czech and Slovak Republics, El Salvador, France, Hungary, Italy, Nicaragua, Portugal, Russia, South Africa, South Korea, Spain, Uruguay, and Zimbabwe. Fauzia Shariff, "Comparative Chart on the Use of Amnesty Legislation, Truth Commissions and Compensation Mechanisms," 10 *Interights Bulletin* 96-98 (1996).

[13] Art. 2(1), ICCPR ("[e]ach State Party to the present Covenant undertakes to respect and ensure to all individuals within its territory and subject to its jurisdiction the rights recognized in the present Covenant..."); Art. 1(1), ACHR ([t]he States Parties to this Convention undertake to respect the rights and freedoms recognized herein and to ensure to all persons subject to their jurisdiction the free and full exercise of those rights and

(continued...)

effective remedies for their violation.[14] The repetition and consistency of these obligations create a strong presumption that states also have a customary law obligation to provide remedies for human rights violations. Accordingly, governments over the last fifty years have compromised by providing amnesty in conjunction with truth or investigatory

---

[13](...continued)
freedoms..."); Art. 13, ECHR ("[t]he High Contracting Parties shall secure to everyone within their jurisdiction the rights and freedoms defined in Section I of this Convention").

[14] Article 8, Universal Declaration of Human Rights, G.A. Res. 217 (III), U.N. Doc. A/810, at 71 (1948), states:

> [e]veryone has the right to an effective remedy by the competent national tribunals for acts violating the fundamental rights granted him by the constitution or by law.

Article 2(3), ICCPR, states:

> Each State Party to the present Covenant undertakes:
> 1. To ensure that any person whose rights or freedoms as herein recognized are violated shall have an effective remedy, notwithstanding that the violation has been committed by persons acting in an official capacity;
> 2. To ensure that any person claiming such a remedy shall have his right thereto determined by competent judicial, administrative or legislative authorities, or by any other competent authority provided for by the legal system of the State, and to develop the possibilities of judicial remedy;
> 3. To ensure that the competent authorities shall enforce such remedies when granted;

Article 25(1), ACHR, states:

> [e]veryone has the right to simple and prompt recourse, or any other effective recourse, to a competent court or other tribunal for protection against acts that violate his fundamental rights recognized by the constitution or laws of the state concerned or by this Convention, even though such violation may have been committed by persons acting in the course of their official duties.

Article 13, ECHR, states:

> [e]veryone whose rights and freedoms as set forth in this Convention are violated shall have an effective remedy before a national authority notwithstanding that a violation has been committed by persons acting in an official capacity.

commissions,[15] and/or compensation.[16] Besides pecuniary compensation, some governments have provided credit grants, housing, and employment as part of a compensation package.[17] Other mechanisms include the barring of former perpetrators of human rights violations from quasi-state or state positions.[18]

These approaches have had mixed results. Most of these schemes have been unsatisfactory as a matter of both international law and political stability. Both the Inter-American Commission of Human Rights and the UN Human Rights Committee have found amnesty laws to be in conflict with states' international human rights obligations. In reference to the prohibition of torture in Article 7 of the ICCPR, the Human Rights Committee has expressed the view that "[a]mnesties are generally incompatible with the duty of States to investigate [torture]; to guarantee freedom from such acts within their jurisdiction; and to ensure that they do not occur in the future."[19] In examining the amnesty laws of Argentina, El Salvador, and Uruguay, the Inter-American Commission ruled that all three laws violated rights protected by the American Convention, including the obligation to investigate.[20] And, many of those countries – such as El Salvador, Nicaragua, and Russia -- that have enacted amnesty laws in conjunction with other mechanisms have failed to achieve political stability. Even diehard advocates of *realpolitik* recognize that there is "no peace without justice" in the long-run: the long-term success and stability of a successor government to a repressive regime must ensure individualized justice that entails a right to remedies criminal, declarative, compensatory, and injunctive. With the recent establishment of the ICT-Y and ICT-R; the future

---

[15] Truth or investigatory commissions have been used by Argentina, Brazil, Chad, Chile, El Salvador, Ethiopia, Germany, Hungary, Lithuania, Nicaragua, Philippines, South Africa, Uganda, and Zimbabwe. Shariff, *supra*, at n. 19.

[16] Compensatory mechanisms have been used by Albania, Argentina, Bulgaria, Czech and Slovak Republics, Germany, Hungary, Lithuania, Russia, and South Africa. *Id.*

[17] Bulgaria has such a package. *Id.*

[18] The former Czechoslovakia enacted such a law in 1991.

[19] General Comment 20, U.N. Doc. HRI/GEN/1/Rev.3 (1997), para. 15.

[20] Report 28/92 (Argentina), ANNUAL REPORT OF THE INTER-AMERICAN COMMISSION ON HUMAN RIGHTS 1992-1993, OEA, Ser.L/V/II/.83, Doc. 14, corr. 1 (12 March 1993) para. 50, (finding a violation of the right to a fair trial (Art. 8) and the right to judicial protection (Art. 25) "in relation to the obligation of the States to guarantee the full and free exercise of the rights recognized in the Convention (Art. 1.1)"); Report 26/92 (El Salvador), ANNUAL REPORT OF THE INTER-AMERICAN COMMISSION ON HUMAN RIGHTS 1992-1993, OEA, Ser.L/V/II/.83, Doc. 14, corr. 1 (12 March 1993) (finding a violation of the right to life (Art. 4), the right to personal security and integrity (Art. 5), the right to due process (Art. 8) and the right to due judicial protection (Art. 25)); Report 29/92 (Uruguay), ANNUAL REPORT OF THE INTER-AMERICAN COMMISSION ON HUMAN RIGHTS 1992-1993, OEA, Ser.L/V/II/.83, Doc. 14, corr. 1 (12 March 1993) (finding a violation of the right to a fair trial (Art. 8.1), the right to judicial protection (Art. 25), and the obligation to investigate (Art. 1.1).

establishment of the ICC; the Pinochet extradition and domestic prosecution by Spain, France, Belgium; the domestic prosecution of Fidel Castro by France; and the possible prosecution of the Khmer Rouge leadership by Cambodia; the rule of international criminal law has acquired a very real and considerable geo-political force that can be brought to bear on both state and non-state powers.

(8) U.S. courts have rejected the "political question" defense to international crimes. *See, e.g., Abebe-Jira v. Negewo*, 72 F.3d 844, 848 (11th Cir. 1996); *Kadic v. Karadzic*, 70 F.3d 232, 249-50 (2d Cir. 1995). U.S. courts also have rejected the "acts of state" defense. *See, e.g., Hilao v. Estate of Marcos*, 25 F.3d 1467, 1470-72 (9th Cir. 1994); *Kadic v. Karadzic*, 70 F.3d at 250.

B. Private Individuals

C.R. v. United Kingdom
European Court of Human Rights
355 Eur. Ct. H.R. (ser. A) (1995)
21 E.H.R.R. 363 (1996)

. . . .
FACTS:

I.   Particular circumstances of the case

A.   Events leading to charges being brought against the applicant

8. The applicant is a British citizen. His relationship with his wife, whom he married in 1987, was turbulent and came under great strain in 1990 when he became unemployed. In the early evening of 18 September 1990, she told him that for some weeks she had been thinking of leaving him and that she regarded the marriage as over. Prior to that date they had been sleeping separately — according to the applicant, for one night, or according to his wife, for five nights. The applicant did not accept that his wife meant what she said and they had a row following which he ejected her from the house, bruising her arm. She went to her next door neighbours and called the police, who subsequently visited and spoke to both the applicant and his wife separately. Later the same evening she re-entered the house and the applicant had sexual intercourse with her. Shortly afterwards she left the house, having first tried to take their child with her. She went to the neighbours crying and distressed, complaining to them and to the police, whom she telephoned, that she had been raped at knife-point.

9. On 19 September 1990 the applicant was charged with rape, under section 1(1) of the Sexual Offences Act 1956; threatening to kill, contrary to section 16 of the Offences against the Person Act 1861; and assault occasioning actual bodily harm, in breach of section 47 of the latter Act.

B.   Crown Court judgment of 30 July 1990 and Court of Appeal judgment of 14 March 1991 in the case of *R v. R*

10. On 30 July 1990 the defendant in another case, *R v R*, had been sentenced to three years' imprisonment by the Crown Court for attempted rape and assault occasioning actual bodily harm against his wife.   The trial judge, Owen J, had rejected the defendant's submission that he could not be convicted in light of a common law principle stated by Sir Matthew Hale CJ in his *History of the Pleas of the Crown* published in 1736:

> But the husband cannot be guilty of rape committed by himself upon his lawful wife, for by their matrimonial consent and contract the wife hath given up herself in this kind unto her husband, which she cannot retract.

In his judgment ([1991] 1 All E.R. 747.) Mr. Justice Owen noted that it was a statement made in general terms at a time when marriage was indissoluble.   Hale CJ had been expounding the common law as it seemed to him at that particular time and was doing it in a book and not with reference to a particular set of circumstances presented to him in a prosecution.   The bald statement had been reproduced in the first edition of ARCHBOLD ON CRIMINAL PLEADINGS, EVIDENCE AND PRACTICE (1822, p 259) in the following terms: "A husband also cannot be guilty of rape upon his wife."

Owen J further examined a series of court decisions, recognising that a wife's consent to marital intercourse was impliedly given by her at the time of marriage and that the consent could be revoked on certain conditions. (*R. v. Clarence* [1888] 22 Q.B.D. 23, [1886-90] All E.R. 113; *R. v. Clarke* [1949] 2 All E.R. 448; *R. v. Miller* [1954] 2 All E.R. 529; *R. v. Reid* [1972] 2 All E.R. 1350; *R. v. O'Brien* [1974] 3 All E.R. 663; *R. v. Steele* (1976) 65 Cr. App. 22; *R. v. Roberts* [1986] Crim L.R. 188.) . . . .

On the question of what circumstances would suffice in law to revoke the consent, Gwen J noted that it may be brought to an end, firstly, by a court order or equivalent. Secondly, he observed, it was apparent from the Court of Appeal's judgment in the case of *R. v. Steele* ((1976) 65 Cr. App. 22) that the implied consent could be withdrawn by agreement between the parties.   Such an agreement could clearly be implicit; there was nothing in the case law to suggest the contrary.   Thirdly, he was of the view that the common law recognised that a withdrawal of either party from cohabitation, accompanied by a clear indication that consent to sexual intercourse has been terminated, would amount to a revocation of the implicit consent.   He concluded that both the second and third exceptions to the matrimonial immunity against prosecution for rape applied in the case.

11. An appeal to the Court of Appeal, Criminal Division, was dismissed on 14 March 1991.   ([1991] 2 All E.R. 257.) Lord Lane noted that the general proposition of Sir Matthew Hale in his HISTORY OF THE PLEAS OF THE CROWN (1736) that a man could not commit rape upon his wife was generally accepted as a correct statement of the common law at that epoch. Further, Lord Lane made an analysis of previous court decisions, from which it appears that in *R. v. Clarence* (1888), the first reported case of this nature, some judges of the Court for Crown Cases Reserved had objected to the principle.   In the next reported case, *R. v. Clarke* (1949), the trial court had departed from the principle by holding that the husband's immunity was lost in the event of a court order directing that

the wife was no longer bound to cohabit with him. Almost every court decision thereafter had made increasingly important exceptions to the marital immunity. . . .

Lord Lane then critically examined the different strands of interpretation of section 1(1)(a) of the 1976 Act in the case law, including the argument that the term "unlawful" excluded intercourse within marriage from the definition of rape. He concluded:

> . . . (We) do not consider that we are inhibited by the 1976 Act from declaring that the husband's immunity as expounded by Hale CJ no longer exists. We take the view that the time has now arrived when the law should declare that a rapist remains a rapist subject to the criminal law, irrespective of his relationship with his victim.
>
> The remaining and no less difficult question is whether, despite that view, this is an area where the court should step aside to leave the matter to the Parliamentary process. This is not the creation of a new offence, it is the removal of a common law fiction which has become anachronistic and offensive and we consider that it is our duty having reached that conclusion to act upon it.
>
> Had our decision been otherwise and had we been of the opinion that Hale CJ's proposition was still effective, we would nevertheless have ruled that where, as in the instant case, a wife withdraws from cohabitation in such a way as to make it clear to the husband that so far as she is concerned the marriage is at an end, the husband's immunity is lost.

12. On 23 October 1991, on a further appeal by the appellant in the above case, the House of Lords upheld the Court of Appeal's judgment, declaring, *inter alia*, that the general principle that a husband cannot rape his wife no longer formed part of the law of England and Wales. ([1991] 4 All E.R. 481.) It stressed that the common law was capable of evolving in the light of changing social, economic and cultural developments. . . .

II. Relevant domestic law and practice

A. The offence of rape

19. The offence of rape, at common law, was traditionally defined as unlawful sexual intercourse with a woman without her consent by force, fear or fraud. By section 1 of the Sexual Offences Act 1956, "it is a felony for a man to rape a woman".

20. Section 1(1) of the Sexual Offences (Amendment) Act 1976 provides, in so far as it is material, as follows:

> For the purposes of section 1 of the Sexual Offences Act 1956 (which relates to rape) a man commits rape if
>
> -- (a) he has unlawful sexual intercourse with a woman who at the time of the intercourse does not consent to it . . .

21. On 3 November 1994 the Criminal Justice and Public Order Act 1994 replaced the above provisions by inserting new sub-sections to section 1 of the Sexual Offences Act 1956, one of the effects of which was to remove the word "unlawful":

1. (1) It is an offence for a man to rape a woman or another man.

(2) A man commits rape if — (a) he has sexual intercourse with a person . . . who at the time of the intercourse does not consent to it . . .

B.   Marital immunity

22. Until the case of *R v. R* the English courts, on the few occasions when they were confronted with the issue whether directly or indirectly, had always recognised at least some form of immunity attaching to a husband from any charge of rape or attempted rape by reason of a notional or fictional consent to intercourse deemed to have been given by the wife on marriage. . . .

PROCEEDINGS BEFORE THE COMMISSION

28. In his application of 29 March 1992 (No 20166/92) to the Commission, the applicant complained that, in breach of Article 7 of the Convention, he was convicted in respect of conduct, namely the rape upon his wife, which at the relevant time did not, so he submitted, constitute a criminal offence.

29. The Commission declared the application admissible on 14 January 1994. In its report of 27 June 1994, (Article 31) the Commission expressed the opinion that there had been no violation of Article 7(1) of the Convention. (Eleven votes to six.) . . . .

. . . .

DECISION [OF THE EUROPEAN COURT OF HUMAN RIGHTS]:

Alleged violation of Article 7 of the Convention

30.   The applicant complained that his conviction and sentence for rape of his wife constituted retrospective punishment in breach of Article 7 of the Convention, which reads:

1. No one shall be held guilty of any criminal offence on account of any act or omission which did not constitute a criminal offence under national or international law at the time when it was committed. Nor shall a heavier penalty be imposed than the one that was applicable at the time the criminal offence was committed.

2. This Article shall not prejudice the trial and punishment of any person for any act or omission which, at the time when it was committed, was criminal according to the general principles of law recognised by civilised nations.

33/31. The Government and the Commission disagreed with the above contention.

Chapter 6. Individual Culpability & Defenses

A. General principles

32. The guarantee enshrined in Article 7, which is an essential element of the rule of law, occupies a prominent place in the Convention system of protection, as is underlined by the fact that no derogation from it is permissible under Article 15 in time of war or other public emergency. It should be construed and applied, as follows from its object and purpose, in such a way as to provide effective safeguards against arbitrary prosecution, conviction and punishment.

33. Accordingly, as the Court held in its *Kokkinakis v. Greece* judgment of 25 May 1993, [260 Eur. Ct. H.R. (ser. A) at 22 (1993)] Article 7 is not confined to prohibiting the retrospective application of the criminal law to an accused's disadvantage: it also embodies, more generally, the principle that only the law can define a crime and prescribe a penalty (*nullum crimen, nulla poena sine lege*) and the principle that the criminal law must not be extensively construed to an accused's detriment, for instance by analogy. From these principles it follows that an offence must be clearly defined in the law. In its aforementioned judgment the Court added that this requirement is satisfied where the individual can know from the wording of the relevant provision and, if need be, with the assistance of the courts' interpretation of it, what acts and omissions will make him criminally liable. The Court thus indicated that when speaking of "law" Article 7 alludes to the very same concept as that to which the Convention refers elsewhere when using that term, a concept which comprises written as well as unwritten law and implies qualitative requirements, notably those of accessibility and foreseeability. (*See*, as a recent authority, *Tolstoy Miloslavsky v. United Kingdom*, 316 Eur. Ct. H.R. (ser. A) at 71-72 (1995).

34. However clearly drafted a legal provision may be, in any system of law, including criminal law, there is an inevitable element of judicial interpretation. There will always be a need for elucidation of doubtful points and for adaptation to changing circumstances. Indeed, in the United Kingdom, as in the other Convention States, the progressive development of the criminal law through judicial law-making is a well entrenched and necessary part of legal tradition. Article 7 of the Convention cannot be read as outlawing the gradual clarification of the rules of criminal liability through judicial interpretation from case to case, provided that the resultant development is consistent with the essence of the offence and could reasonably be foreseen.

B. Application of the foregoing principles

35. The applicant maintained that the general common law principle that a husband could not be found guilty of rape upon his wife, albeit subject to certain limitations, was still effective on 18 September 1990, when he committed the acts which gave rise to the rape charge. A succession of court decisions before and also after that date for instance on 20 November 1990 in *R v J* had affirmed the general principle of immunity. It was clearly beyond doubt that as at 18 September 1990 no change in the law had been effected, although one was being mooted.

When the House of Commons debated the Bill for the Sexual Offences (Amendment) Act 1976, different views on the marital immunity were expressed. On the advice of the Minister of State to await a report of the Criminal Law Revision Committee, an amendment that would have abolished the immunity was withdrawn and never voted upon.

In its report, which was not presented until 1984, the Criminal Law Revision Committee recommended that the immunity should be maintained and that a new exception should be created.

In 1988, when considering certain amendments to the 1976 Act, Parliament had the opportunity to take out the word "unlawful" in section 1(1)(a) or to introduce a new provision on marital intercourse, but took no action in this respect.

On 17 September 1990 the Law Commission provisionally recommended that the immunity rule be abolished. However, the debate was pre-empted by the Court of Appeal's and the House of Lords' rulings in the case of *R v. R*. In the applicant's submission, these rulings altered the law retrospectively, which would not have been the case had the Law Commission's proposal been implemented by Parliament. Consequently, he concluded, when Parliament in 1994 removed the word "unlawful" from section 1 of the 1976 Act, it did not merely restate the law as it had been in 1976.

36. The applicant further argued that in examining his complaint under Article 7(1) of the Convention, the Court should not consider his conduct in relation to any of the exceptions to the immunity rule. Such exceptions were never contemplated in the national proceedings, Rose J having taken his decision in reliance on the Court of Appeal's ruling of 14 March 1991 in *R v. R* to the effect that the immunity no longer existed. Owen J's decision of 30 July 1990 in *R v. R*, adding implied agreement to terminate consent to intercourse to the list of exceptions, had not been reported by 18 September 1990 and was not a binding authority. In any event, the facts in the present case suggest that no such agreement existed.

37. Should a foreseeability test akin to that under Article 10(2) apply in the instant case, the applicant was of the opinion that it had not been satisfied. Although the Court of Appeal and the House of Lords did not create a new offence or change the basic ingredients of the offence of rape, they were extending an existing offence to include conduct which until then was excluded by the common law. They could not be said to have adapted the law to a new kind of conduct but rather to a change of social attitudes. To extend the criminal law, solely on such a basis, to conduct which was previously lawful was precisely what Article 7 of the Convention was designed to prevent. Moreover, the applicant stressed, it was impossible to specify with precision when the change in question had occurred. In September 1990, change by judicial interpretation was not foreseen by the Law Commission, which considered that a Parliamentary enactment would be necessary.

38. The Government and the Commission were of the view that by September 1990 there was significant doubt as to the validity of the alleged marital immunity for rape. This was an area where the law had been subject to progressive development and there were strong indications that still wider interpretation by the courts of the inroads on the immunity was probable. In particular, given the recognition of women's equality of status with men in marriage and outside it and of their autonomy over their own bodies, the adaptation of the ingredients of the offence of rape was reasonably foreseeable, with appropriate legal advice, to the applicant. He was not convicted of conduct which did not constitute a criminal offence at the time when it was committed.

In addition, the Government pointed out, on the basis of the agreed facts Owen J had found that there was an implied agreement between the applicant [CR] and his wife to separation and to withdrawal of the consent to intercourse. The circumstances in his case were thus covered by the exceptions to the immunity already stated by the English courts.

39. The Court notes that the applicant's conviction for rape was based on the statutory offence of rape in section 1 of the 1956 Act, as further defined in section 1(1) of the 1976 Act. The applicant does not dispute that the conduct for which he was convicted would have constituted rape within the meaning of the statutory definition of rape as applicable at the time, had the victim not been his wife. His complaint under Article 7 of the Convention relates solely to the fact that in deciding on 18 April 1991 that the applicant had a case to answer on the rape charge, Rose J followed the Court of Appeal's ruling of 14 March 1991 in the case of *R v. R* which declared that the immunity no longer existed.

40. It is to be observed that a crucial issue in the judgment of the Court of Appeal in *R v. R* related to the definition of rape in section 1(1)(a) of the 1976 Act: "unlawful sexual intercourse with a woman who at the time of the intercourse does not consent to it". The question was whether "removal" of the marital immunity would conflict with the statutory definition of rape, in particular whether it would be prevented by the word "unlawful". The Court of Appeal carefully examined various strands of interpretation of the provision in the case law, including the argument that the term "unlawful" excluded intercourse within marriage from the definition of rape. In this connection, the Court recalls that it is in the first place for the national authorities, notably the courts, to interpret and apply national law. (*See* for instance, *Kemmache v. France* [296 Eur. Ct. H.R. (ser. A) at 86-87 (1995)].) It sees no reason to disagree with the Court of Appeal's conclusion, which was subsequently upheld by the House of Lords, that the word "unlawful" in the definition of rape was merely surplusage and did not inhibit them from "removing a common law fiction which had become anachronistic and offensive" and from declaring that "a rapist remains a rapist subject to the criminal law, irrespective of his relationship with his victim.

41. The decisions of the Court of Appeal and then the House of Lords did no more than continue a perceptible line of case law development dismantling the immunity of a husband from prosecution for rape upon his wife. There was no doubt under the law as it stood on 18 September 1990 that a husband who forcibly had sexual intercourse with his wife could, in various circumstances, be found guilty of rape. Moreover, there was an evident evolution, which was consistent with the very essence of the offence, of the criminal law through judicial interpretation towards treating such conduct generally as within the scope of the offence of rape. This evolution had reached a stage where judicial recognition of the absence of immunity had become a reasonably foreseeable development of the law.

42. The essentially debasing character of rape is so manifest that the result of the decisions of the Court of Appeal and the House of Lords — that the applicant could be convicted of attempted rape, irrespective of his relationship with the victim — cannot be said to be at variance with the object and purpose of Article 7 of the Convention, namely to ensure that no-one should be subjected to arbitrary prosecution, conviction or punishment. What is more, the abandonment of the unacceptable idea of a husband being immune against prosecution for rape of his wife was in conformity not only with a civilised concept of marriage but also, and above all, with the fundamental objectives of the Convention, the very essence of which is respect for human dignity and human freedom.

43. Consequently, by following the Court of Appeal's ruling in *R v. R* in the applicant's case, Rose J did not render a decision permitting a finding of guilt incompatible with Article 7 of the Convention.

44. Having reached this conclusion, the Court does not find it necessary to enquire into whether the facts in the applicant's case were covered by the exceptions to the immunity rule already made by the English courts before 18 September 1990.

45. In short, the Court, like the Government and the Commission, finds that the Crown Court's decision that the applicant could not invoke immunity to escape conviction and sentence for rape upon his wife did not give rise to a violation of his rights under Article 7(1) of the Convention.

For these reasons, THE COURT unanimously

Holds that there has been no violation of Article 7(1) of the Convention.

Questions & Comments

(1) Consider the following excerpt from the concurring opinion by Liddy, C.

> 11. One of the rights guaranteed by the Convention is the right to private life, including integrity of the person, and including the right of a woman to effective measures by means of criminal law provisions whereby there is deterrence against rape. (*X. and Y. v. the Netherlands* [91 Eur. Ct. H.R. (ser. A) (1986)].) This right was identified by the Court as long ago as 1985.

International criminal law historically has addressed international conflicts in which state actors are the persons (or organizations) held criminally liable. On the other hand, international human rights law has created international criminal culpability for private individuals, as seen in both *X. & Y. v. The Netherlands* and *C.R. v. United Kingdom*. Clearly, the right to private life guaranteed in many human rights treaties has allowed the recognition of private individual criminal culpability.

Under the Statutes of the ICT-Y, ICT-R, and ICC, genocide is an act "committed with intent to destroy, in whole or *in part*, a national, ethnical, racial or religious group" (emphasis provided). How many persons belonging to one of these groups constitutes a sufficient "part" in order to rise to the level on an international crime? In light of the private individual criminal culpability recognized by the aforementioned cases, would it be possible for a private individual, acting alone, to be found guilty of genocide for murdering *one* person on the basis of their victim's nationality, ethnicity, race or religion?

(2) Consider the following:

> Like the Ninth and Thirteenth Amendments, but unlike the Fourteenth Amendment and some civil rights legislation, international human rights law does not contain limiting words such as "state," "state action," or "under color of law." Consequently, international human rights law can operate under the

Supremacy Clause to create or transform duties in various sectors of domestic law, including . . . criminal law . . . .

Jordan J. Paust, *The Other Side of Right: Private Duties Under Human Rights Law*, 5 HARV. HUM. RTS. J. 51, 53 n.10 (1992).

How would you argue on behalf of the family of a victim murdered on the basis of her race that the U.S. federal (or state) government has a customary international law duty to prosecute her killer as a perpetrator of genocide?

PART THREE: INTERNATIONAL CRIMES

Charter of the International Military Tribunal

Article 6

. . . .

The following acts, or any of them, are crimes coming within the jurisdiction of the Tribunal for which there shall be individual responsibility:

(a) CRIMES AGAINST PEACE: namely, planning, preparation, initiation or waging of a war of aggression, or a war in violation of international treaties, agreements or assurances, or participation in a common plan or conspiracy for the accomplishment of any of the foregoing;

(b) WAR CRIMES: namely, violations of the laws or customs of war. Such violations shall include, but not be limited to, murder, ill-treatment or deportation to slave labor or for any other purpose of civilian population of or in occupied territory, murder or ill-treatment of prisoners of war or persons on the seas, killing of hostages, plunder of public or private property, wanton destruction of cities, towns or villages, or devastation not justified by military necessity;

(c)CRIMES AGAINST HUMANITY: namely, murder, extermination, enslavement, deportation, and other inhumane acts committed against any civilian population, before or during the war; or persecutions on political, racial or religious grounds in execution of or in connection with any crime within the jurisdiction of the Tribunal, whether or not in violation of the domestic law of the country where perpetrated.

. . . .

Statutes of the International Criminal Tribunals and Court

Statute of the International Criminal Court

Article 5
Crimes within the jurisdiction of the Court

1. The jurisdiction of the Court shall be limited to the most serious crimes of concern to the international community as a whole. The Court has jurisdiction in accordance with this Statute with respect to the following crimes:

(a) The crime of genocide;
(b) Crimes against humanity;
(c) War crimes;
(d) The crime of aggression.

2. The Court shall exercise jurisdiction over the crime of aggression once a provision is adopted in accordance with articles 121 and 123 defining the crime and setting out the conditions under which the Court shall exercise jurisdiction with respect to this crime.

Such a provision shall be consistent with the relevant provisions of the Charter of the United Nations.

Article 6
Genocide

For the purpose of this Statute, "genocide" means any of the following acts committed with intent to destroy, in whole or in part, a national, ethnical, racial or religious group, as such:

(a) Killing members of the group;
(b) Causing serious bodily or mental harm to members of the group;
(c) Deliberately inflicting on the group conditions of life calculated to bring about its physical destruction in whole or in part;
(d) Imposing measures intended to prevent births within the group;
(e) Forcibly transferring children of the group to another group.

Article 7
Crimes against humanity

1. For the purpose of this Statute, "crime against humanity" means any of the following acts when committed as part of a widespread or systematic attack directed against any civilian population, with knowledge of the attack:

(a) Murder;
(b) Extermination;
(c) Enslavement;
(d) Deportation or forcible transfer of population;
(e) Imprisonment or other severe deprivation of physical liberty in violation of fundamental rules of international law;
(f) Torture;
(g) Rape, sexual slavery, enforced prostitution, forced pregnancy, enforced sterilization, or any other form of sexual violence of comparable gravity;
(h) Persecution against any identifiable group or collectivity on political, racial, national, ethnic, cultural, religious, gender as defined in paragraph 3, or other grounds that are universally recognized as impermissible under international law, in connection with any act referred to in this paragraph or any crime within the jurisdiction of the Court;
(i) Enforced disappearance of persons;
(j) The crime of apartheid;
(k) Other inhumane acts of a similar character intentionally causing great suffering, or serious injury to body or to mental or physical health.

2. For the purpose of paragraph 1:

(a) "Attack directed against any civilian population" means a course of conduct involving the multiple commission of acts referred to in paragraph 1 against any civilian population, pursuant to or in furtherance of a State or organizational policy to commit such attack;

(b) "Extermination" includes the intentional infliction of conditions of life, *inter alia* the deprivation of access to food and medicine, calculated to bring about the destruction of part of a population;

(c) "Enslavement" means the exercise of any or all of the powers attaching to the right of ownership over a person and includes the exercise of such power in the course of trafficking in persons, in particular women and children;

(d) "Deportation or forcible transfer of population" means forced displacement of the persons concerned by expulsion or other coercive acts from the area in which they are lawfully present, without grounds permitted under international law;

(e) "Torture" means the intentional infliction of severe pain or suffering, whether physical or mental, upon a person in the custody or under the control of the accused; except that torture shall not include pain or suffering arising only from, inherent in or incidental to, lawful sanctions;

(f) "Forced pregnancy" means the unlawful confinement, of a woman forcibly made pregnant, with the intent of affecting the ethnic composition of any population or carrying out other grave violations of international law. This definition shall not in any way be interpreted as affecting national laws relating to pregnancy;

(g) "Persecution" means the intentional and severe deprivation of fundamental rights contrary to international law by reason of the identity of the group or collectivity;

(h) "The crime of apartheid" means inhumane acts of a character similar to those referred to in paragraph 1, committed in the context of an institutionalized regime of systematic oppression and domination by one racial group over any other racial group or groups and committed with the intention of maintaining that regime;

(i) "Enforced disappearance of persons" means the arrest, detention or abduction of persons by, or with the authorization, support or acquiescence of, a State or a political organization, followed by a refusal to acknowledge that deprivation of freedom or to give information on the fate or whereabouts of those persons, with the intention of removing them from the protection of the law for a prolonged period of time.

3. For the purpose of this Statute, it is understood that the term "gender" refers to the two sexes, male and female, within the context of society. The term "gender" does not indicate any meaning different from the above.

Article 8
War crimes

1. The Court shall have jurisdiction in respect of war crimes in particular when committed as a part of a plan or policy or as part of a large-scale commission of such crimes.

2. For the purpose of this Statute, "war crimes" means:

(a) Grave breaches of the Geneva Conventions of 12 August 1949, namely, any of the following acts against persons or property protected under the provisions of the relevant Geneva Convention:

(i) Wilful killing;
(ii) Torture or inhuman treatment, including biological experiments;
(iii) Wilfully causing great suffering, or serious injury to body or health;
(iv) Extensive destruction and appropriation of property, not justified by military necessity and carried out unlawfully and wantonly;
(v) Compelling a prisoner of war or other protected person to serve in the forces of a hostile Power;
(vi) Wilfully depriving a prisoner of war or other protected person of the rights of fair and regular trial;
(vii) Unlawful deportation or transfer or unlawful confinement;
(viii) Taking of hostages.

(b) Other serious violations of the laws and customs applicable in international armed conflict, within the established framework of international law, namely, any of the following acts:

(i) Intentionally directing attacks against the civilian population as such or against individual civilians not taking direct part in hostilities;
(ii) Intentionally directing attacks against civilian objects, that is, objects which are not military objectives;
(iii) Intentionally directing attacks against personnel, installations, material, units or vehicles involved in a humanitarian assistance or peacekeeping mission in accordance with the Charter of the United Nations, as long as they are entitled to the protection given to civilians or civilian objects under the international law of armed conflict;
(iv) Intentionally launching an attack in the knowledge that such attack will cause incidental loss of life or injury to civilians or damage to civilian objects or widespread, long-term and severe damage to the natural environment which would be clearly excessive in relation to the concrete and direct overall military advantage anticipated;
(v) Attacking or bombarding, by whatever means, towns, villages, dwellings or buildings which are undefended and which are not military objectives;
(vi) Killing or wounding a combatant who, having laid down his arms or having no longer means of defence, has surrendered at discretion;
(vii) Making improper use of a flag of truce, of the flag or of the military insignia and uniform of the enemy or of the United Nations, as well as of the distinctive emblems of the Geneva Conventions, resulting in death or serious personal injury;
(viii) The transfer, directly or indirectly, by the Occupying Power of parts of its own civilian population into the territory it occupies, or the deportation or transfer of all or parts of the population of the occupied territory within or outside this territory;

(ix) Intentionally directing attacks against buildings dedicated to religion, education, art, science or charitable purposes, historic monuments, hospitals and places where the sick and wounded are collected, provided they are not military objectives;

(x) Subjecting persons who are in the power of an adverse party to physical mutilation or to medical or scientific experiments of any kind which are neither justified by the medical, dental or hospital treatment of the person concerned nor carried out in his or her interest, and which cause death to or seriously endanger the health of such person or persons;

(xi) Killing or wounding treacherously individuals belonging to the hostile nation or army;

(xii) Declaring that no quarter will be given;

(xiii) Destroying or seizing the enemy's property unless such destruction or seizure be imperatively demanded by the necessities of war;

(xiv) Declaring abolished, suspended or inadmissible in a court of law the rights and actions of the nationals of the hostile party;

(xv) Compelling the nationals of the hostile party to take part in the operations of war directed against their own country, even if they were in the belligerent's service before the commencement of the war;

(xvi) Pillaging a town or place, even when taken by assault;

(xvii) Employing poison or poisoned weapons;

(xviii) Employing asphyxiating, poisonous or other gases, and all analogous liquids, materials or devices;

(xix) Employing bullets which expand or flatten easily in the human body, such as bullets with a hard envelope which does not entirely cover the core or is pierced with incisions;

(xx) Employing weapons, projectiles and material and methods of warfare which are of a nature to cause superfluous injury or unnecessary suffering or which are inherently indiscriminate in violation of the international law of armed conflict, provided that such weapons, projectiles and material and methods of warfare are the subject of a comprehensive prohibition and are included in an annex to this Statute, by an amendment in accordance with the relevant provisions set forth in articles 121 and 123;

(xxi) Committing outrages upon personal dignity, in particular humiliating and degrading treatment;

(xxii) Committing rape, sexual slavery, enforced prostitution, forced pregnancy, as defined in article 7, paragraph 2 (f), enforced sterilization, or any other form of sexual violence also constituting a grave breach of the Geneva Conventions;

(xxiii) Utilizing the presence of a civilian or other protected person to render certain points, areas or military forces immune from military operations;

(xxiv) Intentionally directing attacks against buildings, material, medical units and transport, and personnel using the distinctive emblems of the Geneva Conventions in conformity with international law;

(xxv) Intentionally using starvation of civilians as a method of warfare by depriving them of objects indispensable to their survival, including wilfully impeding relief supplies as provided for under the Geneva Conventions;

(xxvi) Conscripting or enlisting children under the age of fifteen years into the national armed forces or using them to participate actively in hostilities.

(c) In the case of an armed conflict not of an international character, serious violations of article 3 common to the four Geneva Conventions of 12 August 1949, namely, any of the following acts committed against persons taking no active part in the hostilities, including members of armed forces who have laid down their arms and those placed *hors de* combat by sickness, wounds, detention or any other cause:

(i) Violence to life and person, in particular murder of all kinds, mutilation, cruel treatment and torture;
(ii) Committing outrages upon personal dignity, in particular humiliating and degrading treatment;
(iii) Taking of hostages;
(iv) The passing of sentences and the carrying out of executions without previous judgement pronounced by a regularly constituted court, affording all judicial guarantees which are generally recognized as indispensable.

(d) Paragraph 2 (c) applies to armed conflicts not of an international character and thus does not apply to situations of internal disturbances and tensions, such as riots, isolated and sporadic acts of violence or other acts of a similar nature.
(e) Other serious violations of the laws and customs applicable in armed conflicts not of an international character, within the established framework of international law, namely, any of the following acts:

(i) Intentionally directing attacks against the civilian population as such or against individual civilians not taking direct part in hostilities;
(ii) Intentionally directing attacks against buildings, material, medical units and transport, and personnel using the distinctive emblems of the Geneva Conventions in conformity with international law;
(iii) Intentionally directing attacks against personnel, installations, material, units or vehicles involved in a humanitarian assistance or peacekeeping mission in accordance with the Charter of the United Nations, as long as they are entitled to the protection given to civilians or civilian objects under the law of armed conflict;
 (iv) Intentionally directing attacks against buildings dedicated to religion, education, art, science or charitable purposes, historic monuments, hospitals and places where the sick and wounded are collected, provided they are not military objectives;
(v) Pillaging a town or place, even when taken by assault;
(vi) Committing rape, sexual slavery, enforced prostitution, forced pregnancy, as defined in article 7, paragraph 2 (f), enforced sterilization, and any other form of sexual violence also constituting a serious violation of article 3 common to the four Geneva Conventions;
(vii) Conscripting or enlisting children under the age of fifteen years into armed forces or groups or using them to participate actively in hostilities;

(viii) Ordering the displacement of the civilian population for reasons related to the conflict, unless the security of the civilians involved or imperative military reasons so demand;

(ix) Killing or wounding treacherously a combatant adversary;

(x) Declaring that no quarter will be given;

(xi) Subjecting persons who are in the power of another party to the conflict to physical mutilation or to medical or scientific experiments of any kind which are neither justified by the medical, dental or hospital treatment of the person concerned nor carried out in his or her interest, and which cause death to or seriously endanger the health of such person or persons;

(xii) Destroying or seizing the property of an adversary unless such destruction or seizure be imperatively demanded by the necessities of the conflict;

(f) Paragraph 2 (e) applies to armed conflicts not of an international character and thus does not apply to situations of internal disturbances and tensions, such as riots, isolated and sporadic acts of violence or other acts of a similar nature. It applies to armed conflicts that take place in the territory of a State when there is protracted armed conflict between governmental authorities and organized armed groups or between such groups.

3. Nothing in paragraphs 2 (c) and (d) shall affect the responsibility of a Government to maintain or re-establish law and order in the State or to defend the unity and territorial integrity of the State, by all legitimate means.

Statute of the International Tribunal for the Former Yugoslavia

Article 1
Competence of the International Tribunal

The International Tribunal shall have the power to prosecute persons responsible for serious violations of international humanitarian law committed in the territory of the former Yugoslavia since 1991 in accordance with the provisions of the present Statute.

Article 2
Grave breaches of the Geneva Conventions of 1949

The International Tribunal shall have the power to prosecute persons committing or ordering to be committed grave breaches of the Geneva Conventions of 12 August 1949, namely the following acts against persons or property protected under the provisions of the relevant Geneva Convention:

(a) wilful killing;

(b) torture or inhuman treatment, including biological experiments;

(c) wilfully causing great suffering or serious injury to body or health;

(d) extensive destruction and appropriation of property, not justified by military necessity and carried out unlawfully and wantonly;

(e) compelling a prisoner of war or a civilian to serve in the forces of a hostile power;
(f) wilfully depriving a prisoner of war or a civilian of the rights of fair and regular trial;
(g) unlawful deportation or transfer or unlawful confinement of a civilian;
(h) taking civilians as hostages.

Article 3
Violations of the laws or customs of war

The International Tribunal shall have the power to prosecute persons violating the laws or customs of war. Such violations shall include, but not be limited to:

(a) employment of poisonous weapons or other weapons calculated to cause unnecessary suffering;
(b) wanton destruction of cities, towns or villages, or devastation not justified by military necessity;
(c) attack, or bombardment, by whatever means, of undefended towns, villages, dwellings, or buildings;
(d) seizure of, destruction or wilful damage done to institutions dedicated to religion, charity and education, the arts and sciences, historic monuments and works of art and science;
(e) plunder of public or private property.

Article 4
Genocide

1. The International Tribunal shall have the power to prosecute persons committing genocide as defined in paragraph 2 of this article or of committing any of the other acts enumerated in paragraph 3 of this article.

2. Genocide means any of the following acts committed with intent to destroy, in whole or in part, a national, ethnical, racial or religious group, as such:

(a) killing members of the group;
(b) causing serious bodily or mental harm to members of the group;
(c) deliberately inflicting on the group conditions of life calculated to bring about its physical destruction in whole or in part;
(d) imposing measures intended to prevent births within the group;
(e) forcibly transferring children of the group to another group.

3. The following acts shall be punishable:

(a) genocide;
(b) conspiracy to commit genocide;
(c) direct and public incitement to commit genocide;
(d) attempt to commit genocide;
(e) complicity in genocide.

Article 5
Crimes against humanity

The International Tribunal shall have the power to prosecute persons responsible for the following crimes when committed in armed conflict, whether international or internal in character, and directed against any civilian population:

(a) murder;
(b) extermination;
(c) enslavement;
(d) deportation;
(e) imprisonment;
(f) torture;
(g) rape;
(h) persecutions on political, racial and religious grounds;
(i) other inhumane acts.

Statute of the International Criminal Tribunal for Rwanda

Article 1
Competence of the International Tribunal for Rwanda

The International Tribunal for Rwanda shall have the power to prosecute persons responsible for serious violations of international humanitarian law committed in the territory of Rwanda and Rwandan citizens responsible for such violations committed in the territory of neighbouring States, between 1 January 1994 and 31 December 1994, in accordance with the provisions of the present Statute.

Article 2
Genocide

1. The International Tribunal for Rwanda shall have the power to prosecute persons committing genocide as defined in paragraph 2 of this article or of committing any of the other acts enumerated in paragraph 3 of this article.

2. Genocide means any of the following acts committed with intent to destroy, in whole or in part, a national, ethnical, racial or religious group, as such:

(a) Killing members of the group;
(b) Causing serious bodily or mental harm to members of the group;
(c) Deliberately inflicting on the group conditions of life calculated to bring about its physical destruction in whole or in part;
(d) Imposing measures intended to prevent births within the group;
(e) Forcibly transferring children of the group to another group.

100

3. The following acts shall be punishable:

(a) Genocide;
(b) Conspiracy to commit genocide;
(c) Direct and public incitement to commit genocide;
(d) Attempt to commit genocide;
(e) Complicity in genocide.

Article 3
Crimes against humanity

The International Tribunal for Rwanda shall have the power to prosecute persons responsible for the following crimes when committed as part of a widespread or systematic attack against any civilian population on national, political, ethnic, racial or religious grounds:

(a) Murder;
(b) Extermination;
(c) Enslavement;
(d) Deportation;
(e) Imprisonment;
(f) Torture;
(g) Rape;
(h) Persecutions on political, racial and religious grounds;
(i) Other inhumane acts.

Article 4
Violations of Article 3 common to the
Geneva Conventions and of Additional Protocol II

The International Tribunal for Rwanda shall have the power to prosecute persons committing or ordering to be committed serious violations of Article 3 common to the Geneva Conventions of 12 August 1949 for the Protection of War Victims, and of Additional Protocol II thereto of 8 June 1977. These violations shall include, but shall not be limited to:

(a) Violence to life, health and physical or mental well-being of persons, in particular murder as well as cruel treatment such as torture, mutilation or any form of corporal punishment;
(b) Collective punishments;
(c) Taking of hostages;
(d) Acts of terrorism;
(e) Outrages upon personal dignity, in particular humiliating and degrading treatment, rape, enforced prostitution and any form of indecent assault;
(f) Pillage;

(g) The passing of sentences and the carrying out of executions without previous judgement pronounced by a regularly constituted court, affording all the judicial guarantees which are recognized as indispensable by civilized peoples;
(h) Threats to commit any of the foregoing acts.

Convention on the Prevention and Punishment of the Crime of Genocide

Article II

In the present Convention, genocide means any of the following acts committed with intent to destroy, in whole or in part, a national, ethnical, racial or religious group, as such:

(a) Killing members of the group;
(b) Causing serious bodily or mental harm to members of the group;
(c) Deliberately inflicting on the group conditions of life calculated to bring about its physical destruction in whole or in part;
(d) Imposing measures intended to prevent births within the group;
(e) Forcibly transferring children of the group to another group.

Article III

The following acts shall be punishable:

(a) Genocide;
(b) Conspiracy to commit genocide;
(c) Direct and public incitement to commit genocide;
(d) Attempt to commit genocide;
(e) Complicity in genocide.

Human Rights Treaties

Universal Declaration of Human Rights

Article 4.

No one shall be held in slavery or servitude; slavery and the slave trade shall be prohibited in all their forms.

Article 5.

No one shall be subjected to torture or to cruel, inhuman or degrading treatment or punishment.

International Covenant on Civil and Political Rights

Article 7

No one shall be subjected to torture or to cruel, inhuman or degrading treatment or punishment. In particular, no one shall be subjected without his free consent to medical or scientific experimentation.

Article 8

1. No one shall be held in slavery; slavery and the slave-trade in all their forms shall be prohibited.

2. No one shall be held in servitude.

3.   (a) No one shall be required to perform forced or compulsory labour.

(b) Paragraph 3 (a) shall not be held to preclude, in countries where imprisonment with hard labour may be imposed as a punishment for a crime, the performance of hard labour in pursuance of a sentence to such punishment by a competent court.

(c) For the purpose of this paragraph the term "forced or compulsory labour" shall not include:

(i)   Any work or service, not referred to in sub-paragraph (b), normally required of a person who is under detention in consequence of a lawful order of a court, or of a person during conditional release from such detention;

(ii)   Any service of a military character and, in countries where conscientious objection is recognized, any national service required by law of conscientious objectors;

(iii)   Any service exacted in cases of emergency or calamity threatening the life or well-being of the community;

(iv)   Any work or service which forms part of normal civil obligations.

European Convention on Human Rights

Article 3

No one shall be subjected to torture or to inhuman or degrading treatment or punishment.

Article 4

1. No one shall be held in slavery or servitude.

2. No one shall be required to perform forced or compulsory labour.

. . . .

American Convention on Human Rights

Article 5. RIGHT TO HUMANE TREATMENT.

1. Every person has the right have his physical, mental, and moral integrity respected.

2. No one shall be subjected to torture or to cruel, inhuman, or degrading punishment or treatment. All persons deprived of their liberty shall be treated with respect for the inherent dignity of the human person.

. . . .

Article 6. FREEDOM FROM SLAVERY.

1. No one shall be subject to slavery or to involuntary servitude, which are prohibited in all their forms, as are the slave trade and traffic in women.

2. No one shall be required to perform forced or compulsory labor. This provision shall not be interpreted to mean that, in those countries in which the penalty established for certain crimes is deprivation of liberty at forced labor, the carrying out of such a sentence imposed by a competent court is prohibited. Forced labor shall not adversely affect the dignity or the physical or intellectual capacity of the prisoner.

3. For the purposes of this article, the following do not constitute forced or compulsory labor:

a. Work or service normally required of a person imprisoned in execution of a sentence or formal decision passed by the competent judicial authority; such work or service shall be carried out under the supervision and control of public authorities, and any persons performing such work or service shall not be placed at the disposal of any private party, company, or juridical person;

b. Military service and, in countries in which conscientious objectors are recognized, national service that the law may provide for in lieu of military service;

c. Service exacted in time of danger or calamity that threatens the existence or the well-being of the community; or

d. Work or service that forms part of normal civic obligations.

Treaties & Statutes

Convention Against Torture and Other Cruel, Inhuman or Degrading Treatment or Punishment

Article 1

1. For the purposes of this Convention, torture means any act by which severe pain or suffering, whether physical or mental, is intentionally inflicted on a person for such purposes as obtaining from him or a third person information or a confession, punishing him for an act he or a third person has committed or is suspected of having committed, or intimidating or coercing him or a third person, or for any reason based on discrimination of any kind, when such pain or suffering is inflicted by or at the instigation of or with the consent or acquiescence of a public official or other person acting in an official capacity. It does not include pain or suffering arising only from, inherent in or incidental to lawful sanctions.

2. This article is without prejudice to any international instrument or national legislation which does or may contain provisions of wider application.

Inter-American Convention to Prevent and Punish Torture

Article 2

For the purposes of this Convention, torture shall be understood to be any act intentionally performed whereby physical or mental pain or suffering is inflicted on a person for purposes of criminal investigation, as a means of intimidation, as personal punishment, as a preventive measure, as a penalty, or for any other purpose. Torture shall also be understood to be the use of methods upon a person intended to obliterate the personality of the victim or to diminish his physical or mental capacities, even if they do not cause physical pain or mental anguish.

The concept of torture shall not include physical or mental pain or suffering that is inherent in or solely the consequence of lawful measures, provided that they do not include the performance of the acts or use of the methods referred to in this article.

Article 3

The following shall be held guilty of the crime of torture:

a. A public servant or employee who acting in that capacity orders, instigates or induces the use of torture, or who directly commits it or who, being able to prevent it, fails to do so.

b. A person who at the instigation of a public servant or employee mentioned in subparagraph (a) orders, instigates or induces the use of torture, directly commits it or is an accomplice thereto.

Inter-American Convention on the Forced Disappearance of Persons

Article II

For the purposes of this Convention, forced disappearance is considered to be the act of depriving a person or persons of his or their freedom, in whatever way, perpetrated by agents of the state or by persons or groups of persons acting with the authorization, support, or acquiescence of the state, followed by an absence of information or a refusal to acknowledge that deprivation of freedom or to give information on the whereabouts of that person, thereby impeding his or her recourse to the applicable legal remedies and procedural guarantees.

African [Banjul] Charter on Human and Peoples' Rights

Article 4

Human beings are inviolable. Every human being shall be entitled to respect for his life and the integrity of his person. No one may be arbitrarily deprived of this right.

Article 5

Every individual shall have the right to the respect of the dignity inherent in a human being and to the recognition of his legal status. All forms of exploitation and degradation of man particularly slavery, slave trade, torture, cruel, inhuman or degrading punishment and treatment shall be prohibited.

Convention on Human Rights and Fundamental Freedoms of the Commonwealth of Independent States

Article 3

No one shall be subjected to torture or to cruel, inhuman or degrading treatment or punishment. No one shall be subjected to medical or scientific experiments without his free consent.

Article 4

1. No one shall be held in slavery or servitude.
2. No one shall be constrained to perform forced or compulsory labour.
3. The term "forced or compulsory labour" as used in the present Article shall not include:

a. any work required to be done in the ordinary course of detention imposed in accordance with the provisions of Article 5 of this Convention or during conditional release from such detention;

b.   any service of a military character or, in the case of Contracting Parties recognising the right of conscientious objection on political or religious/ethical grounds, service exacted instead of compulsory military service;

c.   any service exacted in the case of an emergency or calamity threatening the life or well-being of the community;

d.   any work or service which forms part of the normal civic obligations;

e.   the fulfilment by parents to create the necessary conditions for their children, and by children who have reached the age of majority to support parents unable to work and requiring assistance.

Arab Charter on Human Rights

Article 13

A.   The State parties shall protect every person in their territory from physical or psychological torture, or from cruel, inhuman, degrading treatment. [The State parties] shall take effective measures to prevent such acts; performing or participating in them shall be considered a crime punished by law.

B.   No medical or scientific experimentation shall be carried-out on any person without his free consent.

Inter-American Convention on the Prevention, Punishment and Eradication of Violence Against Women ("Convention of Belem Do Para")

Article I

For the purposes of this Convention, violence against women shall be understood as any act or conduct, based on gender, which causes death or physical, sexual or psychological harm or suffering to women, whether in the public or the private sphere.

Article 2

Violence against women shall be understood to include physical, sexual and psychological violence:

a. that occurs within the family or domestic unit or within any other interpersonal relationship, whether or not the perpetrator shares or has shared the same residence with the woman, including, among others, rape, battery and sexual abuse;

b. that occurs in the community and is perpetrated by any person, including, among others, rape, sexual abuse, torture, trafficking in persons, forced prostitution, kidnapping and sexual harassment in the workplace, as well as in educational institutions, health facilities or any other place; and

c. that is perpetrated or condoned by the state or its agents regardless of where it occurs.

CHAPTER II
RIGHTS PROTECTED

Article 3

Every woman has the right to be free from violence in both the public and private spheres.

❖ ❖ ❖

Other international crimes include slavery,[1] sea piracy and aircraft hijacking,[2] taking of hostages,[3] and trafficking in prostitution[4] and narcotics.[5]

---

[1] International Slavery Convention of 1926, adopted 25 September 1926 (entered into force 9 March 1927), amended by Protocol, adopted 7 December 1953 (entered into force as amended 7 July 1955; Supplementary Convention on the Abolition of Slavery, the Slave Trade, and Institutions and Practices Similar to Slavery, 226 U.N.T.S. 3 (entered into force 30 April 1957).

[2] 1970 Hague Convention for the Suppression of Unlawful Seizure of Aircraft, T.I.A.S. No. 7192 (entered into force 14 October 1971).

[3] International Convention Against Taking of Hostages, adopted 17 December 1979, G.A. Res. 146 (XXXIV) (1979), 18 I.L.M. 1456 (1979) (entered into force 3 June 1983).

[4] 1950 Convention for the Suppression of the Traffic in Persons and of the Exploitation of the Prostitution of Others, adopted 21 March 1950 (entered into force, 25 July 1951).

[5] 1961 Single Convention on Narcotic Drugs, 520 U.N.T.S. 151 (1961).

Chapter 7. War Crimes, Crimes Against Peace and Humanity, and Grave Breaches of the Geneva Conventions

The Prosecutor v. Dusko Tadic (Final Judgment)
Case No. IT-94-1-T
Trial Chamber
International Criminal Tribunal for the Former Yugoslavia
7 May 1997

[Tadic was indicted for committing grave breaches of the Geneva Conventions (*viz.*, wilful killing, torture or inhuman treatment, and wilfully causing great suffering or serious injury to body and health), violations of the laws and customs of war (*viz.*, murder and cruel treatment), and crimes against humanity (*viz.*, murder, persecution, and inhumane acts) at Kozarac and the Omarska concentration camp in the former Yugoslavia in June 1992. He was arrested in Germany in February 1994 and turned over to the ICT-Y. He pleaded not guilty.

The Chamber of the ICT-Y examined the testimony of dozens of witnesses and documentary evidence. The following excerpts from the Chamber's judgment address the international law governing the substantive offenses.]

557. Having considered the evidence offered at trial, it is now appropriate to discuss the law relating to the offences charged.

558. The competence of this International Tribunal and hence of this Trial Chamber is determined by the terms of the Statute. Article 1 of the Statute confers power to prosecute persons responsible for serious violations of international humanitarian law committed in the territory of the former Yugoslavia since 1991. The Statute then, in Articles 2, 3, 4 and 5, specifies the crimes under international law over which the International Tribunal has jurisdiction. In the present case, only Articles 2, 3 and 5 are relevant. . . .

559. Each of the relevant Articles of the Statute, either by its terms or by virtue of the customary rules which it imports, proscribes certain acts when committed "within the context of" an "armed conflict". Article 2 of the Statute directs the Trial Chamber to the grave breaches regime of the Geneva Conventions which applies only to armed conflicts of an international character and to offences committed against persons or property regarded as "protected", in particular civilians in the hands of a party to a conflict of which they are not nationals[ ]. Article 3 of the Statute directs the Trial Chamber to those sources of customary international humanitarian law that comprise the "laws or customs of war". Article 3 is a general provision covering, subject to certain conditions, all violations of international humanitarian law which do not fall under Article 2 or are not covered by Articles 4 or 5. This includes violations of the rules contained in Article 3 common to the Geneva Conventions ("Common Article 3"), applicable to armed conflicts in general, with which the accused has been charged under Article 3 of the Statute[ ]. Article 5 of the Statute directs the Trial Chamber to crimes against humanity proscribed by customary international humanitarian law. By virtue of the Statute, those crimes must also occur in the context of an armed conflict, whether international or non-international in character. An armed conflict exists for the purposes of the application of Article 5 if it is found to exist for the purposes of either Article 2 or Article 3.[ ]

560. Consequently, it is necessary to show, first, that an armed conflict existed at all relevant times in the territory of the Republic of Bosnia and Herzegovina and, secondly, that the acts of the accused were committed within the context of that armed conflict and for the application of Article 2, that the conflict was international in character and that the offences charged were committed against protected persons.

561. According to [*Prosecutor v. Duško Tadic*, Appeals Chamber Decision on the Defence Motion for Interlocutory Appeal on Jurisdiction, Int'l Crim. Trib.-Yugo. (2 Oct. 1995) (hereinafter "the *Appeals Chamber Decision*)], the test for determining the existence of such a conflict is that

> an armed conflict exists whenever there is a resort to armed force between States or protracted armed violence between governmental authorities and organized armed groups or between such groups within a State[ ].

562. The test applied by the Appeals Chamber to the existence of an armed conflict for the purposes of the rules contained in Common Article 3 focuses on two aspects of a conflict; the intensity of the conflict and the organization of the parties to the conflict. In an armed conflict of an internal or mixed character, these closely related criteria are used solely for the purpose, as a minimum, of distinguishing an armed conflict from banditry, unorganized and short-lived insurrections, or terrorist activities, which are not subject to international humanitarian law[ ]. Factors relevant to this determination are addressed in the Commentary to Geneva Convention for the Amelioration of the Condition of the Wounded and Sick in Armed Forces in the Field, Convention I, ("*Commentary*, Geneva Convention I") [ ].

. . . .

568. Having regard then to the nature and scope of the conflict in the Republic of Bosnia and Herzegovina and the parties involved in that conflict, and irrespective of the relationship between the Federal Republic of Yugoslavia (Serbia and Montenegro) and the Bosnian Serb forces, the Trial Chamber finds that, at all relevant times, an armed conflict was taking place between the parties to the conflict in the Republic of Bosnia and Herzegovina of sufficient scope and intensity for the purposes of the application of the laws or customs of war embodied in Article 3 common to the four Geneva Conventions of 12 August 1949, applicable as it is to armed conflicts in general, including armed conflicts not of an international character.

. . . .

578. According to the Appeals Chamber, the Statute specifically restricts the prosecution of grave breaches to those committed against "persons or property protected under the provisions of the relevant Geneva Conventions". In this case, each of the victims of the crimes alleged to have been committed by the accused were civilians caught up in the ongoing armed conflict in the Republic of Bosnia and Herzegovina. Some of the victims were in towns and villages captured by the [Bosnian Serb forces], while others fell victim to the acts of the accused while detained at one of the camps established in opstina Prijedor to facilitate the ethnic cleansing of that area. As such, their status under the Geneva Conventions is governed by the terms of Article 4 of Geneva Convention Relative to the Protection of Civilian Persons in Time of War ("Geneva Convention IV"), which

defines those civilians who fall under the protection of that Convention ("protected persons") as follows:

> Persons protected by the Convention are those who, at a given moment and in any manner whatsoever, find themselves, in case of a conflict or occupation, in the hands of a Party to the conflict or Occupying Power of which they are not nationals[ ].

The central question is thus whether at all relevant times the victims of the accused were in the hands of "a Party to the conflict or Occupying Power of which they are not nationals". Implicit in this expression is a threefold requirement. The first and second requirements are that the victims be "in the hands of" a "Party to the conflict or Occupying Power". The third is that the civilian victims not be nationals of that Party or Occupying Power.

[The Chamber found that Tadic's victims were not "protected persons" because they were nationals (Bosnian Muslims and Croats) of the Occupying Power (Bosnian Serbs) even though the army of the Federal Republic of Yugoslavia (Serbia and Montenegro) earlier had occupied the Republic of Bosnia and Herzegovina and earlier had supported the Bosnian Serb forces.]

608. The consequence of this finding, as far as this trial is concerned, is that, since Article 2 of the Statute is applicable only to acts committed against "protected persons" within the meaning of the Geneva Conventions, and since it cannot be said that any of the victims, all of whom were civilians, were at any relevant time in the hands of a party to the conflict of which they were not nationals, the accused must be found not guilty of the counts which rely upon [Article 2's "grave breaches" provision].

609. Article 3 of the Statute directs the Trial Chamber to the laws or customs of war, being that body of customary international humanitarian law not covered by Articles 2, 4 or 5 of the Statute. As previously noted, that body of law includes the regime of protection established under Common Article 3 applicable to armed conflicts not of an international character, as a reflection of elementary considerations of humanity, and which is applicable to armed conflicts in general[ ]. Two aspects must be considered. First, there are the requirements imposed by Article 3 of the Statute for the inclusion of a law or custom of war within the jurisdiction of this International Tribunal. Secondly, there are the additional requirements for the applicability of the proscriptive rules contained in paragraph 1 of Common Article 3 in addition to the elements of the proscribed acts contained therein.[ ]

610. According to the Appeals Chamber, the conditions that must be satisfied to fulfil the requirements of Article 3 of the Statute are:

> (i) the violation must constitute an infringement of a rule of international humanitarian law;
> (ii) the rule must be customary in nature or, if it belongs to treaty law, the required conditions must be met;

(iii) the violation must be "serious", that is to say, it must constitute a breach of a rule protecting important values, and the breach must involve grave consequences for the victim . . . ; and

(iv) the violation of the rule must entail, under customary or conventional law, the individual criminal responsibility of the person breaching the rule[ ].

Those requirements apply to any and all laws or customs of war which Article 3 covers.

611. In relation to requirements (i) and (ii), it is sufficient to note that the Appeals Chamber has held, on the basis of [*Military and Paramilitary Activities in and against Nicaragua (Nicaragua v. United States)*, Int'l Ct. J. (1986)], that Common Article 3 satisfies these requirements as part of customary international humanitarian law[ ].

612. While, for some laws or customs of war, requirement (iii) may be of particular relevance, each of the prohibitions in Common Article 3: against murder; the taking of hostages; outrages upon personal dignity, in particular humiliating and degrading treatment; and the passing of sentences and the carrying-out of executions without previous judgment pronounced by a regularly constituted court, affording all the judicial guarantees which are recognized as indispensable by civilised peoples, constitute, as the Court put it, "elementary considerations of humanity", the breach of which may be considered to be a "breach of a rule protecting important values" and which "must involve grave consequences for the victim". Although it may be possible that a violation of some of the prohibitions of Common Article 3 may be so minor as to not involve "grave consequences for the victim", each of the violations with which the accused has been charged clearly does involve such consequences.

613. Finally, in relation to the fourth requirement, namely that the rule of customary international humanitarian law imposes individual criminal responsibility, the Appeals Chamber held in the *Appeals Chamber Decision* that

customary international law imposes criminal liability for serious violations of common Article 3, as supplemented by other general principles and rules on the protection of victims of internal armed conflict, and for breaching certain fundamental principles and rules regarding means and methods of combat in civil strife.

Consequently, this Trial Chamber has the competence to hear and determine the charges against the accused under Article 3 of the Statute relating to violations of the customary international humanitarian law applicable to armed conflicts, as found in Common Article 3.[ ] The rules contained in paragraph 1 of Common Article 3 proscribe a number of acts which: (i) are committed within the context of an armed conflict; (ii) have a close connection to the armed conflict; and (iii) are committed against persons taking no active part in hostilities. The first and second of these requirements have already been dealt with above. Consequently, the Trial Chamber turns to the third requirement.

615. The customary international humanitarian law regime governing conflicts not of an international character extends protection, from acts of murder, torture and other acts proscribed by Common Article 3, to:

> Persons taking no active part in the hostilities, including members of armed forces who have laid down their arms and those placed *hors de combat* by sickness, wounds, detention, or any other cause . . . without any adverse distinction founded on race, colour, religion or faith, sex, birth or wealth, or any other similar criteria . . . .

This protection embraces, at the least, all of those protected persons covered by the grave breaches regime applicable to conflicts of an international character: civilians, prisoners of war, wounded and sick members of the armed forces in the field and wounded sick and shipwrecked members of the armed forces at sea. Whereas the concept of "protected person" under the Geneva Conventions is defined positively, the class of persons protected by the operation of Common Article 3 is defined negatively. For that reason, the test the Trial Chamber has applied is to ask whether, at the time of the alleged offence, the alleged victim of the proscribed acts was directly taking part in hostilities, being those hostilities in the context of which the alleged offences are said to have been committed. If the answer to that question is negative, the victim will enjoy the protection of the proscriptions contained in Common Article 3.

616. It is unnecessary to define exactly the line dividing those taking an active part in hostilities and those who are not so involved. It is sufficient to examine the relevant facts of each victim and to ascertain whether, in each individual's circumstances, that person was actively involved in hostilities at the relevant time. Violations of the rules contained in Common Article 3 are alleged to have been committed against persons who, on the evidence presented to this Trial Chamber, were captured or detained by Bosnian Serb forces, whether committed during the course of the armed take-over of the Kozarac area or while those persons were being rounded-up for transport to each of the camps in opstina Prijedor. Whatever their involvement in hostilities prior to that time, each of these classes of persons cannot be said to have been taking an active part in the hostilities. Even if they were members of the armed forces of the Government of the Republic of Bosnia and Herzegovina or otherwise engaging in hostile acts prior to capture, such persons would be considered "members of armed forces" who are "placed *hors de combat* by detention". Consequently, these persons enjoy the protection of those rules of customary international humanitarian law applicable to armed conflicts, as contained in Article 3 of the Statute.

617. For the purposes of the application of the rules of customary international humanitarian law contained in Common Article 3, this Trial Chamber finds, in the present case, that: (i) an armed conflict existed at all relevant times in relation to the alleged offences; (ii) each of the victims of the acts charged was a person protected by those provisions being a person taking no active part in the hostilities; and (iii) the offences charged were committed within the context of that armed conflict. Accordingly, the requirements of Article 3 of the Statute are met.

[Article 5 Crimes Against Humanity]
. . . .
623. . . . [S]ince the Nürnberg Charter, the customary status of the prohibition against crimes against humanity and the attribution of individual criminal responsibility for their

commission have not been seriously questioned. It would seem that this finding is implicit in *the Appeals Chamber Decision* which found that "[i]t is by now a settled rule of customary international law that crimes against humanity do not require a connection to international armed conflict"[ ].

. . . .

626. Article 5 of the Statute grants the International Tribunal jurisdiction to prosecute crimes against humanity only "when committed in armed conflict" (whether international or internal) and they must be "directed against any civilian population". These conditions contain within them several elements. The Prosecution argues that the elements of crimes against humanity are: (1) that the accused committed one of the acts enumerated in Article 5; (2) the acts were committed during an armed conflict; (3) at the time of the commission of the acts or omissions there was an ongoing widespread or systematic attack directed against a civilian population; and (4) the accused knew or had reason to know that by his acts or omission, he was participating in the attack on the population. The Defence for the most part agrees with these elements, although it argues that: (1) the crimes must be committed *in* an armed conflict; and (2) the attack must be widespread *and* systematic. The Trial Chamber's determination of the conditions of applicability, as elaborated below, is that, first, "when committed in armed conflict" necessitates the existence of an armed conflict and a nexus between the act and that conflict. Secondly, "directed against any civilian population" is interpreted to include a broad definition of the term "civilian". It furthermore requires that the acts be undertaken on a widespread or systematic basis and in furtherance of a policy. The *Report of the Secretary-General* and the interpretation of several Security Council members reveal the additional requirement that all relevant acts must be undertaken on discriminatory grounds. Finally, the perpetrator must have knowledge of the wider context in which his act occurs.

627. Article 5 of the Statute, addressing crimes against humanity, grants the International Tribunal jurisdiction over the enumerated acts "when committed in armed conflict". The requirement of an armed conflict is similar to that of Article 6(c) of the Nürnberg Charter which limited the Nürnberg Tribunal's jurisdiction to crimes against humanity committed "before or during the war", although in the case of the Nürnberg Tribunal jurisdiction was further limited by requiring that crimes against humanity be committed "in execution of or in connection with" war crimes or crimes against peace[ ]. Despite this precedent, the inclusion of the requirement of an armed conflict deviates from the development of the doctrine after the Nürnberg Charter, beginning with Control Council Law No. 10, which no longer links the concept of crimes against humanity with an armed conflict. As the Secretary-General stated: "Crimes against humanity are aimed at any civilian population and are prohibited regardless of whether they are committed in an armed conflict, international or internal in character."[ ] In the Statute of the International Tribunal for Rwanda the requirement of an armed conflict is omitted, requiring only that the acts be committed as part of an attack against a civilian population[ ]. The Appeals Chamber has stated that, by incorporating the requirement of an armed conflict, "the Security Council may have defined the crime in Article 5 more narrowly than necessary under customary international law"[ ], having stated earlier that "[s]ince customary international law no longer requires any nexus between crimes against humanity and armed conflict . . . Article 5 was intended to reintroduce this nexus for the purposes

of this Tribunal."[ ] Accordingly, its existence must be proved, as well as the link between the act or omission charged and the armed conflict.

628. The Appeals Chamber, as discussed in greater detail in Section VI. A of this Opinion and Judgment, stated that "an armed conflict exists whenever there is a resort to armed force between States or protracted armed violence between governmental authorities and organized armed groups or between such groups within a State."[ ] Consequently, this is the test which the Trial Chamber has applied and it has concluded that the evidence establishes the existence of an armed conflict.

629. The next issue which must be addressed is the required nexus between the act or omission and the armed conflict. The Prosecution argues that to establish the nexus necessary for a violation of Article 5 it is sufficient to demonstrate that the crimes were committed at some point in the course or duration of an armed conflict, even if such crimes were not committed in direct relation to or as part of the conduct of hostilities, occupation, or other integral aspects of the armed conflict. In contrast the Defence argues that the act must be committed "in" armed conflict.

630. The Statute does not elaborate on the required link between the act and the armed conflict. Nor, for that matter, does the *Appeals Chamber Decision,* although it contains several statements that are relevant in this regard. First is the finding, noted above, that the Statute is more restrictive than custom in that "customary international law no longer requires any nexus between crimes against humanity and armed conflict"[ ]. Accordingly, it is necessary to determine the degree of nexus which is imported by the Statute by its inclusion of the requirement of an armed conflict. This, then, is a question of statutory interpretation.

631. The *Appeals Chamber Decision* is relevant to this question of statutory interpretation. In addressing Article 3 the Appeals Chamber noted that where interpretative declarations are made by Security Council members and are not contested by other delegations "they can be regarded as providing an authoritative interpretation" of the relevant provisions of the Statute[ ]. Importantly, several permanent members of the Security Council commented that they interpret "when committed in armed conflict" in Article 5 of the Statute to mean "during a period of armed conflict"[ ]. These statements were not challenged and can thus, in line with the *Appeals Chamber Decision,* be considered authoritative interpretations of this portion of Article 5.[ ]

632. The Appeals Chamber, in dismissing the Defence argument that the concept of armed conflict covers only the precise time and place of actual hostilities, said: "It is sufficient that the alleged crimes were closely related to the hostilities occurring in other parts of the territories controlled by the parties to the conflict"[ ]. Thus it is not necessary that the acts occur in the heat of battle. . . .

633. On the basis of the foregoing the Trial Chamber accepts, with some caveats, the Prosecution proposition that it is sufficient for purposes of crimes against humanity that the act occurred in the course or duration of an armed conflict. The first such caveat, a seemingly obvious one, is that the act be linked geographically as well as temporally with the armed conflict. In this regard it is important to note that the Appeals Chamber found that:

the temporal and geographic scope of both internal and international armed conflicts extends beyond the exact time and place of hostilities.

. . . .

International humanitarian law applies from the initiation of such armed conflicts and extends beyond the cessation of hostilities until a general conclusion of peace is reached; or, in the case of internal conflicts, a peaceful settlement is achieved. Until that moment, international humanitarian law continues to apply in the whole territory of the warring States or, in the case of internal conflicts, the whole territory under the control of a party, whether or not actual combat takes place there.

634. Secondly, the act and the conflict must be related or, to reverse this proposition, the act must not be *unrelated* to the armed conflict, must not be done for purely personal motives of the perpetrator. This is further discussed below in regard to the level of intent required.

635. The requirement in Article 5 that the enumerated acts be "directed against any civilian population" contains several elements. The inclusion of the word "any" makes it clear that crimes against humanity can be committed against civilians of the same nationality as the perpetrator or those who are stateless, as well as those of a different nationality. However, the remaining aspects, namely the definition of a "civilian" population and the implications of the term "population", require further examination.

636. That the prohibited act must be committed against a "civilian" population itself raises two aspects: what must the character of the targeted population be and how is it to be determined whether an individual victim qualifies as a civilian such that acts taken against the person constitute crimes against humanity?

637. The Statute does not provide any guidance regarding the definition of "civilian" nor, for that matter, does the *Report of the Secretary-General*. The Prosecution in its pre-trial brief argues that the term "civilian" covers "all non-combatants within the meaning of common Article 3 to the [Geneva] Conventions" because of the finding that the language of Common Article 3 reflects "elementary considerations of humanity" which are "applicable under customary international law to any armed conflict"[ ]. The Defence agrees that "civilians" under Article 5 covers all non-combatants, arguing however that the concept of "non-combatants" is not always clear in application. The Defence notes that particularly in situations such as that in Bosnia and Herzegovina, "where groups are mobilising without necessarily being under the direct control of the central government," there is a "grey area" between combatants and non-combatants. Thus the Defence concludes that the notion of non-combatants may not be sufficiently defined to determine in all cases whether the victims were civilians.

638. Regarding the first aspect, it is clear that the targeted population must be of a predominantly civilian nature. The presence of certain non-civilians in their midst does not change the character of the population.[1]

---

[1] *See* Article 50(3) of the Protocol Additional to the Geneva Conventions of 12 August 1949, and relating to the Protection of Victims of International Armed Conflicts ("Protocol I") (ICRC, Geneva, 1977); *see also Fédération Nationale des Déportés et*
(continued...)

639. The second aspect, determining which individual[s] of the targeted population qualify as civilians for purposes of crimes against humanity, is not, however, quite as clear. Common Article 3, the language of which reflects "elementary considerations of humanity" which are "applicable under customary international law to any armed conflict"[ ], provides that in an armed conflict "not of an international character" Contracting States are obliged "as a minimum" to comply with the following: "Persons taking no active part in the hostilities, including members of armed forces who have laid down their arms and those placed *hors de combat* by sickness, wounds, detention, or any other cause, shall in all circumstances be treated humanely . . . ." Protocol Additional to the Geneva Conventions of 12 August 1949, and Relating to the Protection of Victims in International Armed Conflicts (Protocol I)[ ] defines civilians by the exclusion of prisoners of war and armed forces, considering a person a civilian in case of doubt. However, this definition of civilians contained in Common Article 3 is not immediately applicable to crimes against humanity because it is a part of the laws or customs of war and can only be applied by analogy. The same applies to the definition contained in Protocol I and the *Commentary,* Geneva Convention IV, on the treatment of civilians, both of which advocate a broad interpretation of the term "civilian". They, and particularly Common Article 3, do, however, provide guidance in answering the most difficult question: specifically, whether acts taken against an individual who cannot be considered a traditional "non-combatant" because he is actively involved in the conduct of hostilities by membership in some form of resistance group can nevertheless constitute crimes against humanity if they are committed in furtherance or as part of an attack directed against a civilian population.

640. In this regard the United Nations War Crimes Commission stated in reference to Article 6(c) of the Nürnberg Charter that "[t]he words '*civilian* population' appear to indicate that 'crimes against humanity' are restricted to inhumane acts committed against civilians as opposed to members of the armed forces . . ."[ ]. In contrast, the Supreme Court of the British zone determined that crimes against humanity were applicable in all cases where the perpetrator and the victim were of the same nationality, regardless of whether the victim was civilian or military[ ]. Similarly, the possibility of considering members of the armed forces as potential victims of crimes against humanity was recognized as early as 1946[ ]. The Commission of Experts Established Pursuant to Security Council Resolution 780 ("Commission of Experts") observed: "It seems obvious that article 5 applies first and foremost to civilians, meaning people who are not combatants. This, however, should not lead to any quick conclusions concerning people who at one particular point in time did bear arms."[ ] The Commission of Experts then provided an example based on the situation in the former Yugoslavia and concluded: "A Head of a family who under such circumstances tries to protect his family gun-in-hand does not thereby lose his status as a civilian. Maybe the same is the case for the sole

---

[1](...continued)
Internés Résistants et Patriotes and Others v. Barbie (*Barbie* case); Final Report of the Commission of Experts Established Pursuant to Security Council Resolution 780 (1992), ("*Final Report of the Commission of Experts*"), paras. 77-78, U.N. Doc. S/1994/674.

policeman or local defence guard doing the same, even if they joined hands to try to prevent the cataclysm."[ ]

641. Precisely this issue was considered in the case of *Fédération Nationale des Déportés et Internés Résistants et Patriotes and Others v. Barbie* (*Barbie* case). In this case the *Chambre d'accusation* of the Court of Appeal of Lyons ordered that an indictment for crimes against humanity be issued against Klaus Barbie, head of the Gestapo of Lyons during the Second World War, but only for "persecutions against innocent Jews", and held that prosecution was barred by the statute of limitations for crimes committed by Barbie against combatants who were members of the Resistance or whom Barbie thought were members of the Resistance, even if they were Jewish, because these acts could only constitute war crimes and not crimes against humanity[ ]. The order of the examining magistrate along the same lines was confirmed by the *Cour d'Assises* and an appeal was lodged. On appeal the *Cour de Cassation* quashed and annulled the judgment in part, holding that members of the Resistance could be victims of crimes against humanity as long as the necessary intent for crimes against humanity was present[ ]. As the court stated, "[n]either the driving force which motivated the victims, nor their possible membership of the Resistance, excludes the possibility that the accused acted with the element of intent necessary for the commission of crimes against humanity."[ ] Thus, according to the *Cour de Cassation,* not only was the general population considered to be one of a civilian character despite the presence of Resistance members in its midst but members of the Resistance themselves could be considered victims of crimes against humanity if the other requisite elements are met.[ ]

642. While instructive, it should be noted that the court in the *Barbie* case was applying national legislation that declared crimes against humanity not subject to statutory limitation, although the national legislation defined crimes against humanity by reference to the United Nations resolution of 13 February 1946, which referred back to the Nürnberg Charter . . . ; and the fact that a crime against humanity is an international crime was relied upon to deny the accused's appeal on the bases of disguised extradition[ ] and an elapsed statute of limitations[ ].

643. Despite the limitations inherent in the use of these various sources, from Common Article 3 to the *Barbie* case, a wide definition of civilian population, as supported by these sources, is justified. Thus the presence of those actively involved in the conflict should not prevent the characterization of a population as civilian and those actively involved in a resistance movement can qualify as victims of crimes against humanity. As noted by Trial Chamber I of the International Tribunal in its Review of the Indictment Pursuant to Rule 61 of the Rules of Procedure and Evidence in *The Prosecutor v. Mile Msksic, Miroslav Radic, and Veselin Sljivancanin* ("*Vukovar Hospital Decision*")[2], although crimes against humanity must target a civilian population, individuals who at one time performed acts of resistance may in certain circumstances be victims of crimes against humanity[ ]. In the context of that case patients in a hospital, either civilians or

---

[2] *The Prosecutor v. Mile Msksic, Miroslav Radic, and Veselin Sljivancanin,* Review of the Indictment Pursuant to Rule 61 of the Rules of Procedure and Evidence, Case No. IT-95-13-R61, T.Ch.I, 3 Apr. 1996.

resistance fighters who had laid down their arms, were considered victims of crimes against humanity[ ].

644. The requirement in Article 5 of the Statute that the prohibited acts must be directed against a civilian "population" does not mean that the entire population of a given State or territory must be victimised by these acts in order for the acts to constitute a crime against humanity. Instead the "population" element is intended to imply crimes of a collective nature and thus exclude single or isolated acts which, although possibly constituting war crimes or crimes against national penal legislation, do not rise to the level of crimes against humanity[ ]. As explained by this Trial Chamber in its *Decision on the Form of the Indictment*, the inclusion in Article 5 of the requirement that the acts "be 'directed against any civilian population' ensures that what is to be alleged will not be one particular act but, instead, a course of conduct."[ ] The purpose of this requirement was clearly articulated by the United Nations War Crimes Commission when it wrote that:

> Isolated offences did not fall within the notion of crimes against humanity. As a rule systematic mass action, particularly if it was authoritative, was necessary to transform a common crime, punishable only under municipal law, into a crime against humanity, which thus became also the concern of international law. Only crimes which either by their magnitude and savagery or by their large number or by the fact that a similar pattern was applied at different times and places, endangered the international community or shocked the conscience of mankind, warranted intervention by States other than that on whose territory the crimes had been committed, or whose subjects had become their victims.[ ]

Thus the emphasis is not on the individual victim but rather on the collective, the individual being victimised not because of his individual attributes but rather because of his membership of a targeted civilian population. This has been interpreted to mean, as elaborated below, that the acts must occur on a widespread or systematic basis, that there must be some form of a governmental, organizational or group policy to commit these acts and that the perpetrator must know of the context within which his actions are taken, as well as the requirement imported by the Secretary-General and members of the Security Council that the actions be taken on discriminatory grounds[ ].

645. The Prosecution argues that the term "population" in Article 5 contemplates that by his actions the accused participated in a widespread or systematic attack against a relatively large victim group, as distinct from isolated or random acts against individuals. The Defence, while generally in agreement, argues that in order to constitute a crime against humanity the violations must be both widespread and systematic.

646. While this issue has been the subject of considerable debate, it is now well established that the requirement that the acts be directed against a civilian "population" can be fulfilled if the acts occur on either a widespread basis or in a systematic manner. Either one of these is sufficient to exclude isolated or random acts. The *Report of the Secretary-General* stipulates that crimes against humanity "refer to inhumane acts of a very serious nature . . . committed as part of a widespread or systematic attack against any civilian population"[ ]. The Defence points to the fact that later in that same paragraph the Secretary-General states that in the conflict in the former Yugoslavia rape occurred on a

"widespread and systematic" basis as support for its proposition that both widespreadness and systematicity are required. However, in the Trial Chamber's view, this passage is no more than a reflection of the situation as the Secretary-General saw it, as was the well-known finding by the Nürnberg Tribunal that "[t]he persecution of the Jews at the hands of the Nazi Government has been proved in the greatest detail before the Tribunal. It is a record of *consistent and systematic* inhumanity on the greatest scale."[ ]

647. In addition to the *Report of the Secretary-General* numerous other sources support the conclusion that widespreadness and systematicity are alternatives. For example, Trial Chamber I came to this conclusion in the Vukovar Hospital Decision.[ ] The Report of the Ad Hoc Committee on the Establishment of a Permanent International Criminal Court provides that crimes against humanity "usually involved a widespread or systematic attack against the civilian population rather than isolated offences"[3]. Article 18 of the International Law Commission Draft Code of Crimes Against the Peace and Security of Mankind[ ] ("I.L.C. Draft Code") requires that the act be committed "in a systematic manner or on a large scale" and explicitly states that these are two alternative requirements. Similarly in its 1994 Report the International Law Commission stated that "the definition of crimes against humanity encompasses inhumane acts of a very serious character involving widespread *or* systematic violations aimed at the civilian population", although it also stated that "[t]he hallmarks of such crimes lie in their large-scale *and* systematic nature", and that the "particular forms of unlawful acts (murder, enslavement, deportation, torture, rape, imprisonment etc.) are less crucial to the definition [sic] the factors of scale and deliberate policy."[ ] Despite this seeming inconsistency the prevailing opinion was for alternative requirements, as is evident from the article addressing crimes against humanity in the 1991 Report of the International Law Commission which was entitled "Systematic or mass violations of human rights"[ ].

648. It is therefore the desire to exclude isolated or random acts from the notion of crimes against humanity that led to the inclusion of the requirement that the acts must be directed against a civilian "population", and either a finding of widespreadness, which refers to the number of victims, or systematicity, indicating that a pattern or methodical plan is evident, fulfils this requirement. As explained by the commentary to the I.L.C. Draft Code:

> (3) The opening clause of this definition establishes the two general conditions which must be met for one of the prohibited acts to qualify as a crime against humanity covered by the present Code. The first condition requires that the act was "committed in a systematic manner or on a large scale". This first condition consists of two alternative requirements... Consequently, an act could constitute a crime against humanity if either of these conditions is met.

The commentary to the I.L.C. Draft Code further explains these requirements and their origins. It states:

---

[3] *Report of the Committee on the Establishment of a Permanent International Criminal Court* ("Report of the Ad Hoc Committee"), U.N. Doc. G.A.O.R. A/50/22 (1995) at 17.

The first alternative requires that the inhumane acts *be committed in a systematic manner* meaning pursuant to a preconceived plan or policy. The implementation of this plan or policy could result in the repeated or continuous commission of inhumane acts. The thrust of this requirement is to exclude a random act that was not committed as part of a broader plan or policy. The Nürnberg Charter did not include such a requirement. None the less the Nürnberg Tribunal emphasized that the inhumane acts were committed as part of the *policy of terror* and were "in many cases . . . organized and systematic" in considering whether such acts constituted crimes against humanity.

(4) The second alternative requires that the inhumane acts be *committed on a large scale* meaning that the acts are directed against a multiplicity of victims. This requirement excludes an isolated inhumane act committed by a perpetrator acting on his own initiative and directed against a single victim. The Nürnberg Charter did not include this second requirement either. None the less the Nürnberg Tribunal further emphasized that the policy of terror was "certainly carried out on a vast scale" in its consideration of inhumane acts as possible crimes against humanity. . . . The term "large scale" in the present text . . . is sufficiently broad to cover various situations involving multiplicity of victims, for example, as a result of the cumulative effect of a series of inhumane acts or the singular effect of an inhumane act of extraordinary magnitude[ ].

649. A related issue is whether a single act by a perpetrator can constitute a crime against humanity. A tangential issue, not at issue before this Trial Chamber, is whether a single act in and of itself can constitute a crime against humanity. This issue has been the subject of intense debate, with the jurisprudence immediately following the Second World War being mixed. The American tribunals generally supported the proposition that a massive nature was required[4], while the tribunals in the British Zone came to the opposite conclusion, finding that the mass element was not essential to the definition, in respect of either the number of acts or the number of victims and that "what counted was not the mass aspect, but the link between the act and the cruel and barbarous political system, specifically, the Nazi regime"[5]. Clearly, a single act by a perpetrator taken within the context of a widespread or systematic attack against a civilian population entails individual criminal responsibility and an individual perpetrator need not commit numerous

---

[4] *See* the *Trial of Josef Altstötter and Others ("Justice case")*, Vol. VI, Law Reports of Trials of War Criminals (U.N. War Crimes Commission London, 1949) *("Law Reports")* 79-80 *and see* the *Trial of Fredrich Flick and Five Others ("Flick* case"), Vol. IX, *Law Reports,* 51, in which isolated cases of atrocities and persecution were held to be excluded from the definition of crimes against humanity.

[5] Report of I.L.C. Special Rapporteur D. Thiam, Ybk I.L.C. 1986, Vol. II, I.L.C. A/CN.4/466 (*"Report of the Special Rapporteur"*), para. 93, referring to the conclusion of Henri Meyrowitz.

offences to be held liable. Although it is correct that isolated, random acts should not be included in the definition of crimes against humanity, that is the purpose of requiring that the acts be directed against a civilian *population* and thus "[e]ven an isolated act can constitute a crime against humanity if it is the product of a political system based on terror or persecution"[ ]. The decision of Trial Chamber I of the International Tribunal in the *Vukovar Hospital Decision* is a recent recognition of the fact that a single act by a perpetrator can constitute a crime against humanity. In that decision the Trial Chamber stated:

> 30. Crimes against humanity are to be distinguished from war crimes against individuals. In particular, they must be widespread or demonstrate a systematic character. However, as long as there is a link with the widespread or systematic attack against a civilian population, a single act could qualify as a crime against humanity. As such, an individual committing a crime against a single victim or a limited number of victims might be recognized as guilty of a crime against humanity if his acts were part of the specific context identified above[ ].

Additional support is found in national cases adjudicating crimes arising from the Second World War where individual acts by perpetrators were held to constitute crimes against humanity.[6]

650. Another related issue is whether the widespread or systematic acts must be taken on, for example, racial, religious, ethnic or political grounds, thus requiring a discriminatory intent for all crimes against humanity and not only persecution. The law in this area is quite mixed. Many commentators and national courts have found that some form of discriminatory intent is inherent in the notion of crimes against humanity, and thus required for the "inhumane acts" group, as well as persecution, because the acts are taken against the individual as a result of his membership in a group that is for some reason targeted by the perpetrator[7].

651. This requirement of discrimination was not contained in the Nürnberg Charter, which clearly recognized two categories of crimes against humanity: those related to inhumane acts such as murder, extermination, enslavement and deportation; and persecution on political, racial or religious grounds. Nor can support for this position be found in Control Council Law No. 10, as well as cases taken on the basis of this law, such as those concerning medical experiments where criminal medical experiments on non-German nationals, both prisoners of war and civilians, including Jews and "asocial"

---

[6] *See, e.g.,* cases 2, 4, 13, 14, 15, 18, 23, 25, 31 and 34 of Entscheidungen Des Obersten Gerichtshofes Für Die Britische Zone in Strafsachen, Vol. I.

[7] *See, e.g., Barbie case supra, the Final Report of the Commission of Experts,* para. 84, *supra,* J. Graven, *Les crimes contre l'humanité,* Receuil de Cours (1950) and Catherine Grynfogel, *Le concept de crime contre l'humanité: Hier, aujourd'hui et demain,* Revue de Droit Pénal et de Criminologie 13 (1994); *but see* Leila Sadat Wexler, *The Interpretation of the Nuremberg Principles by the French Court of Cassation: From Touvier to Barbie and Back Again,* 32 Colum. J. Trans. L. 289 (1994).

persons were considered war crimes and crimes against humanity, as was the program of euthanasia for "incurables" which was extended to the Jews[8]. Likewise, the Tokyo Charter does not contain this requirement. The analysis of the Nürnberg Charter and Judgment prepared by the United Nations shortly after the trial of the major war criminals stated:

It might perhaps be argued that the phrase "on political, racial or religious grounds" refers not only to persecutions but also to the first type of crimes against humanity. The British Chief Prosecutor possibly held that opinion as he spoke of "murder, extermination, enslavement, persecution on political racial or religious grounds". This interpretation, however, seems hardly to be warranted by the English wording and still less by the French text. . . . Moreover, in its statement with regard to von Schirach's guilt the Court designated the crimes against humanity as "murder, extermination, enslavement, deportation, and other inhumane acts" and "persecutions on political, racial or religious grounds"[9].

652. Additionally this requirement is not contained in the Article on crimes against humanity in the I.L.C. Draft Code nor does the Defence challenge its exclusion in the Prosecution's definition of the offence. Significantly, discriminatory intent as an additional requirement for all crimes against humanity was not included in the Statute of this International Tribunal as it was in the Statute for the International Tribunal for Rwanda[ ], the latter of which has, on this very point, recently been criticised. Nevertheless, because the requirement of discriminatory intent on national, political, ethnic, racial or religious grounds for all crimes against humanity was included in the *Report of the Secretary-General*[ ], and since several Security Council members stated that they interpreted Article 5 as referring to acts taken on a discriminatory basis[ ], the Trial Chamber adopts the requirement of discriminatory intent for all crimes against humanity under Article 5. Factually, the inclusion of this additional requirement that the inhumane acts must be taken on discriminatory grounds is satisfied by the evidence discussed above that the attack on the civilian population was conducted against only the non-Serb portion of the population because they were non-Serbs.

653. As mentioned above the reason that crimes against humanity so shock the conscience of mankind and warrant intervention by the international community is because they are not isolated, random acts of individuals but rather result from a deliberate attempt to target a civilian population. Traditionally this requirement was understood to mean that

---

[8] *See* the Medical Case, Vol. II Trials of War Criminals before the Nuernberg Military Tribunals under Control Council Law No. 10, 181, 196-98 (Washington: US Govt. Printing Office 1950).

[9] Memorandum of the Secretary-General on the Charter and Judgment of the Nürnberg Tribunal, 67.

there must be some form of policy to commit these acts. As explained by the Netherlands *Hoge Raad* in *Public Prosecutor v. Menten*[10]:

> The concept of 'crimes against humanity' also requires — although this is not expressed in so many words in the above definition Article 6(c) of the Nürnberg Charter — that the crimes in question form a part of a system based on terror or constitute a link in a consciously pursued policy directed against particular groups of people [ ].

Importantly, however, such a policy need not be formalized and can be deduced from the way in which the acts occur. Notably, if the acts occur on a widespread or systematic basis that demonstrates a policy to commit those acts, whether formalized or not. Although some doubt the necessity of such a policy the evidence in this case clearly establishes the existence of a policy.

654. An additional issue concerns the nature of the entity behind the policy. The traditional conception was, in fact, not only that a policy must be present but that the policy must be that of a State, as was the case in Nazi Germany. The prevailing opinion was, as explained by one commentator, that crimes against humanity, as crimes of a collective nature, require a State policy "because their commission requires the use of the state's institutions, personnel and resources in order to commit, or refrain from preventing the commission of, the specified crimes described in Article 6(c) [of the Nürnberg Charter]"[ ]. While this may have been the case during the Second World War, and thus the jurisprudence followed by courts adjudicating charges of crimes against humanity based on events alleged to have occurred during this period, this is no longer the case. As the first international tribunal to consider charges of crimes against humanity alleged to have occurred after the Second World War, the International Tribunal is not bound by past doctrine but must apply customary international law as it stood at the time of the offences. In this regard the law in relation to crimes against humanity has developed to take into account forces which, although not those of the legitimate government, have *de facto* control over, or are able to move freely within, defined territory. The Prosecution in its pre-trial brief argues that under international law crimes against humanity can be committed on behalf of entities exercising *de facto* control over a particular territory but without international recognition or formal status of a *de jure* state, or by a terrorist group or organization. The Defence does not challenge this assertion, which conforms with recent statements regarding crimes against humanity.

655. For example, Trial Chamber I of the International Tribunal stated in relation to crimes against humanity in its Review of the Indictment Pursuant to Rule 61 of the Rules of Procedure and Evidence in *Prosecutor v. Dragan Nikolic*: "Although they need not be related to a policy established at State level, in the conventional sense of the term, they cannot be the work of isolated individuals alone."[11] The I.L.C. Draft Code is more explicit

---

[10] 75 I.L.R. 362-63 (1987).

[11] *The Prosecutor v. Dragan Nikolic,* Review of the Indictment Pursuant to Rule 61 of the Rules of Procedure and Evidence, Case No. IT-94-2-R61, para. 26, T.Ch.I, 20 Oct.

(continued...)

in this regard. It contains the requirement that in order to constitute a crime against humanity the enumerated acts must be "instigated or directed by a Government or by any organization or group". The commentary clarifies that by stating:

> This alternative is intended to exclude the situation in which an individual commits an inhumane act while acting on his own initiative pursuant to his own criminal plan in the absence of any encouragement or direction from either a Government or a group or organization. This type of isolated criminal conduct on the part of a single individual would not constitute a crime against humanity. . . . The instigation or direction of a Government or *any* organization or group, which may or may not be affiliated with a Government, gives the act its great dimension and makes it a crime against humanity imputable to private persons or agents of a State[ ].

Thus, according to the International Law Commission, the acts do not even have to be directed or instigated by a group in permanent control of territory. It is important to keep in mind that the 1996 version of the I.L.C. Draft Code contains the final text of the article on crimes against humanity adopted by the International Law Commission[ ], which was established pursuant to General Assembly resolution 174 (II) and whose members are elected by the General Assembly. Importantly, the commentary to the draft articles of the Draft Code prepared by the International Law Commission in 1991, which were transmitted to Governments for their comments and observations, acknowledges that non-State actors are also possible perpetrators of crimes against humanity. It states that

> [i]t is important to point out that the draft article does not confine possible perpetrators of the crimes [crimes against humanity] to public officials or representatives alone . . . the article does not rule out the possibility that private individuals with de facto power or organized in criminal gangs or groups might also commit the kind of systematic or mass violations of human rights covered by the article; in that case, their acts would come under the draft Code[ ].

Similarly, the United States Court of Appeals for the Second Circuit recently recognized that "non-state actors" could be liable for committing genocide, the most egregious form of crimes against humanity, as well as war crimes[12]. Therefore, although a policy must exist to commit these acts, it need not be the policy of a State.

656. As discussed above in relation to the nexus, the act must not be unrelated to the armed conflict. This contains two aspects. First, it is the occurrence of the act within the context of a widespread or systematic attack on a civilian population that makes the act a crime against humanity as opposed to simply a war crime or crime against national penal

---

[11](...continued)
1995.

[12] *Kadic v. Karadzic,* 70 F.3d 232 (2nd Cir. 1995), *cert. denied,* 64 U.S.L.W. 3832 (18 Jun. 1996).

legislation, thus adding an additional element, and therefore in addition to the intent to commit the underlying offence the perpetrator must know of the broader context in which his act occurs. Secondly, the act must not be taken for purely personal reasons unrelated to the armed conflict.

657. Regarding the first aspect, the knowledge by the accused of the wider context in which his act occurs, the approach taken by the majority in *R. v. Finta*,[13] in Canada is instructive. In that case the majority decided that "[t]he mental element required to be proven to constitute a crime against humanity is that the accused was aware of or wilfully blind to facts or circumstances which would bring his or her acts within crimes against humanity. However, it would not be necessary to establish that the accused knew that his actions were inhumane."[ ] While knowledge is thus required, it is examined on an objective level and factually can be implied from the circumstances. Several cases arising under German penal law following the Second World War are relevant in this regard. In a case decided by the *Spruchgericht* at Stade, Germany, the accused, who had been stationed near the concentration camp at Buchenwald, was assumed to have known that numerous persons were deprived of their liberty there on political grounds[14]. In addition, it is not necessary that the perpetrator has knowledge of exactly what will happen to the victims and several German cases stressed the fact that denunciations, without more, constitute crimes against humanity[15]. One case in particular is relevant. In that case two accused in 1944 informed the police that the director of the company for which they both worked had criticised Hitler. After the denouncement the director was arrested, temporarily released and then arrested again and brought to a concentration camp. Both of the accused were acquitted due to a lack of "mens rea" as they had not had either a concrete idea of the consequences of their action or an "abominable attitude". However, the *Obersten Gerichthofes* ("OGH") remanded the case to the trial court, finding that a crime against humanity does not require either a concrete idea of the consequences or an "abominable attitude".

658. As for the second aspect, that the act cannot be taken for purely personal reasons unrelated to the armed conflict, while personal motives may be present they should not be the sole motivation for the act. Again one of the German cases arising from the Second World War is relevant. In that case the accused had denounced his wife for her pro-Jewish, anti-Nazi remarks. The OGH found it sufficient that with the purpose of separating from his wife the accused had ensured that the Gestapo knew about her anti-Nazi remarks and that the connection between the action of the accused and the "despotism of the Nazi Regime" was established because the victim was denounced for her anti-Nazi attitude. The OGH found that he had committed a crime against humanity because his behaviour fitted into the plan of persecution against Jews in Germany and that

---

[13] [1994] 1 R.C.S., 701.

[14] Case No 38, Annual Digest and Reports of Public International Law Cases for the Year 1947, 100-101 (Butterworth & Co., London 1951).

[15] *See, e.g.,* Vol. I Entscheidungen des Obersten Gerichtshofes Für Die Britische Zone in Strafsachen, case 2, 6-10; case 4, 19-25; case 23, 91-95; case 25, 105-110; case 31, 122-126; case 34, 141-143.

although his intent was only to harm this one individual, it was closely related to the general mass persecution of the Jews.[16]

659. Thus if the perpetrator has knowledge, either actual or constructive, that these acts were occurring on a widespread or systematic basis and does not commit his act for purely personal motives completely unrelated to the attack on the civilian population, that is sufficient to hold him liable for crimes against humanity. Therefore the perpetrator must know that there is an attack on the civilian population, know that his act fits in with the attack and the act must not be taken for purely personal reasons unrelated to the armed conflict.

660. As discussed, this Trial Chamber has found that an armed conflict existed in the territory of opstina Prijedor at the relevant time and that an aspect of this conflict was a policy to commit inhumane acts against the civilian population of the territory, in particular the non-Serb population, in the attempt to achieve the creation of a Greater Serbia. In furtherance of this policy these inhumane acts were committed against numerous victims and pursuant to a recognisable plan. As such the conditions of applicability for Article 5 are satisfied: the acts were directed against a civilian population on discriminatory grounds, they were committed on both a widespread basis and in a systematic fashion pursuant to a policy and they were committed in the context of, and related to, an armed conflict.

. . . .

[The Chamber then applied the foregoing legal analysis to its factual findings. Tadic was found guilty of violating the laws and customs of war, and of crimes against humanity.

❖ ❖ ❖

Questions & Comments

(1) Outline the constitutive elements necessary for making out a violation of (i) the laws and customs of war and (ii) crimes against humanity as formulated by the ICT-Y Statute and *The Tadic Case.*

(2) The ICC Statute defines "crime against humanity" as

> any of the following acts when committed as part of a widespread or systematic attack directed against any civilian population, with knowledge of the attack: . . . (h) Persecution against any identifiable group or collectivity on . . . grounds that are universally recognized as impermissible under international law, in connection with any act referred to in this paragraph or any crime within the jurisdiction of the Court . . . .

Art. 7, ICC Statute. What other bases of persecution may be universally impermissible under international law? What about persecution of gay, lesbian, and/or bisexual persons? Consider that several regional and global tribunals have ruled that anti-sodomy related domestic laws are unlawful. *See, e.g., Toonen v. Australia,* UN Hum. Rts. Ctte., Communication No. 488/1992, views adopted 31 March 1994, U.N. Doc.

---

[16] OGHBZ, Decision of the District Court (Landgericht) Hamburg of 11 Nov. 1948, STS 78/48, Justiz und NS-Verbrechen II, 1945-1966, 491, 499 (unofficial translation).

CCPR/C/50/D/488 (1992) (criminalization of homosexual activity violative of international right to privacy); *Dudgeon v. United Kingdom*, 45 Eur. Ct. H.R. (ser. A) (1981) (same); *Modinos v. Cyprus*, 259 Eur. Ct. H.R. (ser. A) (1993) (extending protection to carnal knowledge "against the order of nature"); *Norris v. Ireland*, 142 Eur. Ct. H.R. (ser. A) (1988) (protection extended to anal intercourse between adult men). Do these cases establish a customary international legal right against the criminalization of gay/lesbian/bisexual activity? Does a widespread persecution against these persons constitute a crime against humanity? Does a customary international legal protection have to be a "universally" recognized legal protection whose violation rises to the level of a "crime against humanity"? Does "universal" mean that every state must recognize the protected class? Does the persistent objector rule create an exception to the universality requirement?

Consider U.S. law. Under U.S. law, for a particular norm to have the status of customary international law, the norm must be "universal, definable and obligatory." *Zuncax v. Gramajo*, 886 F. Supp. 162, 184 (D. Mass. 1991) (citing *Forti v. Suarez-Mason*, 672 F. Supp. 1531, 1540 (N.D. Cal. 1987)). However, it is not necessary to define every aspect of what might comprise the norm to be "fully defined and universally agreed upon." *Id.* at 187. Therefore, because the right to privacy is a customary international law norm that includes the right of same-sex adults to participate in private, consensual sexual activity, this right also should be guaranteed by customary international law. Accordingly, does this conclusion establish that the systematic persecution of gays, lesbians, and/or bisexuals is a crime against humanity?

Chapter 8. Genocide

The Prosecutor v. Jean-Paul Akayesu
Case No. ICTR-96-4-T
Trial Chambers Judgment
International Criminal Tribunal for Rwanda
2 September 1998

. . . .

Genocide (Article 2 of the Statute)

6.3.1. Genocide

Article 2 of the Statute stipulates that the Tribunal shall have the power to prosecute persons responsible for genocide, direct and public incitement to commit genocide, attempt to commit genocide and complicity in genocide.

In accordance with the said provisions of the Statute, the Prosecutor has charged Akayesu with the crimes legally defined as genocide (count 1), complicity in genocide (count 2) and incitement to commit genocide (count 4).

Crime of Genocide, punishable under Article 2(3)(a) of the Statute

The definition of genocide, as given in Article 2 of the Tribunal's Statute, is taken verbatim from Articles 2 and 3 of the Convention on the Prevention and Punishment of the Crime of Genocide (the "Genocide Convention"). It states:

"Genocide means any of the following acts committed with intent to destroy, in whole or in part, a national, ethnical, racial or religious group, as such:

(a) Killing members of the group;
(b) Causing serious bodily or mental harm to members of the group;
(c) Deliberately inflicting on the group conditions of life calculated to bring about its physical destruction in whole or in part;
(d) Imposing measures intended to prevent births within the group;
(e) Forcibly transferring children of the group to another group."

The Genocide Convention is undeniably considered part of customary international law, as can be seen in the opinion of the International Court of Justice on the provisions of the Genocide Convention, and as was recalled by the United Nations' Secretary-General in his Report on the establishment of the International Criminal Tribunal for the former Yugoslavia.

The Chamber notes that Rwanda acceded, by legislative decree, to the Convention on Genocide on 12 February 1975. Thus, punishment of the crime of genocide did exist in Rwanda in 1994, at the time of the acts alleged in the Indictment, and the perpetrator was liable to be brought before the competent courts of Rwanda to answer for this crime.

Contrary to popular belief, the crime of genocide does not imply the actual extermination of [a] group in its entirety, but is understood as such once any one of the acts mentioned in Article 2(2)(a) through 2(2)(e) is committed with the specific intent to destroy "in whole or in part" a national, ethnical, racial or religious group.

Genocide is distinct from other crimes inasmuch as it embodies a special intent or *dolus specialis*. Special intent of a crime is the specific intention, required as a constitutive element of the crime, which demands that the perpetrator clearly seeks to produce the act charged. Thus, the special intent in the crime of genocide lies in "the intent to destroy, in whole or in part, a national, ethnical, racial or religious group, as such".

Thus, for a crime of genocide to have been committed, it is necessary that one of the acts listed under Article 2(2) of the Statute be committed, that the particular act be committed against a specifically targeted group, it being a national, ethnical, racial or religious group. Consequently, in order to clarify the constitutive elements of the crime of genocide, the Chamber will first state its findings on the acts provided for under Article 2(2)(a) through Article 2(2)(e) of the Statute, the groups protected by the Genocide Convention, and the special intent or *dolus specialis* necessary for genocide to take place.

Killing members of the group (paragraph (a)):

With regard to Article 2(2)(a) of the Statute, like in the Genocide Convention, the Chamber notes that the said paragraph states "*meurtre*" in the French version while the English version states "killing". The Trial Chamber is of the opinion that the term "killing" used in the English version is too general, since it could very well include both intentional and unintentional homicides, whereas the term "*meurtre*", used in the French version, is more precise. It is accepted that there is murder when death has been caused with the intention to do so, as provided for, incidentally, in the Penal Code of Rwanda which stipulates in its Article 311 that "Homicide committed with intent to cause death shall be treated as murder".

Given the presumption of innocence of the accused, and pursuant to the general principles of criminal law, the Chamber holds that the version more favourable to the accused should be upheld and finds that Article 2(2)(a) of the Statute must be interpreted in accordance with the definition of murder given in the Penal Code of Rwanda, according to which "*meurtre*" (killing) is homicide committed with the intent to cause death. The Chamber notes in this regard that the *travaux préparatoires* of the Genocide Convention, show that the proposal by certain delegations that premeditation be made a necessary condition for there to be genocide, was rejected, because some delegates deemed it unnecessary for premeditation to be made a requirement; in their opinion, by its constitutive physical elements, the very crime of genocide, necessarily entails premeditation.

Causing serious bodily or mental harm to members of the group (paragraph b).

Causing serious bodily or mental harm to members of the group does not necessarily mean that the harm is permanent and irremediable.

In the Adolf Eichmann case, who was convicted of crimes against the Jewish people, genocide under another legal definition, the District Court of Jerusalem stated in its judgment of 12 December 1961, that serious bodily or mental harm of members of the group can be caused "by the enslavement, starvation, deportation and persecution [...] and by their detention in ghettos, transit camps and concentration camps in conditions which were designed to cause their degradation, deprivation of their rights as human beings, and to suppress them and cause them inhumane suffering and torture".

For purposes of interpreting Article 2 (2)(b) of the Statute, the Chamber takes serious bodily or mental harm, without limiting itself thereto, to mean acts of torture, be they bodily or mental, inhumane or degrading treatment, persecution.

Deliberately inflicting on the group conditions of life calculated to bring about its physical destruction in whole or in part (paragraph c):

The Chamber holds that the expression deliberately inflicting on the group conditions of life calculated to bring about its physical destruction in whole or in part, should be construed as the methods of destruction by which the perpetrator does not immediately kill the members of the group, but which, ultimately, seek their physical destruction.

For purposes of interpreting Article 2(2)(c) of the Statute, the Chamber is of the opinion that the means of deliberate inflicting on the group conditions of life calculated to bring about its physical destruction, in whole or part, include, *inter alia*, subjecting a group of people to a subsistence diet, systematic expulsion from homes and the reduction of essential medical services below minimum requirement.

Imposing measures intended to prevent births within the group (paragraph d).

For purposes of interpreting Article 2(2)(d) of the Statute, the Chamber holds that the measures intended to prevent births within the group, should be construed as sexual mutilation, the practice of sterilization, forced birth control, separation of the sexes and prohibition of marriages. In patriarchal societies, where membership of a group is determined by the identity of the father, an example of a measure intended to prevent births within a group is the case where, during rape, a woman of the said group is deliberately impregnated by a man of another group, with the intent to have her give birth to a child who will consequently not belong to its mother's group.

Furthermore, the Chamber notes that measures intended to prevent births within the group may be physical, but can also be mental. For instance, rape can be a measure intended to prevent births when the person raped refuses subsequently to procreate, in the same way that members of a group can be led, through threats or trauma, not to procreate.

Forcibly transferring children of the group to another group (paragraph e).

With respect to forcibly transferring children of the group to another group, the Chamber is of the opinion that, as in the case of measures intended to prevent births, the objective is not only to sanction a direct act of forcible physical transfer, but also to sanction acts of threats or trauma which would lead to the forcible transfer of children from one group to another.

Since the special intent to commit genocide lies in the intent to "destroy, in whole or in part, a national, ethnical, racial or religious group, as such", it is necessary to consider a definition of the group as such. Article 2 of the Statute, just like the Genocide

Convention, stipulates four types of victim groups, namely national, ethnical, racial or religious groups.

On reading through the *travaux préparatoires* of the Genocide Convention, it appears that the crime of genocide was allegedly perceived as targeting only "stable" groups, constituted in a permanent fashion and membership of which is determined by birth, with the exclusion of the more "mobile" groups which one joins through individual voluntary commitment, such as political and economic groups. Therefore, a common criterion in the four types of groups protected by the Genocide Convention is that membership in such groups would seem to be normally not challengeable by its members, who belong to it automatically, by birth, in a continuous and often irremediable manner.

Based on the *Nottebohm* decision rendered by the International Court of Justice, the Chamber holds that a national group is defined as a collection of people who are perceived to share a legal bond based on common citizenship, coupled with reciprocity of rights and duties.

An ethnic group is generally defined as a group whose members share a common language or culture.

The conventional definition of racial group is based on the hereditary physical traits often identified with a geographical region, irrespective of linguistic, cultural, national or religious factors.

The religious group is one whose members share the same religion, denomination or mode of worship.

Moreover, the Chamber considered whether the groups protected by the Genocide Convention, echoed in Article 2 of the Statute, should be limited to only the four groups expressly mentioned and whether they should not also include any group which is stable and permanent like the said four groups. In other words, the question that arises is whether it would be impossible to punish the physical destruction of a group as such under the Genocide Convention, if the said group, although stable and membership is by birth, does not meet the definition of any one of the four groups expressly protected by the Genocide Convention. In the opinion of the Chamber, it is particularly important to respect the intention of the drafters of the Genocide Convention, which according to the *travaux préparatoires*, was patently to ensure the protection of any stable and permanent group.

As stated above, the crime of genocide is characterized by its *dolus specialis*, or special intent, which lies in the fact that the acts charged, listed in Article 2 (2) of the Statute, must have been "committed with intent to destroy, in whole or in part, a national, ethnical, racial or religious group, as such".

Special intent is a well-known criminal law concept in the Roman-continental legal systems. It is required as a constituent element of certain offences and demands that the perpetrator have the clear intent to cause the offence charged. According to this meaning, special intent is the key element of an intentional offence, which offence is characterized by a psychological relationship between the physical result and the mental state of the perpetrator.

As observed by the representative of Brazil during the *travaux préparatoires* of the Genocide Convention,

"genocide [is] characterised by the factor of particular intent to destroy a group. In the absence of that factor, whatever the degree of atrocity of an act and however similar it might be to the acts described in the convention, that act could still not be called genocide."

With regard to the crime of genocide, the offender is culpable only when he has committed one of the offences charged under Article 2(2) of the Statute with the clear intent to destroy, in whole or in part, a particular group. The offender is culpable because he knew or should have known that the act committed would destroy, in whole or in part, a group.

In concrete terms, for any of the acts charged under Article 2 (2) of the Statute to be a constitutive element of genocide, the act must have been committed against one or several individuals, because such individual or individuals were members of a specific group, and specifically because they belonged to this group. Thus, the victim is chosen not because of his individual identity, but rather on account of his membership of a national, ethnical, racial or religious group. The victim of the act is therefore a member of a group, chosen as such, which, hence, means that the victim of the crime of genocide is the group itself and not only the individual.

The perpetration of the act charged therefore extends beyond its actual commission, for example, the murder of a particular individual, for the realisation of an ulterior motive, which is to destroy, in whole or part, the group of which the individual is just one element.

On the issue of determining the offender's specific intent, the Chamber considers that intent is a mental factor which is difficult, even impossible, to determine. This is the reason why, in the absence of a confession from the accused, his intent can be inferred from a certain number of presumptions of fact. The Chamber considers that it is possible to deduce the genocidal intent inherent in a particular act charged from the general context of the perpetration of other culpable acts systematically directed against that same group, whether these acts were committed by the same offender or by others. Other factors, such as the scale of atrocities committed, their general nature, in a region or a country, or furthermore, the fact of deliberately and systematically targeting victims on account of their membership of a particular group, while excluding the members of other groups, can enable the Chamber to infer the genocidal intent of a particular act.

Trial Chamber I of the International Criminal Tribunal for the former Yugoslavia also stated that the specific intent of the crime of genocide

> "may be inferred from a number of facts such as the general political doctrine which gave rise to the acts possibly covered by the definition in Article 4, or the repetition of destructive and discriminatory acts. The intent may also be inferred from the perpetration of acts which violate, or which the perpetrators themselves consider to violate the very foundation of the group -- acts which are not in themselves covered by the list in Article 4(2) but which are committed as part of the same pattern of conduct".

Thus, in the matter brought before the International Criminal Tribunal for the former Yugoslavia, the Trial Chamber, in its findings, found that "this intent derives from the combined effect of speeches or projects laying the groundwork for and justifying the acts, from the massive scale of their destructive effect and from their specific nature, which aims at undermining what is considered to be the foundation of the group".

6.3.2. Complicity in Genocide

The Crime of Complicity in Genocide, punishable under Article 2(3)e) of the Statute

Under Article 2(3)e) of the Statute, the Chamber shall have the power to prosecute persons who have committed complicity in genocide. The Prosecutor has charged Akayesu with such a crime under count 2 of the Indictment.

Principle VII of the "Nuremberg Principles" reads

"complicity in the commission of a crime against peace, a war crime, or a crime against humanity as set forth in Principle VI is a crime under international law."

Thus, participation by complicity in the most serious violations of international humanitarian law was considered a crime as early as Nuremberg.

The Chamber notes that complicity is viewed as a form of criminal participation by all criminal law systems, notably, under the Anglo-Saxon system (or Common Law) and the Roman-Continental system (or Civil Law). Since the accomplice to an offence may be defined as someone who associates himself in an offence committed by another, complicity necessarily implies the existence of a principal offence.

According to one school of thought, complicity is "borrowed criminality" (*criminalité d'emprunt*). In other words, the accomplice borrows the criminality of the principal perpetrator. By borrowed criminality, it should be understood that the physical act which constitutes the act of complicity does not have its own inherent criminality, but rather it borrows the criminality of the act committed by the principal perpetrator of the criminal enterprise. Thus, the conduct of the accomplice emerges as a crime when the crime has been consummated by the principal perpetrator. The accomplice has not committed an autonomous crime, but has merely facilitated the criminal enterprise committed by another.

Therefore, the issue before the Chamber is whether genocide must actually be committed in order for any person to be found guilty of complicity in genocide. The Chamber notes that, as stated above, complicity can only exist when there is a punishable, principal act, in the commission of which the accomplice has associated himself. Complicity, therefore, implies a predicate offence committed by someone other than the accomplice.

Consequently, the Chamber is of the opinion that in order for an accused to be found guilty of complicity in genocide, it must, first of all, be proven beyond a reasonable doubt that the crime of genocide has, indeed, been committed.

The issue thence is whether a person can be tried for complicity even where the perpetrator of the principal offence himself has not being tried. Under Article 89 of the Rwandan Penal Code, accomplices

"may be prosecuted even where the perpetrator may not face prosecution for personal reasons, such as double jeopardy, death, insanity or non-identification" [unofficial translation].

As far as the Chamber is aware, all criminal systems provide that an accomplice may also be tried, even where the principal perpetrator of the crime has not been identified, or where, for any other reasons, guilt could not be proven.

The Chamber notes that the logical inference from the foregoing is that an individual cannot thus be both the principal perpetrator of a particular act and the accomplice thereto. An act with which an accused is being charged cannot, therefore, be characterized both as an act of genocide and an act of complicity in genocide as pertains to this accused. Consequently, since the two are mutually exclusive, the same individual cannot be convicted of both crimes for the same act.

As regards the physical elements of complicity in genocide (*actus reus*), three forms of accomplice participation are recognized in most criminal Civil Law systems: complicity by instigation, complicity by aiding and abetting, and complicity by procuring means. It should be noted that the Rwandan Penal Code includes two other forms of participation, namely, incitement to commit a crime through speeches, shouting or threats uttered in public places or at public gatherings, or through the sale or dissemination, offer for sale or display of written material or printed matter in public places or at pubic gatherings, or through the public display of placards or posters, and complicity by harbouring or aiding a criminal. Indeed, according to Article 91 of the Rwandan Penal Code:

"An accomplice shall mean:

1. A person or persons who by means of gifts, promises, threats, abuse of authority or power, culpable machinations or artifice, directly incite(s) to commit such action or order(s) that such action be committed.

2. A person or persons who procure(s) weapons, instruments or any other means which are used in committing such action with the knowledge that they would be so used.

3. A person or persons who knowingly aid(s) or abet(s) the perpetrator or perpetrators of such action in the acts carried out in preparing or planning such action or in effectively committing it.

4. A person or persons who, whether through speeches, shouting or threats uttered in public places or at public gatherings, or through the sale or dissemination, offer for sale or display of written material or printed matter in public places or at pubic gatherings or through the public display of placards or posters, directly incite(s) the perpetrator or perpetrators to commit such an action without prejudice to the penalties applicable to those who incite others to commit offences, even where such incitement fails to produce results.

5. A person or persons who harbour(s) or aid(s) perpetrators under the circumstances provided for under Article 257 of this Code." [unofficial translation]

The Chamber notes, first of all, that the said Article 91 of the Rwandan Penal Code draws a distinction between "instigation" (*instigation*), on the one hand, as provided for by paragraph 1 of said Article, and "incitation" (*incitement*), on the other, which is referred to in paragraph 4 of the same Article. The Chamber notes in this respect that, as pertains to the crime of genocide, the latter form of complicity, *i.e.* by incitement, is the offence which under the Statute is given the specific legal definition of "direct and public incitement to commit genocide," punishable under Article 2(3)c), as distinguished from "complicity in genocide." The findings of the Chamber with respect to the crime of direct and public incitement to commit genocide will be detailed below. That said, instigation, which according to Article 91 of the Rwandan Penal Code, assumes the form of incitement or instruction to commit a crime, only constitutes complicity if it is accompanied by, "gifts, promises, threats, abuse of authority or power, machinations or culpable artifice". In other words, under the Rwandan Penal Code, unless the instigation is accompanied by one of the aforesaid elements, the mere fact of prompting another to commit a crime is not punishable as complicity, even if such a person committed the crime as a result.

The ingredients of complicity under Common Law do not appear to be different from those under Civil Law. To a large extent, the forms of accomplice participation, namely "aid and abet, counsel and procure", mirror those conducts characterized under Civil Law as "*l'aide et l'assistance, la fourniture des moyens*".

Complicity by aiding or abetting implies a positive action which excludes, in principle, complicity by failure to act or omission. Procuring means is a very common form of complicity. It covers those persons who procured weapons, instruments or any other means to be used in the commission of an offence, with the full knowledge that they would be used for such purposes.

For the purposes of interpreting Article 2(3)e) of the Statute, which does not define the concept of complicity, the Chamber is of the opinion that it is necessary to define complicity as per the Rwandan Penal Code, and to consider the first three forms of criminal participation referred to in Article 91 of the Rwandan Penal Code as being the elements of complicity in genocide, thus:

complicity by procuring means, such as weapons, instruments or any other means, used to commit genocide, with the accomplice knowing that such means would be used for such a purpose;

complicity by knowingly aiding or abetting a perpetrator of a genocide in the planning or enabling acts thereof;

complicity by instigation, for which a person is liable who, though not directly participating in the crime of genocide crime, gave instructions to commit genocide, through gifts, promises, threats, abuse of authority or power, machinations or culpable artifice, or who directly incited to commit genocide.

The intent or mental element of complicity implies in general that, at the moment he acted, the accomplice knew of the assistance he was providing in the commission of the principal offence. In other words, the accomplice must have acted knowingly.

Moreover, as in all criminal Civil law systems, under Common law, notably English law, generally, the accomplice need not even wish that the principal offence be committed. In the case of *National Coal Board v. Gamble*, Justice Devlin stated

> "an indifference to the result of the crime does not of itself negate abetting. If one man deliberately sells to another a gun to be used for murdering a third, he may be indifferent about whether the third lives or dies and interested only the cash profit to be made out of the sale, but he can still be an aider and abettor."

In 1975, the English House of Lords also upheld this definition of complicity, when it held that willingness to participate in the principal offence did not have to be established. As a result, anyone who knowing of another's criminal purpose, voluntarily aids him or her in it, can be convicted of complicity even though he regretted the outcome of the offence.

As far as genocide is concerned, the intent of the accomplice is thus to knowingly aid or abet one or more persons to commit the crime of genocide. Therefore, the Chamber is of the opinion that an accomplice to genocide need not necessarily possess the *dolus specialis* of genocide, namely the specific intent to destroy, in whole or in part, a national, ethnic, racial or religious group, as such.

Thus, if for example, an accused knowingly aided or abetted another in the commission of a murder, while being unaware that the principal was committing such a murder, with the intent to destroy, in whole or in part, the group to which the murdered victim belonged, the accused could be prosecuted for complicity in murder, and certainly not for complicity in genocide. However, if the accused knowingly aided and abetted in the commission of such a murder while he knew or had reason to know that the principal was acting with genocidal intent, the accused would be an accomplice to genocide, even though he did not share the murderer's intent to destroy the group.

This finding by the Chamber comports with the decisions rendered by the District Court of Jerusalem on 12 December 1961 and the Supreme Court of Israel on 29 May 1962 in the case of Adolf Eichmann. Since Eichmann raised the argument in his defence that he was a 'small cog' in the Nazi machine, both the District Court and the Supreme Court dealt with accomplice liability and found that,

> "[...] even a small cog, even an insignificant operator, is under our criminal law liable to be regarded as an accomplice in the commission of an offence, in which case he will be dealt with as if he were the actual murderer or destroyer.

The District Court accepted that Eichmann did not personally devise the "Final Solution" himself, but nevertheless, as the head of those engaged in carrying out the "Final Solution" -- "acting in accordance with the directives of his superiors, but [with] wide discretionary powers in planning operations on his own initiative," he incurred individual criminal liability for crimes against the Jewish people, as much as his superiors. Likewise, with respect to his subordinates who actually carried out the executions, "[...] the legal and moral responsibility of he who delivers up the victim to his death is, in our opinion, no smaller, and may be greater, than the responsibility of he who kills the victim with his own hands". The District Court found that participation in the extermination plan with knowledge of the plan rendered the person liable As an accomplice to the extermination of all [...] victims from 1941 to 1945, irrespective of the extent of his participation".

The findings of the Israeli courts in this case support the principle that the *mens rea*, or special intent, required for complicity in genocide is knowledge of the genocidal plan, coupled with the *actus reus* of participation in the execution of such plan. Crucially, then, it does not appear that the specific intent to commit the crime of genocide, as reflected in the phrase "with intent to destroy, in whole or in part, a national, ethnical, racial or religious group, as such," is required for complicity or accomplice liability.

In conclusion, the Chamber is of the opinion that an accused is liable as an accomplice to genocide if he knowingly aided or abetted or instigated one or more persons in the commission of genocide, while knowing that such a person or persons were committing genocide, even though the accused himself did not have the specific intent to destroy, in whole or in part, a national, ethnical, racial or religious group, as such.

At this juncture, the Chamber will address another issue, namely that which, with respect to complicity in genocide covered under Article 2(3)(e) of the Statute, may arise from the forms of participation listed in Article 6 of the Statute entitled, "Individual Criminal Responsibility," and more specifically, those covered under paragraph 1 of the same Article. Indeed, under Article 6(1), "A person who planned, instigated, ordered, committed or otherwise aided and abetted in the planning, preparation or execution of a crime referred to in articles 2 to 4 of the present Statute, shall be individually responsible for the crime." Such forms of participation, which are summarized in the expression "[...] or otherwise aided or abetted [...]," are similar to the material elements of complicity, though they in and of themselves, characterize the crimes referred to in Articles 2 to 4 of the Statute, which include namely genocide.

Consequently, where a person is accused of aiding and abetting, planning, preparing or executing genocide, it must be proven that such a person acted with specific genocidal intent, *i.e.* the intent to destroy, in whole or in part, a national, ethnical, racial or religious group as such, whereas, as stated above, there is no such requirement to establish accomplice liability in genocide.

Another difference between complicity in genocide and the principle of abetting in the planning, preparation or execution a genocide as per Article 6(1), is that, in theory, complicity requires a positive act, *i.e.* an act of commission, whereas aiding and abetting may consist in failing to act or refraining from action. Thus, in the *Jefferson* and *Coney* cases, it was held that 'The accused [...] only accidentally present [...] must know that his presence is actually encouraging the principal(s)". Similarly, the French Court of Cassation found that,

> "A person who, by his mere presence in a group of aggressors provided moral support to the assailants, and fully supported the criminal intent of the group, is liable as an accomplice" [unofficial translation].

The International Criminal Tribunal for the Former Yugoslavia also concluded in the *Tadic* judgment that:

> "if the presence can be shown or inferred, by circumstantial or other evidence, to be knowing and to have a direct and substantial effect on the commission of

the illegal act, then it is sufficient on which to base a finding of participation and assign the criminal culpability that accompanies it."

. . . .

[Later in its decision, the Chambers applied the foregoing legal analysis to the facts in the case.]
7.8. Count 1 - Genocide, Count 2 - Complicity in Genocide

Count 1 relates to all the events described in the Indictment. The Prosecutor submits that by his acts alleged in paragraphs 12 to 23 of the Indictment, Akayesu committed the crime of genocide, punishable under Article 2(3)(a) of the Statute.

Count 2 also relates to all the acts alleged in paragraphs 12 to 23 of the Indictment. The Prosecutor alleges that, by the said acts, the accused committed the crime of complicity in genocide, punishable under Article 2(3)(e) of the Statute.

In its findings on the applicable law, the Chamber indicated supra that, in its opinion, the crime of genocide and that of complicity in genocide were two distinct crimes, and that the same person could certainly not be both the principal perpetrator of, and accomplice to, the same offence. Given that genocide and complicity in genocide are mutually exclusive by definition, the accused cannot obviously be found guilty of both these crimes for the same act. However, since the Prosecutor has charged the accused with both genocide and complicity in genocide for each of the alleged acts, the Chamber deems it necessary, in the instant case, to rule on counts 1 and 2 simultaneously, so as to determine, as far as each proven fact is concerned, whether it constituted genocide or complicity in genocide.

Hence the question to be addressed is against which group the genocide was allegedly committed. Although the Prosecutor did not specifically state so in the Indictment, it is obvious, in the light of the context in which the alleged acts were committed, the testimonies presented and the Prosecutor's closing statement, that the genocide was committed against the Tutsi group. Article 2(2) of the Statute, like the Genocide Convention, provides that genocide may be committed against a national, ethnical, racial or religious group. In its findings on the law applicable to the crime of genocide supra, the Chamber considered whether the protected groups should be limited to only the four groups specifically mentioned or whether any group, similar to the four groups in terms of its stability and permanence, should also be included. The Chamber found that it was necessary, above all, to respect the intent of the drafters of the Genocide Convention which, according to the *travaux préparatoires*, was clearly to protect any stable and permanent group.

In the light of the facts brought to its attention during the trial, the Chamber is of the opinion that, in Rwanda in 1994, the Tutsi constituted a group referred to as "ethnic" in official classifications. Thus, the identity cards at the time included a reference to "*ubwoko*" in Kinyarwanda or "*ethnie*" (ethnic group) in French which, depending on the case, referred to the designation Hutu or Tutsi, for example. The Chamber further noted that all the Rwandan witnesses who appeared before it invariably answered spontaneously and without hesitation the questions of the Prosecutor regarding their ethnic identity. Accordingly, the Chamber finds that, in any case, at the time of the alleged events, the

Tutsi did indeed constitute a stable and permanent group and were identified as such by all.

In the light of the foregoing, with respect to each of the acts alleged in the Indictment, the Chamber is satisfied beyond reasonable doubt, based on the factual findings it has rendered regarding each of the events described in paragraphs 12 to 23 of the Indictment, of the following:

The Chamber finds that, as pertains to the acts alleged in paragraph 12, it has been established that, throughout the period covered in the Indictment, Akayesu, in his capacity as *bourgmestre*, was responsible for maintaining law and public order in the commune of Taba and that he had effective authority over the communal police. Moreover, as "leader" of Taba commune, of which he was one of the most prominent figures, the inhabitants respected him and followed his orders. Akayesu himself admitted before the Chamber that he had the power to assemble the population and that they obeyed his instructions. It has also been proven that a very large number of Tutsi were killed in Taba between 7 April and the end of June 1994, while Akayesu was *bourgmestre* of the Commune. Knowing of such killings, he opposed them and attempted to prevent them only until 18 April 1994, date after which he not only stopped trying to maintain law and order in his commune, but was also present during the acts of violence and killings, and sometimes even gave orders himself for bodily or mental harm to be caused to certain Tutsi, and endorsed and even ordered the killing of several Tutsi.

In the opinion of the Chamber, the said acts indeed incur the individual criminal responsibility of Akayesu for having ordered, committed, or otherwise aided and abetted in the preparation or execution of the killing of and causing serious bodily or mental harm to members of the Tutsi group. Indeed, the Chamber holds that the fact that Akayesu, as a local authority, failed to oppose such killings and serious bodily or mental harm constituted a form of tacit encouragement, which was compounded by being present to such criminal acts.

With regard to the acts alleged in paragraphs 12 (A) and 12 (B) of the Indictment, the Prosecutor has shown beyond a reasonable doubt that between 7 April and the end of June 1994, numerous Tutsi who sought refuge at the Taba Bureau communal were frequently beaten by members of the Interahamwe[1] on or near the premises of the Bureau communal. Some of them were killed. Numerous Tutsi women were forced to endure acts of sexual violence, mutilations and rape, often repeatedly, often publicly and often by more than one assailant. Tutsi women were systematically raped, as one female victim testified to by saying that "each time that you met assailants, they raped you". Numerous incidents of such rape and sexual violence against Tutsi women occurred inside or near the Bureau communal. It has been proven that some communal policemen armed with guns and the accused himself were present while some of these rapes and sexual violence were being committed. Furthermore, it is proven that on several occasions, by his presence, his attitude and his utterances, Akayesu encouraged such acts, one particular witness testifying that Akayesu, addressed the Interahamwe who were committing the rapes and said that

---

[1] [The Interahamwe was the militia of the Mouvement révolutionnaire national pour le développement [MRND]. Ed.'s note.]

"never ask me again what a Tutsi woman tastes like". In the opinion of the Chamber, this constitutes tacit encouragement to the rapes that were being committed.

In the opinion of the Chamber, the above-mentioned acts with which Akayesu is charged indeed render him individually criminally responsible for having abetted in the preparation or execution of the killings of members of the Tutsi group and the infliction of serious bodily and mental harm on members of said group.

The Chamber found supra, with regard to the facts alleged in paragraph 13 of the Indictment, that the Prosecutor failed to demonstrate beyond reasonable doubt that they are established.

As regards the facts alleged in paragraphs 14 and 15 of the Indictment, it is established that in the early hours of 19 April 1994, Akayesu joined a gathering in Gishyeshye and took this opportunity to address the public; he led the meeting and conducted the proceedings. He then called on the population to unite in order to eliminate what he referred to as the sole enemy: the accomplices of the Inkotanyi; and the population understood that he was thus urging them to kill the Tutsi. Indeed, Akayesu himself knew of the impact of his statements on the crowd and of the fact that his call to fight against the accomplices of the Inkotanyi would be understood as exhortations to kill the Tutsi in general. Akayesu who had received from the Interahamwe documents containing lists of names did, in the course of the said gathering, summarize the contents of same to the crowd by pointing out in particular that the names were those of RPF accomplices. He specifically indicated to the participants that Ephrem Karangwa's name was on of the lists. Akayesu admitted before the Chamber that during the period in question, that to publicly label someone as an accomplice of the RPF would put such a person in danger. The statements thus made by Akayesu at that gathering immediately led to widespread killings of Tutsi in Taba.

Concerning the acts with which Akayesu is charged in paragraphs 14 and 15 of the Indictment, the Chamber recalls that it has found supra that they constitute direct and public incitement to commit genocide, a crime punishable under Article 2(3)(c) of the Statute as distinct from the crime of genocide.

With respect to the Prosecutor's allegations in paragraph 16 of the Indictment, the Chamber is satisfied beyond a reasonable doubt that on 19 April 1994, Akayesu on two occasions threatened to kill victim U, a Tutsi woman, while she was being interrogated. He detained her for several hours at the Bureau communal, before allowing her to leave. In the evening of 20 April 1994, during a search conducted in the home of victim V, a Hutu man, Akayesu directly threatened to kill the latter. Victim V was thereafter beaten with a stick and the butt of a rifle by a communal policeman called Mugenzi and one Francois, a member of the Interahamwe militia, in the presence of the accused. One of victim V's ribs was broken as a result of the beating.

In the opinion of the Chamber, the acts attributed to the accused in connection with victims U and V constitute serious bodily and mental harm inflicted on the two victims. However, while Akayesu does incur individual criminal responsibility by virtue of the acts committed against victim U, a Tutsi , for having committed or otherwise aided and abetted in the infliction of serious bodily and mental harm on a member of the Tutsi group, such acts as committed against victim V were perpetrated against a Hutu and cannot, therefore, constitute a crime of genocide against the Tutsi group.

Regarding the acts alleged in paragraph 17, the Prosecutor has failed to satisfy the Chamber that they were proven beyond a reasonable doubt.

As for the allegations made in paragraph 18 of the Indictment, it is established that on or about 19 April 1994, Akayesu and a group of men under his control were looking for Ephrem Karangwa and destroyed his house and that of his mother . They then went to search the house of Ephrem Karangwa's brother-in-law, in Musambira commune and found his three brothers there. When the three brothers, namely Simon Mutijima, Thaddee Uwanyiligira and Jean-Chrysostome, tried to escape, Akayesu ordered that they be captured, and ordered that they be killed, and participated in their killing.

The Chamber holds that these acts indeed render Akayesu individually criminally responsible for having ordered, committed, aided and abetted in the preparation or execution of the killings of members of the Tutsi group and the infliction of serious bodily and mental harm on members of said group.

Regarding the allegations in paragraph 19, the Chamber is satisfied that it has been established that on or about 19 April 1994, Akayesu took from Taba communal prison eight refugees from Runda commune, handed them over to Interahamwe militiamen and ordered that they be killed. They were killed by the Interahamwe using various traditional weapons, including machetes and small axes, in front of the Bureau communal and in the presence of Akayesu who told the killers "do it quickly". The refugees were killed because they were Tutsi.

The Chamber holds that by virtue of such acts, Akayesu incurs individual criminal liability for having ordered, aided and abetted in the perpetration of the killings of members of the Tutsi group and in the infliction of serious bodily and mental harm on members of said group.

The Prosecutor has proved that, as alleged in paragraph 20 of the Indictment, on that same day, Akayesu ordered the local people to kill intellectuals and to look for one Samuel, a professor who was then brought to the Bureau communal and killed with a machete blow to the neck. Teachers in Taba commune were killed later, on Akayesu's instructions. The victims included the following: Tharcisse Twizeyumuremye, Theogene, Phoebe Uwineze and her fiancé whose name is unknown. They were killed on the road in front of the Bureau communal by the local people and the Interahamwe with machetes and agricultural tools. Akayesu personally witnessed the killing of Tharcisse.

In the opinion of the Chamber, Akayesu is indeed individually criminally responsible by virtue of such acts for having ordered, aided and abetted in the preparation or execution of the killings of members of the Tutsi group and in the infliction of serious bodily and mental harm on members of said group.

The Chamber finds that the acts alleged in paragraph 21 have been proven. It has been established that on the evening of 20 April 1994, Akayesu, and two Interahamwe militiamen and a communal policeman, one Mugenzi, who was armed at the time of the events in question, went to the house of Victim Y, a 69 year old Hutu woman, to interrogate her on the whereabouts of Alexia , the wife of Professor Ntereye. During the questioning which took place in the presence of Akayesu, the victim was hit and beaten several times. In particular, she was hit with the barrel of a rifle on the head by the communal policeman. She was forcibly taken away and ordered by Akayesu to lie on the ground. Akayesu himself beat her on her back with a stick. Later on, he had her lie down in front of a vehicle and threatened to drive over her if she failed to give the information he sought.

Although the above acts constitute serious bodily and mental harm inflicted on the victim, the Chamber notes that they were committed against a Hutu woman. Consequently, they cannot constitute acts of genocide against the Tutsi group.

As regards the allegations in paragraphs 22 and 23 of the Indictment, the Chamber is satisfied beyond reasonable doubt that on the evening of 20 April 1994, in the course of an interrogation, Akayesu forced victim W to lay down in front of a vehicle and threatened to drive over her . That same evening, Akayesu, accompanied by Mugenzi, a communal policeman, and one Francois, an Interahamwe militiaman, interrogated victims Z and Y. The accused put his foot on the face of victim Z, causing the said victim to bleed, while the police officer and the militiaman beat the victim with the butt of their rifles. The militiaman forced victim Z to beat victim Y with a stick. The two victims were tied together, causing victim Z to suffocate. Victim Z was also beaten on the back with the blade of a machete.

The Chamber holds that by virtue of the above-mentioned acts Akayesu is individually criminally responsible for having ordered, committed, aided and abetted in the preparation or infliction of serious bodily or mental harm on members of the Tutsi group.

From the foregoing, the Chamber is satisfied beyond a reasonable doubt, that Akayesu is individually criminally responsible, under Article 6(1) of the Statute, for having ordered, committed or otherwise aided and abetted in the commission of the acts described above in the findings made by the Chamber on paragraphs 12, 12A, 12B, 16, 18, 19, 20, 22 and 23 of the Indictment, acts which constitute the killing of members of the Tutsi group and the infliction of serious bodily and mental harm on members of said group.

Since the Prosecutor charged both genocide and complicity in genocide with respect to each of the above-mentioned acts, and since, as indicated supra, the Chamber is of the opinion that these charges are mutually exclusive, it must rule whether each of such acts constitutes genocide or complicity in genocide.

In this connection, the Chamber recalls that, in its findings on the applicable law, it held that an accused is an accomplice to genocide if he or she knowingly and wilfully aided or abetted or instigated another to commit a crime of genocide, while being aware of his genocidal plan, even where the accused had no specific intent to destroy, in whole or in part, a national, ethnical, racial or religious group, as such. It also found that Article 6(1) of the Statute provides for a form of participation through aiding and abetting which, though akin to the factual elements of complicity, nevertheless entails, in and of itself, the individual responsibility of the accused for the crime of genocide, in particular, where the accused had the specific intent to commit genocide, that is, the intent to destroy a particular group; this latter requirement is not needed where an accomplice to genocide is concerned.

Therefore, it is incumbent upon the Chamber to decide, in this instant case, whether or not Akayesu had a specific genocidal intent when he participated in the above-mentioned crimes, that is, the intent to destroy, in whole or in part, a group as such.

As stated in its findings on the law applicable to the crime of genocide, the Chamber holds the view that the intent underlying an act can be inferred from a number of facts. The Chamber is of the opinion that it is possible to infer the genocidal intention that presided over the commission of a particular act, inter alia, from all acts or utterances of the accused, or from the general context in which other culpable acts were perpetrated systematically against the same group, regardless of whether such other acts were committed by the same perpetrator or even by other perpetrators.

First of all, regarding Akayesu's acts and utterances during the period relating to the acts alleged in the Indictment, the Chamber is satisfied beyond reasonable doubt, on the basis of all evidence brought to its attention during the trial, that on several occasions the accused made speeches calling, more or less explicitly, for the commission of genocide. The Chamber, in particular, held in its findings on Count 4, that the accused incurred individual criminal responsibility for the crime of direct and public incitement to commit genocide. Yet, according to the Chamber, the crime of direct and public incitement to commit genocide lies in the intent to directly lead or provoke another to commit genocide, which implies that he who incites to commit genocide also has the specific intent to commit genocide: that is, to destroy, in whole or in part, a national, ethnical, racial or religious group, as such.

Furthermore, the Chamber has already established that genocide was committed against the Tutsi group in Rwanda in 1994, throughout the period covering the events alleged in the Indictment. Owing to the very high number of atrocities committed against the Tutsi, their widespread nature not only in the commune of Taba, but also throughout Rwanda, and to the fact that the victims were systematically and deliberately selected because they belonged to the Tutsi group, with persons belonging to other groups being excluded, the Chamber is also able to infer, beyond reasonable doubt, the genocidal intent of the accused in the commission of the above-mentioned crimes.

With regard, particularly, to the acts described in paragraphs 12(A) and 12(B) of the Indictment, that is, rape and sexual violence, the Chamber wishes to underscore the fact that in its opinion, they constitute genocide in the same way as any other act as long as they were committed with the specific intent to destroy, in whole or in part, a particular group, targeted as such. Indeed, rape and sexual violence certainly constitute infliction of serious bodily and mental harm on the victims and are even, according to the Chamber, one of the worst ways of inflict harm on the victim as he or she suffers both bodily and mental harm. In light of all the evidence before it, the Chamber is satisfied that the acts of rape and sexual violence described above, were committed solely against Tutsi women, many of whom were subjected to the worst public humiliation, mutilated, and raped several times, often in public, in the Bureau Communal premises or in other public places, and often by more than one assailant. These rapes resulted in physical and psychological destruction of Tutsi women, their families and their communities. Sexual violence was an integral part of the process of destruction, specifically targeting Tutsi women and specifically contributing to their destruction and to the destruction of the Tutsi group as a whole.

The rape of Tutsi women was systematic and was perpetrated against all Tutsi women and solely against them. A Tutsi woman, married to a Hutu, testified before the Chamber that she was not raped because her ethnic background was unknown. As part of the propaganda campaign geared to mobilizing the Hutu against the Tutsi, the Tutsi women were presented as sexual objects. Indeed, the Chamber was told, for an example, that before being raped and killed, Alexia, who was the wife of the Professor, Ntereye, and her two nieces, were forced by the Interahamwe to undress and ordered to run and do exercises "in order to display the thighs of Tutsi women". The Interahamwe who raped Alexia said, as he threw her on the ground and got on top of her, "let us now see what the vagina of a Tutsi woman tastes like". As stated above, Akayesu himself, speaking to the Interahamwe who were committing the rapes, said to them: "don't ever ask again what a Tutsi woman tastes like". This sexualized representation of ethnic identity graphically illustrates that Tutsi women were subjected to sexual violence because they were Tutsi. Sexual violence was a step in the process of destruction of the Tutsi group - destruction of the spirit, of the will to live, and of life itself.

On the basis of the substantial testimonies brought before it, the Chamber finds that in most cases, the rapes of Tutsi women in Taba, were accompanied with the intent to kill those women. Many rapes were perpetrated near mass graves where the women were taken to be killed . A victim testified that Tutsi women caught could be taken away by peasants and men with the promise that they would be collected later to be executed. Following an act of gang rape, a witness heard Akayesu say "tomorrow they will be killed" and they were actually killed. In this respect, it appears clearly to the Chamber that the acts of rape and sexual violence, as other acts of serious bodily and mental harm committed against the Tutsi, reflected the determination to make Tutsi women suffer and to mutilate them even before killing them, the intent being to destroy the Tutsi group while inflicting acute suffering on its members in the process.

In light of the foregoing, the Chamber finds firstly that the acts described supra are indeed acts as enumerated in Article 2 (2) of the Statute, which constitute the factual elements of the crime of genocide, namely the killings of Tutsi or the serious bodily and mental harm inflicted on the Tutsi. The Chamber is further satisfied beyond reasonable doubt that these various acts were committed by Akayesu with the specific intent to destroy the Tutsi group, as such. Consequently, the Chamber is of the opinion that the acts alleged in paragraphs 12, 12A, 12B, 16, 18, 19, 20, 22 and 23 of the Indictment and proven above, constitute the crime of genocide, but not the crime of complicity; hence, the Chamber finds Akayesu individually criminally responsible for genocide.

. . . .

[Earlier in its decision, the ICT-R addressed the charge of incitement.]

6.3.3. Direct and Public Incitement to Commit Genocide

. . . .

Under count 4, the Prosecutor charges Akayesu with direct and public incitement to commit genocide, a crime punishable under Article 2(3)(c) of the Statute.

Perhaps the most famous conviction for incitement to commit crimes of international dimension was that of Julius Streicher by the Nuremberg Tribunal for the virulently anti-Semitic articles which he had published in his weekly newspaper DER STÜRMER. The Nuremberg Tribunal found that: "Streicher's incitement to murder and extermination, at the time when Jews in the East were being killed under the most horrible conditions, clearly constitutes persecution on political and racial grounds in connection with War Crimes, as defined by the Charter, and constitutes a Crime against Humanity".

At the time the Convention on Genocide was adopted, the delegates agreed to expressly spell out direct and public incitement to commit genocide as a specific crime, in particular, because of its critical role in the planning of a genocide, with the delegate from the USSR stating in this regard that, "It was impossible that hundreds of thousands of people should commit so many crimes unless they had been incited to do so and unless the crimes had been premeditated and carefully organized. He asked how in those circumstances, the inciters and organizers of the crime could be allowed to escape punishment, when they were the ones really responsible for the atrocities committed".

Under Common law systems, incitement tends to be viewed as a particular form of criminal participation, punishable as such. Similarly, under the legislation of some Civil law countries, including Argentina, Bolivia, Chili, Peru, Spain, Uruguay and Venezuela, provocation, which is similar to incitement, is a specific form of participation in an offence; but in most Civil law systems, incitement is most often treated as a form of complicity.

The Rwandan Penal Code is one such legislation. Indeed, as stated above, in the discussion on complicity in genocide, it does provide that direct and public incitement or provocation is a form of complicity. In fact, Article 91 subparagraph 4 provides that an accomplice shall mean " A person or persons who, whether through speeches, shouting or threats uttered in public places or at public gatherings, or through the sale or dissemination, offer for sale or display of written material or printed matter in public places or at public gatherings or through the public display of placards or posters, directly incite(s) the perpetrator or perpetrators to commit such an action without prejudice to the penalties applicable to those who incite others to commit offences, even where such incitement fails to produce results".

Under the Statute, direct and public incitement is expressly defined as a specific crime, punishable as such, by virtue of Article 2(3)(c). With respect to such a crime, the Chamber deems it appropriate to first define the three terms: incitement, direct and public.

Incitement is defined in Common law systems as encouraging or persuading another to commit an offence. One line of authority in Common law would also view threats or other forms of pressure as a form of incitement. As stated above, Civil law systems punish direct and public incitement assuming the form of provocation, which is defined as an act intended to directly provoke another to commit a crime or a misdemeanour through speeches, shouting or threats, or any other means of audiovisual communication. Such a provocation, as defined under Civil law, is made up of the same elements as direct and public incitement to commit genocide covered by Article 2 of the Statute, that is to say it is both direct and public.

The public element of incitement to commit genocide may be better appreciated in light of two factors: the place where the incitement occurred and whether or not assistance was selective or limited. A line of authority commonly followed in Civil law systems would regard words as being public where they were spoken aloud in a place that were public by definition. According to the International Law Commission, public incitement is characterized by a call for criminal action to a number of individuals in a public place or to members of the general public at large by such means as the mass media, for example, radio or television. It should be noted in this respect that at the time Convention on Genocide was adopted, the delegates specifically agreed to rule out the possibility of including private incitement to commit genocide as a crime, thereby underscoring their commitment to set aside for punishment only the truly public forms of incitement.

The "direct" element of incitement implies that the incitement assume a direct form and specifically provoke another to engage in a criminal act, and that more than mere vague or indirect suggestion goes to constitute direct incitement. Under Civil law systems, provocation, the equivalent of incitement, is regarded as being direct where it is aimed at causing a specific offence to be committed. The prosecution must prove a definite causation between the act characterized as incitement, or provocation in this case, and a specific offence. However, the Chamber is of the opinion that the direct element of incitement should be viewed in the light of its cultural and linguistic content. Indeed, a particular speech may be perceived as "direct" in one country, and not so in another, depending on the audience. The Chamber further recalls that incitement may be direct, and nonetheless implicit. Thus, at the time the Convention on Genocide was being drafted, the Polish delegate observed that it was sufficient to play skillfully on mob psychology by casting suspicion on certain groups, by insinuating that they were responsible for economic or other difficulties in order to create an atmosphere favourable to the perpetration of the crime.

The Chamber will therefore consider on a case-by-case basis whether, in light of the culture of Rwanda and the specific circumstances of the instant case, acts of incitement can be viewed as direct or not, by focusing mainly on the issue of whether the persons for whom the message was intended immediately grasped the implication thereof.

In light of the foregoing, it can be noted in the final analysis that whatever the legal system, direct and public incitement must be defined for the purposes of interpreting Article 2(3)(c), as directly provoking the perpetrator(s) to commit genocide, whether through speeches, shouting or threats uttered in public places or at public gatherings, or through the sale or dissemination, offer for sale or display of written material or printed matter in public places or at public gatherings, or through the public display of placards or posters, or through any other means of audiovisual communication.

The *mens rea* required for the crime of direct and public incitement to commit genocide lies in the intent to directly prompt or provoke another to commit genocide. It implies a desire on the part of the perpetrator to create by his actions a particular state of mind necessary to commit such a crime in the minds of the person(s) he is so engaging. That is to say that the person who is inciting to commit genocide must have himself the specific intent to commit genocide, namely, to destroy, in whole or in part, a national, ethnical, racial or religious group, as such.

Therefore, the issue before the Chamber is whether the crime of direct and public incitement to commit genocide can be punished even where such incitement was unsuccessful. It appears from the *travaux préparatoires* of the Convention on Genocide that the drafters of the Convention considered stating explicitly that incitement to commit genocide could be punished, whether or not it was successful. In the end, a majority decided against such an approach. Nevertheless, the Chamber is of the opinion that it cannot thereby be inferred that the intent of the drafters was not to punish unsuccessful acts of incitement. In light of the overall *travaux*, the Chamber holds the view that the drafters of the Convention simply decided not to specifically mention that such a form of incitement could be punished.

There are under Common law so-called inchoate offences, which are punishable by virtue of the criminal act alone, irrespective of the result thereof, which may or may not have been achieved. The Civil law counterparts of inchoate offences are known as [*infractions formelles*] (acts constituting an offence per se irrespective of their results), as opposed to [*infractions matérielles*] (strict liability offences). Indeed, as is the case with inchoate offenses, in [*infractions formelles*], the method alone is punishable. Put another way, such offenses are "deemed to have been consummated regardless of the result achieved [unofficial translation]" contrary to [*infractions matérielles*]. Indeed, Rwandan lawmakers appear to characterize the acts defined under Article 91(4) of the Rwandan Penal Code as so-called [*infractions formelles*], since provision is made for their punishment even where they proved unsuccessful. It should be noted, however, that such offences are the exception, the rule being that in theory, an offence can only be punished in relation to the result envisaged by the lawmakers. In the opinion of the Chamber, the fact that such acts are in themselves particularly dangerous because of the high risk they carry for society, even if they fail to produce results, warrants that they be punished as an exceptional measure. The Chamber holds that genocide clearly falls within the category of crimes so serious that direct and public incitement to commit such a crime must be punished as such, even where such incitement failed to produce the result expected by the perpetrator.

. . . .

[Later in its decision, the Chambers applied the facts to the foregoing legal analysis.]

7.5 Count 4 - Direct and Public Incitement to Commit Genocide

Count 4 deals with the allegations described in paragraphs 14 and 15 of the Indictment, relating, essentially, to the speeches that Akayesu reportedly made at a meeting held in Gishyeshye on 19 April 1994. The Prosecutor alleges that, through his speeches, Akayesu committed the crime of direct and public incitement to commit genocide, a crime punishable under Article 2(3)(c) of the Statute.

The Trial Chamber made the following factual findings on the events described in paragraphs 14 and 15 of the Indictment. The Chamber is satisfied beyond a reasonable doubt that: (i) Akayesu, in the early hours of 19 April 1994, joined a crowd of over 100 people which had gathered around the body of a young member of the Interahamwe in Gishyeshye. (ii) He seized that opportunity to address the people and, owing, particularly, to his functions as *bourgmestre* and his authority over the population, he led the gathering and the proceedings. (iii) It has been established that Akayesu then clearly urged the population to unite in order to eliminate what he termed the sole enemy: the accomplices of the Inkotanyi. (iv) On the basis of consistent testimonies heard throughout the proceedings and the evidence of Dr. Ruzindana, appearing as expert witness on linguistic matters, the Chamber is satisfied beyond a reasonable doubt that the population understood Akayesu's call as one to kill the Tutsi. Akayesu himself was fully aware of the impact of his speech on the crowd and of the fact that his call to fight against the accomplices of the Inkotanyi would be construed as a call to kill the Tutsi in general. (v) During the said meeting, Akayesu received from the Interahamwe documents which included lists of names, and read from the lists to the crowd by stating, in particular, that the names were those of RPF accomplices. (vi) Akayesu testified that the lists contained, especially, the name of Ephrem Karangwa, whom he named specifically, while being fully aware of the consequences of doing so. Indeed, he admitted before the Chamber that, at the time of the events alleged in the Indictment, to label anyone in public as an accomplice of the RPF would put such a person in danger. (vii) The Chamber is of the opinion that there is a causal relationship between Akayesu's speeches at the gathering of 19 April 1994 and the ensuing widespread massacres of Tutsi in Taba.

From the foregoing, the Chamber is satisfied beyond a reasonable doubt that, by the above-mentioned speeches made in public and in a public place, Akayesu had the intent to directly create a particular state of mind in his audience necessary to lead to the destruction of the Tutsi group, as such. Accordingly, the Chamber finds that the said acts constitute the crime of direct and public incitement to commit genocide, as defined above.

In addition, the Chamber finds that the direct and public incitement to commit genocide as engaged in by Akayesu, was indeed successful and did lead to the destruction of a great number of Tutsi in the commune of Taba.

❖ ❖ ❖

Questions & Comments

(1) Could private arms dealers who provide weapons to persons committing genocide be considered guilty of complicity?

(2) Consider the following excerpt from ICT-Y Trial Chamber's decision in *The Prosecutor v. Furundzija*:

12. The application of the Appeals Chamber's finding by the Defence is flawed. All grave breaches [of the Geneva Conventions] are violations of the laws and customs of war. Theoretically, they can be charged as both if the criteria are satisfied. However, there is a general principle of international law (the doctrine of speciality/*lex specialis derogat generali*) which provides that in a choice between two provisions where one has a broader scope and completely encompasses the other, the more specific charge should be chosen. Nevertheless, the situation at hand is not one where the Trial Chamber is faced with different charges under separate articles of the Statute. The Prosecution has already made a choice and has withdrawn the specific charge alleging grave breaches of the Geneva Conventions. It is the finding of the Trial Chamber that the Prosecution is justified in relying on the residual clause to ensure that no serious violation of international humanitarian law escapes the jurisdiction of the International Tribunal. This is fully in line with the reasoning of the Appeals Chamber Decision.

The Prosecutor v. Furundzija, Int'l Crim Trib.-Yugo, Decision on the Defendant's Motion to Dismiss Counts 13 and 14 of the Indictment (Lack of Subject Matter Jurisdiction, Order of 29 May 1998, at § 12. Recall that genocide is considered a crime against humanity. *Prosecutor v. Tadic*, at § 655. Does the international law doctrine of speciality preclude the possibility that someone can be held culpable for both genocide and crimes against humanity?

(3) Note that neither the ICC Statute, ICT-Y Statute, ICT-R Statute, nor the Genocide Convention includes those harmful acts perpetrated against political groups – unlike the London Agreement establishing the IMT.

Chapter 9. Forced Disappearances

Velásquez Rodríguez v. Honduras
Inter-American Court of Human Rights
Judgment of July 29, 1988, Ser. C No. 4

[Reproduced in Chapter 4]

❖ ❖ ❖

Questions & Comments

(1)   Forced disappearances are considered crimes against humanity by both the Inter-American Court in *Velásquez Rodríguez v. Honduras* and the ICC Statute. However, to be considered crimes under the ICC Statute, these disappearances must be committed as part of a widespread or systematic attack directed against a civilian population. Does the Inter-American Court in *Velásquez Rodríguez v. Honduras* require such a condition for a disappearance to create both state liability and individual culpability? See § 147(d). Can some international human rights violations -- such as a disappearance or sexual assault (see *X. & Y. v. The Netherlands* below) that are not crimes against humanity because they are not part of a widespread or systemic attack on a civilian population still be considered international crimes because they entail international criminal liability for the state as well as individual culpability for the individual perpetrator?

(2)   Note that the Inter-American Convention on the Forced Disappearance of Persons does not include disappearances perpetrated by political organizations as does the ICC Statute.

(3)   If you were a prosecutor, how would you prove the commission of a disappearance without a body? How would you defend?

Chapter 10. Sexual Violence

The Prosecutor v. Jean-Paul Akayesu
Case No. ICTR-96-4-T
Chambers Judgment
International Criminal Tribunal for Rwanda
2 September 1998

Factual Findings[1]

Having carefully reviewed the testimony of the Prosecution witnesses regarding sexual violence, the Chamber finds that there is sufficient credible evidence to establish beyond a reasonable doubt that during the events of 1994, Tutsi girls and women were subjected to sexual violence, beaten and killed on or near the bureau communal premises, as well as elsewhere in the commune of Taba. Witness H, Witness JJ, Witness OO, and Witness NN all testified that they themselves were raped, and all, with the exception of Witness OO, testified that they witnessed other girls and women being raped. Witness J, Witness KK and Witness PP also testified that they witnessed other girls and women being raped in the commune of Taba. Hundreds of Tutsi, mostly women and children, sought refuge at the bureau communal during this period and many rapes took place on or near the premises of the bureau communal - Witness JJ was taken by Interahamwe[2] from the refuge site near the bureau communal to a nearby forest area and raped there. She testified that this happened often to other young girls and women at the refuge site. Witness JJ was also raped repeatedly on two separate occasions in the cultural center on the premises of the bureau communal, once in a group of fifteen girls and women and once in a group of ten girls and women. Witness KK saw women and girls being selected and taken by the Interahamwe to the cultural center to be raped. Witness H saw women being raped outside the compound of the bureau communal, and Witness NN saw two Interahamwes take a woman and rape her between the bureau communal and the cultural center. Witness OO was taken from the bureau communal and raped in a nearby field. Witness PP saw three women being raped at Kinihira, the killing site near the bureau communal, and Witness NN found her younger sister, dying, after she had been raped at the bureau communal. Many other instances of rape in Taba outside the bureau communal - in fields, on the road, and in or just outside houses - were described by Witness J, Witness H, Witness OO, Witness KK, Witness NN and Witness PP. Witness KK and Witness PP also described other acts of sexual violence which took place on or near the premises of the bureau communal - the forced undressing and public humiliation of girls and women. The Chamber notes that much of the sexual violence took place in front of large numbers of people, and that all of it was directed against Tutsi women.

---

[1] [The accused, Jean-Paul Akayesu, was the *bourgmestre* or mayor of the commune of Taba and had effective authority over the communal police. Ed.'s note.]

[2] [The Interahamwe was the militia of the Mouvement révolutionnaire national pour le développement [MRND]. Ed.'s note.]

With a few exceptions, most of the rapes and all of the other acts of sexual violence described by the Prosecution witnesses were committed by Interahamwe. . . . . [W]ith regard to all evidence of rape and sexual violence which took place on or near the premises of the bureau communal, the perpetrators were all identified as Interahamwe. Interahamwe are also identified as the perpetrators of many rapes which took place outside the bureau communal . . . . There is no suggestion in any of the evidence that the Accused or any communal policemen perpetrated rape, and both Witness JJ and Witness KK affirmed that they never saw the Accused rape anyone.

In considering the role of the Accused in the sexual violence which took place and the extent of his direct knowledge of incidents of sexual violence, the Chamber has taken into account only evidence which is direct and unequivocal. Witness H testified that the Accused was present during the rape of Tutsi women outside the compound of the bureau communal, but as she could not confirm that he was aware that the rapes were taking place, the Chamber discounts this testimony in its assessment of the evidence. Witness PP recalled the Accused directing the Interahamwe to take Alexia and her two nieces to Kinihira, saying "Don't you know where killings take place, where the others have been killed?" The three women were raped before they were killed, but the statement of the Accused does not refer to sexual violence and there is no evidence that the Accused was present at Kinihira. For this reason, the Chamber also discounts this testimony in its assessment of the evidence.

On the basis of the evidence set forth herein, the Chamber finds beyond a reasonable doubt that the Accused had reason to know and in fact knew that sexual violence was taking place on or near the premises of the bureau communal, and that women were being taken away from the bureau communal and sexually violated. There is no evidence that the Accused took any measures to prevent acts of sexual violence or to punish the perpetrators of sexual violence. In fact there is evidence that the Accused ordered, instigated and otherwise aided and abetted sexual violence. The Accused watched two Interahamwe drag a woman to be raped between the bureau communal and the cultural center. The two commune policemen in front of his office witnessed the rape but did nothing to prevent it. On the two occasions Witness JJ was brought to the cultural center of the bureau communal to be raped, she and the group of girls and women with her were taken past the Accused, on the way. On the first occasion he was looking at them, and on the second occasion he was standing at the entrance to the cultural center. On this second occasion, he said, "Never ask me again what a Tutsi woman tastes like." Witness JJ described the Accused in making these statements as "talking as if someone were encouraging a player." More generally she stated that the Accused was the one "supervising" the acts of rape. When Witness OO and two other girls were apprehended by Interahamwe in flight from the bureau communal, the Interahamwe went to the Accused and told him that they were taking the girls away to sleep with them. The Accused said "take them." The Accused told the Interahamwe to undress Chantal and march her around. He was laughing and happy to be watching and afterwards told the Interahamwe to take her away and said "you should first of all make sure that you sleep with this girl." The Chamber considers this statement as evidence that the Accused ordered and instigated sexual violence, although insufficient evidence was presented to establish beyond a reasonable doubt that Chantal was in fact raped.

Chapter 10. Sexual Violence

In making its factual findings, the Chamber has carefully considered the cross-examination by the Defence of Prosecution witnesses and the evidence presented by the Defence. With regard to cross-examination, the Chamber notes that the Defence did not question the testimony of Witness J or Witness H on rape at all, although the Chamber itself questioned both witnesses on this testimony. Witness JJ, OO, KK, NN and PP were questioned by the Defence with regard to their testimony of sexual violence, but the testimony itself was never challenged. Details such as where the rapes took place, how many rapists there were, how old they were, whether the Accused participated in the rapes, who was raped and which rapists used condoms were all elicited by the Defence, but at no point did the Defence suggest to the witnesses that the rapes had not taken place. The main line of questioning by the Defence with regard to the rapes and other sexual violence, other than to confirm the details of the testimony, related to whether the Accused had the authority to stop them. In cross-examination of the evidence presented by the Prosecution, specific incidents of sexual violence were never challenged by the Defence.

[The Law]

6.4. Crimes against Humanity (Article 3 of the Statute)

Crimes against Humanity - Historical development

Crimes against humanity were recognized in the Charter and Judgment of the Nuremberg Tribunal, as well as in Law No. 10 of the Control Council for Germany. Article 6(c) of the Charter of Nuremberg Tribunal defines crimes against humanity as

> murder, extermination, enslavement, deportation, and other inhumane acts committed against any civilian population, before or during the war, or persecutions on political, racial or religious grounds in execution of or in connexion with any crime within the jurisdiction of the Chamber, whether or not in violation of the domestic law of the country where perpetrated.

Article II of Law No. 10 of the Control Council Law defined crimes against humanity as:

> Atrocities and Offenses, including but not limited to murder, extermination, enslavement, deportation, imprisonment, torture, rape, or other inhumane acts committed against any civilian population or persecution on political, racial or religious grounds, whether or not in violation of the domestic laws of the country where perpetrated.

Crimes against humanity are aimed at any civilian population and are prohibited regardless of whether they are committed in an armed conflict, international or internal in character. In fact, the concept of crimes against humanity had been recognised long before Nuremberg. On 28 May 1915, the Governments of France, Great Britain and Russia made a declaration regarding the massacres of the Armenian population in Turkey, denouncing them as "crimes against humanity and civilisation for which all the members of the

Turkish government will be held responsible together with its agents implicated in the massacres". The 1919 Report of the Commission on the Responsibility of the Authors of the War and on Enforcement of Penalties formulated by representatives from several States and presented to the Paris Peace Conference also referred to "offences against . . . the laws of humanity".

These World War I notions derived, in part, from the Martens clause of the Hague Convention (IV) of 1907, which referred to "the usages established among civilised peoples, from the laws of humanity, and the dictates of the public conscience". In 1874, George Curtis called slavery a "crime against humanity". Other such phrases as "crimes against mankind" and "crimes against the human family" appear far earlier in human history (*see* 12 N.Y.L. SCH. J. HUM. RTS 545 (1995)).

The Chamber notes that, following the Nuremberg and Tokyo trials, the concept of crimes against humanity underwent a gradual evolution in the *Eichmann, Barbie, Touvier* and *Papon* cases.

In the *Eichmann* case, the accused, Otto Adolf Eichmann, was charged with offences under Nazi and Nazi Collaborators (punishment) Law, 5710/1950, for his participation in the implementation of the plan know as "the Final Solution of the Jewish problem". Pursuant to Section I (b) of the said law:

> Crime against humanity means any of the following acts: murder, extermination, enslavement, starvation or deportation and other inhumane acts committed against any civilian population , and persecution on national, racial, religious or political grounds.

The district court in the Eichmann stated that crimes against humanity differs from genocide in that for the commission of genocide special intent is required. This special intent is not required for crimes against humanity. Eichmann was convicted by the District court and sentenced to death. Eichmann appealed against his conviction and his appeal was dismissed by the supreme court.

In the *Barbie* case, the accused, Klaus Barbie, who was the head of the Gestapo in Lyons from November 1942 to August 1944, during the wartime occupation of France, was convicted in 1987 of crimes against humanity for his role in the deportation and extermination of civilians. Barbie appealed in cassation, but the appeal was dismissed. For the purposes of the present Judgment, what is of interest is the definition of crimes against humanity employed by the Court. The French Court of Cassation, in a Judgment rendered on 20 December 1985, stated:

> Crimes against humanity, within the meaning of Article 6(c) of the Charter of the International Military Tribunal annexed to the London Agreement of 8 August 1945, which were not subject to statutory limitation of the right of prosecution, even if they were crimes which could also be classified as war crimes within the meaning of Article 6(b) of the Charter, were inhumane acts and persecution committed in a systematic manner in the name of a State practising a policy of ideological supremacy, not only against persons by reason of their membership of a racial or religious community, but also against the opponents of that policy, whatever the form of their opposition. (Words italicized by the Court)

154

This was affirmed in a Judgment of the Court of Cassation of 3 June 1988, in which the Court held that:

> The fact that the accused, who had been found guilty of one of the crimes enumerated in Article 6(c) of the Charter of the Nuremberg Tribunal, in perpetrating that crime took part in the execution of a common plan to bring about the deportation or extermination of the civilian population during the war, or persecutions on political, racial or religious grounds, constituted not a distinct offence or an aggravating circumstance but rather an essential element of the crime against humanity, consisting of the fact that the acts charged were performed in a systematic manner in the name of a State practising by those means a policy of ideological supremacy. (Emphasis added)

The definition of crimes against humanity developed in Barbie was further developed in the *Touvier* case. In that case, the accused, Paul Touvier, had been a high-ranking officer in the Militia (Milice) of Lyons, which operated in "Vichy" France during the German occupation. He was convicted of crimes against humanity for his role in the shooting of seven Jews at Rillieux on 29 June 1994 as a reprisal for the assassination by members of the Resistance, on the previous day, of the Minister for Propaganda of the "Vichy" Government.

The Court of Appeal applied the definition of crimes against humanity used in Barbie, stating that:

> The specific intent necessary to establish a crime against humanity was the intention to take part in the execution of a common plan by committing, in a systematic manner, inhuman acts or persecutions in the name of a State practising a policy of ideological supremacy.

Applying this definition, the Court of Appeal held that Touvier could not be guilty of crimes against humanity since he committed the acts in question in the name of the "Vichy" State, which was not a State practising a policy of ideological supremacy, although it collaborated with Nazi Germany, which clearly did practice such a policy.

The Court of Cassation allowed appeal from the decision of the Court of Appeal, on the grounds that the crimes committed by the accused had been committed at the instigation of a Gestapo officer, and to that extent were linked to Nazi Germany, a State practising a policy of ideological supremacy against persons by virtue of their membership of a racial or religious community. Therefore the crimes could be categorised as crimes against humanity. Touvier was eventually convicted of crimes against humanity by the Cour d'Assises des Yvelines on 20 April 1994.

The definition of crimes against humanity used in Barbie was later affirmed by the ICTY in its *Vukovar Rule 61 Decision* of 3 April 1996 (IT-95-13-R61), to support its finding that crimes against humanity applied equally where the victims of the acts were members of a resistance movement as to where the victims were civilians:

> 29. ... Although according to the terms of Article 5 of the Statute of this Tribunal Y combatants in the traditional sense of the term cannot be victims of a crime

against humanity, this does not apply to individuals who, at one particular point in time, carried out acts of resistance. As the Commission of Experts, established pursuant to Security Council resolution 780, noted, "it seems obvious that Article 5 applies first and foremost to civilians, meaning people who are not combatants. This, however, should not lead to any quick conclusions concerning people who at one particular point in time did bear arms. . . . Information of the overall circumstances is relevant for the interpretation of the provision in a spirit consistent with its purpose." (Doc S/1994/674, para. 78).

This conclusion is supported by case law. In the *Barbie* case, the French Cour de Cassation said that:

"inhumane acts and persecution which, in the name of a State practising a policy of ideological hegemony, were committed systematically or collectively not only against individuals because of their membership in a racial or religious group but also against the adversaries of that policy whatever the form of the opposition" could be considered a crime against humanity. (Cass. Crim. 20 December 1985).

Article 7 of the Statute of the International Criminal Court defines a crime against humanity as any of the enumerated acts committed as part of a widespread of systematic attack directed against any civilian population, with knowledge of the attack. These enumerated acts are murder; extermination; enslavement; deportation or forcible transfer of population; imprisonment or other severe deprivation of physical liberty in violation of fundamental rules of international law; torture; rape, sexual slavery, enforced prostitution, forced pregnancy, enforced sterilization, or any other form of sexual violence of comparable gravity; persecution against any identifiable group or collectively on political, racial, national, ethnic, cultural, religious, gender or other grounds that are universally recognised as impermissible under international law, in connection with any act referred to in this article or any other crime within the jurisdiction of the Court; enforced disappearance of persons; the crime of apartheid; other inhumane acts of a similar character intentionally causing great suffering , or serious injury to body or mental or physical health.

Crimes against Humanity in Article 3 of the Statute of the Tribunal

The Chamber considers that Article 3 of the Statute confers on the Chamber the jurisdiction to prosecute persons for various inhumane acts which constitute crimes against humanity. This category of crimes may be broadly broken down into four essential elements, namely:

(i) the act must be inhumane in nature and character, causing great suffering, or serious injury to body or to mental or physical health;
(ii) the act must be committed as part of a wide spread or systematic attack;
(iii) the act must be committed against members of the civilian population;
(iv) the act must be committed on one or more discriminatory grounds, namely, national, political, ethnic, racial or religious grounds.

The act must be committed as part of a wide spread or systematic attack.

The Chamber considers that it is a prerequisite that the act must be committed as part of a wide spread or systematic attack and not just a random act of violence. The act can be part of a widespread or systematic attack and need not be a part of both.

The concept of "widespread" may be defined as massive, frequent, large scale action, carried out collectively with considerable seriousness and directed against a multiplicity of victims. The concept of "systematic" may be defined as thoroughly organised and following a regular pattern on the basis of a common policy involving substantial public or private resources. There is no requirement that this policy must be adopted formally as the policy of a state. There must however be some kind of preconceived plan or policy.

The concept of "attack" maybe defined as a unlawful act of the kind enumerated in Article 3(a) to (I) of the Statute, like murder, extermination, enslavement *etc*. An attack may also be non violent in nature, like imposing a system of apartheid, which is declared a crime against humanity in Article 1 of the Apartheid Convention of 1973, or exerting pressure on the population to act in a particular manner, may come under the purview of an attack, if orchestrated on a massive scale or in a systematic manner.

The act must be directed against the civilian population

The Chamber considers that an act must be directed against the civilian population if it is to constitute a crime against humanity. Members of the civilian population are people who are not taking any active part in the hostilities, including members of the armed forces who laid down their arms and those persons placed *hors de combat* by sickness, wounds, detention or any other cause. Where there are certain individuals within the civilian population who do not come within the definition of civilians , this does not deprive the population of its civilian character.

The act must be committed on discriminatory grounds

The Statute stipulates that inhumane acts committed against the civilian population must be committed on "national, political, ethnic, racial or religious grounds." Discrimination on the basis of a person's political ideology satisfies the requirement of "political" grounds as envisaged in Article 3 of the Statute. For definitions on national, ethnic, racial or religious grounds . . . .

Inhumane acts committed against persons not falling within any one of the discriminatory categories could constitute crimes against humanity if the perpetrator's intention was to further his attacks on the group discriminated against on one of the grounds mentioned in Article 3 of the Statute. The perpetrator must have the requisite intent for the commission of crimes against humanity.

The enumerated acts

Article 3 of the Statute sets out various acts that constitute crimes against humanity, namely: murder; extermination; enslavement; deportation; imprisonment; torture; rape; persecution on political, racial and religious grounds; and; other inhumane acts. Although the category of acts that constitute crimes against humanity are set out in Article 3, this category is not exhaustive. Any act which is inhumane in nature and character may constitute a crime against humanity, provided the other elements are met. This is evident in (i) which caters for all other inhumane acts not stipulated in (a) to (h) of Article 3.

The Chamber notes that the accused is indicted for murder, extermination, torture, rape and other acts that constitute inhumane acts. The Chamber in interpreting Article 3 of the Statute, shall focus its discussion on these acts only.

. . . .

Rape

Considering the extent to which rape constitute crimes against humanity, pursuant to Article 3(g) of the Statute, the Chamber must define rape, as there is no commonly accepted definition of this term in international law. While rape has been defined in certain national jurisdictions as non-consensual intercourse, variations on the act of rape may include acts which involve the insertion of objects and/or the use of bodily orifices not considered to be intrinsically sexual.

The Chamber considers that rape is a form of aggression and that the central elements of the crime of rape cannot be captured in a mechanical description of objects and body parts. The Convention against Torture and Other Cruel, Inhuman and Degrading Treatment or Punishment does not catalogue specific acts in its definition of torture, focusing rather on the conceptual frame work of state sanctioned violence. This approach is more useful in international law. Like torture, rape is used for such purposes as intimidation, degradation, humiliation, discrimination, punishment, control or destruction of a person. Like torture, rape is a violation of personal dignity, and rape in fact constitutes torture when inflicted by or at the instigation of or with the consent or acquiescence of a public official or other person acting in an official capacity.

The Chamber defines rape as a physical invasion of a sexual nature, committed on a person under circumstances which are coercive. Sexual violence which includes rape, is considered to be any act of a sexual nature which is committed on a person under circumstances which are coercive. This act must be committed:

(a) as part of a wide spread or systematic attack;
(b) on a civilian population;
(c) on certain catalogued discriminatory grounds, namely: national, ethnic, political, racial, or religious grounds.

. . . .

[Legal Findings]

7.7. Count 13 (rape) and Count 14 (other inhumane acts) - Crimes against Humanity

In the light of its factual findings with regard to the allegations of sexual violence set forth in paragraphs 12A and 12B of the Indictment, the Tribunal considers the criminal responsibility of the Accused on Count 13, crimes against humanity (rape), punishable by Article 3(g) of the Statute of the Tribunal and Count 14, crimes against humanity (other inhumane acts), punishable by Article 3(i) of the Statute.

Chapter 10. Sexual Violence

In considering the extent to which acts of sexual violence constitute crimes against humanity under Article 3(g) of its Statute, the Tribunal must define rape, as there is no commonly accepted definition of the term in international law. The Tribunal notes that many of the witnesses have used the term "rape" in their testimony. At times, the Prosecution and the Defence have also tried to elicit an explicit description of what happened in physical terms, to document what the witnesses mean by the term "rape". The Tribunal notes that while rape has been historically defined in national jurisdictions as non-consensual sexual intercourse, variations on the form of rape may include acts which involve the insertion of objects and/or the use of bodily orifices not considered to be intrinsically sexual. An act such as that described by Witness KK in her testimony - the Interahamwes thrusting a piece of wood into the sexual organs of a woman as she lay dying - constitutes rape in the Tribunal's view.

The Tribunal considers that rape is a form of aggression and that the central elements of the crime of rape cannot be captured in a mechanical description of objects and body parts. The Tribunal also notes the cultural sensitivities involved in public discussion of intimate matters and recalls the painful reluctance and inability of witnesses to disclose graphic anatomical details of sexual violence they endured. The United Nations Convention Against Torture and Other Cruel, Inhuman and Degrading Treatment or Punishment does not catalogue specific acts in its definition of torture, focusing rather on the conceptual framework of state-sanctioned violence. The Tribunal finds this approach more useful in the context of international law. Like torture, rape is used for such purposes as intimidation, degradation, humiliation, discrimination, punishment, control or destruction of a person. Like torture, rape is a violation of personal dignity, and rape in fact constitutes torture when it is inflicted by or at the instigation of or with the consent or acquiescence of a public official or other person acting in an official capacity.

The Tribunal defines rape as a physical invasion of a sexual nature, committed on a person under circumstances which are coercive. The Tribunal considers sexual violence, which includes rape, as any act of a sexual nature which is committed on a person under circumstances which are coercive. Sexual violence is not limited to physical invasion of the human body and may include acts which do not involve penetration or even physical contact. The incident described by Witness KK in which the Accused ordered the Interahamwe to undress a student and force her to do gymnastics naked in the public courtyard of the bureau communal, in front of a crowd, constitutes sexual violence. The Tribunal notes in this context that coercive circumstances need not be evidenced by a show of physical force. Threats, intimidation, extortion and other forms of duress which prey on fear or desperation may constitute coercion, and coercion may be inherent in certain circumstances, such as armed conflict or the military presence of Interahamwe among refugee Tutsi women at the bureau communal. Sexual violence falls within the scope of "other inhumane acts", set forth Article 3(i) of the Tribunal's Statute, "outrages upon personal dignity," set forth in Article 4(e) of the Statute, and "serious bodily or mental harm," set forth in Article 2(2)(b) of the Statute.

The Tribunal notes that as set forth by the Prosecution, Counts 13-15 are drawn on the basis of acts as described in paragraphs 12(A) and 12(B) of the Indictment. The allegations in these paragraphs of the Indictment are limited to events which took place "on or near the bureau communal premises." Many of the beatings, rapes and murders established by the evidence presented took place away from the bureau communal premises, and therefore the Tribunal does not make any legal findings with respect to these incidents pursuant to Counts 13, 14 and 15.

The Tribunal also notes that on the basis of acts described in paragraphs 12(A) and 12(B), the Accused is charged only pursuant to Article 3(g) (rape) and 3(i) (other inhumane acts) of its Statute, but not Article 3(a) (murder) or Article 3(f) (torture). Similarly, on the basis of acts described in paragraphs 12(A) and 12(B), the Accused is charged only pursuant to Article 4(e) (outrages upon personal dignity) of its Statute, and not Article 4(a) (violence to life, health and physical or mental well-being of persons, in particular murder as well as cruel treatment such as torture, mutilation or any form of corporal punishment). As these paragraphs are not referenced elsewhere in the Indictment in connection with these other relevant Articles of the Statute of the Tribunal, the Tribunal concludes that the Accused has not been charged with the beatings and killings which have been established as Crimes Against Humanity or Violations of Article 3 Common to the Geneva Conventions. The Tribunal notes, however, that paragraphs 12(A) and 12(B) are referenced in Counts 1-3, Genocide and it considers the beatings and killings, as well as sexual violence, in connection with those counts.

The Tribunal has found that the Accused had reason to know and in fact knew that acts of sexual violence were occurring on or near the premises of the bureau communal and that he took no measures to prevent these acts or punish the perpetrators of them. The Tribunal notes that it is only in consideration of Counts 13, 14 and 15 that the Accused is charged with individual criminal responsibility under Section 6(3) of its Statute. As set forth in the Indictment, under Article 6(3) "an individual is criminally responsible as a superior for the acts of a subordinate if he or she knew or had reason to know that the subordinate was about to commit such acts or had done so and the superior failed to take the necessary and reasonable measures to prevent such acts or punish the perpetrators thereof." Although the evidence supports a finding that a superior/subordinate relationship existed between the Accused and the Interahamwe who were at the bureau communal, the Tribunal notes that there is no allegation in the Indictment that the Interahamwe, who are referred to as "armed local militia," were subordinates of the Accused. This relationship is a fundamental element of the criminal offence set forth in Article 6(3). The amendment of the Indictment with additional charges pursuant to Article 6(3) could arguably be interpreted as implying an allegation of the command responsibility required by Article 6(3). In fairness to the Accused, the Tribunal will not make this inference. Therefore, the Tribunal finds that it cannot consider the criminal responsibility of the Accused under Article 6(3).

The Tribunal finds, under Article 6(1) of its Statute, that the Accused, by his own words, specifically ordered, instigated, aided and abetted the following acts of sexual violence:

(i) the multiple acts of rape of ten girls and women, including Witness JJ, by numerous Interahamwe in the cultural center of the bureau communal; (ii) the rape of Witness OO by an Interahamwe named Antoine in a field near the bureau communal; (iii) the forced undressing and public marching of Chantal naked at the bureau communal.

Chapter 10. Sexual Violence

The Tribunal finds, under Article 6(1) of its Statute, that the Accused aided and abetted the following acts of sexual violence, by allowing them to take place on or near the premises of the bureau communal, while he was present on the premises in respect of (i) and in his presence in respect of (ii) and (iii), and by facilitating the commission of these acts through his words of encouragement in other acts of sexual violence, which, by virtue of his authority, sent a clear signal of official tolerance for sexual violence, without which these acts would not have taken place:

> (i) the multiple acts of rape of fifteen girls and women, including Witness JJ, by numerous Interahamwe in the cultural center of the bureau communal; (ii) the rape of a woman by Interahamwe in between two buildings of the bureau communal, witnessed by Witness NN; (iii) the forced undressing of the wife of Tharcisse after making her sit in the mud outside the bureau communal, as witnessed by Witness KK;

The Tribunal finds, under Article 6(1) of its Statute, that the Accused, having had reason to know that sexual violence was occurring, aided and abetted the following acts of sexual violence, by allowing them to take place on or near the premises of the bureau communal and by facilitating the commission of such sexual violence through his words of encouragement in other acts of sexual violence which, by virtue of his authority, sent a clear signal of official tolerance for sexual violence, without which these acts would not have taken place:

> (i) the rape of Witness JJ by an Interahamwe who took her from outside the bureau communal and raped her in a nearby forest; (ii) the rape of the younger sister of Witness NN by an Interahamwe at the bureau communal; (iii) the multiple rapes of Alexia, wife of Ntereye, and her two nieces Louise and Nishimwe by Interahamwe near the bureau communal; (iv) the forced undressing of Alexia, wife of Ntereye, and her two nieces Louise and Nishimwe, and the forcing of the women to perform exercises naked in public near the bureau communal.

The Tribunal has established that a widespread and systematic attack against the civilian ethnic population of Tutsis took place in Taba, and more generally in Rwanda, between April 7 and the end of June, 1994. The Tribunal finds that the rape and other inhumane acts which took place on or near the bureau communal premises of Taba were committed as part of this attack.

COUNT 13

The Accused is judged criminally responsible under Article 3(g) of the Statute for the following incidents of rape:

> (i) the rape of Witness JJ by an Interahamwe who took her from outside the bureau communal and raped her in a nearby forest; (ii) the multiple acts of rape of fifteen girls and women, including Witness JJ, by numerous Interahamwe in

the cultural center of the bureau communal; (iii) the multiple acts of rape of ten girls and women, including Witness JJ, by numerous Interahamwe in the cultural center of the bureau communal; (iv) the rape of Witness OO by an Interahamwe named Antoine in a field near the bureau communal; (v) the rape of a woman by Interahamwe in between two buildings of the bureau communal, witnessed by Witness NN; (vi) the rape of the younger sister of Witness NN by an Interahamwe at the bureau communal; (vii) the multiple rapes of Alexia, wife of Ntereye, and her two nieces Louise and Nishimwe by Interahamwe near the bureau communal.

COUNT 14

The Accused is judged criminally responsible under Article 3(i) of the Statute for the following other inhumane acts:

(i) the forced undressing of the wife of Tharcisse outside the bureau communal, after making her sit in the mud, as witnessed by Witness KK; (ii) the forced undressing and public marching of Chantal naked at the bureau communal; (iii) the forced undressing of Alexia, wife of Ntereye, and her two nieces Louise and Nishimwe, and the forcing of the women to perform exercises naked in public near the bureau communal.

. . . .

❖ ❖ ❖

X. & Y. v. The Netherlands
European Court of Human Rights
91 Eur. Ct. H.R. (ser. A) (1985)
8 E.H.R.R. 235 (1986)

[*Reproduced in* Chapter 4]

❖ ❖ ❖

Questions & Comments

(1)   As noted earlier in regard to forced disappearances (Chap. 9), some human rights violations that are not crimes against humanity because they are not part of a widespread or systemic attack on a civilian population may still entail international criminal liability for the state as well as individual culpability for the individual perpetrator. Does *X.& Y. v. The Netherlands* undercut this claim because the European Court only declared that an investigation was required?

(2)   In *The Prosecutor v. Delalic and Delic (The Celebici Case)*, Case No. IT-96-21-T, Int'l Crim. Trib.-Yugo., Judgment (16 November 1998), the Trial Chamber stated that "there can be no question that acts of rape may constitute torture under customary law". What kinds of rape or other sexual assault would not rise to the level of torture? Consider

the European Court of Human Rights' analysis of the difference between torture and inhuman or degrading treatment in *Ireland v. United Kingdom*: "Torture constitutes an aggravated and deliberate form of cruel, inhuman or degrading treatment or punishment." 25 Eur. Ct. H.R. (ser. A) at § 167 (1978) (quoting UNGA Res. No. 3452). Is there any form of sexual assault that is *not* an aggravated and deliberate form of degrading treatment?

(2) Other international cases addressing sexual assault include *Loayza Tamayo Case*, Inter-Am. Ct. H.R. (Ser. C) (1998); *Rivas Quintanilla v. El Salvador*, Case 10.772, Rep. No. 6/94, Inter-Am. Cm. H.R., OEA/Ser.L/V/II.85 Doc. 9 rev. at 181 (1994) (state duty to investigate, identify, prosecute, and punish state actors responsible for rape of child).

PART FOUR: CRIMINAL PROCEDURE

Treaties and Statutes

Universal Declaration of Human Rights

Article 9.

No one shall be subjected to arbitrary arrest, detention or exile.

Article 10.

Everyone is entitled in full equality to a fair and public hearing by an independent and impartial tribunal, in the determination of his rights and obligations and of any criminal charge against him.

Article 11.

(1) Everyone charged with a penal offence has the right to be presumed innocent until proved guilty according to law in a public trial at which he has had all the guarantees necessary for his defence.

(2) No one shall be held guilty of any penal offence on account of any act or omission which did not constitute a penal offence, under national or international law, at the time when it was committed. Nor shall a heavier penalty be imposed than the one that was applicable at the time the penal offence was committed.

International Covenant on Civil and Political Rights

Article 9

1. Everyone has the right to liberty and security of person. No one shall be subjected to arbitrary arrest or detention. No one shall be deprived of his liberty except on such grounds and in accordance with such procedure as are established by law.

2. Anyone who is arrested shall be informed, at the time of arrest, of the reasons for his arrest and shall be promptly informed of any charges against him.

3. Anyone arrested or detained on a criminal charge shall be brought promptly before a judge or other officer authorized by law to exercise judicial power and shall be entitled to trial within a reasonable time or to release. It shall not be the general rule that persons awaiting trial shall be detained in custody, but release may be subject to guarantees to appear for trial, at any other stage of the judicial proceedings, and, should occasion arise, for execution of the judgement.

4. Anyone who is deprived of his liberty by arrest or detention shall be entitled to take proceedings before a court, in order that that court may decide without delay on the lawfulness of his detention and order his release if the detention is not lawful.

5. Anyone who has been the victim of unlawful arrest or detention shall have an enforceable right to compensation.

Article 14

1. All persons shall be equal before the courts and tribunals. In the determination of any criminal charge against him, or of his rights and obligations in a suit at law, everyone shall be entitled to a fair and public hearing by a competent, independent and impartial tribunal established by law. The Press and the public may be excluded from all or part of a trial for reasons of morals, public order (*ordre public*) or national security in a democratic society, or when the interest of the private lives of the parties so requires, or to the extent strictly necessary in the opinion of the court in special circumstances where publicity would prejudice the interests of justice; but any judgement rendered in a criminal case or in a suit at law shall be made public except where the interest of juvenile persons otherwise requires or the proceedings concern matrimonial disputes or the guardianship of children.

2. Everyone charged with a criminal offence shall have the right to be presumed innocent until proved guilty according to law.

3. In the determination of any criminal charge against him, everyone shall be entitled to the following minimum guarantees, in full equality:

(a) To be informed promptly and in detail in a language which he understands of the nature and cause of the charge against him;

(b) To have adequate time and facilities for the preparation of his defence and to communicate with counsel of his own choosing;

(c) To be tried without undue delay;

(d) To be tried in his presence, and to defend himself in person or through legal assistance of his own choosing; to be informed, if he does not have legal assistance, of this right; and to have legal assistance assigned to him, in any case where the interests of justice so require, and without payment by him in any such case if he does not have sufficient means to pay for it;

(e) To examine, or have examined the witnesses against him and to obtain the attendance and examination of witnesses on his behalf under the same conditions as witnesses against him;

(f) To have the free assistance of an interpreter if he cannot understand or speak the language used in court;

(g) Not to be compelled to testify against himself or to confess guilt.

4. In the case of juvenile persons, the procedure shall be such as will take account of their age and the desirability of promoting their rehabilitation.

5. Everyone convicted of a crime shall have the right to his conviction and sentence being reviewed by a higher tribunal according to law.

6. When a person has by a final decision been convicted of a criminal offence and when subsequently his conviction has been reversed or he has been pardoned on the ground that a new or newly discovered fact shows conclusively that there has been a miscarriage of justice, the person who has suffered punishment as a result of such conviction shall be compensated according to law, unless it is proved that the non-disclosure of the unknown fact in time is wholly or partly attributable to him.

7. No one shall be liable to be tried or punished again for an offence for which he has already been finally convicted or acquitted in accordance with the law and penal procedure of each country.

Article 15

1. No one shall be held guilty of any criminal offence on account of any act or omission which did not constitute a criminal offence, under national or international law, at the time when it was committed. Nor shall a heavier penalty be imposed than the one that was applicable at the time when the criminal offence was committed. If, subsequent to the commission of the offence, provision is made by law for the imposition of a lighter penalty, the offender shall benefit thereby.

2. Nothing in this article shall prejudice the trial and punishment of any person for any act or omission which, at the time when it was committed was criminal according to the general principles of law recognized by the community of nations.

European Convention on Human Rights

Article 5

1. Everyone has the right to liberty and security of person. No one shall be deprived of his liberty save in the following cases and in accordance with a procedure prescribed by law:

(a) the lawful detention of a person after conviction by a competent court;

(b) the lawful arrest or detention of a person for non-compliance with the lawful order of a court or in order to secure the fulfilment of any obligation prescribed by law;

(c) the lawful arrest or detention of a person effected for the purpose of bringing him before the competent legal authority of reasonable suspicion of having committed and offence or when it is reasonably considered necessary to prevent his committing an offence or fleeing after having done so;

(d) the detention of a minor by lawful order for the purpose of educational supervision or his lawful detention for the purpose of bringing him before the competent legal authority;

(e) the lawful detention of persons for the prevention of the spreading of infectious diseases, of persons of unsound mind, alcoholics or drug addicts, or vagrants;

(f) the lawful arrest or detention of a person to prevent his effecting an unauthorized entry into the country or of a person against whom action is being taken with a view to deportation or extradition.

2. Everyone who is arrested shall be informed promptly, in a language which he understands, of the reasons for his arrest and the charge against him.

3. Everyone arrested or detained in accordance with the provisions of paragraph 1(c) of this article shall be brought promptly before a judge or other officer authorized by law to exercise judicial power and shall be entitled to trial within a reasonable time or to release pending trial. Release may be conditioned by guarantees to appear for trial.

4. Everyone who is deprived of his liberty by arrest or detention shall be entitled to take proceedings by which the lawfulness of his detention shall be decided speedily by a court and his release ordered if the detention is not lawful.

5. Everyone who has been the victim of arrest or detention in contravention of the provisions of this article shall have an enforceable right to compensation.

Article 6

1. In the determination of his civil rights and obligations or of any criminal charge against him, everyone is entitled to a fair and public hearing within a reasonable time by an independent and impartial tribunal established by law. Judgement shall be pronounced publicly by the press and public may be excluded from all or part of the trial in the interest of morals, public order or national security in a democratic society, where the interests of juveniles or the protection of the private life of the parties so require, or the extent strictly necessary in the opinion of the court in special circumstances where publicity would prejudice the interests of justice.

2. Everyone charged with a criminal offence shall be presumed innocent until proved guilty according to law.

3. Everyone charged with a criminal offence has the following minimum rights:

(a) to be informed promptly, in a language which he understands and in detail, of the nature and cause of the accusation against him;

(b) to have adequate time and the facilities for the preparation of his defence;

(c) to defend himself in person or through legal assistance of his own choosing or, if he has not sufficient means to pay for legal assistance, to be given it free when the interests of justice so require;

(d) to examine or have examined witnesses against him and to obtain the attendance and examination of witnesses on his behalf under the same conditions as witnesses against him;

(e) to have the free assistance of an interpreter if he cannot understand or speak the language used in court.

Article 7

1. No one shall be held guilty of any criminal offence on account of any act or omission which did not constitute a criminal offence under national or international law at the time when it was committed. Nor shall a heavier penalty be imposed than the one that was applicable at the time the criminal offence was committed.

2. This article shall not prejudice the trial and punishment of any person for any act or omission which, at the time when it was committed, was criminal according the general principles of law recognized by civilized nations.

European Convention on Human Rights, Protocol No. 7

Article 2

1. Everyone convicted of a criminal offence by a tribunal shall have the right to have conviction or sentence reviewed by a higher tribunal. The exercise of this right, including the grounds on which it may be exercised, shall be governed by law.

2. This right may be subject to exceptions in regard to offences of a minor character, as prescribed by law, or in cases in which the person concerned was tried in the first instance by the highest tribunal or was convicted following an appeal against acquittal.

Article 4

1. No one shall be liable to be tried or punished again in criminal proceedings under the jurisdiction of the same State for an offence for which he has already been finally acquitted or convicted in accordance with the law and penal procedure of the State.

2. The provisions of the preceding paragraph shall not prevent the re-opening of the case in accordance with the law and penal procedure of the State concerned, if there is evidence of new or newly discovered facts, or if there has been a fundamental defect in the previous proceedings, which could affect the outcome of the case.

3. No derogation from this Article shall be made under Article 15 of the Convention.

American Declaration on the Rights and Duties of Man

Article XVIII. Right to a fair trial.

Every person may resort to the courts to ensure respect for his legal rights. There should likewise be available to him a simple, brief procedure whereby the courts will protect him from acts of authority that, to his prejudice, violate any fundamental constitutional rights.

Article XXVI. Right to due process of law.

Every accused person is presumed to be innocent until proved guilty.

Every person accused of an offense has the right to be given an impartial and public hearing, and to be tried by courts previously established in accordance with pre-existing laws, and not to receive cruel, infamous or unusual punishment.

American Convention on Human Rights

Article 7. RIGHT TO PERSONAL LIBERTY.

1. Every person has the right to personal liberty and security.

2. No one shall be deprived of his physical liberty except for the reasons and under the conditions established beforehand by the constitution of the State Party concerned or by a law established pursuant thereto.

3. No one shall be subject to arbitrary arrest or imprisonment.

4. Anyone who is detained shall be informed of the reasons for his detention and shall be promptly notified of the charge or charges against him.

5. Any person detained shall be brought promptly before a judge or other officer authorized by law to exercise judicial power and shall be entitled to trial within a reasonable time or to be released without prejudice to the continuation of the proceedings. His release may be subject to guarantees to assure his appearance for trial.

6. Anyone who is deprived of his liberty shall be entitled to recourse to a competent court, in order that the court may decide without delay on the lawfulness of his arrest or detention and order his release if the arrest or detention is unlawful. In States Parties

whose laws provide that anyone who believes himself to be threatened with deprivation of his liberty is entitled to recourse to a competent court in order that it may decide on the lawfulness of such threat, this remedy may not be restricted or abolished. The interested party or another person in his behalf is entitled to seek these remedies.

7. No one shall be detained for debt. This principle shall not limit the orders of a competent judicial authority issued for nonfulfillment of duties of support.

Article 8. RIGHT TO A FAIR TRIAL.

1. Every person has the right to a hearing, with due guarantees and within a reasonable time, by a competent, independent, and impartial tribunal, previously established by law, in the substantiation of any accusation of a criminal nature made against him or for the determination of his rights and obligations of a civil, labor, fiscal, or any other nature.

2. Every person accused of a criminal offense has the right to be presumed innocent so long as his guilt has not been proven according to law. During the proceedings, every person is entitled, with full equality, to the following minimum guarantees:

   a.   The right of the accused to be assisted without charge by a translator or interpreter, if he does not understand or does not speak the language of the tribunal or court;

   b.   Prior notification in detail to the accused of the charges against him;

   c.   Adequate time and means for the preparation of his defense;

   d.   The right of the accused to defend himself personally or to be assisted by legal counsel of his own choosing. and to communicate freely and privately with his counsel;

   e.   The inalienable right to be assisted by counsel provided by the State, paid or not as the domestic law provides, if the accused does not defend himself personally or engage his own counsel within the time period established by law;

   f.   The right of the defense to examine witnesses present in the court and to obtain the appearance, as witnesses, of experts or other persons who may throw light on the facts;

   g.   The right not to be compelled to be a witness against himself or to plead guilty; and

   h.   The right to appeal the judgment to a higher court.

3. A confession of guilt by the accused shall be valid only if it is made without coercion of any kind.

4. An accused person acquitted by a nonappealable judgment shall not be subjected to a new trial for the same cause.

5. Criminal proceedings shall be public, except insofar as may be necessary to protect the interests of justice.

Article 9. FREEDOM FROM "EX POST FACTO" LAWS.

No one shall be convicted of any act or omission that did not constitute a criminal offense, under the applicable law, at the time it was committed. A heavier penalty shall not be imposed than the one that was applicable at the time the criminal offense was committed. If subsequent to the commission of the offense the law provides for the imposition of a lighter punishment, the guilty person shall benefit therefrom.

African [Banjul] Charter on Human and Peoples' Rights

Article 6

Every individual shall have the right to liberty and to the security of his person. No one may be deprived of his freedom except for reasons and conditions previously laid down by law. In particular, no one may be arbitrarily arrested or detained.

Article 7

1. Every individual shall have the right to have his cause heard. This comprises: (a) the right to an appeal to competent national organs against acts of violating his fundamental rights as recognized and guaranteed by conventions, laws, regulations and customs in force; (b) the right to be presumed innocent until proved guilty by a competent court or tribunal; (c) the right to defence, including the right to be defended by counsel of his choice; (d) the right to be tried within a reasonable time by an impartial court or tribunal.

2. No one may be condemned for an act or omission which did not constitute a legally punishable offence at the time it was committed. No penalty may be inflicted for an offence for which no provision was made at the time it was committed. Punishment is personal and can be imposed only on the offender.

Convention on Human Rights and Fundamental Freedoms of the Commonwealth of Independent States

Article 5

1. Everyone shall have the right to liberty and security of person. No one shall be deprived of his liberty save in the following cases and in accordance with a procedure established by national legislation;

    a. the lawful detention of a person after conviction by a competent court;

b. the lawful arrest or detention of a person;

c. the lawful detention of a minor for the purpose of referring his case for investigation, sentencing, or trial.

2. Everyone who is arrested shall be informed, at the time of his arrest, in a language he understands, of the reasons for his arrest.

3. Everyone who is deprived of his liberty by arrest or detention, in accordance with national legislation, shall be entitled to have the lawfulness of his arrest or detention examined by a court.

4. Everyone who is deprived of his liberty shall be entitled to humane treatment and to respect for his dignity as a human being.

Persons who have been subjected to unlawful arrest or detention shall be entitled, in accordance with national legislation, to compensation for the damage caused.

Article 6

1. All persons shall be equal before the judicial system.

In the determination of any charge against him, everyone shall be entitled to a fair and public hearing within a reasonable time by an independent and impartial court. The decisions of the court or the sentence shall be pronounced publicly, but all or part of the trial may take place *in camera* for reasons of public order or state secrecy or where the interests of juveniles or the protection of the private life of the parties so require.

2. Everyone charged with a criminal offence shall be presumed innocent until proved guilty according to law.

3. Everyone charged with a criminal offence shall have the following minimum rights:

a. to be informed promptly and in detail, in a language which he understands, of the nature and cause of the accusation against him;

b. to have adequate time and facilities for the preparation of his defence;

c. to defend him in person or through legal assistance of his own choosing or to have legal assistance assigned to him whenever the interests of justice so require, as well as to be provided with legal assistance free of charge in cases specified in national legislation;

d. to make applications to the court concerning the examination of witnesses, the carrying out of investigations, the obtaining of documents, the commissioning of expert appraisals and other procedural acts;

e. to have the free assistance of an interpreter if he cannot understand or speak the language used in court;

f. not to be forced to testify against himself or to plead guilty.

Article 7

1. No one shall be held liable for an act which did not constitute an offence under national legislation or international law at the time when it was committed. Nor shall a heavier penalty by imposed than the one that was applicable at the time the offence was committed. If, after an offence is committed, a law establishes a lesser punishment for it or eliminates liability for it, the new law shall be applicable.

2. No one shall be convicted or punished a second time for an offence for which he has already been convicted or punished in accordance with national legislation. Every convicted person shall be entitled, in accordance with the law, to have the judgment of the court reviewed by a higher judicial body as well as apply for a pardon or request a lighter sentence.

Arab Charter on Human Rights

Article 6

There can be no crime, or punishment, except for what is stipulated in law. Nor can there be any punishment for any acts committed previous to the enactment of that law. The accused benefits from a subsequent law, if it is in his interest.

Article 7

The accused is presumed innocent until proven guilty in a lawful trial where defence rights are guaranteed.

Article 8

Every person has the right to liberty and security of person. No one shall be subjected to arrest or detention or stopped without legal basis and must be brought before the judiciary without delay.

Article 9

Everyone is equal before the judiciary, and the right to judicial recourse is guaranteed for every person, on the territory of a State.

Article 16

No person can be tried twice for the same crime. Anyone against whom such a measure is taken has the right to challenge its legality and request his release. Anyone who is the victim of an illegal arrest or detention has the right to compensation.

Convention on the Rights of the Child

Article 40

1. States Parties recognize the right of every child alleged as, accused of, or recognized as having infringed the penal law to be treated in a manner consistent with the promotion of the child's sense of dignity and worth, which reinforces the child's respect for the human rights and fundamental freedoms of others and which takes into account the child's age and the desirability of promoting the child's reintegration and the child's assuming a constructive role in society.

2. To this end, and having regard to the relevant provisions of international instruments, States Parties shall, in particular, ensure that:

(a) No child shall be alleged as, be accused of, or recognized as having infringed the penal law by reason of acts or omissions that were not prohibited by national or international law at the time they were committed;

(b) Every child alleged as or accused of having infringed the penal law has at least the following guarantees:

(i) To be presumed innocent until proven guilty according to law;

(ii) To be informed promptly and directly of the charges against him or her, and, if appropriate, through his or her parents or legal guardians, and to have legal or other appropriate assistance in the preparation and presentation of his or her defence;

(iii) To have the matter determined without delay by a competent, independent and impartial authority or judicial body in a fair hearing according to law, in the presence of legal or other appropriate assistance and, unless it is considered not to be in the best interest of the child, in particular, taking into account his or her age or situation, his or her parents or legal guardians;

(iv) Not to be compelled to give testimony or to confess guilt; to examine or have examined adverse witnesses and to obtain the participation and examination of witnesses on his or her behalf under conditions of equality;

(v) If considered to have infringed the penal law, to have this decision and any measures imposed in consequence thereof reviewed by a higher competent, independent and impartial authority or judicial body according to law;

(vi) To have the free assistance of an interpreter if the child cannot understand or speak the language used;

(vii) To have his or her privacy fully respected at all stages of the proceedings.

Charter of the International Military Tribunal

Article 16.

In order to ensure fair trial for the Defendants, the following procedure shall be followed:

(a) The Indictment shall include full particulars specifying in detail the charges against the Defendants. A copy of the Indictment and of all the documents lodged with the Indictment, translated into a language which he understands, shall be furnished to the Defendant at reasonable time before the Trial.

(b) During any preliminary examination or trial of a Defendant he will have the right to give any explanation relevant to the charges made against him.

(c) A preliminary examination of a Defendant and his Trial shall be conducted in, or translated into, a language which the Defendant understands.

(d) A Defendant shall have the right to conduct his own defense before the Tribunal or to have the assistance of Counsel.

(e) A Defendant shall have the right through himself or through his Counsel to present evidence at the Trial in support of his defense, and to cross-examine any witness called by the Prosecution.

Article 26.

The judgment of the Tribunal as to the guilt or the innocence of any Defendant shall give the reasons on which it is based, and shall be final and not subject to review.

Statute of the International Criminal Tribunal for Rwanda

Article 9
Non bis in idem

1. No person shall be tried before a national court for acts constituting serious violations of international humanitarian law under the present Statute, for which he or she has already been tried by the International Tribunal for Rwanda.

2. A person who has been tried by a national court for acts constituting serious violations of international humanitarian law may be subsequently tried by the International Tribunal for Rwanda only if:

(a) The act for which he or she was tried was characterized as an ordinary crime; or

(b) The national court proceedings were not impartial or independent, were designed to shield the accused from international criminal responsibility, or the case was not diligently prosecuted.

3. In considering the penalty to be imposed on a person convicted of a crime under the present Statute, the International Tribunal for Rwanda shall take into account the extent to which any penalty imposed by a national court on the same person for the same act has already been served.

Article 20
Rights of the accused

1. All persons shall be equal before the International Tribunal for Rwanda.

2. In the determination of charges against him or her, the accused shall be entitled to a fair and public hearing, subject to article 21 of the Statute.

3. The accused shall be presumed innocent until proved guilty according to the provisions of the present Statute.

4. In the determination of any charge against the accused pursuant to the present Statute, the accused shall be entitled to the following minimum guarantees, in full equality:

(a) To be informed promptly and in detail in a language which he or she understands of the nature and cause of the charge against him or her;
(b) To have adequate time and facilities for the preparation of his or her defence and to communicate with counsel of his or her own choosing;
(c) To be tried without undue delay;
(d) To be tried in his or her presence, and to defend himself or herself in person or through legal assistance of his or her own choosing; to be informed, if he or she does not have legal assistance, of this right; and to have legal assistance assigned to him or her, in any case where the interests of justice so require, and without payment by him or her in any such case if he or she does not have sufficient means to pay for it;
(e) To examine, or have examined, the witnesses against him or her and to obtain the attendance and examination of witnesses on his or her behalf under the same conditions as witnesses against him or her;
(f) To have the free assistance of an interpreter if he or she cannot understand or speak the language used in the International Tribunal for Rwanda;
(g) Not to be compelled to testify against himself or herself or to confess guilt.

Statute of the International Tribunal [For the Former Yugoslavia]

Article 10
Non-bis-in-idem

1. No person shall be tried before a national court for acts constituting serious violations of international humanitarian law under the present Statute, for which he or she has already been tried by the International Tribunal.

2. A person who has been tried by a national court for acts constituting serious violations of international humanitarian law may be subsequently tried by the International Tribunal only if:

(a) the act for which he or she was tried was characterized as an ordinary crime; or
(b) the national court proceedings were not impartial or independent, were designed to shield the accused from international criminal responsibility, or the case was not diligently prosecuted.

3. In considering the penalty to be imposed on a person convicted of a crime under the present Statute, the International Tribunal shall take into account the extent to which any penalty imposed by a national court on the same person for the same act has already been served.

Article 21
Rights of the accused

1. All persons shall be equal before the International Tribunal.

2. In the determination of charges against him, the accused shall be entitled to a fair and public hearing, subject to article 22 of the Statute.

3. The accused shall be presumed innocent until proved guilty according to the provisions of the present Statute.

4. In the determination of any charge against the accused pursuant to the present Statute, the accused shall be entitled to the following minimum guarantees, in full equality:

(a) to be informed promptly and in detail in a language which he understands of the nature and cause of the charge against him;
(b) to have adequate time and facilities for the preparation of his defence and to communicate with counsel of his own choosing;
(c) to be tried without undue delay;
(d) to be tried in his presence, and to defend himself in person or through legal assistance of his own choosing; to be informed, if he does not have legal assistance, of this right; and to have legal assistance assigned to him, in any case where the interests of justice so require, and without payment by him in any such case if he does not have sufficient means to pay for it;
(e) to examine, or have examined, the witnesses against him and to obtain the attendance and examination of witnesses on his behalf under the same conditions as witnesses against him;
(f) to have the free assistance of an interpreter if he cannot understand or speak the language used in the International Tribunal;
(g) not to be compelled to testify against himself or to confess guilt.

Statute of the International Criminal Court

Article 20
Non bis in idem

1. Except as provided in this Statute, no person shall be tried before the Court with respect to conduct which formed the basis of crimes for which the person has been convicted or acquitted by the Court.

2. No person shall be tried before another court for a crime referred to in article 5 for which that person has already been convicted or acquitted by the Court.

3. No person who has been tried by another court for conduct also proscribed under articles 6, 7 or 8 shall be tried by the Court with respect to the same conduct unless the proceedings in the other court:

 (a) Were for the purpose of shielding the person concerned from criminal responsibility for crimes within the jurisdiction of the Court; or
 (b) Otherwise were not conducted independently or impartially in accordance with the norms of due process recognized by international law and were conducted in a manner which, in the circumstances, was inconsistent with an intent to bring the person concerned to justice.

Article 22
Nullum crimen sine lege

1. A person shall not be criminally responsible under this Statute unless the conduct in question constitutes, at the time it takes place, a crime within the jurisdiction of the Court.

2. The definition of a crime shall be strictly construed and shall not be extended by analogy. In case of ambiguity, the definition shall be interpreted in favour of the person being investigated,
prosecuted or convicted.

3. This article shall not affect the characterization of any conduct as criminal under international law independently of this Statute.

Article 23
Nulla poena sine lege

A person convicted by the Court may be punished only in accordance with this Statute.

Article 24
Non-retroactivity ratione personae

1. No person shall be criminally responsible under this Statute for conduct prior to the entry into force of the Statute.

2. In the event of a change in the law applicable to a given case prior to a final judgement, the law more favourable to the person being investigated, prosecuted or convicted shall apply.

Article 55
Rights of persons during an investigation

1. In respect of an investigation under this Statute, a person:

(a) Shall not be compelled to incriminate himself or herself or to confess guilt;
(b) Shall not be subjected to any form of coercion, duress or threat, to torture or to any other form of cruel, inhuman or degrading treatment or punishment; and
(c) Shall, if questioned in a language other than a language the person fully understands and speaks, have, free of any cost, the assistance of a competent interpreter and such translations as are necessary to meet the requirements of fairness;
(d) Shall not be subjected to arbitrary arrest or detention; and shall not be deprived of his or her liberty except on such grounds and in accordance with such procedures as are established in the Statute.

2. Where there are grounds to believe that a person has committed a crime within the jurisdiction of the Court and that person is about to be questioned either by the Prosecutor, or by national authorities pursuant to a request made under Part 9 of this Statute, that person shall also have the following rights of which he or she shall be informed prior to being questioned:

(a) To be informed, prior to being questioned, that there are grounds to believe that he or she has committed a crime within the jurisdiction of the Court;
(b) To remain silent, without such silence being a consideration in the determination of guilt or innocence;
(c) To have legal assistance of the person's choosing, or, if the person does not have legal assistance, to have legal assistance assigned to him or her, in any case where the interests of justice so require, and without payment by the person in any such case if the person does not have sufficient means to pay for it;
(d) To be questioned in the presence of counsel unless the person has voluntarily waived his or her right to counsel.

Article 61

. . . .
3. Within a reasonable time before the hearing, the person shall:

(a) Be provided with a copy of the document containing the charges on which the Prosecutor intends to bring the person to trial; and

(b) Be informed of the evidence on which the Prosecutor intends to rely at the hearing.

. . . .

Article 67
Rights of the accused

1. In the determination of any charge, the accused shall be entitled to a public hearing, having regard to the provisions of this Statute, to a fair hearing conducted impartially, and to the following minimum guarantees, in full equality:

(a) To be informed promptly and in detail of the nature, cause and content of the charge, in a language which the accused fully understands and speaks;

(b) To have adequate time and facilities for the preparation of the defence and to communicate freely with counsel of the accused's choosing in confidence;

(c) To be tried without undue delay;

(d) Subject to article 63, paragraph 2, to be present at the trial, to conduct the defence in person or through legal assistance of the accused's choosing, to be informed, if the accused does not have legal assistance, of this right and to have legal assistance assigned by the Court in any case where the interests of justice so require, and without payment if the accused lacks sufficient means to pay for it;

(e) To examine, or have examined, the witnesses against him or her and to obtain the attendance and examination of witnesses on his or her behalf under the same conditions as witnesses against him or her. The accused shall also be entitled to raise defences and to present other evidence admissible under this Statute;

(f) To have, free of any cost, the assistance of a competent interpreter and such translations as are necessary to meet the requirements of fairness, if any of the proceedings of or documents presented to the Court are not in a language which the accused fully understands and speaks;

(g) Not to be compelled to testify or to confess guilt and to remain silent, without such silence being a consideration in the determination of guilt or innocence;

(h) To make an unsworn oral or written statement in his or her defence; and

(i) Not to have imposed on him or her any reversal of the burden of proof or any onus of rebuttal.

2. In addition to any other disclosure provided for in this Statute, the Prosecutor shall, as soon as practicable, disclose to the defence evidence in the Prosecutor's possession or control which he or she believes shows or tends to show the innocence of the accused, or to mitigate the guilt of the accused, or which may affect the credibility of prosecution evidence. In case of doubt as to the application of this paragraph, the Court shall decide.

Chapter 11. Police Practices

A. Eavesdropping, Search and Seizure, and the Exclusionary Rule

Treaties

Universal Declaration of Human Rights

Article 12.

No one shall be subjected to arbitrary interference with his privacy, family, home or correspondence, nor to attacks upon his honour and reputation. Everyone has the right to the protection of the law against such interference or attacks.

International Covenant on Civil and Political Rights

Article 17

1. No one shall be subjected to arbitrary or unlawful interference with his privacy, family, home or correspondence, nor to unlawful attacks on his honour and reputation.

2. Everyone has the right to the protection of the law against such interference or attacks.

European Convention on Human Rights

ARTICLE 8

1. Everyone has the right to the respect for his private and family life, his home and his correspondence.

2. There shall be no interference by a public authority with the exercise of this right except such as is in accordance with the law and is necessary in a democratic society in the interests of national security, public safety or the economic well-being of the country, for the prevention of disorder or crime, for the protection of health or morals, or for the protection of the rights and freedoms of others.

American Declaration on the Rights and Duties of Man

Article V. Right to protection of honor, personal reputation, and private and family life.

Every person has the right to the protection of the law against abusive attacks upon his honor, his reputation, and his private and family life.

Article IX. Right to inviolability of the home.

Every person has the right to the inviolability of his home.

Article X. Right to the inviolability and transmission of correspondence

Every person has the right to the inviolability and transmission of his correspondence.

American Convention on Human Rights

Article 11. RIGHT TO PRIVACY.

1. Everyone has the right to have his honor respected and his dignity recognized.

2. No one may be the object of arbitrary or abusive interference with his private life, his family, his home, or his correspondence, or of unlawful attacks on his honor or reputation.

3. Everyone has the right to the protection of the law against such interference or attacks.

Convention on Human Rights and Fundamental Freedoms of the Commonwealth of Independent States

Article 9

1. Everyone shall have the right to respect for his private and family life, his home and his correspondence.
2. There shall be no interference by a public authority with the exercise of this right except as is in accordance with the law and is necessary in a democratic society in the interests of national security, public safety, public order, public health and moral or for the protection of the rights and freedoms of others.

Arab Charter on Human Rights

Article 17

Private life is sacred, and violation of that sanctity is a crime. Private life includes family privacy, the sanctity of the home, and the secrecy of correspondence and other forms of private communication.

Convention on the Rights of the Child

Article 16

1. No child shall be subjected to arbitrary or unlawful interference with his or her privacy, family, home or correspondence, nor to unlawful attacks on his or her honour and reputation.

2. The child has the right to the protection of the law against such interference or attacks.

Klass and Others v. Federal Republic of Germany
European Court of Human Rights
28 Eur. Ct. H.R. (ser. A) (1978)
2 E.H.R.R. 214 (1979-80)

. . . .

FACTS:

10. The applicants, who are German nationals, are Gerhard Klass, an *Oberstaatsanwalt*, Peter Lubberger, a lawyer, Jurgen Nussbruch, a judge, Hans-Jurgen Pohl and Dieter Selb, lawyers. All five applicants claim that article 10(2) of the Basic Law (*Grundgesetz*) and a statute enacted in pursuance of that provision, namely the Act of 13 August 1968 on Restrictions on the Secrecy of the Mail, Post and Telecommunications (*Gesetz zur Beschränkung des Brief- Post- und Fernmeldegeheimnisses*, hereinafter referred to as 'the G 10'), are contrary to the Convention. They do not dispute that the State has the right to have recourse to the surveillance measures contemplated by the legislation; they challenge this legislation in that it permits those measures without obliging the authorities in every case to notify the persons concerned after the event, and in that it excludes any remedy before the courts against the ordering and execution of such measures.

11. Before lodging their application with the Commission, the applicants had appealed to the Federal Constitutional Court. By judgment of 15 December 1970, that Court held that article 1(5) (5) of the G 10 was void, being incompatible with the second sentence of article 10(2) of the Basic Law, insofar as it excluded notification of the person concerned about the measures of surveillance even when such notification could be given without jeopardising the purpose of the restriction. The Constitutional Court dismissed the remaining claims. (30 COLLECTED DECISIONS OF THE CONSTITUTIONAL COURT [BVerfGE] 1.)

Since the operative provisions of that judgment have the force of law, the competent authorities are bound to apply the G 10 in the form and subject to the interpretation decided by the Constitutional Court. Furthermore, the Government of the Federal Republic of Germany were prompted by this judgment to propose amendments to the G 10, but the parliamentary proceedings have not yet been completed.

. . . .

DECISION:

. . . .

II. On the alleged violation of Article 8

39. The applicants claim that the contested legislation[,] notably because the person concerned is not informed of the surveillance measures and cannot have recourse to the courts when such measures are terminated, violates Article 8 of the Convention which provides as follows:

1. Everyone has the right to respect for his private and family life, his home and his correspondence.

2. There shall be no interference by a public authority with the exercise of this right except such as is in accordance with the law and is necessary in a democratic society in the interests of national security, public safety or the economic well-being of the country, for the prevention of disorder or crime, for the protection of health or morals or for the protection of the rights and freedoms of others.

40. According to article 10(2) of the Basic Law, restrictions upon the secrecy of the mail, post and telecommunications may be ordered but only pursuant to a statute. Article 1(1) of the G 10 allows certain authorities to open and inspect mail and post, to read telegraphic messages and to monitor and record telephone conversations [citation omitted]. The Court's examination under Article 8 is thus limited to the authorisation of such measures alone and does not extend, for instance, to the secret surveillance effected in pursuance of the Code of Criminal Procedure [citation omitted].

41. The first matter to be decided is whether and, if so, in what respect the contested legislation in permitting the above-mentioned measures of surveillance, constitutes an interference with the exercise of the right guaranteed to the applicants under Article 8(1).

Although telephone conversations are not expressly mentioned in paragraph 1 of Article 18, the Court considers, as did the Commission, that such conversations are covered by the notions of 'private life' and 'correspondence' referred to by this provision.

In its report, the Commission expressed the opinion that the secret surveillance provided for under the German legislation amounted to an interference with the exercise of the right set forth in Article 8(1). Neither before the Commission nor before the Court did the Government contest this issue. Clearly, any of the permitted surveillance measures, once applied to a given individual, would result in an interference by a public authority with the exercise of that individual's right to respect for his private and family life and his correspondence. Furthermore, in the mere existence of the legislation itself, there is involved, for all those to whom the legislation could be applied, a menace of surveillance; this menace necessarily strikes at freedom of communication between users of the postal and telecommunication services and thereby constitutes an 'interference by a public authority' with the exercise of the applicants' right to respect for private and family life and for correspondence.

The Court does not exclude that the contested legislation, and therefore the measures permitted thereunder, could also involve an interference with the exercise of a person's right to respect for his home. However, the Court does not deem it necessary in the present proceedings to decide this point.

42. The cardinal issue arising under Article 8 in the present case is whether the interference so found is justified by the terms of paragraph 2 of the Article. This paragraph, since it provides for an exception to a right guaranteed by the Convention, is to be narrowly interpreted. Powers of secret surveillance of citizens, characterising as they do the police state, are tolerable under the Convention only in so far as strictly necessary for safeguarding the democratic institutions.

43. In order for the 'interference' established above not to infringe Article 8, it must, according to paragraph 2, first of all have been 'in accordance with the law'. This requirement is fulfilled in the present case since the 'interference' results from Acts passed by Parliament, including one Act which was modified by the Federal Constitutional Court,

in the exercise of its jurisdiction, by its judgment of 15 December 1970 (*see* § 11 above). In addition, the Court observes that, as both the Government and the Commission pointed out, any individual measure of surveillance has to comply with the strict conditions and procedures laid down in the legislation itself.

44. It remains to be determined whether the other requisites laid down in paragraph 2 of Article 8 were also satisfied. According to the Government and the Commission, the interference permitted by the contested legislation was 'necessary in a democratic society in the interests of national security' and/or 'for the prevention of disorder or crime'. Before the Court, the Government submitted that the interference was additionally justified 'in the interests of . . . public safety' and 'for the protection of the rights and freedoms of others'.

45. The G 10 defines precisely, and thereby limits, the purposes for which the restrictive measures may be imposed. It provides that, in order to protect against 'imminent dangers' threatening 'the free democratic constitutional order', the existence or security of the Federation or of a Land', 'the security of the [allied] armed forces' stationed on the territory of the Republic or the security of 'the troops of one of the Three Powers stationed in the Land of Berlin', the responsible authorities may authorise the restrictions referred to above [citation omitted].

46. The Court, sharing the view of the Government and the Commission, finds that the aim of the G 10 is indeed to safeguard national security and/or to prevent disorder to crime in pursuance of Article 8(2). In these circumstances, the Court does not deem it necessary to decide whether the further purposes cited by the Government are also relevant.

On the other hand, it has to be ascertained whether the means provided under the impugned legislation for the achievement of the above-mentioned aim remain in all respects within the bounds of what is necessary in a democratic society.

47. The applicants do not object to the German legislation in that it provides for wide-ranging powers of surveillance; they accept such powers, and the resultant encroachment upon the right guaranteed by Article 8(1), as being a necessary means of defence for the protection of the democratic State. The applicants consider, however, that paragraph 2 of Article 8 lays down for such powers certain limits which have to be respected in a democratic society in order to ensure that the society does not slide imperceptibly towards totalitarianism. In their view, the contested legislation lacks adequate safeguards against possible abuse.

48. As the Delegates observed, the Court, in its appreciation of the scope of the protection offered by Article 8, cannot but take judicial notice of two important facts. The first consists of the technical advances made in the means of espionage and, correspondingly, of surveillance; the second is the development of terrorism in Europe in recent years. Democratic societies nowadays find themselves threatened by highly sophisticated forms of espionage and by terrorism, with the result that the State must be able, in order effectively to counter such threats, to undertake the secret surveillance of subversive elements operating within its jurisdiction. The Court has therefore to accept that the existence of some legislation granting powers of secret surveillance over the mail, post and telecommunications is, under exceptional conditions, necessary in a democratic society in the interests of national security and/or for the prevention of disorder or crime.

49. As concerns the fixing of the conditions under which the system of surveillance is to be operated, the Court points out that the domestic legislature enjoys a certain discretion. It is certainly not for the Court to substitute for the assessment of the national authorities any other assessment of what might be the best policy in this field. [citation omitted]

Nevertheless, the Court stresses that this does not mean that the Contracting States enjoy an unlimited discretion to subject persons within their jurisdiction to secret surveillance. The Court, being aware of the danger such a law poses of undermining or even destroying democracy on the ground of defending it, affirms that the Contracting States may not, in the name of the struggle against espionage and terrorism, adopt whatever measures they deem appropriate.

50. The Court must be satisfied that, whatever system of surveillance is adopted, there exist adequate and effective guarantees against abuse. This assessment has only a relative character: it depends on all the circumstances of the case, such as the nature, scope and duration of the possible measures, the grounds required for ordering such measures, the authorities competent to permit, carry out and supervise such measures, and the kind of remedy provided by the national law.

The functioning of the system of secret surveillance established by the contested legislation, as modified by the Federal Constitutional Court's judgment of 15 December 1970, must therefore be examined in the light of the Convention.

51. According to the G 10, a series of limitative conditions have to be satisfied before a surveillance measure can be imposed. Thus, the permissible restrictive measures are confined to cases in which there are factual indications for suspecting a person of planning, committing or having committed certain serious criminal acts; measures may only be ordered if the establishment of the facts by another method is without prospects of success or considerably more difficult; even then, the surveillance may cover only the specific suspect or his presumed 'contact-persons' [citation omitted]. Consequently, so-called exploratory or general surveillance is not permitted by the contested legislation.

Surveillance may be ordered only on written application giving reasons, and such an application may be made only by the head, or his substitute, of certain services; the decision thereon must be taken by a Federal Minister empowered for the purpose by the Chancellor or, where appropriate, by the supreme Land authority [citation omitted]. Accordingly, under the law, there exists an administrative procedure designed to ensure that measure are not ordered haphazardly, irregularly or without due and proper consideration. In addition, although not required by the Act, the competent Minister in practice and except in urgent cases seeks the prior consent of the G 10 Commission [citation omitted].

52. The G 10 also lays down strict conditions with regard to the implementation of the surveillance measures and to the processing of the information thereby obtained. The measures in question remain in force for a maximum of three months and may be renewed only on fresh application; the measures must immediately be discontinued once the required conditions have ceased to exist or the measures themselves are no longer necessary; knowledge and documents thereby obtained may not be used for other ends, and documents must be destroyed as soon as they are no longer needed to achieve the required purpose [citation omitted].

As regards the implementation of the measures, an initial control is carried out by an official qualified or judicial office. This official examines the information obtained from transmitting to the competent services such information as may be used in accordance with the Act and is relevant to the purpose of the measure; he destroys any other intelligence that may have been gathered [citation omitted].

53. Under the G 10, while recourse to the courts in respect of the ordering and implementation of measures of surveillance is excluded, subsequent control or review is provided instead, in accordance with article 10(2) of the Basic Law, by two bodies appointed by the people's elected representatives, namely, the Parliamentary Board and the G 10 Commission.

The competent Minister must, at least once every six months, report on the application of the G 10 to the Parliamentary Board consisting of five members of Parliament; the members of Parliament are appointed by the Bundestag in proportion to the parliamentary groupings, the opposition being represented on the Board. In addition, the Minister is bound every month to provide the G 10 Commission with an account of the measures he has ordered. In practice, he seeks the prior consent of this Commission. The latter decides, *ex officio* or on application by a person believing himself to be under surveillance, on both the legality of and the necessity for the measures in question; if it declares any measures to be illegal or unnecessary, the Minister must terminate them immediately. The Commission members are appointed for the current term of the Bundestag by the Parliamentary Board after consultation with the Government; they are completely dependent in the exercise of their functions and cannot be subject to instructions [citation omitted].

54. The Government maintains that Article 8(2) does not require judicial control of secret surveillance and that the system of review established under the G 10 does effectively protect the rights of the individual. The applicants, on the other hand, qualify this system as a 'form of political control', inadequate in comparison with the principle of judicial control which ought to prevail.

It therefore has to be determined whether the procedures for supervising the ordering and implementation of the restrictive measures are such as to keep the 'interference' resulting from the contested legislation to what is 'necessary in a democratic society'.

55. Review of surveillance may intervene at three stages: when the surveillance is first ordered, while it is being carried out, or after it has been terminated. As regards the first two stages, the very nature and logic of secret surveillance dictate that not only the surveillance itself but also the accompanying review should be effected without the individual's knowledge. Consequently, since the individual will necessarily be prevented from seeking an effective remedy of his own accord or from taking a direct part in any review proceedings, it is essential that the procedures established should themselves provide adequate and equivalent guarantees safeguarding the individual's rights. In addition, the values of a democratic society must be followed as faithfully as possible in the supervisory procedures if the bounds of necessity, within the meaning of Article 8(2), are not to be exceeded. One of the fundamental principles of a democratic society is the rule of law, which is expressly referred to in the Preamble to the Convention. (*See Golder v. United Kingdom,* 18 Eur. Ct. H.R. (ser. A) at 16-17 (1975).). The rule of law implies, *inter alia*, that an interference by the executive authorities with an individual's rights should be subject to an effective control which should normally be assured by the

judiciary, at least in the last resort, judicial control offering the best guarantees of independence, impartiality and a proper procedure.

56. Within the system of surveillance established by the G 10, judicial control was excluded, being replaced by an initial control effected by an official qualified for judicial office and by the control provided by the Parliamentary Board and the G 10 Commission.

The Court considers that, in a field where abuse is potentially so easy in individual cases and could have such harmful consequences for democratic society as a whole, it is in principle desirable to entrust supervisory control to a judge.

Nevertheless, having regard to the nature of the supervisory and other safeguards provided for by the G 10, the Court concludes that the exclusion of judicial control does not exceed the limits of what may be deemed necessary in a democratic society. The Parliamentary Board and the G 10 Commission are independent of the authorities carrying out the surveillance, and are vested with sufficient powers and competence to exercise an effective and continuous control. Furthermore, the democratic character is reflected in the balanced membership of the Parliamentary Board. The opposition is represented on this body and is therefore able to participate in the control of the measures ordered by the competent Minister who is responsible to the Bundestag. The two supervisory bodies may, in the circumstances of the case, be regarded as enjoying sufficient independence to give an objective ruling.

The Court notes in addition that an individual believing himself to be under surveillance has the opportunity of complaining to the G 10 Commission and of having recourse to the Constitutional Court [citation omitted]. However, as the Government conceded, these are remedies which can come into play only in exceptional circumstances.

57. As regards review *a posteriori*, it is necessary to determine whether judicial control, in particular with the individual's participation, should continue to be excluded even after surveillance has ceased. Inextricably linked to this issue is the question of subsequent notification, since there is in principle little scope for recourse to the courts by the individual concerned unless he is advised of the measures taken without his knowledge and thus able retrospectively to challenge their legality.

The applicants' main complaint under Article 8 is in fact that the person concerned is not always subsequently informed after the suspension of surveillance and is not therefore in a position to seek an effective remedy before the courts. Their preoccupation is the danger of measures being improperly implemented without the individual knowing or being able to verify the extent to which his rights have been interfered with. In their view, effective control by the courts after the suspension of surveillance measures is necessary in a democratic society to ensure against abuses; otherwise adequate control of secret surveillance is lacking and the right conferred on individuals under Article 8 is simply eliminated.

In the Government's view, the subsequent notification which must be given since the Federal Constitutional Court's judgment [citation omitted] corresponds to the requirements of Article 8(2). In their submission, the whole efficacy of secret surveillance requires that, both before and after the event, information cannot be divulged if thereby the purpose of the investigation is, or would be retrospectively, thwarted. They stressed that recourse to the courts is no longer excluded after notification has been given, various legal remedies then becoming available to allow the individual, *inter alia*, to seek redress for any injury suffered [citation omitted].

58. In the opinion of the court, it has to be ascertained whether it is even feasible in practice to require subsequent notification in all cases.

The activity or danger against which a particular series of surveillance measures is directed may continue for years, even decades, after the suspension of those measures. Subsequent notification to each individual affected by a suspended measure might well jeopardise the long-term purpose that originally prompted the surveillance. Furthermore, as the Federal Constitutional Court rightly observed, such notification might serve to reveal the working methods and fields of operation of the intelligence services and even possibly to identify their agents. In the Court's view, in so far as the 'interference' resulting from the contested legislation is in principle justified under Article 8(2) [citation omitted], the fact of not informing the individual once surveillance has ceased cannot itself be incompatible with this provision, since it is this very fact which ensures the efficacy of the 'interference'. Moreover, it is to be recalled that, in pursuance of the Federal Constitutional Court's judgment of 15 December 1970, the person concerned must be informed after the termination of the surveillance measures as soon as notification can be made without jeopardising the purpose of the restriction [citation omitted].

59. Both in general and in relation to the question of subsequent notification, the applicants have constantly invoked the danger of abuse as a ground for their contention that the legislation they challenge does not fulfil the requirements of Article 8(2) of the Convention. While the possibility of improper action by a dishonest, negligent or over-zealous official can never be completely ruled out whatever the system, the considerations that matter for the purposes of the Court's present review are the likelihood of such action and the safeguards provided to protect against it.

The Court has examined above [citation omitted] the contested legislation in the light, *inter alia*, of these considerations. The Court notes in particular that the G 10 contains various provisions designed to reduce the effect of surveillance measures to an unavoidable minimum and to ensure that the surveillance is carried out in strict accordance with the law. In the absence of any evidence or indication that the actual practice followed is otherwise, the Court must assume that, in the democratic society of the Federal Republic of Germany, the relevant authorities are properly applying the legislation in issue.

The Court agrees with the Commission that some compromise between the requirements for defending democratic society and individual rights is inherent in the system of the Convention. (*See, mutatis mutandis, Belgian Linquistics Case* [6 Eur. Ct. H.R. (ser. A) at 32 (1968)]) As the Preamble to the Convention states, 'Fundamental Freedoms . . . are best maintained on the one hand by an effective political democracy and on the other by a common understanding and observance of the Human Rights upon which [the Contracting States] depend'. In the context of Article 8, this means that a balance must be sought between the exercise by the individual of the right guaranteed to him under paragraph 1 and the necessity under paragraph 2 to impose secret surveillance for the protection of the democratic society as a whole.

60. In the light of these considerations and of the detailed examination of the contested legislation, the Court concludes that the German legislature was justified to consider the interference resulting from that legislation with the exercise of the right guaranteed by Article 8(1) as being necessary in a democratic society in the interests of

national security and for the prevention of disorder or crime (Art 8(2)). Accordingly, the Court finds no breach of Article 8 of the Convention.

. . . .

❖ ❖ ❖

Questions & Comments

(1) The European Court seems to treat the existence of terrorism as a sufficient reason to by-pass judicial forms of review. In a country like the U.S., however, far more people are killed in violence associated with the drug trade than from terrorism. Would the Court accept non-reviewable surveillance over drug trafficking as well? Is there something about terrorism which requires a different approach?

The European Court stresses the need for adequate guarantees against abuse. Does the administrative procedure provided here seem enough? In the U.S., secret surveillance of mail or telephones requires judicial approval beforehand. Is the inclusion of opposition members of parliament on the oversight board a sufficient alternative to judicial review? In what ways might a parliamentary body be better than judicial oversight? In what ways might judicial oversight be better? Francisco Forrest Martin, *et al.*, 1 INTERNATIONAL HUMAN RIGHTS LAW & PRACTICE: CASES, TREATIES AND MATERIALS 642 (1997).

(2) In *Huvig v. France*, 176-B Eur. Ct. H.R. (ser. A) (1990), the French authorities investigated Jacques Huvig and his wife for tax evasion. As part of the investigation a judge issued a warrant to the gendarmerie to monitor and transcribe all of the Huvig's telephone calls for part of one day and all of another. The telephone taps lasted a total of twenty-eight hours. The Huvigs were eventually tried and convicted of tax evasion although no evidence collected from the telephone taps was used. The Huvigs raised the telephone tap in several motions to dismiss their charges. After their convictions were final, they applied to the European Commission and Court of Human Rights which found an Article 8 violation.

Following their analysis in *Klass*, the Court first considered whether the "interference" with the "right to respect for his private and family life, his home and his correspondence" was "in accordance with the law." Although the application of existing French law to telephone taps was contestable, the Court felt bound to follow the interpretation of French law by the French courts that the judicial warrant was authorized by law. But the Court went on to hold that the exception for interferences "in accordance with the law" is not a mere formal requirement. To approve the surveillance the Court must determine that the authorizing national law meets the convention's norms for the substantive quality of the law, *i.e.*, its accessibility, protectiveness, and foreseeability.

The Court held that unlike *Klass*, the law here did not provide for adequate procedural protection. Specifically, the French law set no temporal limits on the investigation, leaving to police discretion to determine when the public's investigatory needs were met. Under the German "G-10" rules, every surveillance order had to be renewed every three months, requiring reapplication and reconfirmation of the appropriateness of the mission. Even without a requirement of judicial review, Germany's procedures required oversight and responsibility by higher political officials over the information collected and its use by the government. The French surveillance procedures allowed investigators to make their own judgment without the involvement on a continuing basis of higher officials. Francisco Forrest Martin, *et al.*, 1 INTERNATIONAL HUMAN RIGHTS LAW & PRACTICE: CASES, TREATIES AND MATERIALS 642 (1997).

(3) Note that the European Court in *Klass* recognized that the German law could have a chilling effect persons using the mail and telecommunication services.

> [I]n the mere existence of the legislation itself, there is involved, for all those to whom the legislation could be applied, a menace of surveillance; this menace necessarily strikes at freedom of communication between users of the postal and telecommunication services and thereby constitutes an 'interference by a public authority' with the exercise of the applicants' right to respect for private and family life and for correspondence.

Id. at § 41. Article 10, ECHR, guarantees the right to freedom of expression. If the applicant in *Klass* had raised a freedom of expression claim along with his privacy claim, do you think the European Court would have decided this case differently, given the interests involved?

García Pérez v. Peru
Inter-American Commission on Human Rights
Report No. 1/95, Case 11.006
Inter-Am. Cm. H.R. 71,
OEA/Ser.L/V/II.88, Doc. 9 rev. (1995)

. . . .

[T]he petitioners have stated that on the night of April 5, 1992, Army soldiers under the command of General Hermoza Ríos entered the home of [former Peruvian President] Dr. Alan García and unlawfully seized private family papers, such as identification papers, passports, property deeds, tax declarations and legal documents used in the defense of the former President in the case brought against him for the crime of unlawful enrichment.

Article 11 of the American Convention on Human Rights protects the right to privacy and stipulates that no one may be the object of arbitrary or abusive interference in his private life or family.

By explicitly protecting the home and private correspondence of individuals, this article serves to guarantee that the right to privacy will be respected. This protection is consistent with the American Declaration of the Rights and Duties of Man inasmuch as it upholds the inviolability of domicile and private papers as guarantees arbitrary State interference in the private lives of individuals [Arts. IX and X].

However, the right to privacy is not absolute; quite the contrary, exercise of this right is routinely restricted by the domestic laws of States.

The guarantee of the inviolability of the domicile and of private papers must give way when there is a well-substantiated search warrant issued by a competent judicial authority, spelling out the reasons for the measure being adopted and specifying the place to be searched and the objects that will be seized.

The 1979 Constitution of Peru stipulated the inviolability of domicile and of private papers except when an order has been issued by a competent judicial authority authorizing the search, explaining its reasons and, where appropriate, authorizing the seizure of private papers, while respecting the guarantees stipulated by law.[1]

Based on these concepts, the Commission concludes that the warrantless search of Dr. García's home and the seizure of private family papers — actions committed by Peruvian soldiers — were committed in complete disregard of the procedural requirements stipulated in the Constitution. The violation of those requirements indicates that the Government of Peru failed to guarantee to Dr. Alan García and to his family the full exercise of their right to privacy.

The arguments made by the Government of Peru to the effect that the Army soldiers surrounded the residence of Dr. García Perez in order to protect him are, in themselves, insufficient. Protection of a private residence does not call for action by heavily armed soldiers nor for the use of war tanks equipped with canons, small tanks or armored troop carriers.

2. Criminal prosecution for the crime of illegal possession of weapons

As the petitioners indicated, Dr. Alan García Perez is charged in two criminal cases for the illegal possession of weapons, wherein the only incriminating evidence — firearms, munitions and explosives — was unlawfully obtained by searching his private residence, in one case, and the headquarters of the Aprista Party of which the former President is Secretary General in the other case.

Article 8.1 of the American Convention provides that every person has the right to a hearing, with due guarantees, in the substantiation of any action of a criminal nature made against him.

Similarly, Article 8.2 provides that during proceedings, every person is entitled, with full equality, to certain minimum guarantees. The enumeration contained in this clause has been interpreted as a list of the minimum guarantees, but not an exhaustive list. Hence, there are other guarantees recognized in the domestic laws of that State that, although not explicitly included in the text of the Convention, are equally protected under the broad wording of paragraph 1 of Article 8 of the Convention. [note omitted]

. . . . In effect, inviolability of domicile is one of the implicit guarantees of that article. In effect, inviolability of domicile is more than a guarantee of privacy; it is a guarantee of due process inasmuch as it establishes what can be seized, that being incriminating evidence against an individual charged with a crime. When a search of a domicile is conducted without observing the proper constitutional procedures, that guarantee prevents any evidence thus obtained from being used to arrive at a subsequent court decision. Thus, in practice it functions as an exclusionary rule, one that eliminates illegally obtained evidence.

The *raison d'etre* of this guarantee and of the rule excluding evidence obtained by violating that guarantee has been explained by Maier as follows:

---

[1] See Article 2, subparagraphs 7 and 8 of the Constitution in force until December 31, 1993.

The justification of the methods used to arrive at the truth depends upon the observance of juridical rules governing how they can be validly weighed in the proceedings. Not all methods are allowed and authorities must compile evidence according to the discipline imposed by procedural law. The judicial procedures are not mere formalities; instead, since they work directly to protect human dignity, they act as a material category . . .[2]

The proceedings instituted against Dr. García Perez for illegal possession of weapons were based exclusively on unlawfully obtained evidence. The searches conducted of his private residence and of the headquarters of the Aprista Party were effected by means of intimidating tactics by Army troopers, in total disregard for the procedures stipulated by Peru's domestic laws.

For this reason, the Commission considers that the "procedural guarantees" protected by the American Convention were not respected in processing the criminal cases against former President Alan García.

. . . .

[The Commission recommended that the Government undertake the necessary measures to re-establish the "*status quo ante.*"]

❖ ❖ ❖

Questions & Comments

(1) Many supporters of limiting the exclusionary rule in the United States emphasize the importance of truth finding as the central value of the criminal process. Does the Commission reject that view? Does it matter that this case involves highly charged political antagonisms while the typical exclusionary rule case in the United States involves drugs seized from low level dealers and users? Francisco Forrest Martin, *et al.*, 1 INTERNATIONAL HUMAN RIGHTS LAW & PRACTICE: CASES, TREATIES AND MATERIALS 646 (1997).

(2) In *The Prosecutor v. Mucic*, Case No. IT-96-21, Int'l Crim. Trib.-Yugo, Trial Chamber (9 February 1998), the Trial Chamber allowed the admission of documents seized by the Austrian police. The seizure may have entailed minor breaches of the Austrian law on search and seizure. The Trial Chamber allowed the admission because not admitting the evidence "would constitute a dangerous obstacle to the administration of justice." If evidence is obtained illegally by the police, how reliable is that evidence? Consider the ICT-Y's own rules of procedure:

---

[2] Julio B. J. Maier, *Derecho Procesal Penal Argentino*, Buenos Aires, Editorial Hammurabi, 1989, pp. 470 and 471.

Rule 95. Evidence Obtained by Means Contrary to Internationally Protected Human Rights

No evidence shall be admissible if obtained by methods which cast substantial doubt on its reliability or if its admission is antithetical to, and would seriously damage, the integrity of the proceedings.

Rule 95, ICT-Y Rules of Procedure.

How does the ICT-Y's ruling comport with the Inter-American Commission's in *García Pérez v. Peru*? How does the ICT-Y's ruling compare with the ICC Statute:

States Parties shall, in accordance with the provisions of this Part and under *procedures of national law*, comply with requests by the Court to provide the following assistance in relation to investigations or prosecutions:

. . .

(h) The execution of searches and seizures; . . . .

Art. 93, ICC Statute (emphasis provided).

Crèmieux v. France
European Court of Human Rights
256-B Eur. Ct. H.R. (ser. A) (1993)
16 E.H.R.R. 357 (1993)

. . . .

FACTS:

I. The circumstances of the case

6. Mr Paul Crèmieux, a French citizen born in 1908, is retired and lives at his female companion's home in Marseilles. At the material time he was chairman and managing director of SAPVIN, a wholesale wine firm, whose head office is in Marseilles.

A. The house searches and seizures of documents

7. In October 1976, in the course of an investigation into the SODEVIM company, customs officers seized documents relating to business transactions between SAPVIN and foreign firms.

8. Thereafter, from 27 January 1977 to 26 February 1980, the customs authorities carried out 83 investigative operations in the form of interviews and of raids on SAPVIN's head office, on the applicant's home and at other addresses of his and on the homes of other people, during which further items were seized.

Each of the house searches was made under Articles 64 and 454 of the Customs Code. They were conducted by officials from the National Customs Investigations Department ('the DNED') in the presence of a senior police officer (*officier de police judiciaire*); a report was made on each of them and they all led to Mr Crèmieux's being subsequently interviewed.

9. Several such searches were made on 23 January 1979.

One of them began at 7 am at the applicant's Paris home, in his absence. The customs officers were received by Mr Crèmieux's son; they inspected the office and took away 518 documents, some of which, according to Mr Crèmieux, had no connection with the customs investigation. The son initialed the inventory of documents. The applicant, who had arrived at 9.10 am, signed the report together with his son; he denied having been able, as the Government maintained, to go through the documents.

Another search began at 8 am at the home of Mr Crèmieux's female companion, whom, the applicant claimed, the DNED officials had followed into the bathroom when she said she wanted to put on a dressing-gown. Numerous personal papers were seized.

Searches were also made of the homes of other people, who had business relations with the applicant and his company.

10. On 24 January and 17 May 1979, Mr Crèmieux was questioned by customs officers.

On 16 February 1979 they opened the private strongbox he had at SAPVIN's head office and took 17 documents from it.

[Crèmieux applied to the European Commission of Human Rights claiming an Article 8 violation to this right to respect for private life. The Commission found no violation and referred the case to the European Court of Human Rights.]

. . . .

DECISION [OF THE EUROPEAN COURT OF HUMAN RIGHTS]

. . . .

B.   Merits of the complaint

31. The Government conceded that there had been an interference with Mr Crèmieux's right to respect for his private life, and the Commission additionally found that there had been an interference with his right to respect for his home.

Like Mr Crèmieux, the Court considers that all the rights secured in Article 8(1) are in issue, except for the right to respect for family life. It must accordingly be determined whether the interferences in question satisfied the conditions in paragraph 2.

1.   'In accordance with the law'

32. The applicant contended that the interferences had no legal basis. As worded at the time, Article 64 of the Customs Code was, he claimed, contrary to the 1958 Constitution because it did not make house searches and seizures subject to judicial authorisation. Admittedly, its constitutionality could not be reviewed, since it had come into force before the Constitution had. Nevertheless, in the related field of taxation the Constitutional Council had rejected section 89 of the Budget Act for 1984, concerning the investigation of income tax and turnover tax offences, holding, *inter alia*:

While the needs of the Revenue's work may dictate that tax officials should be authorised to make investigations in private places, such investigations can only be conducted in accordance with Article 66 of the Constitution, which makes the judiciary responsible for protecting the liberty of the individual in all its aspects, in particular the inviolability of the home. Provision must be made for judicial participation in order that the judiciary's responsibility and supervisory power may be maintained in their entirety. (Decision no 83-164 DC of 29 December 1983, OFFICIAL GAZETTE (*JOURNAL OFFICIEL*), 30 December 1983, p 3874.)

33. The Government, whose arguments the Commission accepted in substance, maintained that in Article 64 of the Customs Code, as supplemented by a fairly substantial body of case law, the power to search houses was defined very closely and represented a transposition to customs legislation and the regulations governing financial dealings with foreign countries of the power of search provided for in ordinary criminal procedure. Provision was first made for it in an Act of 6 August 1791 and subsequently in a legislative decree of 12 July 1934, and it had been widened in 1945 to cover investigations into exchange-control offences and confirmed on several occasions. In the Government's submission, its constitutionality could not be put in doubt, any more than that of Article 454 of the same code, since review of the constitutionality of statutes took place between their enactment by Parliament and promulgation and was within the sole competence of the Constitutional Council, to the exclusion of all other courts.

As to the 'quality' of the national legal rules *vis-a-vis* the Convention, it was ensured by the precision with which the legislation and case law laid down the scope and manner of exercise of the relevant power, and this eliminated any risk of arbitrariness. Thus, even before the reform of 1986-89, the courts had supervised customs investigations *ex post facto* but very efficiently. And in any case, Article 8 of the Convention contained no requirement that house searches and seizures should be judicially authorised in advance.

34. The Court does not consider it necessary to determine the issue in this instance, as at all events the interferences complained of are incompatible with Article 8 in other respects.

2.   Legitimate aim

35. The Government and the Commission considered that the interferences in question were in the interests of 'the economic well-being of the country' and 'the prevention of crime.'

Notwithstanding the applicant's arguments to the contrary, the Court is of the view that the interferences were in pursuit of at any rate the first of these legitimate aims.

3.   'Necessary in a democratic society'

36. In Mr Crèmieux's submission, the interferences could not be regarded as 'necessary in a democratic society.' Their scope was unlimited and they had also been carried out in an unacceptable manner. In the first place, their sheer scale was, he said, striking: 83 investigative operations spread over three years, although the case was neither serious nor complex and ended with a composition; furthermore, none of the documents removed had proved that any exchange-control offence had been committed.   The

interferences further reflected a lack of discrimination on the part of the customs officers, who took possession of purely private papers and correspondence and lawyer's letters and subsequently returned a very large number of the documents seized, which they deemed unnecessary for the investigation. Lastly, the interferences illustrated the authorities' hounding of the applicant, with the customs searches (*visites domiciliaires*) being turned into thoroughgoing general searches (*perquisitions*).

37. The Government, whose contentions the Commission accepted in substance, argued that house searches and seizures were the only means available to the authorities for investigating offences against the legislation governing financial dealings with foreign countries and thus preventing the flight of capital and tax evasion. In such fields there was a *corpus delicti* only very rarely if at all; the 'physical manifestation' of the offence therefore lay mainly in documents which a guilty party could easily conceal or destroy. Such persons, however, had the benefit of substantial safeguards, strengthened by very rigorous judicial supervision: decision-making by the head of the customs district concerned, the rank of the officers authorised to establish offences, the presence of a senior police officer (*officier de police judiciaire*), the timing of searches, the preservation of lawyers' and doctors' professional secrecy, the possibility of invoking the liability of the public authorities, *etc*. In short, even before the reform of 1986-89, the French system had ensured that there was a proper balance between the requirements of law enforcement and the protection of the rights of the individual.

As regards the circumstances of the case, the Government made two observations. First, the composition agreed to by the authorities was tantamount to acknowledgement by Mr Crèmieux of the offence committed; far from demonstrating that the case was of little importance, it was an efficient procedure commonly used by the customs to obviate more cumbersome proceedings with identical consequences. Secondly, the many house searches had been made necessary by the number of different places where Mr Crèmieux might keep documents.

38. The Court has consistently held that the Contracting States have a certain margin of appreciation in assessing the need for an interference, but it goes hand in hand with European supervision. The exceptions provided for in Article 8(2) are to be interpreted narrowly (*See Klass and Others v. Germany*, 28 Eur. Ct. H.R. (ser. A) at 21 (1978)), and the need for them in a given case must be convincingly established.

39. Undoubtedly, in the field under consideration — the prevention of capital outflows and tax evasion — States encounter serious difficulties owing to the scale and complexity of banking systems and financial channels and to the immense scope for international investment, made all the easier by the relative porousness of national borders. The Court therefore recognises that they may consider it necessary to have recourse to measures such as house searches and seizures in order to obtain physical evidence of exchange-control offences and, where appropriate, to prosecute those responsible. Nevertheless, the relevant legislation and practice must afford adequate and effective safeguards against abuse. (*See*, among other authorities and, *mutatis mutandis, Klass and Others v. Germany*, 28 Eur. Ct. H.R. at 23.)

40. This was not so in the instant case. At the material time — and the Court does not have to express an opinion on the legislative reforms of 1986 and 1989, which were designed to afford better protection for individuals — the customs authorities had very wide powers; in particular, they had exclusive competence to assess the expediency,

number, length and scale of inspections. Above all, in the absence of any requirement of a judicial warrant the restrictions and conditions provided for in law, which were emphasised by the Government, appear too lax and full of loopholes for the interferences in the applicant's right to have been strictly proportionate to the legitimate aim pursued.

41. In sum, there has been a breach of Article 8.

. . . .

❖   ❖   ❖

Questions & Comments

(1) The European Court found that the procedures did little to check the discretion of customs officials. In fact, the existing domestic statutory rules forbade searches at night and required the accompaniment of a municipal officer. What is more important: to limit the occasions on which the police may intrude into private spaces, or to make sure that such intrusions are done with respect for the dignity of the individual? Both are presumably important values in democratic nations but courts often fail to recognize both. The U.S. Supreme Court, for example, has emphasized the person's interest in secrecy rather than their interest in the dignity and autonomy of their private spaces and activities. Thus the Court has reprimanded police officers for reading a product identification serial number on the back of a stereo, even though the police were lawfully in the apartment investigating a shooting incident, but has tended to ignore the quality of police interventions, and especially the routine indignities that young urban males, especially persons of color, experience in street encounters with the police. Compare, *Arizona v. Hicks*, 480 U.S. 321 (1987) (police look at the back of stereo equipment without probable cause violated 4th Amendment) and *Terry v. Ohio*, 392 U.S. 1 (1968) (police do not need probable cause for brief investigative seizures and external "pat-down" type search). Francisco Forrest Martin, *et al.*, 1 INTERNATIONAL HUMAN RIGHTS LAW & PRACTICE: CASES, TREATIES AND MATERIALS 654 (1997).

(2) How would you distinguish this case from *Klass*? Does the Court simply believe that terrorism is a more serious threat to democracy then currency flight? Is that an appropriate call for the Court to make?

(3) In 1986 the law was changed to add extensive new regulations to search and seizure powers of the customs officials. Did this change make it easier for the Court to condemn what was essentially a superseded procedure?

(4) Compare *X. & Y. v. Argentina*, Inter-Am. Cm. H.R., Case No. 10.056, ANNUAL REPORT OF THE INTER-AMERICAN COMMISSION ON HUMAN RIGHTS 1996 50, OEA/Ser.L/V/II/95 Doc. 7 rev. (14 March 1997). In *X. & Y. v. Argentina*, the petitioners (a mother and daughter) complained that prison officials routinely performed vaginal inspections during their prison visits with their husband/father. The petitioners alleged the practice violated their right to privacy. The Commission found that the law allowing such searches failed to specify the conditions or types of visits to which such searches were applicable, thereby allowing very wide discretion for prison officials. Accordingly, the Commission found it doubtful that the legislation was precise enough for the searches to

be "prescribed by law." The Commission held that such inspections must be "absolutely necessary" for achieving the aim of prison security and that no other options exist to achieve that security. If such searches were necessary, prison authorities must obtain a judicial order and the search must be executed by qualified medical personnel.

B. Arrest

Murray v. United Kingdom
European Court of Human Rights
300-A Eur. Ct. H.R. (ser. A) (1994)
19 E.H.R.R. 193 (1995)

. . . .

FACTS:

I.   Particular circumstances of the case

A.   Introduction

9. The six applicants are members of the same family. The first applicant, Mrs. Margaret Murray, and the second applicant, Mr. Thomas Murray, are husband and wife. The other four applicants are their children, namely their son Mark Murray (born in 1964), their twin daughters Alana and Michaela Murray (born in 1967) and a younger daughter Rossina Murray (born in 1970). At the relevant time in 1982 all six applicants resided together in the same house in Belfast, Northern Ireland.

10. On 22 June 1982 two of the first applicant's brothers were convicted in the United States of America ("USA") of arms offences connected with the purchase of weapons for the Provisional Irish Republican Army ("Provisional IRA"). The Provisional IRA is included among the organisations proscribed under the special legislation enacted in the United Kingdom to deal with terrorism in Northern Ireland.

B.   First applicant's arrest

11. On 26 July 1982 at approximately 6.30 am Corporal D, a member of the Women's Royal Army Corps, attended an Army briefing at which she was told that the first applicant was suspected of involvement in the collection of money for the purchase of arms for the IRA in the United States, this being a criminal offence under section 21 of the Northern Ireland (Emergency Provisions) Act 1978 ("the 1978 Act") and section 10 of the Prevention of Terrorism (Temporary Provisions) Act 1976. The corporal was instructed to go to the first applicant's house, arrest her under section 14 of the 1978 Act and bring her back to the Army screening centre at Springfield Road in Belfast.

12. At 7.00 am Corporal D, who was unarmed but accompanied by five armed soldiers, arrived by Army vehicle at the applicants' home. The first applicant herself answered the door and three of the male soldiers, together with Corporal D, entered the house. Corporal D established the identity of the first applicant and asked her to get dressed. Corporal D went upstairs with the first applicant. The other applicants were roused and asked to assemble in the living room. The soldiers did not carry out any search

of the contents of the house, but made written notes as to the interior of the house and recorded personal details concerning the applicants. At about 7.30 am in the hallway of the house Corporal D, with one of the soldiers acting as a witness, said to the first applicant, "As a member of Her Majesty's Forces, I arrest you." On being asked twice by the first applicant under what section, Corporal D replied, "Section 14".

C. First applicant's questioning

13. The first applicant was then driven to the Army screening centre at Springfield Road, Belfast. She was escorted into a building and asked to sit for a short time in a small cubicle. At 8.05 am she was taken before Sergeant B who asked her questions with a view to completing part one of a standard form to record, *inter alia*, details of the arrest and screening procedure and personal details. The first applicant refused to answer any questions save to give her name and she refused to be photographed. The interview ended four minutes later. She was then examined by a medical orderly who endeavoured to establish whether she suffered from certain illnesses, but she again refused to co-operate and did not answer any of his questions.

14. At 8.20 am she was taken to an interview room and questioned by a soldier in civilian clothes in the presence of Corporal D. She was asked, *inter alia*, about her brothers and her contacts with them, but she still refused to answer questions. After the interview, which ended at 9.35 am, she was returned to the reception area and then taken back to the medical orderly who asked her if she had any complaints. She did not reply to this query.

At some stage during her stay in the centre she was photographed without her knowledge or consent. This photograph and the personal details about her, her family and her home were kept on record.

She was released at 9.45 am without being charged.

15. The standard record form, called the "screening pro forma", recorded the first applicant's name, address, nationality, marital and tenancy status, the chronological details about her arrest, the names of the Army personnel involved, the names of the other applicants and their relationship to her, her physique and her attitude to the interview. Under the heading "Additional information . . . concerning the arrestee (as reported by the arresting soldier)", it stated: "Subject is the sister of C . . . M . . . who was arrested in USA. Questioned on the above subject." Nothing however was recorded under the heading "Suspected offence". It noted that the applicant had refused to answer questions and that no information had been gained from the interview.

D. Proceedings before the High Court

16. Some 18 months later, on 9 February 1984, the first applicant brought an action against the Ministry of Defence for false imprisonment and other torts.

17. In those proceedings one of the principal allegations made by the first applicant was that her arrest and detention had been effected unlawfully and for an improper purpose. Her allegations were summarised in the judgment of Murray J given on 25 October 1985:

The plaintiff's counsel launched a series of attacks on the legality of the plaintiff's arrest and detention which varied in thrust between the very broad and the very narrow. In the former class, for example, was an attack in which they alleged that the use of section 14 of the [1978 Act] in this case was an example of what they called "an institutionalised form of unlawful screening" by the military authorities, with the intention of obtaining what Counsel termed "low level intelligence" from the plaintiff, and without (a) any genuine suspicion on the part of those authorities that she had committed a criminal offence or (b) any genuine intention on their part of questioning her about a criminal offence alleged to have been committed by her.

. . . .

19. The evidence given by the first applicant is recorded in a note drafted by the trial judge, there being no transcript of the first day of the trial as a result of a technical mishap with the recording equipment. The first applicant explained how she had found the conditions of her arrest and detention distressing for her. She had been angry but had not used strong language. She testified that whilst at the Army centre she had refused to be photographed, to be weighed by the medical orderly, to sign any documents and to answer questions, whether put by Sergeant B, the medical orderly or the interviewer, apart from giving her name. She had made it clear that she would not be answering any questions. She alleged that Sergeant B had told her in so many words that the Army knew that she had not committed any crime but that her file had been lost and the Army wanted to update it. She said that she had been questioned about her brothers in the United States, their whereabouts and her contacts with them, but not about the purchase of arms for the Provisional IRA or about any offence. She accepted that she had been in contact with her brothers and had been to the United States, including a visit that year (1985). She believed that the Army had wanted to obtain information about her brothers. On leaving the centre, she had told the officials that she would be seeing them in court.

20. As appears from the transcript of her evidence, Corporal D gave an account of her briefing on the morning of the arrest. She stated that at the briefing she had been told the first applicant's name and address and the grounds on which she was wanted for questioning, namely her suspected involvement in the collection of money for the purchase of weapons from America. She testified that "my suspicions were aroused by my briefing, and my belief was that Mrs Murray was suspected of collecting money to purchase arms".

Under cross-examination Corporal D maintained that the purpose of an arrest and detention under section 14 of the 1978 Act was not to gather intelligence but to question a suspected person about an offence. She stated that her suspicion of the first applicant had been formed on the basis of everything she had been told at the briefing and which she had read in a document which had been supplied to her then. Corporal D stated that she would not have effected the arrest unless she had been given the grounds on which she was expected to arrest the person. Under repeated questioning, Corporal D maintained that she had been informed at the briefing, and that she had formed the suspicion, that the applicant had been involved in the collection of money for the purchase of arms from America.

. . . .

22. Sergeant B was examined and cross-examined about his completion of part 1 of the standard record form when standing at the reception desk. He said that the first applicant had stated her name but refused to give her address or date of birth or any further information. He expressly denied the applicant's allegation that he had said to her that he knew she was not a criminal and that he just wanted to update her files which had been lost. He gave evidence that information recorded in 1980 on the occasion of a previous arrest of the first applicant had in any event not been lost, since it had been used to complete the details on the first page of the form when she had refused to answer any questions.

Under cross-examination Sergeant B did not accept that the main purpose of questioning a person arrested under section 14 of the 1978 Act was to gather general information about the background, family and associates of the arrested person. He maintained that persons were only arrested and detained if there existed a suspicion against them of involvement in a criminal offence.

. . . .

24. In his judgment of 25 October 1985 Murray J gave detailed consideration to the evidence of Corporal D and Sergeant B on the one hand and the first applicant on the other. Murray J "could not possibly accept the [first applicant's] evidence" that she had been told by Sergeant B that she was not suspected of any offence and that he was just updating his records. He similarly rejected the applicant's claim that Corporal D at no time genuinely suspected her of having committed an offence. In the light of the evidence of Corporal D herself, who was described as a "transparently honest witness", the judge was quite satisfied that on the basis of her briefing at Musgrave Park she genuinely suspected the [first applicant] of having been involved in the offence of collecting money in Northern Ireland for arms.

25. Murray J also rejected the first applicant's claim that section 14 of the 1978 Act had been used with a view to screening in order to gain low-level intelligence: he accepted the evidence of Corporal D and Sergeant B, which had been tested in cross-examination, that the purpose of the applicant's arrest and detention under the section had been to establish facts concerning the offence of which she was suspected.

Murray J also believed the evidence of Corporal D that there were questions addressed to the matters of which the applicant was suspected. He stated:

As regards the interviewer, the plaintiff accepted that he was interested in the activities of her brothers who shortly before the date of the interview had been convicted on arms charges in the USA connected with the Provisional IRA but the [first applicant], who seems to have been well aware of her rights, obviously had decided not to co-operate with the military staff in the centre. In particular she had decided (it seems) not to answer any of their questions and in this situation, and with the short detention period permitted by the section, there was little that the interviewer or any of the other staff in the centre could do to pursue their suspicions.

. . . .

27. The first applicant's action before the High Court was therefore dismissed.

E.   Proceedings before the Court of Appeal

. . . .

202

29. The Court of Appeal further unanimously rejected the first applicant's complaint that the purpose of her arrest and detention, and the whole purport of her questioning, was a fishing expedition unrelated to the matters of which she was suspected and designed to obtain low-grade intelligence about the applicant and others.

. . . .

F.   Proceedings before the House of Lords

. . . .

32. In the House of Lords the applicant did not pursue the allegation that she had not been arrested on the basis of a genuine and honest suspicion that she had committed an offence.

She did however pursue the complaint, previously raised before the Court of Appeal, that since she was only lawfully arrested at 7.30 am she had been unlawfully detained between 7.00 and 7.30 am The House of Lords found that a person is arrested from the moment he is subject to restraint and that the first applicant was therefore under arrest from the moment that Corporal D identified her on entering the house at 7.00 am. It made no difference that the formal words of arrest were communicated to the applicant by 7.30 am. In this respect Lord Griffiths stated [citation omitted]:

> If the plaintiff had been told she was under arrest the moment she identified herself, it would not have made the slightest difference to the sequence of events before she left the house. It would have been wholly unreasonable to take her off, half-clad, to the Army centre, and the same half-hour would have elapsed while she gathered herself together and completed her toilet and dressing. It would seem a strange result that in these circumstances, whether or not she has an action for false imprisonment should depend upon whether the words of arrest are spoken on entering or leaving the house, when the practical effect of the difference on the plaintiff is non-existent.

33. The first applicant had also maintained that the failure to inform her that she was arrested until the soldiers were about to leave the house rendered the arrest unlawful. This submission was also rejected by the House of Lords. Lord Griffiths held as follows [citation omitted]:

> It is a feature of the very limited power of arrest contained in section 14 that a member of the armed forces does not have to tell the arrested person the offence of which he is suspected, for it is specifically provided by section 14(2) that it is sufficient if he states that he is effecting the arrest as a member of Her Majesty's forces.
>
> Corporal D was carrying out this arrest in accordance with the procedures in which she had been instructed to make a house arrest pursuant to section 14. This procedure appears to me to be designed to make the arrest with the least risk of injury to those involved including both the soldiers and the occupants of the house. When arrests are made on suspicion of involvement with the IRA it would be to close one's eyes to the obvious not to appreciate the risk that the arrest may be forcibly resisted.

The drill the Army follow is to enter the house and search every room for occupants. The occupants are all directed to assemble in one room, and when the person the soldiers have come to arrest has been identified and is ready to leave, the formal words of arrest are spoken just before they leave the house. The Army do not carry out a search for property in the house and, in my view, they would not be justified in doing so. The power of search is given 'for the purpose of arresting a person', not for a search for incriminating evidence. It is however a proper exercise of the power of search for the purpose of effecting the arrest to search every room for other occupants of the house in case there may be those there who are disposed to resist the arrest. The search cannot be limited solely to looking for the person to be arrested and must also embrace a search whose object is to secure that the arrest should be peaceable. I also regard it as an entirely reasonable precaution that all the occupants of the house should be asked to assemble in one room. As Corporal D explained in evidence, this procedure is followed because the soldiers may be distracted by other occupants in the house rushing from one room to another, perhaps in a state of alarm, perhaps for the purpose of raising the alarm and to resist the arrest. In such circumstances a tragic shooting accident might all too easily happen with young, and often relatively inexperienced, armed soldiers operating under conditions of extreme tension. Your Lordships were told that the husband and children either had commenced, or were contemplating commencing, actions for false imprisonment arising out of the fact that they were asked to assemble in the living-room for a short period before the plaintiff was taken from the house. That very short period of restraint when they were asked to assemble in the living room was a proper and necessary part of the procedure for effecting the peaceable arrest of the plaintiff. It was a temporary restraint of very short duration imposed not only for the benefit of those effecting the arrest, but also for the protection of the occupants of the house and would be wholly insufficient to found an action for unlawful imprisonment.

It was in my opinion entirely reasonable to delay speaking the words of arrest until the party was about to leave the house. If words of arrest are spoken as soon as the house is entered before any precautions have been taken to search the house and find the other occupants, it seems to me that there is a real risk that the alarm may be raised and an attempt made to resist arrest, not only by those within the house but also by summoning assistance from those in the immediate neighbourhood. When soldiers are employed on the difficult and potentially dangerous task of carrying out a house arrest of a person suspected of an offence in connection with the IRA, it is I think essential that they should have been trained in the drill they are to follow. It would be impracticable and I think potentially dangerous to leave it to the individual discretion of the particular soldier making the arrest to devise his own procedures for carrying out this unfamiliar military function. It is in everyone's best interest that the arrest is peaceably effected and I am satisfied that the procedures adopted by the Army are sensible, reasonable and designed to bring about the arrest with the minimum of danger and distress to all concerned. I would however add this rider: that if the suspect, for any reason, refuses to accept the fact of restraint in the house he should be informed forthwith that he is under arrest.

34. Before the House of Lords the first applicant also pursued a claim that her period of detention exceeded what was reasonably required to make a decision whether to release her or hand her over to the police. In this regard the applicant complained that the standard record form (the "screening pro forma") constituted an improper basis for questioning a suspect on the ground that it asked questions not directly relevant to the suspected offence; it was also suggested that the evidence did not show that the questioning of the applicant was directed to the matters of which she was suspected. The allegation was unanimously rejected by the House of Lords. Lord Griffiths observed as follows [citation omitted]:

> The member of the forces who carried out the interrogation between 8.20 and 9.35 am was not called as a witness on behalf of the Ministry of Defence. There may have been sound reasons for this decision associated with preserving the confidentiality of interrogating techniques and the identity of the interviewer, but be that as it may, the only evidence of what took place at the interview came from Corporal D and the [first applicant] and it is submitted that this evidence is insufficient to establish that the interview was directed towards an attempt to investigate the suspicion upon which the [applicant] was arrested. Corporal D was present at that interview, she was not paying close attention but she gave evidence that she remembered questions about money which were obviously directed towards the offences of which the [applicant] was suspected. The [applicant] also said she was questioned about her brothers.
>
> The judge also had before him a questionnaire that was completed by the interviewer . . . There is nothing in the questionnaire which the Army may not reasonably ask the suspect together with such particular questions as are appropriate to the particular case . . .
>
> The conclusion of the trial judge that the applicant had not been asked unnecessary or unreasonable questions and the conclusion of the Court of Appeal that the interviewer had attempted to pursue with the applicant the suspicion which had been the occasion of the arrest, but had been unable to make any headway, were held by the House of Lords to be justified on the evidence.

II.   The relevant domestic law and practice

A.   Introduction

35. For more than 20 years the population of Northern Ireland, which totals about 1.5 million people, has been subjected to a campaign of terrorism. During that time thousands of persons in Northern Ireland have been killed, maimed or injured. The campaign of terror has extended to the rest of the United Kingdom and to the mainland of Europe.

The 1978 Act forms part of the special legislation enacted over the years in an attempt to enable the security forces to deal effectively with the threat of terrorist violence.

B.   Entry and search; arrest and detention

36. The first applicant was arrested under section 14 of the 1978 Act, which at the relevant time provided as follows:

(1) A member of Her Majesty's forces on duty may arrest without warrant, and detain for not more than four hours, a person whom he suspects of committing, having committed or being about to commit any offence.

(2) A person effecting an arrest under this section complies with any rule of law requiring him to state the ground of arrest if he states that he is effecting the arrest as a member of Her Majesty's forces.

(3) For the purpose of arresting a person under this section a member of Her Majesty's forces may enter and search any premises or other place —

(a) where that person is, or
(b) if that person is suspected of being a terrorist or of having committed an offence involving the use or possession of an explosive, explosive substance or firearm, where that person is suspected of being.

. . . .

38. The scope and exercise of the section 14 powers were considered by the domestic courts in the proceedings in the present case. The applicable law, as stated by the judgments in these proceedings, is that when the legality of an arrest or detention under section 14 is challenged (whether by way of habeas corpus or in proceedings for damages for wrongful arrest or false imprisonment), the burden lies on the military to justify their acts and, in particular, to establish the following elements:

(a) compliance with the formal requirements for arrest;
(b) the genuineness of the suspicion on which the arrest was based;
(c) that the powers of arrest and detention were not used for any improper purpose such as intelligence-gathering;
(d) that the power of search was used only to facilitate the arrest and not for the obtaining of incriminating evidence;
(e) that those responsible for the arrest and detention did not exceed the time reasonably required to reach a decision whether to release the detainee or hand him over to the police.

. . . .

D.   Standard record form

41. As was confirmed in particular by the Court of Appeal and the House of Lords in the present case, the standard record form (known as the "screening pro forma") was an integral part of the examination of the first applicant following her arrest, and the legal authority for recording certain personal details about her in the form derived from the lawfulness of her arrest, detention and examination under section 14 of the 1978 Act. The implied lawful authority conferred by section 14 of the 1978 Act to record information

about the first applicant equally provided the legal basis for the retention of the information.

PROCEEDINGS BEFORE THE [EUROPEAN COMMISSION OF HUMAN RIGHTS]

42. The applicants applied to the Commission on 28 September 1988 (No 14310/88).

The first applicant complained that her arrest and detention for two hours for questioning gave rise to a violation of Article 5(1) and (2), for which she had no enforceable right to compensation as guaranteed by Article 5(5) . . .

. . . .

All six applicants claimed that the entry into and search of their home by the Army were contrary to their right to respect for their private and family life and their home under Article 8 of the Convention; . . . .

. . . .

44. In its report of 17 February 1993 (Made under Art 31) the Commission expressed the opinion:

(a) in the case of the first applicant, by 11 votes to three there had been a violation of Article 5(1), Article 5(2) by 10 votes to four and Article 5(5) by 11 votes to three;

(b) by 13 votes to one there had been no violation of Article 8 . . . .

. . . .

DECISION [OF THE EUROPEAN COURT OF HUMAN RIGHTS]:

I. General approach

47. The applicants' complaints concern the first applicant's arrest and detention by the Army under special criminal legislation enacted to deal with acts of terrorism connected with the affairs of Northern Ireland. As has been noted in several previous judgments by the Court, the campaign of terrorism waged in Northern Ireland over the last quarter of a century has taken a terrible toll, especially in terms of human life and suffering.

The Court sees no reason to depart from the general approach it has adopted in previous cases of a similar nature. Accordingly, for the purposes of interpreting and applying the relevant provisions of the Convention, due account will be taken of the special nature of terrorist crime, the threat it poses to democratic society and the exigencies of dealing with it. [citations omitted]

II. Alleged violation of Article 5(1) of the Convention

48. The first applicant, Mrs. Margaret Murray, alleged that her arrest and detention by the Army were in breach of Article 5(1) of the Convention, which, in so far as relevant, provides:

Everyone has the right to liberty and security of person. No one shall be deprived of his liberty save in the following cases and in accordance with a procedure prescribed by law:

. . . .

> (c) the lawful arrest or detention of a person effected for the purpose of bringing him before the competent legal authority on reasonable suspicion of having committed an offence . . .;

. . . .

A. Lawfulness

49. Before the Convention institutions the first applicant did not dispute that her arrest and detention were "lawful" under Northern Ireland law and, in particular, "in accordance with a procedure prescribed by law", as required by Article 5(1). . . .

B. "Reasonable suspicion"

50. Mrs. Murray was arrested and detained by virtue of section 14 of the 1978 Act. This provision, as construed by the domestic courts, empowered the Army to arrest and detain persons suspected of the commission of an offence provided, *inter alia*, that the suspicion of the arresting officer was honestly and genuinely held. It is relevant but not decisive that the domestic legislation at the time merely imposed this essentially subjective standard: the Court's task is to determine whether the objective standard of "reasonable suspicion" laid down in Article 5(1) was met in the circumstances of the application of the legislation in the particular case.

51. In its judgment of 30 August 1990 in the case of *Fox, Campbell and Hartley v. United Kingdom*, which was concerned with arrests carried out by the Northern Ireland police under a similarly worded provision of the 1978 Act, the Court stated as follows:

> The 'reasonableness' of the suspicion on which an arrest must be based forms an essential part of the safeguard against arbitrary arrest and detention which is laid down in Article 5 § 1(c) . . . (Having) a 'reasonable suspicion' presupposes the existence of facts or information which would satisfy an objective observer that the person concerned may have committed the offence. What may be regarded as 'reasonable' will however depend upon all the circumstances.

> In this respect, terrorist crime falls into a special category. Because of the attendant risk of loss of life and human suffering, the police are obliged to act with utmost urgency in following up all information, including information from secret sources. Further, the police may frequently have to arrest a suspected terrorist on the basis of information which is reliable but which cannot, without putting in jeopardy the source of the information, be revealed to the suspect or produced in court to support a charge.

> . . . (In) view of the difficulties inherent in the investigation and prosecution of terrorist-type offences in Northern Ireland, the 'reasonableness' of the

suspicion justifying such arrests cannot always be judged according to the same standards as are applied in dealing with conventional crime.

Nevertheless, the exigencies of dealing with terrorist crime cannot justify stretching the notion of 'reasonableness' to the point where the essence of the safeguard secured by Article 5 §1(c) is impaired . . .
. . . .

Certainly Article 5 § 1(c) of the Convention should not be applied in such a manner as to put disproportionate difficulties in the way of the police authorities of the Contracting States in taking effective measures to counter organised terrorism . . . . It follows that the Contracting States cannot be asked to establish the reasonableness of the suspicion grounding the arrest of a suspected terrorist by disclosing the confidential sources of supporting information or even facts which would be susceptible of indicating such sources or their identity.

Nevertheless the Court must be enabled to ascertain whether the essence of the safeguard afforded by Article 5 § 1(c) has been secured. Consequently, the respondent Government have to furnish at least some facts or information capable of satisfying the Court that the arrested person was reasonably suspected of having committed the alleged offence. This is all the more necessary where, as in the present case, the domestic law does not require reasonable suspicion, but sets a lower threshold by merely requiring honest suspicion.

On the facts the Court found in that case that, although the arrest and detention of the three applicants, which lasted respectively 44 hours, 44 hours and 5 minutes and 30 hours and 15 minutes, were based on an honest suspicion, insufficient elements had been furnished by the Government to support the conclusion that there had been a "reasonable suspicion" for the purposes of sub-paragraph (c) of Article 5(1).

52. In the present case the Government maintained that there existed strong and specific grounds, founded on information from a reliable but secret source, for the Army to suspect that Mrs Murray was involved in the collection of funds for terrorist purposes. However, the "primary" information so provided could not be revealed in the interests of protecting lives and personal safety. In the Government's submission, the fact that they had maintained that this was the foundation of the suspicion should be given considerable weight by the Court. They also pointed to a number of other facts capable of supporting, albeit indirectly, the reasonableness of the suspicion, including notably the findings made by the domestic courts in the proceedings brought by Mrs. Murray, the very recent conviction of her brothers in the USA of offences connected with the purchase of weapons for the Provisional IRA, her own visits to the USA and her contacts with her brothers there. They submitted that all these matters taken together provided sufficient facts and information to satisfy an objective observer that there was a reasonable suspicion in the circumstances of the case. Any other conclusion by the Court would, they feared, prohibit arresting authorities from effecting an arrest of a person suspected of being a terrorist based primarily on reliable but secret information and would inhibit the arresting authorities in taking effective measures to counter organised terrorism.

53. The first applicant, on the other hand, considered that the Government had failed to discharge the onus of disclosing sufficient facts to enable the Convention institutions

to conclude that the suspicion grounding her arrest was reasonable or anything more than the "honest" suspicion required under Northern Ireland law. As in the case of *Fox, Campbell and Hartley*, the Government's explanation did not meet the minimum standards set by Article 5(1)(c) for judging the reasonableness of her arrest and detention. She did not accept that the reason advanced for non-disclosure was a genuine or valid one. She in her turn pointed to circumstances said to cast doubt on the reasonableness of the suspicion. Thus, had the suspicion really been reasonable, she would not have been arrested under the four-hour power granted by section 14 of the 1978 Act but under more extensive powers; she would have been questioned by the police, not the Army; time would not have been spent in gathering personal details and in photographing her; she would have been questioned for more than one hour and 15 minutes; she would have been questioned about her own alleged involvement and not just about her brothers in the United States; and she would have been cautioned. In reply to the Government the first applicant contended that the issue which the domestic courts inquired into was not the objective reasonableness of any suspicion but the subjective state of mind of the arresting officer, Corporal D.

54. For the Commission, the Government's explanation in the present case was not materially distinguishable from that provided in the case of *Fox, Campbell and Hartley*. It took the view that no objective evidence to corroborate the unrevealed information had been adduced in support of the suspicion that the first applicant had been involved in collecting money for Provisional IRA arms purchases other than her kinship with her convicted brothers. That, the Commission concluded, was insufficient to satisfy the minimum standard set by Article 5(1)(c).

55. With regard to the level of "suspicion", the Court would note firstly that, as was observed in its judgment in the case of *Brogan and Others v. United Kingdom*, "sub-paragraph (c) of Article 5 § 1 does not presuppose that the [investigating authorities] should have obtained sufficient evidence to bring charges, either at the point of arrest or while [the arrested person is] in custody. Such evidence may have been unobtainable or, in view of the nature of the suspected offences, impossible to produce in court without endangering the lives of others". The object of questioning during detention under sub-paragraph (c) of Article 5(1) is to further the criminal investigation by way of confirming or dispelling the concrete suspicion grounding the arrest. Thus, facts which raise a suspicion need not be of the same level as those necessary to justify a conviction or even the bringing of a charge, which comes at the next stage of the process of criminal investigation.

56. The length of the deprivation of liberty at risk may also be material to the level of suspicion required. The period of detention permitted under the provision by virtue of which Mrs Murray was arrested, namely section 14 of the 1978 Act, was limited to a maximum of four hours.

57. With particular regard to the "reasonableness" of the suspicion, the principles stated in the *Fox, Campbell and Hartley* judgment are to be applied in the present case, although as pointed out in that judgment, the existence or not of a reasonable suspicion in a concrete instance depends ultimately on the particular facts.

58. The Court would firstly reiterate its recognition that the use of confidential information is essential in combating terrorist violence and the threat that organised terrorism poses to the lives of citizens and to democratic society as a whole. [citation

omitted] This does not mean, however, that the investigating authorities have *carte blanche* under Article 5 to arrest suspects for questioning, free from effective control by the domestic courts or by the Convention supervisory institutions, whenever they choose to assert that terrorism is involved.

59. As to the present case, the terrorist campaign in Northern Ireland, the carnage it has caused over the years and the active engagement of the Provisional IRA in that campaign are established beyond doubt. The Court also accepts that the power of arrest granted to the Army by section 14 of the 1978 Act represented a bona fide attempt by a democratically elected parliament to deal with terrorist crime under the rule of law. That finding is not altered by the fact that the terms of the applicable legislation were amended in 1987 as a result of the Baker Report so as to include a requirement that the arrest should be based on reasonable, rather than merely honest, suspicion.

The Court is accordingly prepared to attach some credence to the respondent Government's declaration concerning the existence of reliable but confidential information grounding the suspicion against Mrs Murray.

60. Nevertheless, in the words of the *Fox, Campbell and Hartley* judgment, the respondent Government must in addition "furnish at least some facts or information capable of satisfying the Court that the arrested person was reasonably suspected of having committed the alleged offence". In this connection, unlike in the case of *Fox, Campbell and Hartley*, the Convention institutions have had the benefit of the review that the national courts conducted of the facts and of Mrs. Murray's allegations in the civil proceedings brought by her.

61. It cannot be excluded that all or some of the evidence adduced before the national courts in relation to the genuineness of the suspicion on the basis of which Mrs. Murray was arrested may also be material to the issue whether the suspicion was "reasonable" for the purposes of Article 5(1)(c) of the Convention. At the very least the honesty and bona fides of a suspicion constitute one indispensable element of its reasonableness.

In the action brought by Mrs. Murray against the Ministry of Defence for false imprisonment and other torts, the High Court judge, after having heard the witnesses and assessed their credibility, found that she had genuinely been suspected of having been involved in the collection of funds for the purchase of arms in the United States for the Provisional IRA. The judge believed the evidence of the arresting officer, Corporal D, who was described as a "transparently honest witness", as to what she had been told at her briefing before the arrest. Likewise as found by the judge, although the interview at the Army centre was later in time than the arrest, the line of questioning pursued by the interviewer also tends to support the conclusion that Mrs. Murray herself was suspected of the commission of a specific criminal offence.

62. Some weeks before her arrest two of Mrs Murray's brothers had been convicted in the United States of offences connected with purchase of arms for the Provisional IRA. As she disclosed in her evidence to the High Court, she had visited the United States and had contacts with her brothers there. The offences of which her brothers were convicted were ones that implied collaboration with "trustworthy" persons residing in Northern Ireland.

63. Having regard to the level of factual justification required at the stage of suspicion and to the special exigencies of investigating terrorist crime, the Court finds, in the light of all the above considerations, that there did exist sufficient facts or information

which would provide a plausible and objective basis for a suspicion that Mrs. Murray may have committed the offence of involvement in the collection of funds for the Provisional IRA. On the particular facts of the present case, therefore, the Court is satisfied that, notwithstanding the lower standard of suspicion under domestic law, Mrs. Murray can be said to have been arrested and detained on "reasonable suspicion" of the commission of a criminal offence, within the meaning of sub-paragraph (c) of Article 5(1).

C. Purpose of the arrest

64. In the first applicant's submission, it was clear from the surrounding circumstances that she was not arrested for the purpose of bringing her before a "competent legal authority" but merely for the purpose of interrogating her with a view to gathering general intelligence. She referred to the entries made in her regard on the standard record completed at the Army centre, to the failure of the Army to involve the police in her questioning and to the short (one-hour) period of her questioning.

The Government disputed this contention, pointing to the fact that it was a claim expressly raised by Mrs. Murray in the domestic proceedings and rejected by the trial judge on the basis of evidence which had been tested by cross-examination of witnesses.

The Commission in its report did not find it necessary to examine this complaint in view of its conclusion as to the lack of "reasonable suspicion" for the arrest and detention.

65. Under the applicable law of Northern Ireland the power of arrest and detention granted to the Army under section 14 of the 1978 Act must not be used for any improper purpose such as intelligence-gathering. In the civil action brought by Mrs. Murray against the Ministry of Defence the trial court judge found that on the evidence before him the purpose of her arrest and detention under section 14 of the 1978 Act had been to establish facts concerning the offence of which she was suspected. In reaching this conclusion the trial judge had had the benefit of seeing the various witnesses give their evidence and of evaluating their credibility. He accepted the evidence of Corporal D and Sergeant B as being truthful and rejected the claims of Mrs. Murray, in particular her contention that she had been told by Sergeant B that she was not suspected of any offence and had been arrested merely in order to bring her file up to date. The Court of Appeal, after reviewing the evidence, in turn rejected her argument that the purpose of her arrest and detention had been a "fishing expedition" designed to obtain low-grade intelligence. This argument was not pursued before the House of Lords.

66. The Court's task is to determine whether the conditions laid down by paragraph (c) of Article 5(1), including the pursuit of the prescribed legitimate purpose, have been fulfilled in the circumstances of the particular case. However, in this context it is not normally within the province of the Court to substitute its own finding of fact for that of the domestic courts, which are better placed to assess the evidence adduced before them. [citations omitted] In the present case no cogent elements have been produced by the first applicant in the proceedings before the Convention institutions which could lead the Court to depart from the findings of fact made by the Northern Ireland courts.

67. Mrs. Murray was neither charged nor brought before a court but was released after an interview lasting a little longer than one hour. This does not necessarily mean, however, that the purpose of her arrest and detention was not in accordance with Article 5(1)(c) since "the existence of such a purpose must be considered independently of its

achievement". [citation omitted] As the domestic courts pointed out, in view of her persistent refusal to answer any questions at the Army centre it is not surprising that the authorities were not able to make any headway in pursuing the suspicions against her. It can be assumed that, had these suspicions been confirmed, charges would have been laid and she would have been brought before the competent legal authority.

68. The first applicant also alleged absence of the required proper purpose by reason of the fact that in practice persons arrested by the Army under section 14 were never brought before a competent legal authority by the Army but, if the suspicions were confirmed during questioning, were handed over to the police who preferred charges and took the necessary action to bring the person before a court.

The Court sees little merit in this argument. What counts for the purpose of compliance with Convention obligations is the substance rather than the form. Provided that the purpose of the arrest and detention is genuinely to bring the person before the competent legal authority, the mechanics of how this is to be achieved will not be decisive.

69. The arrest and detention of the first applicant must therefore be taken to have been effected for the purpose specified in paragraph 1(c).

D. Conclusion

70. In conclusion, there has been no violation of Article 5(1) in respect of the first applicant.

III. Alleged violation of Article 5(2) of the Convention

71. The first applicant also alleged a violation of Article 5(2) of the Convention, which provides:

Everyone who is arrested shall be informed promptly, in a language which he understands, of the reasons for his arrest and of any charge against him.

72. The relevant principles governing the interpretation and application of Article 5(2) in cases such as the present one were explained by the Court in its *Fox, Campbell and Hartley* judgment as follows:

Paragraph 2 of Article 5 contains the elementary safeguard that any person arrested should know why he is being deprived of his liberty. This provision is an integral part of the scheme of protection afforded by Article 5: by virtue of paragraph 2 any person arrested must be told, in simple, non-technical language that he can understand, the essential legal and factual grounds for his arrest, so as to be able, if he sees fit, to apply to a court to challenge its lawfulness in accordance with paragraph 4 . . . Whilst this information must be conveyed 'promptly' (in French: '*dans le plus court dèlai*'), it need not be related in its entirety by the arresting officer at the very moment of the arrest. Whether the content and promptness of the information conveyed were sufficient is to be assessed in each case according to its special features.

In that case the Court found on the facts that the reasons for the applicants' arrest had been brought to their attention during their interrogation within a few hours of their arrest. This being so, the requirements of Article 5(2) were held to have been satisfied in the circumstances.

73. The first applicant maintained that at no time during her arrest or detention had she been given any or sufficient information as to the grounds of her arrest. Although she had realised that the Army was interested in her brothers' activities, she had not, she claimed, understood from the interview at the Army centre that she herself was suspected of involvement in fund-raising for the Provisional IRA. The only direct information she was given was the formal formula of arrest pronounced by Corporal D.

74. The Commission similarly took the view that it was impossible to draw any conclusions from what it described as the vague indications given by Corporal D in evidence before the High Court as to whether the first applicant had been able to understand from the interview why she had been arrested. In the Commission's opinion, it had not been shown that the questions asked of Mrs. Murray during her interview were sufficiently precise to constitute the information as to the reasons for arrest required by Article 5(2).

75. According to the Government, on the other hand, it was apparent from the trial evidence that in the interview it was made clear to Mrs. Murray that she was suspected of the offence of collecting money for the Provisional IRA. The Government did not accept the Commission's conclusion on the facts, which was at variance with the findings of the domestic courts. They considered it established that Mrs. Murray had been given sufficient information as to the grounds of her arrest. In the alternative, even if insufficient information had been given to her to avail herself of her right under Article 5(4) of the Convention to take legal proceedings to test the lawfulness of her detention, she had suffered no prejudice thereby which would give rise to a breach of Article 5(2) since she had been released rapidly, before any determination of the lawfulness of her detention could have taken place.

76. It is common ground that, apart from repeating the formal words of arrest required by law, the arresting officer, Corporal D, also told Mrs. Murray the section of the 1978 Act under which the arrest was being carried out. This bare indication of the legal basis for the arrest, taken on its own, is insufficient for the purposes of Article 5(2). [citation omitted]

77. During the trial of Mrs. Murray's action against the Ministry of Defence, evidence as to the interview at the Army centre was given by Mrs. Murray and Corporal D, but not by the solider who had conducted the interview. Mrs. Murray testified that she had been questioned about her brothers in the United States and about her contacts with them but not about the purchase of arms for the Provisional IRA or about any offence. Corporal D did not have a precise recollection as to the content of the questions put to Mrs. Murray. This is not perhaps surprising since the trial took place over three years after the events — Mrs. Murray having waited 18 months before bringing her action — and Corporal D, although present, had not taken an active part in the interview. Corporal D did however remember that questions had been asked about money and about America and the trial judge found her to be a "transparently honest witness". Shortly before the arrest two of Mrs. Murray's brothers had, presumably to the knowledge of all concerned

in the interview, been convicted in the United States of offences connected with the purchase of weapons for the Provisional IRA.

In the Court's view, it must have been apparent to Mrs. Murray that she was being questioned about her possible involvement in the collection of funds for the purchase of arms for the Provisional IRA by her brothers in the United States. Admittedly, "there was never any probing examination of her collecting money" — to use the words of the trial judge — but, as the national courts noted, this was because of Mrs. Murray's declining to answer any questions at all beyond giving her name. The Court therefore finds that the reasons for her arrest were sufficiently brought to her attention during her interview.

78. Mrs. Murray was arrested at her home at 7.00 am and interviewed at the Army centre between 8.20 am and 9.35 am on the same day. In the context of the present case this interval cannot be regarded as falling outside the constraints of time imposed by the notion of promptness in Article 5(2).

79. In view of the foregoing findings it is not necessary for the Court to examine the Government's alternative submission.

80. In conclusion, there was no breach of Article 5(2) in respect of the first applicant.

. . . .

V. Alleged violation of Article 8 of the Convention

83. All six applicants claimed to be the victims of a violation of Article 8 of the Convention, which provides:

1. Everyone has the right to respect for his private and family life, his home and his correspondence.

2. There shall be no interference by a public authority with the exercise of this right except such as is in accordance with the law and is necessary in a democratic society in the interests of national security, public safety or the economic well-being of the country, for the prevention of disorder or crime, for the protection of health or morals, or for the protection of the rights and freedoms of others.

A. Arguments before the Court

84. The first applicant complained of the manner in which she was treated both in her home and at the Army centre; in the latter connection she objected to the recording of personal details concerning herself and her family, as well as the photograph which was taken of her without her knowledge or consent. All six applicants contended that the entry into and search of their family home by the Army, including the confinement of the second, third, fourth, fifth and sixth applicants for a short while in one room, violated Article 8.

85. Both the Government and the Commission considered that the matters complained of were justified under paragraph 2 of Article 8 as being lawful measures necessary in a democratic society for the prevention of crime in the context of the fight against terrorism in Northern Ireland.

B. Interference

86. It was not contested that the impugned measures interfered with the applicants' exercise of their right to respect for their private and family life and their home.

C. "In accordance with the law"

87. On the other hand, the applicants did not concede that the resultant interferences had been "in accordance with the law". They disputed that the impugned measures all formed an integral part of Mrs. Murray's arrest and detention or that the domestic courts had affirmed their lawfulness, in particular as concerns the retention of the records including the photograph of Mrs. Murray.

88. Entry into and search of a home by Army personnel such as occurred in the present case were explicitly permitted by section 14(3) of the 1978 Act for the purpose of effecting arrests under that section. The Court of Appeal upheld the legality of the search in the present case. The short period of restraint endured by the other members of Mrs. Murray's family when they were asked to assemble in one room was held by the House of Lords to be a necessary and proper part of the procedure of arrest of Mrs. Murray. The Court of Appeal and the House of Lords also confirmed that the Army's implied lawful authority under section 14 extended to interrogating a detained person and to recording personal details of the kind contained in the standard record form. It is implicit in the judgments of the national courts that the retention of such details was covered by the same lawful authority derived from section 14. The taking and, by implication, also the retention of a photograph of the first applicant without her consent had no statutory basis but, as explained by the trial court judge and the Court of Appeal, were lawful under the common law.

The impugned measures thus had a basis in domestic law. The Court discerns no reason, on the material before it, for not concluding that each of the various measures was "in accordance with the law", within the meaning of Article 8(2).

D. Legitimate aim

89. These measures undoubtedly pursued the legitimate aim of the prevention of crime.

E. Necessity in a democratic society

90. It remains to be determined whether they were necessary in a democratic society and, in particular, whether the means employed were proportionate to the legitimate aim pursued. In this connection it is not for the Court to substitute for the assessment of the national authorities its own assessment of what might be the best policy in the field of investigation of terrorist crime. [citation omitted] A certain margin of appreciation in deciding what measures to take both in general and in particular cases should be left to the national authorities.

91. The present judgment has already adverted to the responsibility of an elected government in a democratic society to protect its citizens and its institutions against the

threats posed by organised terrorism and to the special problems involved in the arrest and detention of persons suspected of terrorist-linked offences. These two factors affect the fair balance that is to be struck between the exercise by the individual of the right guaranteed to him or her under paragraph 1 of Article 8 and the necessity under paragraph 2 for the State to take effective measures for the prevention of terrorist crimes. [citation omitted]

92. The domestic courts held that Mrs. Murray was genuinely and honestly suspected of the commission of a terrorist-linked crime. The European Court, for its part, has found on the evidence before it that this suspicion could be regarded as reasonable for the purposes of sub-paragraph (c) Article 5(1). The Court accepts that there was in principle a need both for powers of the kind granted by section 14 of the 1978 Act and, in the particular case, to enter and search the home of the Murray family in order to arrest Mrs. Murray.

Furthermore, the "conditions of extreme tension", as Lord Griffiths put it in his speech in the House of Lords, under which such arrests in Northern Ireland have to be carried out must be recognised. The Court notes the analysis of Lord Griffiths, when he said:

> The search cannot be limited solely to looking for the person to be arrested and must also embrace a search whose object is to secure that the arrest should be peaceable. I . . . regard it as an entirely reasonable precaution that all the occupants of the house should be asked to assemble in one room . . . It is in everyone's best interest that the arrest is peaceably effected and I am satisfied that the procedures adopted by the Army are sensible, reasonable and designed to bring about the arrest with the minimum of danger and distress to all concerned.

These are legitimate considerations which go to explain and justify the manner in which the entry into and search of the applicants' home were carried out. The Court does not find that, in relation to any of the applications, the means employed by the authorities in this regard were disproportionate to the aim pursued.

93. Neither can it be regarded as falling outside the legitimate bounds of the process of investigation of terrorist crime for the competent authorities to record and retain basic personal details concerning the arrested person or even other persons present at the time and place of arrest. None of the personal details taken during the search of the family home or during Mrs. Murray's stay at the Army centre would appear to have been irrelevant to the procedures of arrest and interrogation. Similar conclusions apply to the taking and retention of a photograph of Mrs. Murray at the Army centre. In this connection too, the Court does not find that the means employed were disproportionate to the aim pursued.

94. In the light of the particular facts of the case, the Court finds that the various measures complained of can be regarded as having been necessary in a democratic society for the prevention of crime, within the meaning of Article 8(2).

F. Conclusion

95. In conclusion there has been no violation of Article 8 in respect of any of the applicants.

. . . .

For these reasons, THE COURT

1. Holds, by 14 votes to four, that there has been no breach of Article 5(1) of the Convention in respect of the first applicant;

2. Holds, by 13 votes to five, that there has been no breach of Article 5(2) of the Convention in respect of the first applicant;

. . . .

4. Holds, by 15 votes to three, that there has been no breach of Article 8 of the Convention in respect of any of the applicants . . . .

❖ ❖ ❖

Questions & Comments

(1) The most striking aspect of ECHR law governing arrests is that only "reasonable suspicion" is required -- not probable cause, as under U.S. law. *Spinelli v. United States*, 393 U.S. 410 (1969). Under U.S. law, reasonable suspicion is sufficient only for "stop and frisks." *Terry v. Ohio*, 392 U.S. 1 (1968). Neither the Inter-American Court nor Inter-American Commission has addressed the required evidentiary requirement for lawful arrest. On the other hand, the UN Human Rights Committee has opined that only reasonable suspicion is required. *See* M.J. Bossuyt, GUIDE TO THE "TRAVAUX PRÈPARATOIRES" OF THE INTERNATIONAL COVENANT ON CIVIL AND POLITICAL RIGHTS 187-219 (1987) (detailing the ICCPR's drafting history and the Committee's Art. 9 comments).

(2) There are several troubling aspects about the European Court's decision in *Murray v. United Kingdom*. Mrs. Murray's arrest was based on her brothers' convictions in the U.S. and her visit to them. Is it not reasonable and lawful that a sister would visit her brothers if they had been detained? Furthermore, does her brothers' convictions and her visit really form sufficient grounds for reasonable suspicion of her raising funds for the IRA? If these factors constituted sufficient grounds for reasonable suspicion, then anyone who ever visited a prisoner could be stopped, arrested, and detained for questioning.

Although the European Court made reference to secret sources of information upon which the U.K. authorities' reasonable suspicion was based, neither the European Court nor the U.K. courts examined the veracity and basis of knowledge of the secret source. How does this comport with the European Court's other caselaw addressing the right to the examination of witnesses and documents? See Chapter 12(C).

Under U.S. law, to establish probable cause, a judge must examine the totality of circumstances, including the "veracity" and "basis of knowledge" of confidential sources. *Illinois v. Gates*, 462 U.S. 213 (1983). Even under a "reasonable suspicion" standard, such as provided by *Terry v. Ohio*, "specific and articulatable facts" must be produced.

In *Murray v. United Kingdom*, no comparable analyses of the secret source's information was undertaken by either the U.K. courts or European Court.

> [I]n the words of the *Fox, Campbell and Hartley* judgment, the respondent Government must in addition "furnish at least some facts or information capable of satisfying the Court that the arrested person was reasonably suspected of having committed the alleged offence". In this connection, unlike in the case of *Fox, Campbell and Hartley*, the Convention institutions have had the benefit of the review that the national courts conducted of the facts and of Mrs. Murray's allegations in the civil proceedings brought by her.

Murray v. United Kingdom, 300-A Eur. Ct. H.R. at § 60 (1994). Did the European Court fail to exercise the appropriate level of "European supervision" given that this case turns of an important factual issue?

Another troubling aspect of the European Court's decision is that while the European Court provided background as to the civil strife in Northern Ireland and accordingly recognized the need to combat IRA terrorism, it did not see fit to discuss the well-established terrorist practices[3] of the U.K.'s police and military and the concomitant need to combat state terrorism. The use of terror — whether by rousing and holding family members in a room where they could be subjected to physical or other threats or by arresting Mrs. Murray — is often effective in extracting information from persons whom are not the subject of reasonable suspicion of committing crimes. In rejecting Mrs. Murray's argument that the purpose of her arrest and detention had been a "fishing expedition" designed to obtain low-grade intelligence, the Court seems to have effectively sanctioned the use of coercive measures against innocent persons in criminal investigations.

Does the fact that Mrs. Murray was released after a very brief interrogation in which no information was elicited throw into question the government's claim of "reasonable suspicion" of criminal activity? If she truly was suspected of terrorist-related activity, wouldn't the government have an interest in detaining her until she answered the questions put to her? If the government had held her until she agreed to answer the questions, would this constitute a violation under the European Convention? Francisco Forrest Martin, *et al.*, 1 INTERNATIONAL HUMAN RIGHTS LAW & PRACTICE: CASES, TREATIES AND MATERIALS 488-89 (1997).

(3) For another right to liberty case dealing with Northern Ireland, *see, e.g., Fox, Campbell, and Hartley v. United Kingdom*, 182 Eur. Ct. H.R. (ser. A) (1990).

---

[3] In *Ireland v. United Kingdom*, 24 Eur. Ct. H.R. (ser. A) (1978), the European Court itself found that the U.K. authorities had as a matter of policy used interrogation methods that constituted inhuman and degrading treatment in violation of Article 3, ECHR. Also, recall the case of the Guildford Four in which unlawful coercive interrogation methods were used against suspected IRA terrorists.

(4) Compare *Slijivo v. Republika Srpska (Admissibility and Merits)*, Case No. CH/97/34, Hum. Rts. Chamber-BiH (10 September 1998), in which the Human Rights Chamber for Bosnia and Herzegovina held that arresting authorities need not tell the arrestee the reasons for his/her arrest in its entirety at the moment of arrest.

(5) Compare the strength of the Article 5 right to liberty with that of the Article 8 right to respect for private and family life in the context of arrests within the home or other private places. Does Article 8 provide greater protection to individuals?

(6) Compare the ICC Statute's arrest provisions:

Article 58
Issuance by the Pre-Trial Chamber of a warrant of arrest or a summons to appear

1. At any time after the initiation of an investigation, the Pre-Trial Chamber shall, on the application of the Prosecutor, issue a warrant of arrest of a person if, having examined the application and the evidence or other information submitted by the Prosecutor, it is satisfied that:

> (a) There are reasonable grounds to believe that the person has committed a crime within the jurisdiction of the Court; and
> (b) The arrest of the person appears necessary:
>
>> (i) To ensure the person's appearance at trial,
>> (ii) To ensure that the person does not obstruct or endanger the investigation or the court proceedings, or
>> (iii) Where applicable, to prevent the person from continuing with the commission of that crime or a related crime which is within the jurisdiction of the Court and which arises out of the same circumstances.

2. The application of the Prosecutor shall contain:

> (a) The name of the person and any other relevant identifying information;
> (b) A specific reference to the crimes within the jurisdiction of the Court which the person is alleged to have committed;
> (c) A concise statement of the facts which are alleged to constitute those crimes;
> (d) A summary of the evidence and any other information which establish reasonable grounds to believe that the person committed those crimes; and
> (e) The reason why the Prosecutor believes that the arrest of the person is necessary.

3. The warrant of arrest shall contain:

(a) The name of the person and any other relevant identifying information;

(b) A specific reference to the crimes within the jurisdiction of the Court for which the person's arrest is sought; and

(c) A concise statement of the facts which are alleged to constitute those crimes.

4. The warrant of arrest shall remain in effect until otherwise ordered by the Court.

. . . .

Clearly, the ICC Statute's provisions require more than the "reasonable suspicion" interpretation of the European Court of Human Rights. Does it require more than the reasonable suspicion standard in *Terry v. Ohio*? Does it reach the "probable cause" standard in *Spinelli v. United States*?

C. Court Access for Determining Lawfulness of Arrest and Continuing Detention

Suárez Rosero v. Ecuador
Inter-American Court of Human Rights
Judgment of 12 November 1997

. . . .

34. From an examination of the documents, the witnesses' statements, the expert's report, and the remarks of the State and the Commission in the course of the proceedings, the Court deems the following facts to have been proven:

a. Mr. Rafael Iván Suárez-Rosero was arrested at 2:30 a.m. on June 23, 1992, by officers of the National Police of Ecuador, in connection with police Operation *"Ciclón"*, the aim of which was to *"disband one of the largest international drug-trafficking organizations"*, by a police order issued when residents of the Zámbiza sector of Quito reported that the occupants of a "Trooper" were burning what appeared to be drugs . . . ;

b. Mr. Suárez-Rosero was arrested without a warrant from the competent authority and not *in flagrante delicto* . . . ;

c. on the day of his arrest, Mr. Suárez-Rosero gave an initial statement to police officers in the presence of three prosecutors from the Ministry of Public Affairs. No defense attorney was present during the questioning . . . ;

d. from June 23 to July 23, 1992, Mr. Rafael Iván Suárez-Rosero was held *incommunicado* at the "Quito Number 2" Police Barracks situated at Montúfar and Manabí streets in the city of Quito, in a damp and poorly ventilated cell measuring five meters by three, together with sixteen other persons . . . ;

e. on July 22, 1992, the Commissioner-General of Police of Pichincha ordered the Director of the Men's Social Rehabilitation Center to keep Mr. Suárez-Rosero and other persons in detention until a court had issued an order to the contrary . . . ;

f. on July 23, 1992, Mr. Suárez-Rosero was transferred to the Men's Social Rehabilitation Center of Quito . . . ;

. . . .

i. on August 12, 1992, the Third Criminal Court of Pichincha issued an order of preventive detention against Mr. Suárez-Rosero . . . ;

j. on September 3, 1992, the Third Criminal Court of Pichincha declined to try the case against Mr. Suárez-Rosero and the other persons detained in Operation "*Ciclón*," inasmuch of one of the accused in that case was promoted to the rank of Infantry Major, and transferred the file to the Superior Court of Justice of Quito . . . ;

k. on two occasions, on September 14, 1992, and January 21, 1993, Mr. Suárez-Rosero requested that the order authorizing his preventive detention be revoked . . . ;

l. on November 27, 1992, the President of the Superior Court of Justice of Quito ordered the initiation of the first phase of the pre-trial proceedings. In that order, Mr. Suárez-Rosero was charged with transporting drugs for the purpose of destroying them and hiding the evidence . . . ;

m. on December 9, 1992, the President of the Superior Court of Justice of Quito ordered investigative proceedings to be instituted in connection with the case; these were held between December 29, 1992, and January 13, 1993 . . . ;

n. on March 29, 1993, Mr. Suárez-Rosero filed a writ of habeas corpus with the President of the Supreme Court of Justice of Ecuador, under the provisions of Article 458 of the Code of Criminal Proceedings of Ecuador . . . ;

o. on August 25, 1993, the President of the Superior Court of Justice of Quito requested the Public Prosecutor of Pichincha to render his opinion on Mr. Suárez-Rosero's request to have his detention order revoked . . . ;

p. on January 11, 1994, the Prosecutor of Pichincha rendered an opinion on the request for abrogation of Mr. Suárez-Rosero's detention order (*supra*, subparagraph o.), stating that

> for the time being, the police report which serves as the basis for initiation of the instant criminal case, as well as the preliminary statements, suggests that the accused [...]: Iván Suárez-Rosero [...] appear[s] to be responsible, so that it would be improper to revoke the order for [his] preventive detention .

. . . .

q. on January 26, 1994, Mr. Suárez-Rosero's request to have the preventive detention order against him revoked was denied *(supra*, subparagraph k.) . . . . That same day, the officers who had arrested him were summoned to give statements, but did not appear, nor did they do so when they were again summoned on March 3 and May 9, 1994 . . . ;

r. on June 10, 1994, the President of the Supreme Court of Justice denied the writ of habeas corpus filed by Mr. Suárez-Rosero (*supra*, subparagraph n.), on the ground that

[t]he petition presented [. did] not provide any information showing the category or nature of the proceeding indicating that he was deprived of his liberty, the district in which the President of the Superior Court of Justice that had issued the order was located, the place of detention, the date on which he was deprived of his liberty, the reason, etc., so that it cannot be processed and is therefore denied and ordered to be struck from the list.

. . . .

s. on November 4, 1994, the President of the Superior Court of Justice of Quito declared the preliminary proceedings to be at an end and referred the case to the Public Prosecutor of Pichincha for his final pronouncement . . . . The prosecutor was to make a determination, within six days, but there is no record of the date in which he did so (Art. 235 of the Code of Criminal Proceeding of Ecuador);

t. on July 10, 1995, the President of the Superior Court of Justice of Quito declared open the plenary phase of the case against Mr. Suárez-Rosero, on a charge of being accessory to the crime of drug trafficking. That court also decided that in Mr. Suárez-Rosero's case the requirements of preventive detention had not been met, and ordered his release . . . ;

u. on July 13, 1995, the Public Prosecutor of Pichincha requested the President of the Superior Court of Pichincha to expand his order of July 10, 1995,

so as not to release any person until that order [had been] referred to the Superior Court, in strict compliance with Article 121 of the Law on Narcotic Drugs and Psychotropic Substances

. . . .

v. on July 24, 1995, the President of the Superior Court of Justice of Quito ruled

[the] petition [of the Public Prosecutor of Pichincha of July 13, 1995] to be in order, inasmuch as the norm previously invoked in this type of violation is mandatory, since it deals with the crime of drug trafficking, governed by the Special Law on Narcotic Drugs and Psychotropic Substances [... and that] the order of release granted to accessories and to those whose cases were provisionally suspended should also be reviewed.

Consequently, the units were revised by the First Chamber of the Superior Court of Justice of Quito on July 31, 1995 . . . ;

w. on April 16, 1996, the First Chamber of the Superior Court of Justice of Quito ordered Mr. Suárez-Rosero's release . . . . That order was complied with on April 29, 1996 . . . ;

x. the President of the Superior Court of Justice of Quito, in his judgment of September 9, 1996, decided that Mr. Suárez-Rosero is an accessory [.] to the crime of illegal trafficking in narcotic and drugs and psychotropic substances, defined and punishable under Art. 62 of the Law on Narcotic Drugs and Psychotropic Substances, and that, pursuant to the provisions of Arts. 44 and 88 of the Criminal Code, he was [.] sentenced to two years' imprisonment which he [was to] serve at the Men's Social Rehabilitation Center in [the] city of Quito, and that the time he has remained in preventive [.] detention would be deducted from that sentence.

Mr. Suárez-Rosero was also fined two thousand times the minimum living wage . . . , and

y. at no time was Mr. Suárez-Rosero summoned to appear before a competent judicial authority to be informed of the charges brought against him . . . .
. . . .

VIOLATION OF ARTICLE 7(2) AND 7(3)

38. In its application the Commission asked the Court to declare that Mr. Suárez-Rosero's initial detention was unlawful and arbitrary, in violation of Article 7(2) and 7(3) of the American Convention, since both this instrument and the Ecuadorian laws require such acts to be performed by order of the competent authority in accordance with the procedures and terms established by law. A further requirement, according to the Commission, is that the detention be necessary and reasonable, which has not been proven in this case. Lastly, the Commission argued that during the initial period of Mr. Suárez-Rosero's arrest, he was held in facilities unsuitable for persons in preventive detention.

39. The State, for its part, contended that Mr. Suárez-Rosero's arrest *"was carried out in connection with a lawful inquiry and as a result of actual events, of which he was one of the protagonists."*

40. In its brief of closing arguments the Commission stated that, in the course of the proceeding, not only had Ecuador not denied that Mr. Suárez-Rosero had been arrested in violation of Ecuadorian law, but that, on the contrary, the alternate agent of the State had admitted at the public hearing before the Court that Mr. Suárez-Rosero's arrest had been arbitrary.

41. Ecuador maintained in its closing arguments, on the subject of Mr. Suárez-Rosero's arrest, that "[i]*t is surprised* [...] *that the defendant has described a frightful scenario of detention and arrest and yet he is the only person to have appealed to the Commission to demonstrate such monstrous facts."*

42. Article 7(2) and (3) of the American Convention on Human Rights establishes that

2. No one shall be deprived of his physical liberty except for reasons and under conditions established beforehand by the constitution of the State Party concerned or by a law established pursuant thereto.

3. No one shall be subject to arbitrary arrest or imprisonment.

43. The Court has said that no one may be

deprived of personal liberty except for reasons, or in cases or circumstances expressly described in the law (material aspect), but, moreover, with strict adherence to the procedures objectively defined by it (formal aspect) (*Gangaram Panday Case,* Judgment of January 21, 1994. Series C No. 16, para. 47).

With regard to the formal requirements, the Court observes that the Political Constitution of Ecuador provides in Article 22(19)(h) that:

[n]o one shall be deprived of his liberty except by written order of the competent authority, as appropriate, for the period and according to the procedures prescribed by law, save in the case of *flagrante delicto*, in which case he may not either be held without a trial order for more than twenty-four hours. In either case, he may not be held *incommunicado* for more than twenty-four hours

and that, pursuant to Article 177 of the Code of Criminal Procedure of Ecuador,

[t]he court may issue a writ of preventive imprisonment when it deems it to be necessary, provided the following procedural data are presented:

1. Evidence leading to a presumption of the existence of a crime that warrants the punishment of deprivation of liberty; and,
2. Evidence leading to a presumption that the accused is the author of or accomplice in the crime in question.

The evidence on which the order of imprisonment are based shall be stated in the records.

44. It was not demonstrated in the instant Case that Mr. Suárez-Rosero was apprehended *in flagrante delicto.* His arrest should therefore have been effected with a warrant issued by a competent judicial authority. However, the first judicial proceeding relating to his detention only took place on August 12, 1992 (*supra,* para. 34(i)), that is, over a month after his arrest, in violation of procedures previously established by the Political Constitution and the Code of Criminal Procedure of Ecuador.

45. The Court deems it unnecessary to voice an opinion on the evidence or suspicions that may have led to a detention order. The relevant point is that such an order was only produced in this case long after the victim's arrest. This was expressly acknowledged by the State during the public hearing, when it said that "*Mr. Suárez was the victim of arbitrary detention.*"

46. As to the place in which Mr. Suárez-Rosero was held *incommunicado*, the Court deems it to have been proven that he spent from June 23 to July 23, 1992, at a police station unsuitable as accommodation for a prisoner, according to the Commission and the expert (*supra,* para. 34(d)), in addition to all the violations of the right to liberty to the detriment of Mr. Suárez-Rosero.

47. For the above reasons, the Court finds that the Mr. Suárez-Rosero' arrest and his subsequent detention from June 23, 1992, were carried out in violation of the provisions contained in Article 7(2) and (3) of the American Convention.

* * *

48. The Commission requested the Court to find that the fact that Mr. Suárez-Rosero's *incommunicado* detention for 36 days generated a violation of Article 7(2) of the American Convention, inasmuch as it violated Ecuadorian law, which establishes that such detention may not exceed 24 hours.

49. Ecuador did not challenge that argument in its answer to the application.

50. The Court observes that, pursuant to Article 22(19)(h) of the Political Constitution of Ecuador, the *incommunicado* detention of a person may not exceed 24 hours (*supra*, para. 43). Nevertheless, Mr. Suárez-Rosero was held *incommunicado* from June 23 to July 28, 1992 (*supra*, para. 34(d)), that is, for a total of 35 days in excess of the maximum period established by the Constitution.

51. *Incommunicado* detention is an exceptional measure the purpose of which is to prevent any interference with the investigation of the facts. Such isolation must be limited to the period of time expressly established by law. Even in that case, the State is obliged to ensure that the detainee enjoys the minimum and non-derogable guarantees established in the Convention and, specifically, the right to question the lawfulness of the detention and the guarantee of access to effective defense during his incarceration.

52. The Court, bearing in mind the maximum limit established in the Ecuadorian Constitution, finds that Mr. Rafael Iván Suárez-Rosero's *incommunicado* detention from June 23 to July 28, 1992, violated Article 7(2) of the American Convention.

VIOLATION OF ARTICLE 7(5)

53. The Commission argued in its application that the State had not fulfilled its obligation to bring Mr. Suárez-Rosero before a competent judicial authority, as required by Article 7(5) of the Convention, for, according to the arguments of the petitioner -- not contested by the State before the Commission --, Mr. Suárez-Rosero never appeared in person before such an authority to be informed of the charges against him.

54. In its answer to the application in that regard, Ecuador stated that "*Mr. Suárez-Rosero has been exercising his legal rights to express his views and make his legitimate claims during his legal process.*"

55. Article 7(5) of the American Convention provides that

[a]ny person detained shall be brought promptly before a judge or other officer authorized by law to exercise judicial power and shall be entitled to trial within a reasonable time or to be released without prejudice to the continuation of the proceedings. His release may be subject to guarantees to assure his appearance for trial.

56. The State did not contest the Commission's claim that Mr. Suárez-Rosero never appeared before a judicial authority during the proceeding. The Court therefore deems

that claim to have been proved and rules that this omission on the part of the State constitutes a violation of Article 7(5) of the American Convention.

VIOLATION OF ARTICLES 7(6) AND (25)

57.   The Commission asked the Court to rule that Mr. Suárez-Rosero's *incommunicado* detention violated Article 7(6) of the American Convention in that it denied him contact with the outside world and did not permit him to exercise his right of habeas corpus.

58.   With regard to the aforementioned guarantee, Article 7(6) of the Convention provides that

[a]nyone who is deprived of his liberty shall be entitled to recourse to a competent court, in order that the court may decide without delay on the lawfulness of his arrest or detention and order his release if the arrest or detention is unlawful. In States Parties whose laws provide that anyone who believes himself to be threatened with deprivation of his liberty is entitled to recourse to a competent court in order that it may decide on the lawfulness of such threat, this remedy may not be restricted or abolished. The interested party or another person on his behalf is entitled to seek these remedies.

59.   The Court has already ruled that a detained person must be guaranteed the right of habeas corpus at all times, even when he is being held in exceptional circumstances of *incommunicado* detention established by law. That guarantee is doubly entrenched in the law in Ecuador. Article 28 of the Political Constitution provides that

[a]ny person who believes that he is being unlawfully deprived of his liberty may seek the remedy of habeas corpus. He may exercise this right himself or through another person without the need for written mandate . . .

The Code of Criminal Procedure of that State establishes in Article 458 that

[a]ny person who is charged with infringing the precepts contained in [that] Code and is kept in detention may apply to be released to a higher Court than the one that has ordered the deprivation of his liberty.
[...]
The application shall be made in writing.
[...]
Immediately upon receipt of the application, the Judge who is to hear it shall order the detained person to be brought before him and shall hear his statements, which shall be included in a record which shall be signed by the Judge, the Secretary and the applicant, or, should the applicant be unable to sign, by a witness on his behalf. Thereupon, the Judge shall seek to obtain all the information he deems necessary for the purpose of arriving to a conclusion and ensuring the lawfulness of his decision and shall, within forty-eight hours, decide what he deems to be lawful.

60. The Court observes, first of all, that the aforesaid articles do not restrict access to the remedy of habeas corpus to the persons who are held *incommunicado*; in addition, the Constitution allows that remedy to be sought by any person *"without the need for written mandate."* It also points out that no evidence has been submitted to it to show that Mr. Suárez-Rosero attempted to file such an appeal with a competent authority during his *incommunicado* detention, nor did any other person attempt to do so on his behalf. Consequently, the Court deems the Commission's claim in that regard not to have been proven.

* * *

61. The Commission claimed that Ecuador violated Articles 7(6) and 25 of the American Convention when it denied Mr. Suárez-Rosero the right of habeas corpus. On that point, the Commission claimed that the inordinate time of fourteen and a half months between Mr. Suárez-Rosero's filing the writ of habeas corpus on March 29, 1993, and the ruling on the writ is patently incompatible with the reasonable time provided for in Ecuador's own legislation. It further claimed that the State had therefore failed in its obligation to provide effective judicial recourse. Lastly, the Commission maintained that such recourse was denied for purely procedural reasons, that is, because the petitioner had not indicated the nature of the proceeding or the location of the court that had ordered the detention, nor the place, date or cause of the detention. Such formal requirements are not established in Ecuadorian Law.

62. Ecuador did not contest those arguments in its answer to the application.

63. This Court shares the Commission's view that the right enshrined in Article 7(6) of the American Convention is not exercised with the mere formal existence of the remedies it governs. Those remedies must be effective, since their purpose, in the terms of Article 7(6), is to obtain without delay a decision *"on the lawfulness of* [his] *arrest or detention,"* and, should they be unlawful, to obtain, also without delay, an *"order* [for] *his release"*. The Court has also held that

> [i]n order for habeas corpus to achieve its purpose, which is to obtain a judicial determination of the lawfulness of a detention, it is necessary that the detained person be brought before a competent judge or tribunal with jurisdiction over him. Here habeas corpus performs a vital role in ensuring that a person's life and physical integrity are respected, in preventing his disappearance or the keeping of his whereabouts secret and in protecting him against torture or other cruel, inhuman or degrading punishment or treatment *(Habeas Corpus in Emergency Situations (Arts. 27(2), 25(1) and 7(6) American Convention on Human Rights)*, Advisory Opinion OC-8/87 of January 30, 1987. Series A No. 8, para. 35).

64. As indicated above (*supra,* para. 34.(r)), the Court deems it to have been proven that the writ of habeas corpus filed by Mr. Suárez-Rosero on March 29, 1993, was disposed of by the President of the Supreme Court of Justice of Ecuador on June 10, 1994, that is, more than 14 months after it was filed. This Court also deems it to have been proven that the application was ruled inadmissible, on the ground that Mr. Suárez-Rosero had omitted certain information, whereas, under Ecuadorian Law, such information is not a prerequisite for admissibility.

Chapter 11. Police Practices

65. Article 25 of the American Convention provides that everyone has the right to simple and prompt recourse, or any other effective recourse, to a competent court or tribunal. The Court has ruled that this provision

> constitutes one of the basic pillars not only of the American Convention, but of the very rule of law in a democratic society in the sense of the Convention.

Article 25 is closely linked to the general obligation contained in Article 1(1) of the American Convention, in assigning protective functions to the domestic law of States Parties. The purpose of habeas corpus is not only to ensure respect for the right to personal liberty and physical integrity, but also to prevent the person's disappearance or the keeping of his whereabouts secret and, ultimately, to ensure his right to life (*Castillo Páez Case,* Judgment of November 3, 1997. Series C No. 34, paras. 82 and 83).

66. On the basis of the foregoing, and especially since Mr. Suárez-Rosero did not have access to simple, prompt and effective recourse, the Court finds that the State violated the provisions of Article 7(6) and 25 of the American Convention.

. . . .

❖ ❖ ❖

Questions & Comments

(1) Compare the ICT-Y's decision in *The Prosecutor v. Kupreskic and Others*, Case No. IT-95-16, Int'l Crim. Trib.-Yugo., Trial Chamber, Decision on Motion for Provisional Release filed by Zoran Kupreskic, Mirjan Kupreskic, Drago Josipovic and Dragan Papic (Joined by Marinko Katava and Vladimir Santic (15 December 1997). The Trial Chamber held that "provisional release may only be ordered in extreme and rare circumstances such as where the accused's state of health is incompatible with any form of detention." The Chamber held that four conditions must be met for provisional release: (i) there are exceptional circumstances, (ii) the defendant will appear for trial, (iii) if released, the defendant will not pose a danger to any victim, witness or other person, and (iv) the host country must be heard. The Chamber ruled that a defendant's voluntary surrender did not justify his release from preventive detention.

Why is there a higher standard? Is it because of the crimes involved? What if an ICC defendant is charged with a crime against humanity that consists of one of the less than severe forms of persecution?

(2) Compare *Hill v. Spain*, UN Hum. Rts. Ctte., Communication No. 526/1993, U.N. Doc. CCPR/C/59/D/526/1993 (2 April 1997), in which the UN Human Rights Committee held that the mere fact that the defendant is a foreigner does not of itself imply that s/he must be held in detention pending trial on the mere conjecture that they might leave the state's jurisdiction. In *Hill v. Spain*, the Committee found that the authors, who had been charged with arson and were British citizens, should have been released pending trial.

(3) In *Josip, Bozana and Tomislav Matanovic v. Republika Srpska (Merits)*, Case No. CH/96/1, Hum. Rts. Chamber-BiH (1997), the Human Rights Chamber for Bosnia and Herzegovina in a disappearance case found an Article 5 (right to liberty), ECHR, violation

for the Republika Srpska's failure to produce the applicant after the Dayton Agreement even though he was originally detained before the Agreement.

D. Pre-Trial Publicity and the Presumption of Innocence

Allenet de Ribemont v. France
European Court of Human Rights
308 Eur. Ct. H.R. (1995)
20 E.H.R.R. 557 (1995)

FACTS:
. . . .
8. On 24 December 1976 Mr Jean de Broglie, a Member of Parliament . . . and former minister, was murdered in front of the applicant's home. He had just been visiting his financial adviser, Mr Pierre De Varga, who lived in the same building and with whom Mr Allenet de Ribemont was planning to become the joint owner of a Paris restaurant, "La Rotisserie de la Reine Pedauque". The scheme was financed by means of a loan taken out by the victim. He had passed on the borrowed sum to the applicant, who was responsible for repaying the loan.

9. A judicial investigation was begun into the commission by a person or persons unknown of the offence of intentional homicide. On 27 and 28 December 1976 the crime squad at Paris police headquarters arrested a number of people, including the victim's financial adviser. On 29 December it arrested Mr Allenet de Ribemont.

B. The press conference of 29 December 1976 and the implicating of the applicant

10. On 29 December 1976, at a press conference on the subject of the French police budget for the coming years, the Minister of the Interior, Mr Michel Poniatowski, the Director of the Paris Criminal Investigation Department, Mr Jean Ducret, and the Head of the Crime Squad, Superintendent Pierre Ottavioli, referred to the inquiry that was under way.

11. Two French television channels reported this press conference in their news programmes. The transcript of the relevant extracts reads as follows:

TF1 NEWS

Mr Roger Giquel, newsreader: . . . Be that as it may, here is how all the aspects of the de Broglie case were explained to the public at a press conference given by Mr Michel Poniatowski yesterday evening.

Mr Poniatowski: The haul is complete. All the people involved are now under arrest after the arrest of Mr De Varga-Hirsch. It is a very simple story. A bank loan guaranteed by Mr Jean de Broglie was to be repaid by Mr Varga-Hirsch and Mr de Ribemont.

A journalist: Superintendent, who was the key figure in this case? De Varga?

230

Chapter 11. Police Practices

Mr Ottavioli: I think it must have been Mr De Varga.

Mr Ducret: The instigator, Mr De Varga, and his acolyte, Mr de Ribemont, were the instigators of the murder. The organiser was Detective Sergeant Simone and the murderer was Mr Freche.

Mr Giquel: As you can see, those statements include a number of assertions. That is why the police are now being criticised by Ministry of Justice officials. Although Superintendent Ottavioli and Mr Ducret were careful to (end of recording).

ANTENNE 2 NEWS:

Mr Daniel Bilalian, newsreader: . . . This evening, therefore, the case has been cleared up. The motives and the murderer's name are known.

Mr Ducret: The organiser was Detective Sergeant Simone and the murderer was Mr Freche.

Mr Ottavioli: That is correct. I can . . . [unintelligible] the facts for you by saying that the case arose from a financial agreement between the victim, Mr de Broglie, and Mr Allenet de Ribemont and Mr Varga.

Mr Poniatowski: It is a very simple story. A bank loan guaranteed by Mr Jean de Broglie was to be repaid by Mr Varga-Hirsch and Mr de Ribemont.

A journalist: Superintendent, who was the key figure in this case? De Varga?

Mr Ottavioli: I think it must have been Mr De Varga.

Mr Jean-Francois Luciani, journalist: The loan was guaranteed by a life insurance policy for four hundred million old francs taken out by Jean de Broglie. In the event of his death, the sum insured was to be paid to Pierre De Varga-Hirsch and Allenet de Ribemont. The turning-point came last night when Guy Simone, a police officer, was the first to crack. He admitted that he had organised the murder and had lent a gun to have the MP killed. He also hired the contract killer, Gerard Freche, who was promised three million old francs and who in turn found two people to accompany him. The reasons for their downfall were, first, that Simone's name appeared in Jean de Broglie's diary and, second, that they killed him in front of no 2 rue des Dardanelles. That was not planned. The intention had apparently been to take him somewhere else, but Jean de Broglie perhaps refused to follow his killer. At all events, that was their first mistake. Varga and Ribemont apparently then refused to pay them. That led to the secret meetings in bars, the shadowing by the police and informers -- we know the rest of the story -- and their arrest. The second mistake was made by Simone. Before contacting Freche he approached another contract killer, who turned down the job but apparently talked to other people about it. To catch the killers, the police realistically based their investigation on two simple ideas. Firstly, the murder was committed in the rue des Dardanelles as Jean de Broglie was leaving De Varga's home. There was necessarily a link between the killer and De Varga. Secondly, De Varga's past did not count in his favour and the police regarded him as a rather dubious legal adviser. Those two simple ideas and over sixty investigators led to the discovery of the murderer.

Mr Bilalian: The epilogue to the case coincided with a Cabinet meeting at which the question of public safety was discussed . . .

12. On 14 January 1977 Mr Allenet de Ribemont was charged with aiding and abetting intentional homicide and taken into custody. He was released on 1 March 1977 and a discharge order was issued on 21 March 1980.

[Allenet de Ribemont unsuccessfully sought compensation for the false statements before the French courts.]

. . . .

PROCEEDINGS BEFORE THE COMMISSION

. . . .

100. The Commission concludes unanimously that in this case there has been a violation of Article 6(2) of the Convention;

. . . .

DECISION [OF THE EUROPEAN COURT OF HUMAN RIGHTS]:

I. Alleged Violation of Article 6(2) of the Convention

31. Mr Allenet de Ribemont complained of the remarks made by the Minister of the Interior and the senior police officers accompanying him at the press conference of 29 December 1976. He relied on Article 6(2) of the Convention . . .

. . . .

A. Applicability of Article 6(2)

32. The Government contested, in substance, the applicability of Article 6(2), relying on the *Minelli v. Switzerland* judgment of 25 March 1983. They maintained that the presumption of innocence could be infringed only by a judicial authority, and could be shown to have been infringed only where, at the conclusion of proceedings ending in a conviction, the court's reasoning suggested that it regarded the defendant as guilty in advance.

33. The Commission acknowledged that the principle of presumption of innocence was above all a procedural safeguard in criminal proceedings, but took the view that its scope was more extensive, in that it imposed obligations not only on criminal courts determining criminal charges but also on other authorities.

34. The Court's task is to determine whether the situation found in this case affected the applicant's right under Article 6(2). . . .

35. The presumption of innocence enshrined in paragraph 2 of Article 6 is one of the elements of the fair criminal trial that is required by paragraph 1. . . . It will be violated if a judicial decision concerning a person charged with a criminal offence reflects an

opinion that he is guilty before he has been proved guilty according to law. It suffices, even in the absence of an formal finding, that there is some reasoning suggesting that the court regards the accused as guilty. . . .

However, the scope of Article 6(2) is not limited to the eventuality mentioned by the Government. The Court held that there had been violations of this provision in the *Minelli* . . . case[ ] previously cited, although the national courts concerned had closed the proceedings . . . because the limitation period had expired and had acquitted the applicant in the second. It has similarly held it to be applicable in other cases where the domestic courts did not have to determine the question of guilt. [*See, e.g., Adolph v. Austria.* 4 E.H.R.R. 313.]

Moreover, the Court reiterates that the Convention must be interpreted in such a way as to guarantee rights which are practical and effective as opposed to theoretical and illusory. (See, among other authorities. . . . That also applies to the right enshrined in Article 6(2).

36. The Court considers that the presumption of innocence may be infringed not only by a judge or court but also by other public authorities.

37. At the time of the press conference of 29 December 1976 Mr Allenet de Ribemont had just been arrested by the police. Although he had not yet been charged with aiding and abetting intentional homicide, his arrest and detention in police custody formed part of the judicial investigation begun a few days earlier by a Paris investigating judge and made him a person "charged with a criminal offence" within the meaning of Article 6(2). The two senior police officers present were conducting the inquiries in the case. Their remarks, made in parallel with the judicial investigation and supported by the Minister of the Interior, were explained by the existence of that investigation and had a direct link with it. Article 6(2) therefore applies in this case.

B. Compliance with Article 6(2)

1. Reference to the case at the press conference

38. Freedom of expression, guaranteed by Article 10 of the Convention, includes the freedom to receive and impart information. Article 6(2) cannot therefore prevent the authorities from informing the public about criminal investigations in progress, but it requires that they do so with all the discretion and circumspection necessary if the presumption of innocence is to be respected.

2. Content of the statements complained of

39. Like the applicant, the Commission considered that the remarks made by the Minister of the Interior and, in his presence and under his authority, by the police superintendent in charge of the inquiry and the Director of the Criminal Investigation Department, were incompatible with the presumption of innocence. It noted that in them Mr Allenet de Ribemont was held up as one of the instigators of Mr de Broglie's murder.

40. The Government maintained that such remarks came under the head of information about criminal proceedings in progress and were not such as to infringe the presumption of innocence, since they did not bind the courts and could be proved false by

subsequent investigations. The facts of the case bore this out, as the applicant had not been formally charged until two weeks after the press conference and the investigating judge had eventually decided that there was no case to answer.

41. The Court notes that in the instant case some of the highest-ranking officers in the French police referred to Mr Allenet de Ribemont, without any qualification or reservation, as one of the instigators of a murder and thus an accomplice in that murder. This was clearly a declaration of the applicant's guilt which, firstly, encouraged the public to believe him guilty and, secondly, prejudged the assessment of the facts by the competent judicial authority. There has therefore been a breach of Article 6(2).

. . . .

❖ ❖ ❖

Questions & Comments

(1) How does the European Court's decision in *Allenet de Ribemont v. France* compare with the U.S. law? Can the difference be attributed to the different form of criminal justice system in the U.S.? Can the difference be attributed to the role of the judge in pre-trial proceedings? Is this difference sufficiently material?

(2) Consider the Inter-American Court of Human Rights decision in *Suárez Rosero v. Ecuador* (reproduced above in Chapter 11(C)) in which it addresses the right to the presumption of innocence in a preventive detention case involving drug smuggling:

76. The Court now turns to the argument put forward by the Commission to the effect that the proceeding against Mr. Suárez-Rosero was in breach of the principle of the presumption of innocence, enunciated in Article 8(2) of the American Convention. That Article provides that

[e]very person accussed of a criminal offense has the right to be presumed innocent so long as his guilt has not been proven according to the law [...].

77. This Court is of the view that the principle of the presumption of innocence -- inasmuch as it lays down that a person is innocent until proven guilty -- is founded upon the existence of judicial guarantees. Article 8(2) of the Convention establishes the obligation of the State not to restrict the liberty of a detained person beyond the limits strictly necessary to ensure that he will not impede the efficient development of an investigation and that he will not evade justice; preventive detention is, therefore, a precautionary rather than a punitive measure. This concept is laid down in a goodly number of instruments of international human rights law, including the International Covenant on Civil and Political Rights, which provides that preventive detention should not be the normal practice in relation to persons who are to stand trial (Art. 9(3)). This would be tantamount to anticipating a sentence, which is at odds with universally recognized general principles of law.

Chapter 11. Police Practices

78. The Court considers that Mr. Suárez-Rosero's prolonged preventive detention violated the principle of presumption of innocence, in that he was detained from June 23, 1992, to April 28, 1996, and that the order for his release issued on July 10, 1995, was only executed a year later. In view of the above, the Court rules that the State violated Article 8(2) of the American Convention.

Chapter 12. Trial Due Process Protections

A. Assistance of Legal Counsel

Grant v. Jamaica
UN Human Rights Committee
Communication No. 353/1988
Views adopted 31 March 1994
U.N. Doc. CCPR/C/50/D/353/1988 (1994)

The facts as submitted by the author

1. The author of the communication is Lloyd Grant, a Jamaican citizen awaiting execution at St. Catherine District Prison, Jamaica. . . .

2.1 The author and his brother, Vincent Grant, were tried in the Hanover Circuit Court between 4 and 7 November 1986 for the murder, on 2 October 1985, of one T.M. Both were convicted and sentenced to death. On 5 October 1987, the Court of Appeal of Jamaica dismissed the author's appeal, but acquitted his brother. The author's petition for special leave to appeal to the Judicial Committee of the Privy Council was dismissed on 21 November 1988. With this, it is submitted, all available domestic remedies have been exhausted.

2.2 The author was interrogated by the police on 7 October 1985 in connection with the murder of T.M., who had been killed during a robbery at his home in the parish of Hanover, over 150 miles away from the author's home. The author explained that, while he knew the deceased from the time when he lived in Hanover, he had not visited that town since June 1985 and knew nothing about the crime. He was none the less arrested and placed in custody. On 25 October 1985, the author was placed on an identification parade, where he was identified by the deceased's wife, E.M., whom he also knew. He and Vincent Grant, who was then living in Hanover, were subsequently charged with the murder of T.M.

. . . .

2.4 E.M. testified that, in the afternoon of 1 October 1985, Vincent Grant, whom she had known all her life, entered the shop. Although she spoke to him he remained silent, staring at her house which was opposite the shop. He then left. Subsequently D.S. entered the shop and told her that he had seen Vincent Grant holding a sharp machete and leaning against the gate to her house, watching her banana field, and that two masked men, both carrying machetes, had been in the field. D.S. further told her that, despite the mask, he had recognized Lloyd Grant, who, when asked what they were doing on the M.'s premises, ran away. E.M. further testified that, after having locked the doors and windows of their house, she and her husband retired to bed; a kerosene lamp was left burning in the living room. At approximately 1 a.m., she was woken up by a noise and she went to the living room where she saw two men who immediately assaulted her. At their request, she gave them all the money kept in the house. She was then forced to lie face down on the floor, and one of the men, whom she identified as Lloyd Grant, bent over her, asking her whether she knew him. When she replied in the negative, he stood up and attacked her husband, who had entered the room. A scuffle ensued and her husband fell to the floor. Lloyd Grant, she stated, then proceeded to humiliate and assault her, during which time she had ample opportunity to see his face. E.M. finally testified that, before both men left the premises, they exchanged words with a third man, who was apparently waiting for them outside in the yard.

. . . .

2.6 In court D.S. further testified that, on 2 October 1985, between 2 a.m. and 3 a.m., he was returning home when he saw Vincent and Lloyd Grant and an unidentified third man run away from the *locus in quo*.

2.7 Statements allegedly made by both defendants to the police on 7 and 11 October 1985 were admitted in evidence by the judge after a challenge on the voire dire. Vincent Grant allegedly told the police that he had been forced by his brother to accompany him and another man to T.M.'s house, but that, after both men had entered the premises, he had run away. In his statement, the author identified Vincent Grant as the mastermind behind the robbery and gave details of the burglary and of his entry into T.M.'s house in the company of his brother and a third person. The author further allegedly stated that while he was outside, holding E.M., the third person came out of the house and told him that he had "chopped up" T.M.

2.8 The author put forward an alibi defence. He made an unsworn statement from the dock, claiming that he had been at his home in Kingston with his girlfriend when the crime occurred. He further claimed that he had been forced by the police to sign, on 11 October 1985, a drawn up statement. Vincent Grant also made an unsworn statement from the dock, stating only that, on 2 October 1985, he was at home with his girlfriend, that he went to bed at 5 o'clock and that he knew nothing about the murder.

2.9 With respect to the identification of Vincent Grant (who had not been identified by E.M.), the testimony of D.S. revealed that his sight had been impaired by the darkness. Before the Court of Appeal, Vincent Grant's counsel argued, *inter alia*, that the trial judge had failed to give the jury adequate warning about the dangers of identification evidence and, in addition, failed to relate such direction as he gave on identification to the evidence presented by D.S. The Court of Appeal agreed with counsel that the trial judge overlooked the fact that the identification evidence offered in respect of the two defendants was materially different and that each case required appropriate and specific treatment. The Court of Appeal subsequently acquitted Vincent Grant.

2.10 Author's counsel before the Court of Appeal admitted that "there was overwhelming evidence against his client, especially in the light of E.M.'s testimony", and that, "although he was of the opinion that the trial judge's directions on identification in relation to the author could have been more helpful, he did not believe that any reasonable argument could be mounted in law as to what the trial judge actually said". He further admitted that "the trial judge gave proper directions on common design" and that "overall he could find no arguable ground to urge on behalf of his client". The Court of Appeal agreed with counsel, stating that, in the case of the author, it found no defects in the instructions to the jury by the judge, and that the evidence against him was "overwhelming".

2.11 Throughout his trial and appeal, the author was represented by legal aid lawyers. A London law firm represented him pro bono before the Judicial Committee of the Privy Council.

. . . .

The complaint

. . . .

3.2 In respect of the allegation of unfair trial under article 14 of the Covenant, it is submitted that:

(a) The author did not receive legal advice during the preliminary hearing. It was not until one month prior to the trial that he was assigned a legal aid attorney, who did not consult with him, despite an earlier adjournment for that purpose, until the day before the start of the trial and then only for 40 minutes;

(b) The circumstances of the case were not investigated before the trial began. The attorney did not attempt to secure the testimony of the author's girlfriend, P.D., or of her mother. Although instructed by the author to do so, the attorney failed to contact P.D., whose evidence would have provided an alibi for the author;

(c) The attorney did not argue the issue of reliability of the identification by E.M. If E.M. had been asked when she had last seen the author, it would have been revealed that she had not seen him for about 10 years, when he was fourteen or fifteen years old;

(d) The attorney did not go through the prosecution statements with the author;

(e) Counsel for the appeal effectively abandoned the appeal or failed to pursue it properly. This is said to have prejudiced the author's case before the Judicial Committee of the Privy Council, which acknowledged that there might have been points of law for the Court of Appeal to look into;

(f) Counsel for the appeal also declined to call P.D. It is contended that the author's legal representation was inadequate and in violation of article 14, paragraph 3 (d), in respect of the proceedings before both the Circuit Court and the Court of Appeal.

. . . .

The Committee's admissibility decision

. . . .

5.3 With regard to the allegations of unfair trial, the Committee noted that the author's claims related primarily to the inadequacy of the preparation of his defence and of his representation before the Jamaican courts. It considered that these claims might raise issues under article 14, paragraphs 3 (b), (d) and (e) of the Covenant, which should be examined on the merits.

. . . .

The State party's request for review of admissibility and counsel's comments

. . . .

6.3 With regard to the alleged violations of article 14, paragraphs 3 (b), (d) and (e), the State party refers to an individual opinion appended to the Committee's views in [Communication No. 253/1987 (*Paul Kelly v. Jamaica*), views adopted on 8 April 1991] and submits that the State party's obligation to provide an accused with legal representation cannot extend beyond the duty to act in good faith in assigning counsel to the accused, and that errors of judgement made by court-appointed lawyers cannot be attributed to the State party any more than errors by privately retained lawyers can be. It concludes that the Committee would be applying a double standard if it were to hold court-appointed lawyers accountable to a higher degree of responsibility than their counterparts, and thus hold the State party responsible for their errors of judgement.

. . . .

7.3 As to the inadequacy of the preparation of the author's defence and of his representation before the Jamaican courts, it is submitted that the author was not represented during police interrogation and during the preliminary hearing. In September 1986, he saw the attorney assigned to him for the trial for the first time. She reportedly requested the judge to adjourn the trial, as she needed more time to prepare the defence. The hearing was rescheduled for 3 November 1986. Although upon requesting the adjournment, the attorney promised the author that she would discuss the case with him that evening, she never came to see him. On 3 November 1986, she visited him in the court lockup. During the interview, which lasted for only 40 minutes, she took the first statement from the author; the attorney did not investigate the circumstances of the case prior to the trial nor did she consider the author's alibi defence. The author affirms that during the course of the trial he again met with his attorney, but that she did not carry out his instructions.

7.4 With regard to the attorney's failure to pursue the evidence of the author's girlfriend, counsel forwards an affidavit, dated 4 December 1989, from P.D. and a questionnaire, dated 22 March 1990; P.D. contends that the author was with her during the whole night of 1 to 2 October 1985, and that her mother and one P.M. could have corroborated this evidence. It further appears from her affidavit that, on one of the days of the court hearing, she was informed by the police that her presence was needed, but that she failed to go because she had no money to travel and the police allegedly told her that it had no car available to transport her to the Circuit Court. According to London counsel, the main reason why witnesses were not traced and called was that the legal aid rates were so inadequate that the attorney was not able to make the necessary inquiries and initiate the necessary steps to prepare the author's defence properly.

7.5 As to the conduct of the trial defence itself, it is submitted that the attorney failed properly to challenge the testimony of E.M. and D.S., in particular with regard to their identification of the author, and that she did not make any interventions when counsel for the prosecution put leading questions to the prosecution witnesses.

7.6 With regard to the preparation of the author's defence on appeal, reference is made to the transcript of an annex to the "Privy Council questionnaire for inmate appealing" where the author claims that: "On one occasion D.C. (counsel assigned to him for the purpose of the appeal) came inside the prison and saw about 10 inmates (including myself) and I spoke with him for approximately 20 minutes. During those 20 minutes he asked me if I had any knowledge of the crime and if I have any witness. I also asked him to get my girlfriend in court and he don't". It is submitted that, since D.C. had not represented him at the trial, it was essential for the author to have adequate time to consult with D.C. prior to the hearing of the appeal, and that the amount of time granted for that purpose was wholly inadequate. The above is said to indicate that the author's rights under article 14, paragraph 3 (d) were not respected, since counsel was not of his own choosing.

7.7 With regard to the claim that D.C. abandoned or failed properly to pursue the appeal, reference is made to the written judgement of the Court of Appeal and to a letter, dated 8 February 1988, from D.C. to the Jamaica Council for Human Rights. In his letter, D.C. states that: "I daresay however that the judge's instructions on identification was certainly not the best but the usual safeguards were complied with and on any legal merit I cannot recommend the case for further consideration". According to London counsel, there were several grounds in the case which could have been argued on appeal, such as P.D.'s evidence (had she been called), and the reliability of the identification evidence of E.M. and D.S., especially in light of the fact that the weakness in the latter's identification concerned both defendants. [Footnote omitted]

. . . .

Examination of the merits

. . . .

8.4 Concerning the author's claims relating to the preparation of his defence and his legal representation on trial, the Committee recalls that the right of an accused person to have adequate time and facilities for the preparation of his defence is an important element of the guarantee of a fair trial and an important aspect of the principle of equality of arms. The determination of what constitutes "adequate time" requires an assessment of the circumstances of each case. The Committee notes that the material before it does not disclose whether either the author or his attorney complained to the trial judge that the time or facilities for the preparation of the defence had been inadequate. Nor is there any indication that the author's attorney acted negligently in the conduct of the defence. In this context, the Committee notes that the trial transcript discloses that E.M. and D.S. were thoroughly cross-examined on the issue of identification by the defence. The Committee therefore finds no violations of article 14, paragraphs 3 (b) and (d), in respect of the author's trial.

8.5 The author also contends that he was unable to secure the attendance of witnesses on his behalf, in particular the attendance of his girlfriend, P.D. The Committee notes from the trial transcript that the author's attorney did contact the girlfriend, and, on the second day of the trial, made a request to the judge to have P.D. called to court. The judge then instructed the police to contact this witness, who, as indicated in paragraph 7.4 above, had no means to attend. The Committee is of the opinion that, in the circumstances, and bearing in mind that this is a case involving the death penalty, the judge should have adjourned the trial and issued a subpoena to secure the attendance of P.D. in court. Furthermore, the Committee considers that the police should have made transportation available to her. To the extent that P.D.'s failure to appear in court was attributable to the State party's authorities, the Committee finds that the criminal proceedings against the author were in violation of article 14, paragraphs 1 and 3 (e), of the Covenant.

8.6 The author also claims that the preparation of his defence and his representation before the Court of Appeal were inadequate, and that counsel assigned to him for this purpose was not of his own choosing. The Committee recalls that, while article 14, paragraph 3 (d), does not entitle the accused to choose counsel provided to him free of charge, measures must be taken to ensure that counsel, once assigned, provides effective representation in the interest of justice. This includes consulting with, and informing, the accused if he intends to withdraw an appeal or to argue before the appellate instance that the appeal has no merit. [Communication No. 356/1989 (*Trevor Collins v. Jamaica*), views adopted on 25 March 1993, para. 8.2.] While it is not for the Committee to question counsel's professional judgement that there was no merit in the appeal, it is of the opinion that he should have informed Mr. Grant of his intention not to raise any grounds of appeal, so that Mr. Grant could have considered any other remaining options open to him. In the circumstances, the Committee finds that the author's rights under article 14, paragraphs 3 (b) and (d) were violated in respect of his appeal.

. . . .

10. The Committee is of the view that Mr. Lloyd Grant is entitled to a remedy entailing his release. It requests the State party to provide information, within ninety days, on any relevant measures taken by the State party in compliance with the Committee's views.

❖ ❖ ❖

Questions & Comments

(1) The UN Human Rights Committee has dealt with a variety of due process and legal access issues in numerous death penalty cases from Jamaica, and Trinidad and Tobago. In Jamaica, this phenomenon began in the 1980s when there was a surge in death penalty convictions resulting from an enormous influx of weapons during earlier elections. "Gun Courts" were established which provided little due process protection. For other cases addressing the right to effective legal counsel, *see, e.g., Collins v. Jamaica,* UN Hum. Rts. Ctte., Communication No. 356/1989, views adopted 25 March 1993, U.N.Doc. A/48/40 (Pt. II) (1993) at 85 (court appointed counsel required to consult with client before declining to argue appeal); *Simmonds v. Jamaica,* UN Hum. Rts. Ctte., Communication No. 338/1988, views adopted 23 October 1992, U.N.Doc. A/48/40 (Pt. II) (1993) at 78 (Article 14 violation where appellate counsel did not consult client about grounds of appeal).

(2) The UN Human Rights Committee repeatedly has found violations of the right to effective assistance of counsel where appellate counsel in a death penalty case has stated to an appeals court that his client's appeal has no merit. *Reid v. Jamaica,* UN Hum. Rts. Ctte., Communication No. 250/1987, views adopted 20 July 1990; *Collins v. Jamaica,* UN Hum. Rts. Ctte., Communication No 356/1989, views adopted 25 March 1993. The UN Human Rights Committee has held that due process issues require heightened scrutiny in death penalty cases. Compare *Maxwell v. United Kingdom,* 300-C Eur. Ct. H.R. (ser. A) (1994), in which a legal aid office refused to file an appeal on behalf of the applicant facing a five-year sentence because it believed that the appeal had no merit. The European Court found an Article 6(3)(c) violation because of (i) the limited capacity of the appellant to represent himself without the assistance of counsel before the court of highest instance of appeal, (ii) the importance of the "issue at stake" (*viz.,* a five-year sentence), and (iii) the wide powers of the court to, *e.g.,* affirm, dismiss, or set aside the verdict. In *Maxwell,* the European Court held that this five-year sentence was "above all" the determinative issue for finding an Article 6 legal access violation. Should the UN Human Rights Committee extend their heightened due process scrutiny in death penalty cases to cases in which the "issue at stake" is much lower — as low as a five-year sentence as in *Maxwell?* What factors should the UN Human Rights Committee take into consideration in lowering this standard?

(3) Consider *Boner v. United Kingdom,* 300-B Eur. Ct. H.R. (ser. A) (1994). Boner was charged with assault and armed robbery in Scotland. He received free legal aid. During

241

the trial, a prosecution witness (prior to giving testimony) entered the courtroom and spoke to one of Boner's co-accused, against whom charges subsequently were dropped. A jury convicted Boner. The judge sentenced him to eight years in prison. Boner's lawyer stated that in his view the only possible ground of appeal related to the admissibility of the evidence of the above witness who had inappropriately entered the courtroom. Boner applied to extend legal aid to the appellate proceedings. The Scottish Legal Aid Board refused his application because it believed that the appeal lacked merit. Despite the advice of his solicitor and counsel, Boner decided to proceed with the appeal. Although he had no legal knowledge and had no assistance with his submissions, he presented his own case before the High Court of Justiciary in 1991. The Crown was represented by counsel at this hearing. The Appeal Court held that there was no miscarriage of justice and unanimously dismissed Boner's appeal.

The European Court held that for determining an Article 6 (3) violation, the special features of the proceedings involved must be examined. Account must be taken of the entirety of the proceedings and of the role of the courts therein. In the instant case, the Scottish system grants all persons a right to appeal. No special leave is required. The procedure is not limited to specific grounds; any alleged miscarriage of justice may be challenged.

An independent body (the Scottish Legal Aid Board) determines whether an appellant can obtain free legal assistance. The Scottish government defended its decision to refuse Boner legal aid by stating that in view of professional ethics, Boner could not have found counsel willing to represent him because he had no proper basis for bringing an appeal. They also pointed out that the issues in this case were not particularly complex. The Court, although agreeing with the latter point, held that a certain degree of legal skill and experience is necessary to attack a trial judge's exercise of discretion. That Boner was able to understand the grounds for his appeal and that counsel was not prepared to represent him does not alter the fact that without the services of a legal practitioner he was unable to competently address the court on this legal issue and thus defend himself effectively. The U.K. pointed out that if the Court found a violation, they might have to end their automatic right of appeal. However, the European Court replied that its responsibility was solely to determine whether the system states do choose lead to results which are inconsistent with the requirements of Article 6. In a situation involving a heavy penalty, where an appellant is left to present his own defense unassisted before the highest court of appeal, the system is not in conformity with the requirements of Article 6. In the instant case, given the nature of the proceedings, the wide powers of the High Court, Boner's limited capacity as an unrepresented appellant to present a legal argument and, above all, the importance of the issue at stake in view of the severity of the sentence (8 years imprisonment), the Court considered that the interests of justice required that Boner be granted legal aid for representation at his appeal. The Court concluded that there had been a violation Article 6 (3)(c).

Compare *Boner v. United Kingdom* to the *Lane v. Brown*, 372 U.S. 477 (1963), in which the U.S. Supreme Court found a violation to effective assistance of counsel where the petitioner filed a *habeas corpus* petition challenging his murder conviction, and his publicly-funded counsel refused to file his petition because his attorney believed that his petition had no merit. In *Evitts v. Lucey*, 469 U.S. 387, 394 (1985), the U.S. Supreme Court held that an appellate counsel "must play the role of an active advocate, rather than a mere friend of the court assisting in a detached evaluation of the appellant's claim" in finding a Sixth Amendment violation of right to assistance of counsel. Francisco Forrest Martin, *et al.*, 1 INTERNATIONAL HUMAN RIGHTS LAW & PRACTICE: CASES, TREATIES AND MATERIALS 523-26 (1997).

(4) The above cases were from the U.S., U.K., and Jamaica — countries using adversarial (*vs.* inquisitorial) legal systems. Do you think that either the UN Human Rights Committee or the European Court of Human Rights would take a different position on the right to appellate counsel in criminal cases in an inquisitorial legal system? Why? Francisco Forrest Martin, *et al.*, 1 INTERNATIONAL HUMAN RIGHTS LAW & PRACTICE: CASES, TREATIES AND MATERIALS 526 (1997).

(5) A common complaint of authors in these death penalty cases from Jamaica was their lawyers' failure to call certain witnesses. The UN Human Rights Committee repeatedly held that this failure was not an Article 14 violation of right to effective counsel. The Committee felt that the decision to not call witnesses was a professional judgment call by defense counsel. *See, e.g., Reynolds v. Jamaica*, UN Hum. Rts. Ctte., Communication No. 229/1987, views adopted 8 April 1991, at §6.4; *Sawyers and McLean v. Jamaica*, UN Hum. Rts. Ctte., Communication Nos. 226/1987 and 256/1987, views adopted 11 April 1991, at §13.7.

This rule comports with the general rule, as articulated by CORPUS JURIS SECUNDUM: "the right to counsel is generally not violated due to an attorney's exercise of discretion regarding tactics or strategy, provided the attorney made a reasoned choice." 22 C.J.S. *Effectiveness of Counsel* § 305 (1973) (citations omitted).

However, there is some language in one decision by the UN Human Rights Committee that suggests that this rule may only apply to privately-retained lawyers.

> The Committee is of the opinion that the failure of the author's representative to bring these issues to the attention of the trial judge, which purportedly resulted in the negative outcome of the trial, cannot be attributed to the State party, *since the lawyer was privately retained*. The Committee, therefore, finds no violation of article 14, paragraph 1, of the Covenant in this respect.

Berry v. Jamaica, UN Hum. Rts. Ctte., Communication No. 330/1988, views adopted 7 April 1994, U.N. Doc. CCPR/C/50/D/330/1988 (1994) at §11.3 (emphasis provided). An explanation for the Committee's language here may be that because a defendant does not have a right to choose his legal aid lawyer, the defendant has less control over the management of the case — unlike a privately-retained lawyer who can be dismissed by the client if the client is unhappy with his lawyer's conduct of his case. Also, the Committee may not consider state action to be present in the case of a privately retained lawyer providing ineffective assistance of counsel. Francisco Forrest Martin, *et al.*, 1 INTERNATIONAL HUMAN RIGHTS LAW & PRACTICE: CASES, TREATIES AND MATERIALS 526 (1997).

(6) For the leading U.S. Supreme Court case governing effective assistance of counsel, *see Strickland v. Washington*, 466 U.S. 668 (1984), which sets out a two-part test:

A convicted defendant's claim that counsel's assistance was so defective as to require reversal of a conviction . . . has two components. First, the defendant must show that counsel's performance was deficient. . . . Second, the defendant must show that the deficient performance prejudiced the defense. This requires showing that counsel's errors were so serious as to deprive the defendant of a fair trial, a trial whose result is reliable.

(7) In *Lala v. The Netherlands*, 297-A Eur. Ct. H.R. (ser. A) (1994), the fact that the defendant, in spite of having been properly summoned, does not appear, cannot — even in the absence of an excuse — justify depriving him of his right under Article 6(3) to be defended by counsel. The European Court did not accept the Netherlands' argument that there was no interference because Lala's counsel failed to ask the court's permission to defend him. A State Party has an affirmative duty to provide counsel.Francisco Forrest Martin, *et al.*, 1 INTERNATIONAL HUMAN RIGHTS LAW & PRACTICE: CASES, TREATIES AND MATERIALS 517 (1997).

(8) In *Campbell & Fell v. United Kingdom*, 80 Eur. Ct. H.R. (ser. A) (1984), the European Court found an Article 6(1) violation for the U.K. government's failure to provide legal assistance to prisoners facing prison disciplinary proceedings. Contrast this decision with a U.S. Supreme Court decision which refused to recognize a prisoner's right to counsel in prison disciplinary proceedings — even if there is a likelihood of criminal prosecution for the same acts upon which the disciplinary proceeding is based. *Baxter v. Palmigiano*, 425 U.S. 308 (1976). Is there any material difference between disciplinary and criminal proceedings in the context of right to counsel? Francisco Forrest Martin, *et al.*, 1 INTERNATIONAL HUMAN RIGHTS LAW & PRACTICE: CASES, TREATIES AND MATERIALS 518 (1997).

(9) A critical aspect of the right to legal access is protection from reprisals for exercising this right. In *Hammel v. Madagascar*, UN Hum. Rts. Ctte., Communication No. 155/1983, views adopted 3 April 1987, 2 SELECTED DECISIONS OF THE HUMAN RIGHTS COMMITTEE UNDER THE OPTIONAL PROTOCOL 179, U.N. Doc. CCPR/C/OP/2 (1990), the author of the communication, a French national, practiced law in Madagascar for over thirty years. After defending leaders of the opposition party in Madagascar, he was detained twice, held incommunicado, and eventually deported. The Committee found a violation of the right to assistance of counsel.

(10) The European Court repeatedly has recognized a prisoner's right to correspond privately with his/her lawyer under both Articles 6 (legal assistance) and 8 (privacy of mail). *See e.g., Domenichini v. Italy*, — Eur. Ct. H.R. (ser. A) (1997) (slip opinion); *S. v. Switzerland*, 220 Eur. Ct. H.R. (ser. A) (1992); *Schoenberger and Durmaz Case*, 137 Eur. Ct. H.R. (1989); *Boyle and Rice v. United Kingdom*, 131 Eur. Ct. H.R. (ser. A) (1988); *Silver v. United Kingdom*, 61 Eur. Ct. H.R. (ser. A) (1983); *Golder v. United Kingdom*, 18 Eur. Ct. H.R. (ser. A) (1975).
Under U.S. law, prisoners have a constitutional right to confidential communication with lawyers whether by telephone, mail, or personal meetings. Incoming letters may be opened and inspected for physical contraband in the prisoner's presence, but these letters

cannot be read by prison authorities. *Wolff v. McDonnell*, 418 U.S. 539, 577 (1974). Outgoing letters to lawyers generally may be mailed unopened. *Davidson v. Scully*, 694 F.2d 50, 53 (2d Cir. 1982); *Guajardo v. Estelle*, 580 F.2d 748, 759 (5th Cir. 1978). Furthermore, outgoing mail to lawyers seeking legal representation also cannot be opened or read — even if there is no existing lawyer-client agreement. *Taylor v. Sterrett*, 532 F.2d 462, 474 (5th Cir. 1976). In order for legal mail to receive the protection of confidentiality, it must be marked as legal mail. For U.S. federal prisons, the prison authorities require that the envelopes contain the following exact words: "Special Mail — Open Only in the Presence of the Inmate." Francisco Forrest Martin, *et al.*, 1 INTERNATIONAL HUMAN RIGHTS LAW & PRACTICE: CASES, TREATIES AND MATERIALS 519 (1997).

B. Judicial and Jury Impartiality

Andrews v. United States
Report No. 57/96, Case 11.139
Inter-American Commission on Human Rights
ANNUAL REPORT OF THE
INTER-AMERICAN COMMISSION ON HUMAN RIGHTS 1997
OEA/Ser/L/V/II.98, Doc. 7 rev. (19 February1998)

I. ALLEGATIONS IN PETITION DATED JULY 28, 1992

1. On July 27, 1992, the Commission received a fax communication informing it of the pending execution of Mr. William Andrews by the State of Utah on July 29, 1992, for three counts of Murder . . . .

2. On July 28, 1992 the Commission received a petition filed by Steven W. Hawkins of the LDF Capital Punishment Project; Richard J. Wilson, Director, International Human Rights Clinic, Washington College of Law, American University; and Bartram S. Brown of Chicago-Kent College of Law, on behalf of William Andrews which alleged that he was an African-American male born in Jonesboro, Louisiana, was now a prisoner on death row in Draper Correctional Institution, Draper, Utah, and was scheduled to be executed at or about 12:01 a.m on July 30, 1992. The petition alleged that in 1974, Mr. Andrews was convicted of three counts of first degree murder and two counts of aggravated robbery in the State of Utah, and that he was subsequently sentenced to death on all three counts by the same jury which convicted him.

3. The petitioners further alleged that both the victims and the jurors were Caucasian, and the sole black member of the jury pool was stricken peremptorily by the prosecution during jury selection. Mr. Andrews had left the premises prior to the offenses, and that his co-defendant, fatally shot the victims. His co-defendant, also African-American was executed by the State of Utah in 1987.

4. It is further alleged that a napkin (note) was found among the jurors during a recess of the trial, which stated "Hang the Nigger's" and that Mr. Andrews' attorney requested a mistrial and a right to question jurors concerning the note, but this request was denied by the trial judge. Instead the trial judge admonished the jurors to "ignore communications from foolish people". That the denial of the right to question the jury about the note and

the mistrial coupled with the known racist Mormon Church doctrine was ground for a mistrial and at minimum, a further inquiry into the authorship, and source of the note, exposure of the note to members of the jury or their response to it.

. . . .

II. ARTICLES ALLEGEDLY VIOLATED

8. Articles 3 (k) and 44 (a) of the Organization of American States' Charter. Articles I, (right to life, liberty and personal security) II, (right to equality before the law without distinction as to race), and XXVI (right to an impartial hearing, and not to receive cruel, infamous or unusual punishment) of the American Declaration of the Rights and Duties of Man.

III. THE PETITIONERS REQUEST THAT:

The Inter-American Commission on Human Rights

9. Find that in the trial, sentencing and execution of William Andrews, the United States violated Articles I, II, and XXVI of the American Declaration of the Rights and Duties of Man.

. . . .

IV. PROCEEDINGS BEFORE THE COMMISSION

. . . .

B. Legal Submissions of the Petitioners

18. . . . .The petitioners argued that the courts in the United States did not grant Mr. Andrews an evidentiary hearing to remedy the defect in his trial and sentencing. . . .

. . . .

20. The petitioners argued that the OAS Charter and the American Declaration were violated by the racially discriminatory manner in which the death penalty was imposed in Mr. Andrews' case. The tainted procedure by which Mr. Andrews was found guilty and sentenced to death in this case violated Articles 3 (k) and 44 (a) of the Charter of the OAS. It also violated Mr. Andrews' rights to equality before the law without distinction as to race (Article II) and to an impartial hearing (Article XXVI) under the American Declaration of the Rights and Duties of Man.

21. The petitioners further argued that both the International Court of Justice and the European Commission of Human Rights have found that racial distinctions require that international tribunals examine "more seriously" the purported justifications for differences in treatment based on race. [ ] Systematic racial discrimination has been recognized as a peremptory norm of the customary international law of human rights.[6] Moreover, the importance of freedom from racial discrimination is affirmed under Article 27(1) of the American Convention on Human Rights, which prohibits racial discrimination even in time of war or national emergence.

---

[6] See § 702(f), *Restatement of the Law (Third): The Foreign Relations Law of the United States*, vol. 2 (1987).

22. The petitioners argued that the U.S., as a signatory to several instruments regarding protection of human rights in the Conference on Security and Co-Operation in Europe, agreed that "special measures" must sometimes be taken to assure that the rights of national minorities are protected.

23. The petitioners argued that in the past, this Commission has found that another petitioner did not satisfy a burden to produce sufficient evidence of racial discrimination in a capital trial or death sentence in the United States, the facts presented here and below demonstrate a clear satisfaction of any burden of production which can be said to lie with the petitioner, and should result in a shifting of the burden of proof to the United States to demonstrate the absence of racial prejudice in Mr. Andrews' death sentence.[7]

24. The petitioners also argued that the procedures in the trial and in the review of the death sentence imposed in William Andrew's case, when considered in the context of the racist doctrine of the Mormon Church at the time of Mr. Andrews' trial in Utah, a State which is overwhelming Mormon and white, demonstrate invidious racial discrimination in violation of the OAS Charter and the American Declaration. Mr. Andrews was denied his right to racial equality when his lawyer was denied both a request for a mistral and a right to question jurors concerning a note that was found among them saying, "Hang the Nigger's [sic]." [ ] The very fact that such a note was found with the jury, coupled with the known racist Mormon Church doctrine at the time, was grounds for a mistrial or, at minimum, a further inquiry into the authorship, source of the note, exposure of the note to members of the jury or their response to it. Yet, the trial judge -- who himself was a Mormon -- refused to grant the request, and cut off any questioning of the jury about the note.

25. The petitioners argued that no reviewing court in the United States ever required the production of evidence or the holding of an evidentiary hearing on the issue of the influence of racial prejudice in the trial of William Andrews. These errors require redress as a violation of the law of international human rights. At Mr. Andrews' trial in 1974, the blatantly racist note was brought to the trial judge's attention by a bailiff. The bailiff told the judge that he had been given the note, which was written on a napkin, by a member of the jury over the lunch period. The bailiff was sworn and questioned, but could provide little information beyond hearsay. The bailiff told the judge that a juror had told him that he "found" the note in the jury lunchroom. The bailiff also stated that in his opinion one of the jurors could have written the note.

26. Moreover, the petitioners argued that despite the bailiff's own opinion, the trial judge blindly accepted the explanation of a juror who was never called to the stand to testify. The judge never attempted to determine if the juror's claim that the note was "found" was truthful or not by placing that person on the stand to testify. The judge never saw the juror's demeanor in order to adequately gauge his credibility. The judge's only response to this outrageous incident was to tell the jury to "ignore communications from foolish people."

27. The petitioners also argued that racism alone explains why William Andrews was executed in the State of Utah on July 30, 1992. The denial of his basic human right to be accorded the same level of dignity as that of a person of any other race is clearly the result

---

[7] Celestine Case, Res. No. 23/89, Case 10.031 (Sept. 28, 1989).

of racist Mormon Church doctrine. The State of Utah is overwhelmingly Mormon and white. Although no inquiry into the racial views of the jurors was permitted at the time of the revelation of the note described above, it was unquestionably true that some or all of the members of the jury were Mormons, and that the tenets of their faith guided their determination to sentence Mr. Andrews to death.

28. The petitioners argued that members of the jury were unable to show William Andrews mercy or to render him compassion because their religion taught them that no person of the Negro race was worthy of their sympathy and had been already condemned to Hell by God. Tragically, to have shown Mr. Andrews mercy would have been sacrilegious to those Mormons who comprised the jury. They were duty-bound to sentence him to death by the Apartheid-type teachings of their religious faith. The racist Church doctrine has its origins in Brigham Young, a Prophet of the Mormon Church, who instructed the congregation in 1852 that Black skin was a mark of God's curse upon black people: "I tell you, these people that are commonly called negroes are the children of the old Cain. I know they are, I know that they cannot bear rule in the Priesthood for the curse upon them . . . ."

29. The petitioners argued that, a century later, racist teaching had not changed, but was actually even more virulent. A former First President of the Mormon Church, the Church's spiritual leader, expressly told the congregation in 1949 that Black people were "damned to death by God:" "Why are so many of the inhabitants of the earth cursed with a skin of blackness? It comes in consequence of their fathers rejecting the power of the holy priesthood, and the law of God. They will go down to death." Even with the advent of the Civil Rights Movement in the United States, the Mormon Church still clung in 1969 to its racist ideology, believing that God had demanded that Blacks be treated as inferior beings. The First President told the congregation: "The seeming discrimination by the Church toward the Negro is not something that originated with man; but goes back to the beginning with God." This formal statement was made less than five years before Mr. Andrews was sentenced to death in Utah.

30. The petitioners argued that less than three years before Mr. Andrews was put on trial for his life, a poll conducted in Utah showed that over 70 percent of all Mormons vehemently believed that God had cursed black people to a life in Hell. Instead of appreciating criticism of their pre-Civil War view of Blacks, a third of the Mormons polled believed that there was a "black conspiracy" to destroy the Church.

31. The petitioners argued that in 1974, at the time when William Andrews was tried for a capital offense, Mormon Church doctrine still compelled that the jury show him no mercy because God had shown no mercy on Mr. Andrews' race. It was only in June of 1978, four years after the jury sentenced Mr. Andrews to death, that the First President of the Mormon Church announced that he had experienced a "revelation" and that from that day forward blacks could enter the Kingdom of Heaven. For Mr. Andrews, the "revelation" had come too late. He tried many times unsuccessfully to have Utah and federal courts address the obvious effect of the Church doctrine on his sentence of death, all to no avail.

32. The petitioners argued that the U.S. cannot demonstrate that it did not violate its obligation of racial equality as articulated in the OAS Charter and the American Declaration on the Rights and Duties of Man (hereinafter "American Declaration"), as well as in more recent international human rights instruments to which it has become a

party. The U.S. Government has internationally recognized obligations to racial equality before the law, binding on it in the Inter-American system in which it participates, pursuant to Article II of the American Declaration, as well as Articles 3 (k) and 44 (a) of the OAS Charter, which provide, in relevant part: Article 3 "The American States reaffirm the following principles: . . . (k) The American States proclaim the fundamental rights of the individual without distinction as to race . . ." Article 44. "The Member States . . . agree to dedicate every effort to the application of the following principles and mechanisms: a) All human beings, without distinction as to race, . . . have a right to . . . liberty, dignity, [and] equality of opportunity . . ."

33. The petitioners argued that the "fundamental rights of the individual" referred to in Article 3(k) unquestionably refer to the specific provisions of the American Declaration and its antecedent, the Universal Declaration of Human Rights. The latter instrument specifically protects the right to life (Article 3), the right to equality before the law (Article 7) and the right to due process of law in the face of criminal charges (Article 10). These rights are more specifically developed in the American Declaration. It is particularly noteworthy that the United States recently ratified the International Covenant on Civil and Political Rights. There were no reservations by the United States to Articles 2 and 26, which cover equal treatment under the law.[8] Those rights are non-derogable, pursuant to the provisions of Article 4 (1) of the Covenant. Given its recent affirmation to the right to racial equality before the law, the United States cannot now argue that it has no burden to show adherence to racial equality in the case before the Commission.

34. The petitioners argued that finally, the U.S. has been an active participant in the Conference on Security and Co-Operation in Europe (CSCE). As a full participant in the deliberations of the Conference, the U.S. became a signatory of the Report of the CSCE Meeting of Experts on National Minorities, held in Geneva, Switzerland in 1991. The report states that the participating States "consider that respect for human rights and fundamental freedoms must be accorded on a non-discriminatory basis throughout society."[9] That report, in turn, refers to the concluding document of the Copenhagen conference, in which the states parties, including the United States, agreed to the following: "Persons belonging to national minorities have the right to exercise fully and effectively their human rights and fundamental freedoms without any discrimination and in full equality before the law. The participating States will adopt, where necessary, special measures for the purpose of ensuring to persons belonging to national minorities

---

[8] The U.S. did adopt an understanding with regard to the application of Articles 2 and 26, stating that discrimination based on race is understood in the United States "to be permitted when such distinctions are, at minimum, rationally related to a legitimate governmental objective." See *United States: Senate Committee on Foreign Relations Report on the International Covenant on Civil and Political Rights*, 31 I.L.M. 645, 659 (1992). This understanding applies only when the treaty is sought to be applied domestically and does not affect the obligations of the United States under the international law of human rights.

[9] *Conference on Security and Co-Operation in Europe: Report of the CSCE Meeting of Experts on National Minorities*, 30 I.L.M. 1692, 1696 (1991).

full equality with the other citizens in the exercise and enjoyment of human rights and fundamental freedoms."[10]

35. The petitioners argued that taken as a whole, the U.S. has an internationally recognized obligation to guarantee racial equality before the law. Moreover, when, as here, overwhelming evidence of governmental complicity in racial discrimination is shown, the burden shifts to that government to prove the absence of discrimination in guaranteeing racial equality. The United States cannot discharge that burden here. The Commission should therefore find that the United States has violated its obligations to racial equality as found in the OAS Charter and the American Declaration. William Andrews was denied his right to life and to due process of law by the decision of the U.S. Government to execute him without an impartial hearing on the issue of racial discrimination at his trial. Despite his many claims to fundamental fairness and his ultimate efforts to seek the intervention of this Commission to review his case, William Andrews was executed on July 30, 1992. Mr. Andrews was improperly deprived of his life in violation of Article I of the American declaration. Article I, as it relates to the imposition of the death penalty in criminal proceedings, must be read in conjunction with Article XXVI, paragraph 2, which guarantees due process in such proceedings.

. . . .

37. The petitioners argued that Mr. Andrews' right to an impartial hearing was violated in his trial, and more importantly, in his sentencing. In complete disregard of universal notions of an impartial trial, no state or federal court ever granted Mr. Andrews the right to inquire into the origins of the racist note. The Supreme Court of the United States would not grant review of Mr. Andrews' case. Justices Marshall and Brennan were the lone dissenters, calling the note "a vulgar incident of lynch-mob racism reminiscent of Reconstruction days." *Andrews v. Shulsen*, 485 U.S. 919, 920 (1988) (dissent from denial of certiorari). Justice Marshall described the denial of basic due process by pointing out that Mr. Andrews merely sought an evidentiary hearing to determine the origins of the note, and that "the Constitution [of the United States], not to mention common decency, require[d] no less than this modest procedure."*Id.* Justice Marshall gave examples of obvious questions about the note that have never been answered: "Was it one or more of [Mr. Andrews'] jurors who drew a black man hanging on a gallows and attached the inscription, "Hang the Niggers"? How many other jurors saw the incendiary drawing before it was turned over to the bailiff? Might it have had any effect on the deliberations?" *Id.* These questions remain unanswered to this day.

38. The petitioners argued that because no court granted Mr. Andrews the right to question the jurors about the note, the worst scenario cannot be ruled out: the entire jury was involved in the drawing of the note and joked about it before finally giving it to the bailiff; the judge then joined in their conspiracy by telling them to "ignore communications by foolish people." It cannot be ruled out that a "lynch-mob atmosphere" existed within the jury which sentenced Mr. Andrews to death since he has never been accorded a hearing. The failure of the U.S. Government to afford a hearing on the issue of racial

---

[10] *Document of the Copenhagen Meeting of the Conference on the Human Dimension of the CSCE*, 29 I.L.M. 1305, 1318 (1990).

discrimination, and its subsequent execution of William Andrews, constitute a violation of Articles I and XXVI of the American Declaration.

. . . .

C. United States Government's Response to Petition

. . . .

62.. . .[T]he United States argued that it rejected the petitioner's effort to shift the burden of proof by claiming a presumptive violation of human rights. [The petitioner] contends that because the United States has a duty under the Charter and the Declaration to secure rights without discrimination based on race, the United States accordingly has an affirmative duty to demonstrate that it did not violate that duty to Mr. Andrews. Pet. at 14. Not only is this argument legally unavailing, it is unsupported by any factual basis. The petition alleges "overwhelming evidence of governmental complicity" but provides no evidence of such "complicity" whatsoever, apart from the fact that the State of Utah successfully prosecuted Mr. Andrews for his role in an especially gruesome crime. The burden remains upon the petitioner to demonstrate the violations [the petitioner] alleges; that effort proves no more successful in this petition than it was for over a decade in the U.S. Court System.

63. The United States argued that the first and arguably most compelling element of petitioner's claim that Mr. Andrews' trial, sentencing and execution were fatally tainted by racially-motivated discrimination turns on the discovery by a juror of a note bearing a racist slur (an apparent copy of which is appended to the petition). According to the judicial record, the juror found the note while on a lunch break in a restaurant when s/he overturned the napkin on the back of which the note had been sketched. Although the jury had been sequestered during the break, there was no indication that the note had been written by a juror or circulated or discussed among members of the jury. Moreover, the note was promptly disclosed to the bailiff, who in turn brought it to the attention of the trial judge.

64. The United States argued that immediately thereafter, the Court held a hearing at which the bailiff was sworn and testified as to the circumstances of the discovery; defendants and counsel were present. Upon conclusion of the hearing, the Court denied defendants' motion to sequester the jury completely and thereafter admonished the jury to ignore such communications. Contrary to the implications of the petition, the trial judge did not fail to respond to the "napkin incident;" in point of fact, the court investigated the incident promptly and determined that it had not resulted in any prejudice to the defendants. Mr. Andrews' attorneys made their objections at the time; they were fully considered by the trial judge and were overruled.

. . . .

66. Generalized Racism - The United States argued that the petition alleged that Mr. Andrews was deprived of his right to a fair and impartial jury free from outside influence because the State of Utah was at the time (and remains) overwhelmingly Mormon and white, the jurors were all white, some or all of them "unquestionably" were Mormons, and they were "compelled" by the Mormon Churchs "racist doctrine" to sentence him to death. Petitioner adduces no evidence whatsoever for these conclusory allegations. While s/he argues that Mr. Andrews was denied an impartial hearing on the issue of racial discrimination at his trial (pet. at 17), s/he admits that "the obvious effect of the Church

doctrine on [Mr. Andrews'] sentence to death" was present to the Utah and federal courts, "many times unsuccessfully, all to no avail."

67. The United States argued that the petitioners were entirely correct on this last point. It is clear that Mr. Andrews raised the issue of outside influence with the courts on numerous occasions, and that the courts repeatedly examined the claim and determined that his constitutional right to a fair and impartial jury had not been transgressed. [ ] The fact is that Mr. Andrews failed to convince any court that his assertions concerning the lack of a fair trial had any merit.

68. As to the racial composition of the jury, the United States bears noting that Andrews and his co-defendants themselves objected to the only African-American who was a member of the jury panel; perhaps because that panel member was a law enforcement officer and knew several members of the Ogden Police Department, the attorneys for Andrews and Pierre both objected to him and the State stipulated to his removal for cause. In any event, this claim too was considered by the courts and rejected on the merits.[ ] Moreover, the third defendant, Keith Roberts, was also an African-American and the only defendant represented by and African-American attorney at trial; surely, if racist doctrine had prevented the jury from reaching an impartial decision or had "compelled" its members to impose capital punishment, he would also have received the death penalty. [ ]

. . . .

[The Inter-American Commission found the petition admissible.]

. . . .

b. The United States Government's Argument on Merits

. . . .

117. . . . .It argued that the burden of proof always remains on the accuser who has the burden of proving that discrimination occurred. While the burden of producing evidence may shift to the accused government to prove lack of discriminatory animus, it does not shift until and unless a prima facie case is made that discrimination exists. It argued that the Commission understands this because in the Celestine case, the Commission held that the burden of production was on the petitioner to prove a prima facie case. Only then does the burden shift. In the Case of Willie L. Celestine supra, para. 45 at 72, the Commission said: "in its opinion, the petitioner has not provided sufficient evidence that the statistical studies presented make a prima facie case to prove the allegations of racial/ethnic discrimination and partiality in the imposition of the death penalty such as to shift the burden of proof (sic) to the United States Government."

118. The Government argued further that there was no credible evidence that any of the twelve jurors, let alone all of them were racist, or that any one connected to the case was racist. The sole African-American juror was peremptorily challenged by the State only after the defense challenged him for cause which was denied by the trial court judge. The prosecution obliged the defendants by peremptorily challenging him for them. The evidence reflected that the jury was impartial, and that the napkin incident did not reflect that the jury was racist. While the person who left the napkin was no doubt racist, there is no evidence that his or her racist appeal to the jury incited the juror who saw it to be racist, it was promptly handed over to the bailiff and the judge reflected awareness of the impropriety of the message. No one, including counsel for Andrews and counsel for the

co-defendants asked the judge to voir dire the jury after the incident occurred, nor was it necessary after the napkin incident.

119. The Government stated that the admonition to the jury was appropriate. The judge told them: "Occasionally some foolish person will try to communicate with you. Please disregard the communications from foolish persons and ignore the same."[ ]. It argued that treatment of the third co-defendant reflected that the jury was not racist. Keith Roberts, the third co-defendant, was also charged with murder. He was not convicted of murder, let alone sentenced to death. Yet he was African American, and his counsel was African American. The attorneys for the other two co-defendants were not African American. Had the jury truly been racist, it would have found Keith Roberts guilty of murder and sentenced him to death, regardless of his scope of involvement.

120. The Government argued further that there was substantial evidence of Andrews' guilt at trial. To find "racial" ethnic discrimination in this case, the Commission would have to find that there was no other possible basis for the jury's decision to convict Andrews. It stated that there was substantial and appropriate appellate review of Andrews' claims, and that the allegation of racism was being used as an indirect means to attempt to abolish the death penalty.

. . . .

e. Other Submissions

. . . .

138. The Commission received a 31 page Amicus Commissae brief from . . . Rights International . . . which [argued] that disclosure of specific evidence of possible juror racial bias or taint requires the trial judge to examine each juror individually in order to ensure tribunal impartiality as well as to fulfill the State-Party's affirmative duty to eliminate racial discrimination. This requires the State under both international and domestic law to avoid not only bias in fact but also the appearance of bias. International law employs an "objective test" and the domestic law of countries using juries in criminal cases also requires states to avoid the appearance of bias in their tribunals.[ ]

. . . .

VI. ANALYSIS [BY THE INTER-AMERICAN COMMISSION]

A. Did Mr. Andrews Have a Fair and Impartial Hearing?

147. Article XXVI of the American Declaration, paragraph 2 provides: "Every person accused of an offense has the right to be given an impartial and public hearing, and to be tried by courts previously established in accordance with pre-existing laws, and not to receive cruel, infamous or unusual punishment." . . . .

148. . . . Upon examining all arguments, documentary and testimonial evidence including exhibits submitted to it, the Commission notes that: Mr. Andrews was tried, convicted, sentenced, and executed by the State of Utah on three counts of first degree murder, and two counts of aggravated robbery, which occurred after he participated in the robbery of a radio store. He was tried in the State of Utah where the teaching of the Mormon church doctrine prevailing at the time of his trial, was that all black people were damned to death by God and were inferior beings. This doctrine was changed after the trial and conviction of the victim, Mr. Andrews.

. . . .

b) Proceedings in the Trial Court/Napkin

i. The Bailiff's Testimony

150. The Commission, upon examining the trial transcript of the proceedings referring to the "notation on the napkin," noted, that a hearing was held in the afternoon session of the trial proceedings, on the renewal of a motion to sequester the jury and a motion for a mistrial by the co-defendants attorney, including William Andrews' attorney in the absence of the jury, after the jurors returned from lunch. The trial transcript of the testimony of the bailiff, Thomas R. Linox, to whom the napkin was given by a member of the juror reveals the following:

> On the day in question, November 4, 1974, he was in the company of the jurors in Lee's restaurant where they went for lunch on that day, shortly after they had been seated a Mr. Weaver, one of the jurors said, "bailiff I have some evidence for you...", and gave him a napkin. The bailiff said that "myself as well as some of the other people thought it was one of Mr. Weaver's jokes, he is quite a hilarious gentleman. So I went up there very honestly at first thinking I was just humoring a joke and that is when he produced that napkin with the writing that you see on it.[footnote omitted]

> He had not seen the napkin prior to the time that he had handed it to him, and stated that the napkin was with Mr. Weaver's regular place setting, the blank portion of the napkin showing to anyone who would have cared to walk along the table. It had the appearance of any other napkin until, according to him, he turned it over to open it up and that is when he saw the writing that the judge had before him. The bailiff read the words on the napkin "hang the niggers," and described the drawing on the napkin as "a character of a gallows and a stick figure hanging therefrom."

151. The bailiff was asked the following questions:

> "Was this, [People's] exhibit No.4, discussed or shown to other prospective jurors?"[ ] He replied: "I do believe the people immediately to the left and the right of Mr. Weaver would have had to have seen it. I couldn't say with any degree of certainty." The bailiff was then asked: "After the napkin was handed to you, what, if any conversations existed between jurors and yourself or Mr. Weaver and other jurors, in your presence?" He responded: "Nothing pertinent to that. They felt it was that important that I should have it to show the court and nothing more was discussed. There was no comments one way or another about it. There was some concern shown on the part of some of the jurors who asked me directly, 'do you think this will affect our present situation as far as where we are eating or what the court may do about this.' I said, I have no idea. That is a matter for the court to decide." [footnote omitted]

152. Upon further examination the bailiff was asked by Mr. Davis:

"Mr. Linox, do you think perhaps one of the jurors themselves could have drawn that? Are you able to make such a conclusion that it was possible or not? That is what I want to know?" He responded, "Mr. Davis, I say it is possible, that small amount, that much time could have lapsed." [ ]

ii. The Trial Court's Action

153. The Court asked the bailiff the following question:

"Did I tell you to say anything to Mr. Weaver?" The bailiff stated that: "You did" and stated that "I admonished Mr. Weaver not to mention the incident any further, to let the issue die." The judge then asked the bailiff, "have you been able to do that?" the bailiff responded, "I have." The judge then asked the bailiff, "did he say anything to you?" the bailiff responded, "he said he would." [ ]

154. There is language in the trial transcript which shows concern expressed by a defense attorney. He requested of the Court that, "the jury be sequestered, that they be put under guard that would guard against influencing this jury which is accumulative now, with the talk in the hallway, now this action."[ ] The trial court denied the motions to sequester the jury and for a new trial and stated that "the only thing that this kind of foolishness can do is cause the trial to start all over again. It is that foolish, but I will deny your motions at this time."[ ]

c) Appellate Review of Mr. Andrews' Case

. . . .

156. The United States Supreme Court denied Mr. Andrew's motion for certiorari. However, two of the Justices, Marshall and Brennan in the Supreme Court dissented. The note was referred to as "a vulgar incident of lynch-mob racism reminiscent of Reconstruction days."[ ] Justice Marshal referred to the denial of due process by stating that Mr. Andrews merely sought an evidentiary hearing to determine the origins of the note, and that "the Constitution [of the United States], not to mention common decency, require[d] no less than this modest procedure."[ ] Justice Marshall stated:

Was it one or more of [Mr. Andrews'] jurors who drew a black man hanging on a gallows and attached the inscription, "Hang the niggers"? How many other jurors saw the incendiary drawing before it was turned over to the bailiff? Might it have had any effect on the deliberations? [ ]

d) United States Domestic Law

157. The Fifth Amendment of the Constitution of the United States of America 1787 provides: "No person shall be held to answer for a capital, or otherwise infamous crime . . . nor deprived of life, . . . without due process of law . . . ." The Sixth Amendment provides: "In all criminal prosecutions, the accused shall enjoy the right to a speedy and

public trial, by an impartial jury . . . ." The Commission notes the principles enunciated by the Courts in the United States. The United States Supreme Court held in the *Rosales-Lopez v. United States*, that a "reasonable possibility" of juror bias is sufficient to find reversible error for a federal court's refusal to ask venire-persons about possible racial bias."[11] Jury misconduct concerning outside influences must be fully investigated to determine if any misconduct actually occurred and whether or not it was prejudicial.[12] Failure to hold a hearing in these cases constitutes an abuse of discretion and is thus reversible error.[ ]

158. The Code of Criminal Procedure for the State of Utah requires the Court to admonish the jury at each adjournment . . . that it is their duty not to converse among themselves nor with any one else on any subject connected with the trial, and not to form or express any opinion thereon until the case is finally submitted to them.[ ] Under the Code jurors can be challenged in the State of Utah on "peremptory" grounds, and for "cause" (for bias-opinion) and can be examined as to such bias-opinion[ ] by the Court. Such challenges are made prior to the commencement of a trial.

e) The International Standard on Impartiality

159. The international standard on the issue of "judge and juror impartiality" employs an objective test based on "reasonableness, and the appearance of impartiality." The United Nations Committee to Eliminate Racial Discrimination has held that a reasonable suspicion of bias is sufficient for juror disqualification, and stated that: "it is incumbent upon national judicial authorities to investigate the issue and to disqualify the juror if there is a suspicion that the juror might be biased."[13] The Commission notes that in the European System of Human Rights an objective test was enunciated in the cases of *Piersack v. Belgium,*[14] and *Gregory v. United Kingdom.*[15]

---

[11] 451 U.S. 182 (1981).

[12] [*United States v. Harris*, 908 F.2d 728, 733 (11th Cir. 1990); *United States v. Brantley*, 733 F.2d 1429, 1439 (11th Cir. 1984), *cert. denied*, 470 U.S. 1006 (1984)].

[13] *Narrainen v. Norway*, UN Ctte. Elim Racial Discrim., Communication No. 3/1991, views adopted 15 March 1994. In that case a Norwegian citizen of Tamil origin, who was charged with a drug-related offense, complained that he had not obtained a fair and impartial trial. He alleged that racial views had played a large part in the decision against him, pointing to a statement of one of the jurors that people such as him, living on taxpayers' money, should be sent back from where they had come, and alleged that slurs were made about the color of his skin.

[14] 5 HRR 169 (1982). The European Court of Human Rights held that there was a violation of Article 6 of the European Convention which guarantees the right to a fair and impartial trial. The European Commission stated that: "Whilst impartiality normally denotes absence of prejudice or bias, its existence or otherwise can . . . be tested in various ways. A distinction can be drawn in this context between a subjective approach, that is endeavoring to ascertain the personal conviction of a given judge in a given case, and an
(continued...)

160. In the case of *Remli v. France* the European Court of Human Rights referred to the principles laid down in its case-law concerning the independence and impartiality of tribunals, which applied to jurors as they did to professional and lay judges and found that there had been a violation of Article 6(1) of the European Convention For the Protection of Human Rights and Fundamental Freedoms.[16] That Article provides that: "In the determination of his civil rights and obligations or of any criminal charge against him,

---

[14](...continued)
objective approach, that is determining whether he offered guarantees sufficient to exclude any legitimate doubt in this respect."

[15] 16 H.R.L.J. 238 (1995). In this case an Afro-Caribbean male had been convicted of armed robbery. During jury deliberations, the trial judge received a handwritten note for a juror stating: "Jury showing racial overtones 1 member to be excused." The trial judge redirected the jury and did not hold an evidentiary hearing. The European Commission found the case admissible and found that the defendant essentially makes the case that it was clear from the jury note that there was, at the very least, a strong objective indication of racial bias within the jury. It looked at the international standard and stated:

> [i]f the possibility of bias on the part of the juror comes to the attention of the trial judge in the course of a trial, the trial judge should consider whether there is actual bias or not (subjective test). If this has not been established, that trial judge or appeal court must then consider whether there is "a real danger of bias affecting the mind of the relevant juror or jurors" (objective test). Note, the real danger test originated in the English common law in the case of *R. v. Gough*, 4 A.E.R. (Court of Appeal, Criminal Division 1992).

However, the European Commission concluded that the judge's detailed and careful redirection of the jury was sufficient. The *Gregory* case is now before the European Court of Human Rights.

[16] [1996] HRCD Vol. VII No. 7, European Court of Human Rights: Judgments, at 608-613. Judgment was delivered on April 23, 1996. The case involves the trial of an Algerian national in France for escape, during which a prison guard was struck and killed. The applicant and another person (both of them were of North African origin) were tried and convicted for international homicide and attempted escape in the Rhone Assize Court. The applicant was sentenced to life imprisonment on April 14, 1989. He submitted evidence that during his trial, a person overheard one of the jurors say, "What's more, I'm a racist." That person so certified in writing, and defense counsel asked that the court take formal note of the racist remark, and that the court append the written statement to the record. The trial court refused the first request but granted the second. As to the first request, the Assize judge stated that it was "not able to take formal note of events alleged to have occurred out of its presence."

everyone is entitled to a fair and public hearing . . .by an independent and impartial tribunal established by law . . . ."

161. The European Court considered that Article 6(1) of the Convention imposed an obligation on every national court to check whether, as constituted, it was "an impartial tribunal" within the meaning of that provision where, as in the instant case, that was disputed on a ground that did not immediately appear to be manifestly devoid of merit. In Remli's case the Rhone Assize Court had not made any such check, thereby depriving Mr. Remli of the possibility of remedying, if it had proved necessary, a situation contrary to the requirements of the Convention.[17]

162. The Commission has noted the United States Government's argument that the admonishment by the trial court to the jury to disregard communications from foolish people was appropriate. It has also noted its argument that the jury was not racist because Mr. Andrews' co-defendant, Keith Roberts, who was African American, and whose counsel was African American and also charged with murder, was not convicted of murder, nor sentenced to death; and the attorneys for the other two co-defendants were not African American. The Commission finds that these factors are not dispositive of whether the United States violated the Articles of the American Declaration as pertaining to Mr. William Andrews' right to an "impartial hearing." The Commission has also noted that Mr. Andrews' other co-defendant who was African American was convicted and sentenced to death by the State of Utah, and executed in 1987.

163. The United States Government's evidence produced at the hearing on the merits of the case before the Commission through the testimony of its own witness Mr. Yocum, Assistant Attorney General of Utah substantiates the petitioners' case. Mr. Yocum testified that the jury members were not questioned by the trial judge about the note. The trial judge held a hearing, but only the bailiff was questioned. The judge denied the motion for a mistrial and proceeded to trial with the same members of the jury.

164. Conclusion: The Commission finds that the United States has not disputed that a napkin was found by one of the jurors, and given to the bailiff (who took the jurors to lunch in a restaurant) with words written in black stating "hang the nigger's" and a figure drawn in black hanging therefrom. Nor has it disputed that the napkin was brought to the attention of the trial judge who questioned the bailiff as to its origin.

165. The Commission finds that in assessing the totality of the facts in an objective and reasonable manner the evidence indicates that Mr. Andrews did not receive an impartial hearing because there was a reasonable appearance of "racial bias" by some

---

[17] In Remli's case the Rhone Assize Court dismissed the application without even examining the evidence submitted to it, on the ground that it was "not able to take formal note of events alleged to have occurred out of its presence." Nor had it ordered that evidence should be taken to verify what had been reported and, if had been established, take formal note of it as requested by the defence, although it could have done so. The applicant had been unable either to have the juror in question replaced by one of the additional jurors or to rely on the fact in issue in support of his appeal on points of law. Nor had he been able to challenge the juror, since the jury had been finally empaneled and no appeal lay against the Assize Court's judgment other than on points of law. *Id.* at 612.

members of the jury, and the omission of the trial court to voir dire the jury tainted his trial and resulted in him being convicted, sentenced to death and executed. The record before the Commission reflects ample evidence of "racial basis."

166. First, Mr. Andrews was a black male, and was tried by an all white jury some of whom were members of the Mormon Church and adhered to its teachings that black people were inferior beings.[18] The transcript reveals that the bailiff testified that when the juror told him he had some evidence for him, both the bailiff and some of the other jurors thought that it was one of the juror's jokes which they were humoring and there was discussion among the jurors concerning the "napkin."[ ]

167. Second, was the conduct and manner, in which the note was handed to the bailiff by the juror. (See trial transcript, the bailiff thought he was humoring a joke.) The note depicts racial words "hang the nigger's," written on the napkin that was given to the Court. (See the opinions of Justices Brennan and Marshall.) The trial transcript states "Hang the Niggers," and the drawing on the napkin was described by the bailiff as "a gallows and a stick figure hanging therefrom."[ ] The transcript refers to express language by the bailiff, that the jurors who were immediate to the left and the right of Mr. Weaver, (the juror who found the napkin) would have had to have seen it. The jurors asked the bailiff, if it would affect their present situation and what the court may do about it.[ ] The bailiff himself stated under oath that it was possible that one of the jurors could have drawn that note because "that small amount, that much time could have elapsed".[ ]

168. Third, the admonishment by the trial court to the jury was inadequate. The trial judge at the very least if he did not want to grant a mistrial, should have conducted an evidentiary hearing of the jury members to ascertain whether some of them had seen the note and they had been influenced by it. The trial judge instead, warned them against foolish people, and questioned the bailiff and left such an important and fundamental issue for the bailiff, whom he instructed to admonish the juror who found the note. The trial judge appeared to be more concerned to continue the trial with the same members of the jury without questioning them, as to whether they had seen the note, and denied both motions to sequester the jury and for a mistrial.

169. Fourth, in addition to the note being found, there is language in the trial transcript which indicates the concern expressed by the defense attorneys, that two things had occurred during the trial, "the talk in the hallway, and the note," which would influence the jury members in their deliberations and in making their decisions, and which language had become accumulative.

170. It should be noted that while it is not the function of the Inter-American Commission on Human Rights to act as a quasi-judicial fourth instance court and to review the holdings of the domestic courts of the OAS member states,[ ] it is mandated by its Statute and its Regulations to examine petitions alleging violations of human rights under the American Declaration against member States who are not parties to the American Convention.[ ]

171. The Commission finds that Mr. Andrews did not receive an impartial trial because there was evidence of "racial bias" present during his trial, and because the trial court failed to conduct an evidentiary hearing of the jury in order to ascertain whether

---

[18] In Davis County, Utah, 73.9% of the people who resided there were Mormons.

members of the jury found the napkin as the juror claimed or whether the jurors themselves wrote and drew the racial words on the napkin. If the note did not originate from the jurors and was "found" by the juror then the trial court could have inquired of the jurors by conducting an evidentiary hearing as to whether they would be influenced or their judgment impaired by the napkin depicting the racial words and drawing so that they would be unable to try the case impartially. Had the Court conducted the hearing it would have had the possibility of remedying, if it had proved necessary so to do, a situation contrary to the requirements of the American Declaration.

172. Therefore, the Commission finds the United States in violation of Article XXVI, paragraph 2, of the American Declaration, because Mr. Andrews had the right to receive an impartial hearing as provided by the Article, and he did not receive an impartial trial in United States Courts. In capital punishment cases, the States Parties have an obligation to observe rigorously all the guarantees for an impartial trial. . . .

❖   ❖   ❖

Questions & Comments

(1) The U.S. federal government and the State of Utah failed to stay Andrews' execution. The U.S. government had taken the position that the American Declaration is not legally binding on the U.S. Recently, Pres. Clinton issued an executive order that states in part:

> It shall also be the policy and practice of the Government of the United States to promote respect for international human rights, both in our relationships with all other countries and by working with and strengthening the various international mechanisms for the promotion of human rights, including, *inter alia*, those of the United Nations, the International Labor Organization, and the Organization of American States.

Sec. 1(b), Exec. Order No. 13107, Implementation of Human Rights Treaties (10 Dec. 1998), 63 F.R. 68991 (1998). Does the U.S.' new policy of promoting respect for international human rights by working with and strengthening the Inter-American Commission entail compliance with the Commission's future requests for stays? What about compliance with the Commission's recommendations?

Assuming that a stay is issued – but the U.S. does not comply with the Commission's recommendations – and you go into federal or state court to order state compliance with the Commission's recommendation as evidence of customary international law, how would you argue such a claim?

(2)   Consider *Rizvanovic v. Federation of Bosnia & Herzegovina (Admissibility and Merits)*, Case No. CH/97/59, Hum. Rts. Chamber-BiH (12 June 1998), in which the Human Rights Chamber for Bosnia and Herzegovina in a death penalty case found that because members of a military court were "operating in a situation of conflict where outside pressure on its members was likely" and were subject to dismissal on the proposal of the Ministry of Defence, these factors could give rise to legitimate doubts as to whether the court meet the standard of independence required in a death penalty case. Accordingly, the Chamber concluded that the military court lacked a sufficient appearance of

independence and the applicant could not be executed on order from this military court.

Is there a higher standard for death penalty cases in the international law governing judicial impartiality and independence? Should there be?

C. Examination of Witnesses and Documents

Harward v. Norway
UN Human Rights Committee
Communication No. 451/1991
Views adopted 15 July 1994
U.N. Doc. CCPR/C/51/D/451/1991 (1994)

. . . .

2.1 The author [a British citizen] states that he was arrested on 27 September 1986 in Tenerife, Spain, and informed that his extradition had been requested on suspicion of drug trafficking. He was kept in detention until his extradition on 21 August 1987 to Norway. He submits that, at that time, he was still waiting for the outcome of the appeal against his extradition, which he had filed with the Spanish Constitutional Court.

2.2 In Norway, the author was charged with having imported a considerable quantity of heroin into the country during 1985 and 1986. A legal-aid lawyer, who spoke only little English, was appointed. On 31 August 1987, a formal indictment was issued against him and his co-defendants, including his two brothers.

2.3 The trial started on 12 October 1987, in the Eidsivating High Court. On 3 November 1987, the author and his co-defendants were found guilty as charged; the author, who claims to be innocent, was sentenced to 10 years' imprisonment. On 25 March 1988, the Supreme Court rejected the author's appeal.

The complaint:

. . . .

3.3 The author further claims to be a victim of a violation of article 14, paragraph 3(a), of the Covenant, since he was allegedly misinformed about the charges against him in Spain. He further submits that the 1,100 document pages used in the trial against him were in the Norwegian language, which he did not understand; only the indictment and a small proportion of the other papers were translated.

3.4 The author also claims that article 14, paragraph 3(b), was violated in his case. He claims that he was hindered in the preparation of his defence because the indictment was issued only six weeks before the start of the trial and his lawyer's request to have all documents pertaining to the case translated was refused. He further alleges that his defence was obstructed, since the most damaging evidence against him was only introduced during the trial, and not included in the documents which were available beforehand. According to the author, this evidence consisted of uncorroborated and unsigned statements made by his co-defendants during their detention in solitary confinement, in the absence of an interpreter or lawyer.

. . . .

Issues and proceedings before the Committee:

. . . .

9.2 The Committee notes that the facts, to which the parties agree, show that Mr. Harward was assigned a lawyer on 28 August 1987 and that the trial against him started on 12 October 1987, that the indictment, the statements of co-defendants to the Norwegian police and the court records were provided in written translation to the author, and that the author's defence counsel had access to the entire case file. It is also undisputed that an interpreter was available to the defence for all meetings between counsel and Mr. Harward and that simultaneous interpretation was provided during the court hearings.

9.3 The Committee further notes that the State party has argued that not all documents in the case file were of relevance to the defence and that only fifteen documents were presented by the prosecution in Court and therefore available to the jurors, out of which only four police reports were not available in English or in English translation. The Committee has also taken note of counsel's argument that all documents in the case file, although not presented during the trial, were of relevance to the defence, since they had been used by the police and the prosecution in their preparation of the trial.

9.4 Article 14 of the Covenant protects the right to a fair trial. An essential element of this right is that an accused must have adequate time and facilities to prepare his defence, as is reflected in paragraph 3(b) of article 14. Article 14, however, does not contain an explicit right of an accused to have direct access to all documents used in the preparation of the trial against him in a language he can understand. The question before the Committee is whether, in the specific circumstances of the author's case, the failure of the State party to provide written translations of all the documents used in the preparation of the trial has violated Mr. Harward's right to a fair trial, more specifically his right under article 14, paragraph 3(b), to have adequate facilities to prepare his defence.

9.5 In the opinion of the Committee, it is important for the guarantee of fair trial that the defence has the opportunity to familiarize itself with the documentary evidence against an accused. However, this does not entail that an accused who does not understand the language used in court, has the right to be furnished with translations of all relevant documents in a criminal investigation, provided that the relevant documents are made available to his counsel. The Committee notes that Mr. Harward was represented by a Norwegian lawyer of his choice, who had access to the entire file, and that the lawyer had the assistance of an interpreter in his meetings with Mr. Harward. Defence counsel therefore had opportunity to familiarize himself with the file and, if he thought it necessary, to read out Norwegian documents to Mr. Harward during their meetings, so that Mr. Harward could take note of its contents through interpretation. If counsel would have deemed the time available to prepare the defence (just over six weeks) inadequate to familiarize himself with the entire file, he could have requested a postponement of the trial, which he did not do. The Committee concludes that, in the particular circumstances of the case, Mr. Harward's right to a fair trial, more specifically his right to have adequate facilities to prepare his defence, was not violated.

9.6 The Human Rights Committee, acting under article 5, paragraph 4, of the Optional Protocol to the International Covenant on Civil and Political Rights, is of the view that the facts before it do not reveal a violation of any of the articles of the Covenant.

❖ ❖ ❖

Questions & Comments

(1)   The European Court has held that Article 6(3)(c) requires that State Parties pay for translation costs — even though the criminal defendant eventually was convicted. *Luedicke, Belkaçem and Koç v. Federal Republic of Germany*, 29 Eur. Ct. H. R. (ser. A) (1978); *Öztürk v. Federal Republic of Germany*, 73 Eur. Ct. H.R. (ser. A) (1984).

(2)   Consider the rules governing the production of evidence for the International Criminal Tribunal for the Former Yugoslavia.

Section 4: Production of Evidence

Rule 66   Disclosure by the Prosecutor

(A) Subject to the provisions of Rules 53 and 69, the Prosecutor shall make available to the defence in a language which the accused understands

(i) within thirty days of the initial appearance of the accused, copies of the supporting material which accompanied the indictment when confirmation was sought as well as all prior statements obtained by the Prosecutor from the accused, and

(ii) within the time-limit prescribed by the Trial Chamber or by the pre-trial Judge appointed pursuant to Rule 65 ter, copies of the statements of all witnesses whom the Prosecutor intends to call to testify at trial; copies of the statements of additional prosecution witnesses shall be made available to the defence when a decision is made to call those witnesses.

(B) The Prosecutor shall on request, subject to Sub-rule (C), permit the defence to inspect any books, documents, photographs and tangible objects in the Prosecutor's custody or control, which are material to the preparation of the defence, or are intended for use by the Prosecutor as evidence at trial or were obtained from or belonged to the accused.

(C)   Where information is in the possession of the Prosecutor, the disclosure of which may prejudice further or ongoing investigations, or for any other reasons may be contrary to the public interest or affect the security interests of any State, the Prosecutor may apply to the Trial Chamber sitting in camera to be relieved from the obligation to disclose pursuant to Sub-rule (B). When making such application the Prosecutor shall provide the Trial Chamber (but only the Trial Chamber) with the information that is sought to be kept confidential.

Rule 67   Reciprocal Disclosure

(A) As early as reasonably practicable and in any event prior to the commencement of the trial:

(i) the Prosecutor shall notify the defence of the names of the witnesses that the Prosecutor intends to call in proof of the guilt of the accused and in rebuttal of any defence plea of which the Prosecutor has received notice in accordance with Sub-rule (ii) below;

(ii) the defence shall notify the Prosecutor of its intent to offer:

> (a) the defence of alibi; in which case the notification shall specify the place or places at which the accused claims to have been present at the time of the alleged crime and the names and addresses of witnesses and any other evidence upon which the accused intends to rely to establish the alibi;

> (b) any special defence, including that of diminished or lack of mental responsibility; in which case the notification shall specify the names and addresses of witnesses and any other evidence upon which the accused intends to rely to establish the special defence.

(B) Failure of the defence to provide notice under this Rule shall not limit the right of the accused to testify on the above defences.

(C) If the defence makes a request pursuant to Sub-rule 66 (B), the Prosecutor shall be entitled to inspect any books, documents, photographs and tangible objects, which are within the custody or control of the defence and which it intends to use as evidence at the trial.

(D) If either party discovers additional evidence or material which should have been produced earlier pursuant to the Rules, that party shall promptly notify the other party and the Trial Chamber of the existence of the additional evidence or material.

Rule 68 Disclosure of Exculpatory Evidence

The Prosecutor shall, as soon as practicable, disclose to the defence the existence of evidence known to the Prosecutor which in any way tends to suggest the innocence or mitigate the guilt of the accused or may affect the credibility of prosecution evidence.

Rules of Procedure and Evidence, International Criminal Tribunal for the Former Yugoslavia, U.N. Doc. IT/32/Rev. 14 (as amended 9 & 10 July 1998).

(3) Compare U.S. law on the prosecution's duty to disclose. In *Brady v. Maryland*, 373 U.S. 83 (1963), the U.S. Supreme Court held that "the suppression by the prosecution of evidence favorable to an accused upon request violates due process where the evidence is material either to guilt or punishment." *Id.* at 87. A prosecutor is not required to deliver his entire file to defense counsel. *United States v. Bagley*, 105 S. Ct. 3375 (1985). The level of "materiality" required is a "reasonable probability" that the evidence will contribute to guilt or punishment. *Id.*

Note that the ICT-Y requires a level of materiality "which in any way tends to suggest the innocence or mitigate the guilt of the accused or may affect the credibility of prosecution evidence." Rule 68, ROP of ICT-Y. Are both the European Court's decision in *Edwards v. United Kingdom* (reproduced below) and the U.S. Supreme Court's caselaw out-of-step with the ICT-Y's rules on the prosecution's duty to disclose evidence to the defense? Are there any good reasons for this difference? Francisco Forrest Martin, *et al.*, 1 INTERNATIONAL HUMAN RIGHTS LAW & PRACTICE: CASES, TREATIES AND MATERIALS 577 (1997).

(4) Consider Rule 70 of the ICT-Y's Rules of Procedure:

Rule 70 Matters not Subject to Disclosure

(A) Notwithstanding the provisions of Rules 66 and 67, reports, memoranda, or other internal documents prepared by a party, its assistants or representatives in connection with the investigation or preparation of the case, are not subject to disclosure or notification under those Rules.

(B) If the Prosecutor is in possession of information which has been provided to the Prosecutor on a confidential basis and which has been used solely for the purpose of generating new evidence, that initial information and its origin shall not be disclosed by the Prosecutor without the consent of the person or entity providing the initial information and shall in any event not be given in evidence without prior disclosure to the accused.

(C) If, after obtaining the consent of the person or entity providing information under this Rule, the Prosecutor elects to present as evidence any testimony, document or other material so provided, the Trial Chamber, notwithstanding Rule 98, may not order either party to produce additional evidence received from the person or entity providing the initial information, nor may the Trial Chamber for the purpose of obtaining such additional evidence itself summon that person or a representative of that entity as a witness or order their attendance. A Trial Chamber may not use its power to order the attendance of witnesses or to require production of documents in order to compel the production of such additional evidence.

(D) If the Prosecutor calls a witness to introduce in evidence any information provided under this Rule, the Trial Chamber may not compel that witness to answer any question relating to the information or its origin, if the witness declines to answer on grounds of confidentiality.

(E) The right of the accused to challenge the evidence presented by the Prosecution shall remain unaffected subject only to the limitations contained in Sub-rules (C) and (D).

(F) The Trial Chamber may order upon an application by the accused or defence counsel that, in the interests of justice, the provisions of this Rule shall apply *mutatis mutandis* to specific information in the possession of the accused.

(G) Nothing in Sub-rule (C) or (D) above shall affect a Trial Chamber's power under Rule 89 (D) to exclude evidence if its probative value is substantially outweighed by the need to ensure a fair trial.

(5)   In *The Prosecutor v. Blaskic*, Case No. IT-95-14, Int'l Crim. Trib.-Yugo., Trial Chamber (19 January 1998), the Trial Chamber rejected the defense claim that the admission of documents written by persons who did not appear as witnesses violated his right to examine witnesses against him. Compare the European Court of Human Rights decision in *Mantovanelli v. France*, – Eur. Ct. H.R. (ser. A) (1997), in which the Court held that the applicants' inability to have their lawyers present at the interviews held by an independent expert appointed by an administrative court and to have an opportunity to inspect numerous documents to which the expert's report referred, violated their right to a fair hearing. The Court noted that the right to a fair hearing guaranteed by Article 6(1), ECHR, included the right to adversarial proceedings. Most importantly, the Court noted that expert's report contained technical knowledge outside the administrative judge expertise. Can the difference between the European Court's decision and the ICT-Y's be attributed to the character of evidence in both cases?

Edwards v. United Kingdom
European Court of Human Rights
247-B Eur. Ct. H. R. (ser. A) (1992)
E.H.R.R. 417 (1993)

. . . .
FACTS:

. . . .
A. The trial and appeal proceedings

6. On 9 November 1984 the applicant was convicted at Sheffield Crown Court, *inter alia*, of one count of robbery and two counts of burglary. The jury's decision was by a majority verdict of ten to two. He received a sentence of imprisonment of ten years for the robbery, and two sentences of eight years each for the burglary offences. All three sentences were to be served concurrently.

The evidence against the applicant consisted of detailed oral admissions that he had allegedly made to the police concerning his involvement in the three offences. According to the police he was questioned on three separate occasions and contemporaneous notes were taken of his statements. However, he had declined to sign them.

His defence during the trial was to maintain that these statements had been concocted by the police. He protested his innocence pointing out that he had not denied his numerous misdeeds in the past. The only witnesses called by the defence during the trial were the two police officers who had interviewed him.

. . . .

8. The victim of the robbery (Miss Sizer) which took place on 14 April 1984 was a lady of 82 years of age who was awakened from her sleep to find a man standing over her. Before having her hands tied behind her back and being blindfolded she was able to take a quick glance at him. She remained tied up until she was freed the next morning. In a statement to the police she gave a description of the man which corresponded with the applicant and stated that she thought she would recognise him again. She was not called as a witness during the trial but her written statement was read to the jury.

The two counts of burglary related to separate incidents which occurred on 19 April and 10 June 1984 also involving the home of an elderly woman. On the latter occasion the police arrested the applicant's co-defendant in the vicinity. It was his statement to the police which lead to the applicant's arrest.

9. On 16 May 1985, the applicant petitioned the Secretary of State for the Home Department with complaints against police officers who had investigated his case and given evidence at his trial. An independent police investigation was ordered in the course of which certain facts came to the applicant's attention. On 3 December 1985, the applicant applied for leave to appeal against conviction out of time. The police report (The Carmichael Report), dated 5 December 1985, was delivered to the Police Complaints Authority which directed it to the Director of Public Prosecutions. The report was requested by the applicant's advisers but its disclosure was refused on the grounds of public interest immunity.

In February 1986, the Director of Public Prosecutions decided that there was insufficient evidence to support criminal charges against the police officers, but recommended that disciplinary charges be brought against three police officers. At the disciplinary hearing, on 13 to 15 June 1988, the tribunal decided that there was no case to answer and dismissed the charges.

B. Reference by the Secretary of State to the Court of Appeal

10. On 21 March 1986, the Secretary of State for the Home Department referred the applicant's case to the Court of Appeal (Criminal Division) under section 17(1)(a) of the Criminal Appeal Act 1968 ('the 1968 Act'). The case was heard on 18 July 1986 and judgment delivered on the same date.

11. The applicant submitted to the Court of Appeal that the verdict should be set aside as unsafe and unsatisfactory because of certain shortcomings in the prosecution case, in particular, that certain information had been withheld by the police. At the trial one of the police witnesses had stated under cross-examination that no fingerprints were found at the scene of the crime. In fact two fingerprints had been found which later turned out to be those of the next door neighbour who was a regular visitor to the house. The applicant had not been informed of this by the prosecution before his trial.

It was argued by the applicant that the police officer had told lies and that his veracity as regards the admission statements was thus called into question.

The Court of Appeal rejected this submission as follows:

> We do not accept that interpretation of Detective Sergeant Hoyland's evidence. We think quite plainly what he was indicating there and intended to indicate was that no fingerprints relating to either of the two alleged burglars

were discovered at the scene: neither the fingerprint of Rose nor the fingerprint of Edwards, the present appellant.

We do not think, had the matter been carried further, it would have been demonstrated that Hoyland was a person who to that extent could not be believed on his own.

12. A further shortcoming complained of by the applicant related to the fact that the police had shown two volumes of photographs of possible burglars (including a photograph of himself) to the elderly victim of the robbery who said that she had caught a fleeting glimpse of the burglar. Her statement, read to the jury, said that she thought she would be able to recognise her assailant. Yet she did not pick out the applicant from the photographs.

This fact was not, however, mentioned by one of the police witnesses who had made a written statement which was read out to the jury and had not been indicated to the applicant before or during his trial. Counsel for the applicant submitted to the Court of Appeal that this omission cast such doubt on the evidence of the prosecution that it might have led the jury to believe that the confession statements had indeed been 'manufactured' by the police as the applicant alleged.

The Court of Appeal also rejected this argument:

> The fact that Miss Sizer had a fleeting glimpse of her assailant, and the fact that such identification as she did make was largely directed to other matters of identification rather than his features, leads us to believe that the jury would not have been influenced to act other than they did if they had the full story of the photographs and of Police Constable Esdon's activities with regard to that.

13. The Court of Appeal examined other impugned shortcomings which it did not consider to cast any doubt on the verdict. It was of the opinion that even if these matters had been investigated, it would have made no difference to the outcome.

14. The Court concluded as follows:

> It is clear that there was some slipshod police work in the present case, no doubt because they took the view that here was a man who had admitted these crimes fully, and consequently there was very little need for them to indulge in a further verification of whether what he said was true. Although this is a matter which perhaps casts the police in a somewhat lazy or idle light, we do not think in the circumstances there was anything unsafe or unsatisfactory in the end about these convictions. Consequently, treating this matter as we have to according to section 17 of the Act, we think this appeal fails and must be dismissed.

15. Counsel for the applicant did not request the Court of Appeal to exercise its discretionary power to rehear evidence under section 23 of the 1968 Act with a view, for example, to cross-examining the police officers who gave evidence at the applicant's trial. He considered that there was little prospect of such a request being granted. Nor did he request the Court to order the production of the Carmichael Report.

16. The applicant took advice concerning the possibility of appealing to the House of Lords but was informed, in an opinion of counsel dated 8 September 1986, that there were no grounds on which an appeal could successfully be pursued before the House of Lords.

He petitioned the Secretary of State for Home Affairs on 3 June 1987 without success.   He is currently serving a sentence of two years' imprisonment following his conviction on 26 March 1992 at Sheffield Crown Court on three counts of burglary.

II. Relevant domestic law and practice

A. Duty of prosecution to disclose certain information to the defence

17. Under the Attorney-General's Guidelines issued in December 1981, the prosecution is obliged (subject to specified discretionary exceptions) to disclose to the defence 'unused material,' which includes all witness statements not enclosed in the bundle of statements served on the defence at the stage of committal of the case by the magistrates' court to the Crown Court.

The prosecution is also under a duty to inform the defence of any earlier written or oral statement of a prosecution witness which is inconsistent with evidence given by that witness at the trial. *R v. Clarke* (1930) 22 Cr. App. R. 58.) Consequently where evidence of a prosecution witness is given before the court stating that the witness would recognise the accused again, and the prosecution knows that when shown a photograph of the accused the witness in fact failed to identify him, it is required to inform the prosecution of that fact.

For the purpose, among others, of ensuring compliance with this duty, the Court of Appeal has stated that all the statements which have been taken by the police should be put before counsel for the Crown, and that it should not be left to the police to decide which statements he is to receive. (*R v. Fellowes*, 12 July 1985, unreported)

B. Jury verdicts

18. A jury's verdict may be either unanimous or by a majority. It must be unanimous unless the trial judge, in accordance with section 17 of the Juries Act 1974, has directed, after at least two hours of unsuccessful jury deliberations, that a majority verdict will be accepted. A majority verdict will be effective if, where there are not less than 11 jurors, ten of them agree on the verdict, or, where there are ten jurors, nine of them agree. If the jury do not agree on either a unanimous or majority verdict, they may, at the discretion of the trial judge, be discharged, but such a discharge does not amount to acquittal and the accused may be tried again by a second jury. In the event of a second jury disagreeing, it is common practice for the prosecution formally to offer no evidence.

. . . .

E. New evidence on appeal

21. Section 23 of the 1968 Act provides, *inter alia*, as follows:

(1) For purposes of this part of the Act, the Court of Appeal may, if they think it necessary or expedient in the interests of justice-

(a) order the production of any document, exhibit or other thing connected with the proceedings, the production of which appears to them necessary for the determination of the case;

(b) order any witness who would have been a compellable witness in the proceedings from which the appeal lies to attend for examination and be examined before the Court, whether or not he was called in those proceedings; and

(c) . . .

(2) Without prejudice to subsection (1) above, where evidence is tendered to the Court of Appeal thereunder the Court shall, unless they are satisfied that the evidence, if received, would not afford ground for allowing the appeal, exercise their power of receiving it if --

(a) it appears to them that the evidence is likely to be credible and would have been admissible in the proceedings from which the appeal lies on an issue which is the subject of the appeal; and

(b) they are satisfied that it was not adduced in those proceedings but there is a reasonable explanation for the failure to adduce it.

(3) . . .

It falls to the Court to determine, if necessary, claims by the Crown that documents should not be disclosed on the grounds of public interest in immunity. (*see, inter alia, R v. Judith Ward* (1993) 96 Cr App R 1.)

22. The approach to be adopted by the Court of Appeal when considering under section 2(1)(a) of the 1968 Act whether a trial verdict was unsafe or unsatisfactory was discussed by the Appellate Committee of the House of Lords in the context of a section 17 reference in *Stafford v. Director of Public Prosecutions* [1974] AC 878). Viscount Dilhorne, with whom the other members of the Appellate Committee agreed, stated:

I do not suggest that in determining whether a verdict is unsafe or unsatisfactory, it is a wrong approach for the court to pose the question — 'Might this new evidence have led to the jury returning a verdict of not guilty?' If the court thinks that it would or might, the court will no doubt conclude that the verdict was unsafe or unsatisfactory . . .

It would, in my opinion, be wrong for the court to say: 'In our view this evidence does not give rise to any reasonable doubt about the guilt of the accused. We do not ourselves consider that an unsafe or unsatisfactory verdict was returned but as the jury who heard the case might conceivably have taken a different view from ours, we quash the conviction' for Parliament has, in terms, said that the court should only quash a conviction if, there being no error of law or material irregularity at the trial, 'they think' the verdict was unsafe or unsatisfactory. They have to decide and Parliament has not required them or given them power to quash a verdict if they think that a jury might conceivably reach a different conclusion from that to which they have come. If the court has no reasonable doubt about the verdict, it follows that the court does not think that the jury could have one; and, conversely, if the court says that a jury might in the light of the new evidence have a reasonable doubt, that means that the court has a reasonable doubt.

23. The Court of Appeal has held that the powers under section 23 of the 1968 Act extend to rehearing evidence which has already been given at the trial, if this is necessary or expedient in the interests of justice. The Court has also held that it has a general power under section 23(1) to admit further evidence, not restricted to the circumstances set out in section 23(2). (*R v. Lattimore and Others* (1976) 62 Cr. App. R. 53.) However, it is unusual for the Court of Appeal to exercise that power since it is reluctant to substitute its own findings of fact for those of the jury which has already seen and heard the relevant witness. In practice, the exercise of the power to receive evidence is thus mainly confined to fresh evidence which has arisen since the trial and which the jury did not have the benefit of hearing. No statistics are available on the frequency with which the power to rehear evidence is exercised.

24. In March 1991 the Secretary of State for the Home Department announced the appointment of a Royal Commission on Criminal Justice which is expected to consider, *inter alia*, the general application the 1968 Act.

PROCEEDINGS BEFORE THE COMMISSION

25. In his application before the Commission (No 13071/87) lodged on 29 September 1986, the applicant complained that he had not received a fair trial, in breach of Article 6(1) of the Convention and, in particular, that he was denied the right to cross-examine police witnesses on the basis of the new evidence which had come to light, contrary to Article 6(3)(d). . . .

. . . .

[The European Commission of Human Rights found no violation of Article 6, and it referred the case to the Court.]

. . . .

DECISION [OF THE EUROPEAN COURT OF HUMAN RIGHTS]:

I. Alleged violation of Article 6

29. The applicant complained that he did not receive a fair trial, in breach of Article 6(1) and (3)(d), the relevant parts of which read:

1. In the determination . . . of any criminal charge against him, everyone is entitled to a fair . . . hearing . . . by an independent and impartial tribunal . . .

2. . . . .

3. Everyone charged with a criminal offence has the following minimum rights:
. . . .

(d) to examine or have examined witnesses against him and to obtain the attendance and examination of witnesses on his behalf under the same conditions as witnesses against him.

30. He submitted that the trial proceedings were unfair because of the failure of the police to disclose to the defence (1) the fact that one of the victims, who had made a statement that she thought she would be able to recognise her assailant, had failed to identify the applicant from a police photograph albums and (2) the existence of fingerprints which had been found at the scene of the crime. If his counsel had been aware of these facts he would have been able to attack the credibility of police testimony. Bearing in mind that this was the main evidence against him there existed a possibility that one more juror might have been persuaded that he was innocent which would have led to his acquittal. As a result, the defence was denied an adequate opportunity to examine the police witnesses and was not on an equal footing with the prosecution as required by Article 6(3)(d).

In the applicant's view the proceedings before the Court of Appeal did not remedy the defects at the trial since it neither heard the police witnesses nor called for the production of the report of the independent police investigation (The Carmichael Report) which had not been disclosed to his legal advisers. In consequence, he had two incomplete hearings before two separate courts.

31. The Government maintained that, in determining whether there had been unfairness, the proceedings must be considered as a whole including those before the Court of Appeal. The applicant who had been provided with all the relevant information concerning the undisclosed facts had every opportunity, through his lawyer, to submit to the Court of Appeal that his conviction should be quashed. Moreover, that court had examined his conviction in the light of the new evidence thoroughly and conscientiously but had concluded that it should be upheld. It was not open to the European Court to substitute its judgment on the facts for that of the Court of Appeal. Finally, the Government contended that Article 6(3)(d) was not relevant to the issue of non-disclosure of evidence to the defence which fell more appropriately to be considered under Article 6(1).

32. The Commission was of the view that paragraph (3)(d) was relevant to the applicant's complaint but concluded that, having regard to the proceedings as a whole, there had been no breach of Article 6(1) read in conjunction with this provision.

33. The Court recalls that the guarantees in Article 6(3) are specific aspects of the right to a fair trial set forth in paragraph 1. . . . In the circumstances of the case it finds it unnecessary to examine the relevance of paragraph (3)(d) to the case since the applicant's allegations, in any event, amount to a complaint that the proceedings have been unfair. It will therefore confine its examination to this point.

34. In so doing, the Court must consider the proceedings as a whole including the decisions of the appellate courts. (*see*, amongst other authorities, *Helmers v. Sweden* (1993), at § 31) Moreover, it is not within the province of the European Court to substitute its own assessment of the facts for that of the domestic courts and, as a general rule, it is for these courts to assess the evidence before them. The Court's task is to ascertain whether the proceedings in their entirety, including the way in which evidence was taken, were fair. (*see, inter alia, Vidal v. Belgium*, 235-B Eur. Ct. H.R. (ser. A) (1992) at § 33)

35. The applicant's conviction was based mainly on police evidence, which he contested, that he had confessed to the offences. It subsequently came to light that certain facts had not been disclosed by the police to the defence which would have enabled it to attack the credibility and veracity of police testimony.

36. The Court considers that it is a requirement of fairness under Article 6(1), indeed one which is recognised under English law, that the prosecution authorities disclose to the defence all material evidence for or against the accused and that the failure to do so in the present case gave rise to a defect in the trial proceedings.

However, when this was discovered, the Secretary of State, following an independent police investigation, referred the case to the Court of Appeal, which examined the transcript of the trial including the applicant's alleged confession and considered in detail the impact of the new information on the conviction.

37. In the proceedings before the Court of Appeal the applicant was represented by senior and junior counsel who had every opportunity to seek to persuade the Court that the conviction should not stand in view of the evidence of non-disclosure. Admittedly the police officers who had given evidence at the trial were not heard by the Court of Appeal. It was, nonetheless, open to counsel for the applicant to make an application to the Court — which they chose not to do — that the police officers be called as witnesses.

38. In the course of the hearing before the European Court the applicant claimed, for the first time, that without the disclosure of the Carmichael Report to the applicant or to the Court of Appeal the proceedings, considered as a whole, could not be fair. However, it is not disputed that he could have applied to the Court of Appeal for the production of this report but did not do so. It is no answer to the failure to make such an application that the Crown might have resisted by claiming public interest immunity since such a claim would have been for the Court to determine.

39. Having regard to the above, the Court concludes that the defects of the original trial were remedied by the subsequent procedure before the Court of Appeal. (*see*, in this respect, *Adolf v. Austria* (1982), at §§ 38-41, and *mutatis mutandis*, *DeCubber v. Belgium* (1984), at § 33). Moreover, there is no indication that the proceedings before the Court of Appeal were in any respect unfair. Accordingly there has been no breach of Article 6.

. . . .

Dissenting Opinion of Judge Pettiti (provisional translation)

I did not join the majority in voting that there had not been a breach, as in my opinion there was an undeniable violation of Article 6 of the European Convention on Human Rights.

First, because the Court of Appeal prejudged what the jury's decision would have been if they had had to decide and, secondly, because the essential question raised by the *Edwards* case was that of the principle of public interest immunity, which in English law allows the prosecution, in the public interest, not to disclose or communicate to the defence all the evidence in his possession and to 'reserve' certain evidence. Such non-disclosure took place in the Crown Court. The Court made no express statement of its views on this point and its silence might be understood as approval of this principle, which is not the case. The Court had regard primarily to the failure by the defence to rely on this ground of appeal.

To be sure, it is understandable that the plea of 'defence secrets' or state secrets' should be invoked at the stage of duly authorised telephone taps. (*See Klass v. Germany* (1978); *Malone v. United Kingdom* (1984); *Huvig v. France* (1990); *Kruslin v. France* (1990).)) But once there are criminal proceedings and an indictment, the whole of the evidence, favourable or unfavourable to the defendant, must be communicated to the defence in order to be the subject of adversarial argument in accordance with Article 6 of the Convention. It is conceivable that a hearing may be held *in camera* so as to protect defence secrets or state secrets. In the *Edwards* case such a secret was not even involved; it was simply a question of documents and items of ordinary criminal evidence to the effect that Miss Sizer had not recognised the applicant and that the police had neglected to investigate the fingerprints.

In his memorial the applicant made the following pertinent observations:

> At present the law of England and Wales permits the use in evidence of uncorroborated and disputed confession statements provided that the trial judge gives a suitably worded warning to the jury in relation to the confession. A conviction can be founded on such a confession.
>
> The law in relation to this matter is presently under review by a Royal Commission.
>
> Even if the jury did not accept such a submission, the fact of Miss Sizer's failure to identify the applicant could itself have raised a reasonable doubt as to the identification of the applicant as the offender and accordingly a reasonable doubt as to his guilt.
>
> The applicant asks the Court to note that the jury convicted him by a majority of ten to two, which indicates that two of the jurors entertained reasonable doubts as to the applicant's guilt. Under domestic law, the applicant could not have been convicted if three or more jurors had entertained such doubt. It would have required only one more juror to entertain reasonable doubt in order for the applicant to be acquitted. The evidence which was withheld from the applicant and the jury might have produced such doubt in the mind of one more juror.
>
> The fact that Miss Sizer had not identified the applicant was material obtained by the prosecution but not used by it in its presentation of the case. As such, it should have been disclosed to the applicant under the Attorney-General's Guidelines and applying the principles of domestic law stated in *R v. Bryant* ((1946) 31 Cr. App. R. 146) and *R v. Clark* ((1930) 22 Cr. App. R. 58).
>
> The fact that Miss Sizer had failed to identify the applicant, which fact was known to the police before the trial, was unfairly, and in breach of Article 6(1) and (3)(d) withheld from the applicant.
>
> . . . .

In English criminal proceedings, the prosecution is required to disclose information of the kind referred to above to the defence. It cannot be denied that such information was not disclosed to the applicant in this case. The United Kingdom has failed to put forward any explanation or justification for this failure to adhere to principles of domestic law which ought, if adhered to, to secure compliance with Article 6.

The concealment of exonerating evidence and in other cases the fabrication of evidence have plagued police investigations (remember the Birmingham Six and the *Ward* case).

This shows the importance of the assessment of such a situation in criminal proceedings, and the reservations called for by the decision of the Court of Appeal.

As the defence submitted, the essential point was the credibility of the police officers. Before the Court the applicant argued as follows:

> In those circumstances, it was vital for Mr Edwards to know that, when shown a photograph of the various persons including himself (Mr Edwards), Miss Sizer had failed to pick out Mr Edwards as the offender . . .
>
> . . . .

If I may leave the trial at this stage and move to the Court of Appeal procedure, the applicant accepts the well-established principle in the case law of this Court that in considering the fairness of trial procedure under Article 6, the criminal proceedings taken as a whole must be examined. It is also, however, clear that Article 6 requires a tribunal to carry out a fair and public hearing. In this case no one tribunal considered the case fully and with reference to all of the available material.

The submission of Mr Edwards is that the end result of the procedure, taking the trial and the appeal as one sequence of procedure, was a fragmentary procedure. Neither the individual elements of that procedure nor the procedure as a whole can be described as full and fair. Mr Edwards had two incomplete hearings before two separate courts. The trial hearing was an incomplete hearing in that evidence available to the prosecution was not made available to Mr Edwards. The Court of Appeal was similarly an incomplete hearing. Mr Edwards disagrees with the submission of the United Kingdom that all relevant material was before the Court of Appeal. Mr Edwards reminds the Court that the police conduct of the case against him was investigated by Detective Superintendent Robert Carmichael of the Humberside police force. That investigation followed upon complaints made by Mr Edwards himself about the conduct of the police.

Superintendent Carmichael concluded his report in December 1985. The Carmichael report was submitted to the Police Complaints Authority which in turn submitted the report to the Director of Public Prosecutions. The submission of the report led to the referral of the case to the Court of Appeal by the Secretary of State for Home Affairs.

The Carmichael report should not have been protected by any immunity, and should have been disclosed.

With respect to the failure by the defence to raise this ground of appeal in the Court of Appeal, this argument does not seem to me to be relevant. Such concealment is comparable to a ground of nullity for reasons of public policy in the continental system. Grounds of nullity can and must be raised by the court itself *ex officio*, even if the defence does not rely on them. For one cannot leave to a possibly inexperienced defence alone the burden of ensuring respect for the fundamental procedural rule which prohibits the concealment of documents or evidence. In the continental system such a fault on the part of the police may lead to criminal proceedings for malfeasance in public office. Cases where evidence has been hidden from the trial court have left bitter memories in the history of justice.

It seems clear to me that the Court of Appeal should have raised this ground of nullity of the proceedings of its own motion and remitted the case to a jury without prejudging what that jury's decision would have been, especially as the original jury had reached its decision by ten votes to two and one vote more would have meant an acquittal.

Under the European Convention an old doctrine such as that of 'public interest' must be revised in accordance with Article 6.

The European Court has on numerous occasions stated that it is essential that proceedings are 'adversarial' and the favourable and unfavourable evidence is subjected to adversarial examination. (*see, inter alia, Kostovski v. The Netherlands* (1989); *Cardot v. France* (1991); *Delta v. France*, 191 Eur. Ct. H.R. (ser. A) (1990)) This means that the prosecution must communicate the evidence to the defence. For this reason I find that there was a violation of Article 6 in the present case.

❖ ❖ ❖

Questions & Comments

(1)   The UN Human Rights Committee has held that the state has an affirmative obligation to provide transportation to an alibi witness in a death penalty case. *Grant v. Jamaica*, Communication No. 353/1988, views adopted 31 March 1994, U.N. Doc. CCPR/C/50/D/353/1988 (1994) at § 8.4 (reproduced above in Chapter 12(A)). Would such an affirmative right extend to non-capital cases? Should it?

(2)   In *The Prosecutor v. Blaskic*, Case No. IT-95-14, Int'l Crim. Trib.-Yugo., Trial Chamber (21 January 1998), the Trial Chamber rejected the defense's argument that hearsay evidence was not admissible. The Chamber noted that Rule 89(A) of the Rules of Procedure and Evidence states that "Chambers shall not be bound by national rules of evidence." Accordingly, the Chamber held that

> neither the rules issuing from the common law tradition in respect of the admissibility of hearsay evidence nor the general principle prevailing in the civil law systems, according to which, barring exceptions, all relevant evidence is admissible, including hearsay evidence, because it is the judge who finally takes a decision on the weight to ascribe to it, are directly applicable before this Tribunal. The International Tribunal is, in fact, a *sui generis* institution with its own rules of procedure which do not merely constitute a transposition of national legal systems. The same holds for the conduct of the trial which, contrary to the Defence arguments, is not similar to an adversarial trial, but is moving towards a more hybrid system.

Given the hybrid character of the ICT-Y, in what other areas might the ICT-Y make a ruling that departs from the civil or common law ?

Chapter 12. Trial Due Process Protections

Kostovski v. The Netherlands
European Court of Human Rights
166 Eur. Ct. H. R. (ser. A) (1989)
12 E.H.R.R. 434 (1990)

. . . .

FACTS:

I. The particular circumstances of the case

9. Mr Slobodan Kostovski is a Yugoslav citizen born in 1953. He has a very long criminal record, including convictions for various crimes in the Netherlands, notably armed robbery at a jeweller's shop in 1979 for which he was sentenced to six years' imprisonment.

In November 1980 the Amsterdam District Court (*arrondissements-rechtbank*) had declared admissible a request by Sweden for his extradition to stand trial for serious offences committed in Stockholm in September 1979, namely two armed robberies and assisting in an escape from a court building, involving in each case attempted manslaughter.

On 8 August 1981 the applicant escaped from Scheveningen prison together with one Stanley Hillis and others; he remained on the run until the following April.

10. On 20 January 1982 three masked men conducted an armed raid on a bank in Baarn and made off with a substantial amount of currency and cheques.

Police suspicions centred on Stanley Hillis and his associates because, being on the run, they probably needed money and because some years previously Stanley Hillis had been directly involved in a robbery carried out at the same bank with exactly the same *modus operandi* as the 1982 raid. These suspicions were strengthened on 25 January, when the Amsterdam police received an anonymous telephone call from a man who said:

'A few days ago a hold-up took place at a bank in Baarn. Those responsible for the hold-up are Stanley Hillis, Paul Molhoek and a Yugoslav. Stanley Hillis and the Yugoslav escaped from prison in The Hague in August last year.'

11. On 26 January 1982 a man visited the police in The Hague. The reporting officer drew up, on 18 March, the following account of the interview:

'On 26 January there appeared before me a man who for fear of reprisals desired to remain anonymous but whose identity is known to me. He stated as follows:

"A few months ago four men escaped from the remand centre (*huis van bewaring*) in The Hague, among them a Yugoslav and an Amsterdammer. They are now living with an acquaintance of theirs in Utrecht. I do not know the address. They are also in touch with Paul Molhoek of The Hague. The Yugoslav and the Amsterdammer sometimes spend the night at Aad Denie's home in Paul Krugerlaan in The Hague. Paul Molhoek sleeps there almost every night. The

Yugoslav and the Amsterdammer now drive a blue BMW car; I do not know the registration number. Paul Molhoek drives a new white Mercedes sports car. The Yugoslav, the Amsterdammer and Paul Molhoek carried out a hold-up a few days ago on a bank in Baarn, in the course of which the staff of the bank were locked up. Aad Denie, who otherwise had nothing to do with the affair, takes Paul Molhoek to the two men in Utrecht every day because Paul Molhoek does not have a driving licence. Aad Denie drives a silver-grey BMW car, registration mark 84-PF-88.''

I wish to add that, after being shown various photographs included in the police file, he picked out photos of the following persons: Slobodan Kostovski . . . as being the Yugoslav to whom he had referred; Stanley Marshall Hillis . . . as being the Amsterdammer in question.'

12. On 27 January the Utrecht police, acting on information received that Stanley Hillis was hiding with a brother of Paul Molhoek at an address in that town, conducted a search there. Whilst they found no one, they did find fingerprints of Stanley Hillis and Paul Molhoek.

13. On 23 February 1982 a person visited the police in The Hague. The two reporting officers drew up, on 22 March, the following account of the interview:

'On Tuesday 23 February 1982 there appeared before us a person who for security reasons wishes to remain anonymous but whose identity is known to us. He/she stated that he/she knew that Stanley Hillis, Slobodan Kostovski, Paul Molhoek and Aad Denie, who were known to him/her, were guilty of the armed raid on a branch of the Nederlandse Middenstands Bank at Nieuwstraat 1 in Baarn on or about 19 January 1982. According to the said person, the first three of the aforementioned persons had carried out the raid and Aad Denie had acted as driver or at least he had picked them up in a car after the raid.

The said person also stated that the proceeds of the raid, amounting to about Fl 600,000, had been divided into more or less equal parts by Hillis, Kostovski and Molhoek and that Aad Denie had received a small part thereof. From what he/she said, this would have been about Fl 20,000. The said person also stated that Hillis, Kostovski and Molhoek knew each other from when they were detained in Scheveningen prison.

Hillis and Kostovski escaped from prison on 8 August 1981 and Molhoek was released at a later date. The said person stated that Paul Molhoek lived most of the time with Aad Denie at Paul Krugerlaan 216 in The Hague. Hillis and Kostovski were said to have lived for a while at Oude Gracht 76 in Utrecht, which they had rented in another name. A brother of Paul Molhoek also lived there; he was called Peter. The said person stated in this connection that the Utrecht police had raided the said premises but had not found the abovementioned people. He/she said that Hillis, Kostovski and Molhoek were in a room on a higher floor of the same building in the Oude Gracht at the time of the police raid. The police had not searched that floor. The person in question also stated that Hillis was now believed to be living in Amsterdam.

Paul Molhoek and Hillis were said to meet each other quite regularly there, near Amstel Station, which was their usual meeting place.

According to the person in question, Hillis, Kostovski and Molhoek were in possession of powerful weapons. He/she knew that Hillis and Kostovski each had a Sten gun among other things and that Paul Molhoek had a revolver, possibly a Colt .45.

The person interviewed by us stated that he/she might later be able to provide more details about the abovementioned persons and the offences they had committed.'

14. On 1 April 1982 Stanley Hillis and Slobodan Kostovski were arrested together in Amsterdam. They were in a car driven by one V, who had helped them to escape from prison and had had various contacts with them in and after January 1982.

On his arrest Slobodan Kostovski was in possession of a loaded revolver. Subsequently, firearms were also found in the home of Paul Molhoek, who was arrested on 2 April, in the home of V and in another room in the house previously searched in Utrecht.

Like the applicant, Stanley Hillis, Paul Molhoek, Aad Denie and V all have very long criminal records.

15. A preliminary judicial investigation (*gerechtelijk vooronderzoek*) was instituted in respect of Stanley Hillis, Slobodan Kostovski, Paul Molhoek and Aad Denie. On 8 April 1982 Mr Nuboer, the examining magistrate (*rechter-commissaris*), interviewed, in the presence of the police but in the absence of the public prosecutor and of the applicant and his counsel, the witness who had made a statement to the police in The Hague on 23 February. The magistrate, who did not know the person's identity, considered his/her fear of reprisals to be well-founded and therefore respected his/her wish to remain anonymous. His report on the hearing recorded that the witness made the following sworn statement:

'On 23 February 1982 I made a statement to the police in The Hague which was included in a report drawn up on 22 March 1982. You read out that statement to me. I declared that it is the truth and that I stand by it, on the understanding that I was not aware that the bank in Baarn was at No 1 Nieuwstraat. My knowledge stems from the fact that both Stanley Hillis and Paul Molhoek, as well as Aad Denie, had all told me about the hold-up. They said that they had taken not only cash, but also American travellers' cheques and Eurocheques. I myself saw a number of the Eurocheques.'

16. On 2 June 1982 the examining magistrate wrote to the lawyers acting for those concerned, enclosing copies of the official reports, including the statements of the anonymous person he had seen. He indicated that they could submit written questions on the basis of the statements made, pointing out that they would not be invited to the hearing before him. Amongst those who responded was Mr Kostovski's lawyer, Mrs Spronken, who submitted fourteen questions in a letter of 14 June.

On 22 June, as a result of those questions, the anonymous witness whom Mr Nuboer had heard was interviewed again, this time by Mr Weijsenfeld, an examining magistrate deputising for Mr Nuboer. The police were present but neither the public prosecutor nor the applicant or his counsel was. The magistrate's report of the hearing recorded that the witness — whose anonymity was respected on this occasion also — made the following sworn statement:

'I stand by the statement which I made on 8 April 1982 to the examining magistrate in Utrecht. My answers to the questions posed by Mrs Spronken are as follows.

I am not the person who telephoned anonymously to the police communications centre in Amsterdam on 25 January 1982, nor the person who made a statement on 26 January 1982 at the police station in The Hague. I did not state to the police that I knew that the bank was at Nieuwestraat 1 in Baarn. I knew that it was in Baarn, but not the street. I learned the latter from the police and it was included as being part of my own statement by mistake. Although Mrs Sponken did not ask this, I would add that I did not inform the municipal police in Utrecht.

As regards the questions posed by Van Straelen, I would in the first instance refer to the statement I have just made. I am acquainted with Hillis, Kostovski, Molhoek and Denie and have no doubts as to their identity.'

In the event, only two of Mrs Spronken's fourteen questions, most of which concerned the circumstances in which the witness had obtained his/her information, were answered. In this connection Mr Weijsenfeld added the following in his report:

'The questions sent in, including those from SM Hillis, which have not been answered were either not asked by me, the examining magistrate, in order to preserve the anonymity of the witness, or not answered by the witness for the same reason.'

17. The cases against Stanley Hillis, Slobodan Kostovski and Paul Molhoek came on for trial before the Utrecht District Court on 10 September 1982. Although for procedural reasons each case was dealt with separately and was the subject of a separate judgment, the court held a single sitting, so that the statements made thereat applied to all three suspects.

The witnesses heard in court included the examining magistrates Mr Nuboer and Mr Weijsenfeld and Mr Weijman, one of the police officers who had conducted the interview on 23 February. They had been called at the applicant's request, but the court, pursuant to Article 288 of the Code of Criminal Procedure, did not allow the defence to put to them certain questions designed to clarify the anonymous witnesses' reliability and sources of information, where answers would have revealed the latter's identity.

Mr Nuboer stated that he believed the witness he had heard on 8 April 1982, who had 'made a favourable impression' on him; that he did not know the witness's identity and considered the fear of reprisals advanced in support of his/her wish for anonymity to be a real one; that he believed the witness had made his/her statement to the police voluntarily; and that he had refused an offer by the police for him to interview the man they had seen on 26 January 1982 as he could not guarantee the latter's anonymity.

Mr Weijsenfeld stated that he considered to be 'not unreliable' the witness — whose identity he did not know — whom he had interviewed on 22 June 1982; and that he too regarded the witness's fear of reprisals as well-founded.

Mr Weijman stated that, in his view, the person he had interviewed with a colleague on 23 February 1982 was 'completely reliable' because he/she had also given information on other cases which had proved to be correct. He added that certain parts of that person's statement had been omitted from the official report in order to protect his/her identity.

18. The anonymous witnesses themselves were not heard at the trial. Contrary to a defence submission, the official reports drawn up by the police and the examining magistrates on the hearings of those witnesses were used in evidence. Also the sworn statements made by one of them to the magistrates were read out and designated as statements by a witness made at the trial, in accordance with Article 295 of the Code of Criminal Procedure.

In its judgments of 24 September 1982 the Utrecht District Court recognised, with regard to the use of the statements of the anonymous witnesses, that their sources of information could not be checked, that it could not form an independent view as to their reliability and that the accused were deprived of the possibility of being confronted with them. By way of justification for its decision nevertheless to use this material in evidence the court stated that it had been convinced of Mr Kostovski's guilt, considering that the statements strengthened and partly complemented each other and having regard to the views it had heard as to the reliability of one of the anonymous witnesses. Having also noted that the applicant had previously been found guilty of similar offences, the court convicted him and his co-accused of armed robbery and sentenced each of them to six years' imprisonment.

19. Mr Hillis, Mr Kostovski and Mr Molhoek — who have always denied any involvement in the bank raid — appealed to the Amsterdam Court of Appeal (*Gerechtshof*), which set aside the Utrecht District Court's judgments as it arrived at a different assessment of the evidence. However, after a retrial, at which the three cases were dealt with together, the Court of Appeal, by judgment of 27 May 1983, also convicted the applicant and his co-accused and imposed the same sentences as before.

On 13 May the Court of Appeal had heard a number of the witnesses previously heard at first instance, who stood by their earlier testimony. Like the Utrecht District Court, it had not allowed certain questions by the defence to be answered, where this would have revealed the identity of the anonymous witnesses. The following statement had also been made to the Court of Appeal by Chief Superintendent Alferink of The Hague municipal police:

'Consultations take place before anonymous witnesses are interviewed. It is customary for me to ascertain the identity of the witness to be interviewed in order to assess whether he or she could be in danger. In this case the anonymous witnesses were in real danger. The threat was real. Both witnesses decided to make statements on their own initiative. The public prosecutor was contacted, but I cannot remember who it was. The testimony of anonymous witnesses is offered to the examining magistrate after consultation with the public prosecutor. Both anonymous witnesses made a reliable impression on me.'

The Court of Appeal likewise did not hear the anonymous witnesses but, again contrary to a defence submission, considered the official reports of their interviews with the police and the examining magistrates to be admissible evidence. The court found that the witnesses, who had made their statements on their own initiative, had good reason to fear reprisals; noted that they had made a reliable impression on Mr Alferink and a reasonably reliable one on Mr Nuboer; and took into account the connections between, and the mutual consistency of, the statements in question.

20. On 25 September 1984 the Supreme Court (*Hoge Raad*) dismissed an appeal by the applicant on points of law. It found that the Amsterdam Court of Appeal had adduced sufficient reasons for admitting the reports in question. It also stated that Article 6 of the Convention[19] did not prevent a judge, if he deemed it necessary in the interest of the proper administration of justice, from curtailing to some extent the obligation to answer questions and, notably, from allowing a witness not to answer questions about the identity of persons.

. . . .

II. Relevant domestic law and practice

A. The Code of Criminal Procedure

22. The Dutch Code of Criminal Procedure ('CCP') came into force on 1 January 1926. The citations appearing in the present judgment are taken from the CCP as it stood at the time of the applicant's trials.

23. Article 168 CCP provides that each District Court has one or more examining magistrates to whom criminal cases are entrusted. They are nominated, as for a term of two years, by the competent Court of Appeal from amongst the members of the District Court.

It is open to the public prosecutor, under Article 181 CCP, to request what is called — in order to distinguish it from the subsequent investigation at the trial — a 'preliminary investigation,' which it is the task of an examining magistrate to conduct. In that event the latter will hear the suspect, witnesses and experts as soon as possible and as often as is required. Both the public prosecutor and defence counsel are, in principle, entitled to be present at those hearings and, even if they are absent, to give notice of questions they wish to have put.

The preliminary investigation provides a basis for a decision with regard to the further prosecution of a suspect and also serves to clarify matters which cannot properly be investigated at the trial. The magistrate must act impartially, by collecting also evidence which might exculpate the suspect.

---

[19] Dutch law incorporates the ECHR. Ed.'s note.

If the public prosecutor is of the opinion that the results of the preliminary investigation justify further prosecution, he will notify the suspect and refer the case to the court. The investigation at the trial will then follow.

24. Under Article 338 CCP, a finding that the accused has been proved to have committed the acts with which he is charged may be made by a judge only if he has been so convinced through the investigation at the trial, by 'legal means of evidence.' The latter consist, according to Article 339 CCP, exclusively of (i) what the judge has himself observed; (ii) statements made by the accused; (iii) statements made by a witness; (iv) statements made by an expert; and (v) written documents.

Evidence in the third category is defined in Article 342 CCP, which reads:

'1. A statement by a witness is understood to be his statement, made in the investigation at the trial, of facts or circumstances which he himself has seen or experienced.

2. The judge cannot accept as proven that the defendant has committed the act with which he is charged, solely on the statement of one witness.'

25. Articles 280 and 281-295 CCP contain various provisions concerning the examination of witnesses at the trial, of which the following are of importance in the context of the present case.

(a) The president of the court must ask the witness to state, after his first names and surname, his age, occupation and address; the same obligation is also laid, by Article 190 CCP, on an examining magistrate when he is hearing witnesses.

(b) Articles 284, 285 and 286 CCP make it clear that the accused is entitled to put questions to a witness. As a general rule witnesses are examined first by the president of the court; however, a witness who has not been heard during the preliminary investigation and has been called at the request of the defence will be examined first by the accused and only afterwards by the president. In any event, Article 288 CCP empowers the court 'to prevent a question put by the accused, counsel for the defence or the public prosecutor being answered.'

(c) Article 292 CCP enables the president of the court to order an accused to leave the courtroom so that a witness may be examined out of his presence. If such an order — for which reasons do not have to be given — is made, counsel for the defence may question the witness and 'the accused shall be told immediately what has happened during his absence and only then will the investigation be resumed. Thus, on returning to the courtroom the accused may avail himself of his right, under Article 285 CCP, to put questions to the witness.

26. Article 295 CCP provides for an exception to the rule in Article 342 CCP that witnesses should be heard at the trial. It reads:

'An earlier statement by a witness who, having been sworn in or admonished to speak the truth in accordance with Article 216(2), has died or, in the opinion of the court, is unable to appear at the trial shall be considered as having been made at the trial, on condition that it is read aloud there.'

In connection with witnesses unable to appear at the trial, Article 187 CCP provides:

'If the examining magistrate is of the opinion that there are grounds for assuming that the witness or the expert will not be able to appear at the trial, he shall invite the public prosecutor, the defendant and counsel to be present at the hearing before him, unless, in the interest of the investigation, that hearing cannot be delayed.'

27. The fifth category of evidence listed in Article 339 CCP is defined in Article 344 CCP which, so far as is relevant, reads:

'1. Written documents means:

> '1 . . .;
> 2. official reports and other documents, drawn up in legal form by bodies and persons who have the proper authority and containing their statement of facts or circumstances which they themselves have seen or experienced;
> . . . .
> 5. all other documents; but these are valid only in conjunction with the content of other means of evidence.

2. The judge can accept as proven that the defendant has committed the act with which he is charged, on the official report of an investigating officer.'

An anonymous statement contained in an official police report falls within the scope of sub-paragraph 2o of paragraph 1 of this Article.

B. Criminal procedure in practice

28. In the Netherlands, the procedure in a criminal case follows in actual practice a course that is markedly different from that suggested by the above provisions. This is to a considerable extent due to a leading judgment delivered by the Supreme Court on 20 December 1926, the year in which the CCP came into force. That judgment contains the following rulings, each of which is of importance in the context of the present case:

> (a) for a statement by a witness to be considered as having been made at the trial under Article 295 CCP, it is immaterial whether or not the examining magistrate has complied with Article 187 CCP,
> (b) a deposition by a witness concerning what he was told by another person (hearsay evidence) may be used as evidence, albeit with the utmost caution;
> (c) it is permissible to use as evidence declarations made by the accused or by a witness to a police officer, as recorded in the latter's official report.

29. These rulings permit the use, as 'legal means of evidence' within the meaning of Articles 338 and 339 CCP, of depositions made by a witness not at the trial but before a police officer or the examining magistrate, provided they are recorded in an official report which is read aloud in court. The rulings have had the effect that in practice the

importance of the investigation at the trial — which is never conducted before a jury — has dwindled. In the great majority of cases witnessed are not heard at the trial but either only by the police or also by the examining magistrate.

30. The law does not make the presence of counsel for the defence obligatory during the investigation by the police. The same applies to the preliminary investigation by the examining magistrate. Nowadays, however, most examining magistrates invite the accused and his counsel to attend when they are hearing witnesses.

C. The anonymous witness: case law

31. The CCP contains no express provisions on statements by anonymous witnesses.

However, with the increase in violent, organised crime a need was felt to protect those witnesses who had justification for fearing reprisals, by granting them anonymity. In a series of judgments the Supreme Court has made this possible.

32. A precursor to this development was a judgment of 17 January 1938 in which the Supreme Court held that hearsay evidence could be admitted even if the witness did not name his informant. Decisions to the same effect were handed down in the 1980s.

In a judgment of 5 February 1980, concerning a case where the examining magistrate had granted anonymity to and had heard a witness without the accused or his counsel being present, the Supreme Court held — following its judgment of 20 December 1926 — that non-compliance with Article 187 CCP did not prevent the magistrate's official report being used in evidence, 'albeit with the caution called for when assessing the probative value of such evidence.' The same ruling was made in a judgment of 4 May 1981, concerning a case where the witness had been heard anonymously by both the police and the examining magistrate; on that occasion the Supreme Court also held — in accordance with its abovementioned judgment of 17 January 1938 — that the mere fact that the official reports of the hearings did not name the witness was not an obstacle to their utilisation in evidence, subject to an identical proviso as to caution.

It may be inferred from a judgment of 29 November 1983 that the caution called for does not necessarily imply that anonymous witnesses must also have been heard by the examining magistrate.

The next judgments in the series are those given by the Supreme Court on 25 September 1984 in the cases of Mr Kostovski and his co-accused. They contain the following new elements:

(a) the mere fact that the examining magistrate did not know the identity of the witness does not prevent the use in evidence of the official report of the hearing he conducted;
(b) if the defence contests at the trial the reliability of depositions by an anonymous witness, as recorded in the official report of the hearing of the witness, but the court nevertheless decides to admit them as evidence, it must give reasons justifying that decision.

These principles were confirmed in a judgment of 21 May 1985, which makes it clear that the Supreme Court's review of the reasons given to justify the admission of anonymous statements as evidence is only a marginal one.

D. Law reform

33. In their submissions preceding certain of the Supreme Court's judgments referred to in § 32 above, various Advocates General, whilst recognising that the granting of anonymity to witnesses could not always be avoided and sometimes had to be accepted as the lesser evil, nevertheless voiced concern. The learned writers who annotated the judgments did likewise, stressing the need for the courts to be very cautious indeed. The judgments have, however, also been criticised.

34. In 1983 the Association of Judges expressed disquiet at the increase in cases in which witnesses were threatened and at the growing number of witnesses who refused to testify unless they were granted anonymity. The Association recommended that the legislature should direct its attention to the question of anonymous witnesses.

The Minister of Justice consequently set up in September 1984 an external advisory committee, called 'the Commission on Threatened Witnesses,' to examine the problem. In its report of 11 June 1986, which was later submitted for advice to several bodies concerned with the application of the criminal law, the Commission concluded, with only one member dissenting, as follows:

> 'In some cases one cannot avoid anonymity of witnesses. Reference is made to the fact (which was also pointed out by the Minister) that at present there are forms of organised criminality of a gravity that the legislature of the day would not have considered possible.'

The Commission added that 'in a society governed by the rule of law the interference with, or more accurately the frustration of, the course of justice resulting [from this situation] cannot possibly be accepted.'

The Commission proposed that the law should in principle forbid the use as evidence of statements by anonymous witnesses. It should, however, be possible to make an exception where the witness would run an unacceptable risk if his or her identity were known. In such cases an anonymous statement might be admitted as evidence if the witness had been examined by an examining magistrate, the accused being given a right of appeal against the latter's decision to grant anonymity. The report contains a Bill making the necessary modifications to the CCP (with draft explanatory notes) and comparative data.

According to the Government, initiation of legislation in this area has been deferred pending the Court's decision in the present case.

. . . .

[Kostovski applied to the European Commission of Human Rights, which unanimously found violations to Article 6(1) and 3(d) in that he had not been able to cross-examine the anonymous witnesses or challenge their statements.]

DECISION:

I. Alleged violation of Article 6

37. The essence of Mr Kostovski's claim was that he had not received a fair trial. In this connection he relied mainly on the following provisions of Article 6 of the Convention:

'1. In the determination of . . . any criminal charge against him, everyone is entitled to a fair and public hearing . . . by an independent and impartial tribunal

. . .

. . .

3. Everyone charged with a criminal offence has the following minimum rights:

. . .

(d) to examine or have examined witnesses against him and to obtain the attendance and examination of witnesses on his behalf under the same conditions as witnesses against him;

. . .'

The Commission arrived at the conclusion, which was contested by the Government, that there had been a breach of paragraph (1), taken together with paragraph (3)(d), of Article 6.

38. The source of the applicant's allegation was the use as evidence, by the Utrecht District Court and the Amsterdam Court of Appeal, of reports of statements by two anonymous persons. The latter had been heard by the police and, in one case, also by the examining magistrate but were not themselves heard at either of the trials.

39. It has to be recalled at the outset that the admissibility of evidence is primarily a matter for regulation by national law. Again, as a general rule it is for the national courts to assess the evidence before them.

In the light of these principles the Court sees its task in the present case as being not to express a view as to whether the statements in question were correctly admitted and assessed but rather to ascertain whether the proceedings considered as a whole, including the way in which evidence was taken, were fair.

This being the basic issue, and also because the guarantees in Article 6(3) are specific aspects of the right to a fair trial set forth in paragraph (1), the Court will consider the applicant's complaints from the angle of paragraphs (3)(d) and (1) taken together.

40. The Court notes that only one of the authors of the statements — namely the person whose statements were read out at the trial — was, under Dutch law, regarded as a 'witness.' However, in view of the autonomous interpretation to be given to this term, both authors should be so regarded for the purposes of Article 6(3)(d) of the Convention, since the statements of both of them, whether read out at the trial or not, were in fact before the court and were taken into account by it.

41. In principle, all the evidence must be produced in the presence of the accused at a public hearing with a view to adversarial argument. This does not mean, however, that in order to be used as evidence statements of witnesses should always be made at a public hearing in court: to use as evidence such statements obtained at the pre-trial stage is not

in itself inconsistent with paragraphs (3)(d) and (1) of Article 6, provided the rights of the defence have been respected.

As a rule, these rights require that an accused should be given an adequate and proper opportunity to challenge and question a witness against him, either at the time the witness was making his statement or at some later stage of the proceedings.

42. Yet such an opportunity was not afforded to the applicant in the present case, although there could be no doubt that he desired to challenge and question the anonymous persons involved. Not only were the latter not heard at the trials but also their declarations were taken, whether by the police or the examining magistrate, in the absence of Mr Kostovski and his counsel. Accordingly, at no stage could they be questioned directly by him or on his behalf.

It is true that the defence was able, before both the Utrecht District Court and the Amsterdam Court of Appeal, to question one of the police officers and both of the examining magistrates who had taken the declarations. It was also able, but as regards only one of the anonymous persons, to submit written questions to him/her indirectly through the examining magistrate. However, the nature and scope of the questions it could put in either of these ways was considerably restricted by reason of the decision that the anonymity of the authors of the statements should be preserved.

The latter feature of the case compounded the difficulties facing the applicant. If the defence is unaware of the identity of the person it seeks to question, it may be deprived of the very particulars enabling it to demonstrate that he or she is prejudiced, hostile or unreliable. Testimony or other declarations inculpating an accused may well be designedly untruthful or simply erroneous and the defence will scarcely be able to bring this to light if it lacks the information permitting it to test the author's reliability or cast doubt on his credibility. The dangers inherent in such a situation are obvious.

43. Furthermore, each of the trial courts was precluded by the absence of the anonymous persons from observing their demeanour under questioning and thus forming its own impression of their reliability. The courts admittedly heard evidence on the latter point and no doubt — as is required by Dutch law — they observed caution in evaluating the statements in question, but this can scarcely be regarded as a proper substitute for direct observation.

It is true that one of the anonymous persons was heard by examining magistrates. However, the Court is bound to observe that — in addition to the fact that neither the applicant nor his counsel was present at the interviews — the examining magistrates themselves were unaware of the person's identity, a situation which cannot have been without implications for the testing of his/her reliability. As for the other anonymous person, he was not heard by an examining magistrate at all, but only by the police.

In these circumstances it cannot be said that the handicaps under which the defence laboured were counterbalanced by the procedures followed by the judicial authorities.

44. The Government stressed the fact that case law and practice in the Netherlands in the matter of anonymous evidence stemmed from an increase in the intimidation of witnesses and were based on a balancing of interests of society, the accused and the witnesses. It pointed out that in the present case it had been established that the authors of the statements in question had good reason to fear reprisals.

As on previous occasions the Court does not underestimate the importance of the struggle against organised crime. Yet the Government's line of argument, whilst not without force, is not decisive.

Although the growth in organised crime doubtless demands the introduction of appropriate measures, the Government's submissions appear to the Court to lay insufficient weight on what the applicant's counsel described as 'the interest of everybody in a civilised society in a controllable and fair judicial procedure.' The right to a fair administration of justice holds so prominent a place in a democratic society that it cannot be sacrificed to expediency. The Convention does not preclude reliance, at the investigation stage of criminal proceedings, on sources such as anonymous informants. However, the subsequent use of anonymous statements as sufficient evidence to found a conviction, as in the present case, is a difficult matter. It involved limitations on the rights of the defence which were irreconcilable with the guarantees contained in Article 6. In fact, the Government accepted that the applicant's conviction was based 'to a decisive extent' on the anonymous statements.

45. The Court therefore concludes that in the circumstances of the case the constraints affecting the rights of the defence were such that Mr Kostovski cannot be said to have received a fair trial. There was accordingly a violation of paragraph (3)(d), taken together with paragraph (1), of Article 6.

. . . .

❖   ❖   ❖

Questions & Comments

(1) In a later case, *Doorson v. The Netherlands*, — Eur. Ct. H.R. (ser. A) (1996), the European Court found that the use of anonymous witnesses was compatible with Article 6 if the accused's lawyer was present during the questioning of the witnesses and able to cross-examine these witnesses. While it may have been preferable for accused to have attended the questioning of the witnesses, the presence and participation of his counsel was sufficient for the purposes of Article 6(3)(d), ECHR. In addition, although the witnesses did not identify the accused in person, they did identify him through a photograph that he himself acknowledged to be of himself. Because of the foregoing, the "counterbalancing" procedure followed by the authorities in obtaining the evidence of the witnesses was considered sufficient to have enabled the defense to challenge or impeach their testimony. Furthermore, the national court did not base its finding of guilt solely or even to a decisive extent on the evidence of these anonymous witnesses. Francisco Forrest Martin, *et al.*, 1 INTERNATIONAL HUMAN RIGHTS LAW & PRACTICE: CASES, TREATIES AND MATERIALS 589 (1997).

(2) Compare the ruling governing witness identification issued by the International Criminal Tribunal for the Former Yugoslavia. For the identity of witnesses to be withheld from the accused, the Trial Chamber identified five criteria:

(i) there must exist a "real fear" for the safety of the witness or her/his family;
(ii) the testimony of the witness must be "important enough to the Prosecutor's case . . . to make it unfair . . . to compel the Prosecutor to proceed without it";

(iii) the Trial Chamber must be satisfied that there is no prima facie evidence that the witness is untrustworthy nor partial;

(iv) the ineffectiveness or non-existence of a witness protection program must be taken into account; and

(v) the measures taken "should be strictly necessary" so that the accused suffers "no undue avoidable prejudice."

Furthermore, the Trial Chamber proposed the following procedural safeguards:

(i) the judges must be able to observe the demeanour of the witness in order to assess the reliability of the testimony;

(ii) the judges must know the identity of the witness in order to test the reliability of the witness;

(iii) the defense must be allowed ample opportunity to question the witness on issues unrelated to his/her identity or current whereabouts; and

(iv) the identity of the witness must be released when there are no longer reasons to fear for the witness' security.

International Criminal Tribunal for the Former Yugoslavia, 17 *Bulletin* 6-7 (22 April 1997); *see also The Prosecutor v. Tadic*, Case No. IT-94-1, Decision on Prosecutor's Motion Requesting Protective Measures for Victims and Witnesses, Int'l Crim. Trib.-Yugo. Chamber (18 August 1995); Christine M. Chinkin, *Due Process and Witness Anonymity*, 91 AM. J. INT'L L. 75 (1997).

Do you think this is fair? Consider the underlying reasons for not allowing anonymous witnesses given by the U.S. Supreme Court. In *Smith v. Illinois*, 390 U.S. 129 (1968), the prosecution's key witness was an informer who testified that he had bought heroin from the defendant. This witness identified himself using an alias, and the defense counsel's questions as to his real name and address were rejected by the court. The U.S. Supreme Court held that the trial court's ruling violated the defendant's right to confrontation. The Supreme Court noted that a witnesses' name and address are essential to the defense in opening "countless avenues of in-court examination and out-of-court investigation." *Id.* at 131. Is this concern sufficiently addressed by the ICT-Y and the European Court of Human Rights in *Doorson*? Francisco Forrest Martin, *et al.*, 1 INTERNATIONAL HUMAN RIGHTS LAW & PRACTICE: CASES, TREATIES AND MATERIALS 590 (1997).

(3) The Trial Chamber for the ICT-Y has ruled that in cases of victims of sexual assault testifying, the use of screens to prevent the witness from seeing the accused (but not the accused from seeing the witness) is sufficient. Closed circuit television is not necessary. International Criminal Tribunal for the Former Yugoslavia, 17 *Bulletin* 6 (22 April 1997).

(4) In *Compass v. Jamaica*, Communication No. 375/1989, views adopted 19 October 1993, U.N. Doc. CCPR/C/49/D/375/1989 (1993), the UN Human Rights Committee held that the failure of the trial judge to instruct the jury as to dangers of dock identifications during the trial did not violate the right to a fair trial under Article 14, ICCPR. Relying upon its previous caselaw, the Committee held that the review of jury instructions by the

Committee is beyond the scope of Article 14 — "unless it can be ascertained that the instructions to the jury were clearly arbitrary or amounted to a denial of justice." *Id.* at § 4.6. Do you think that other international tribunals would rule differently?

D. Right Against Self-Incrimination

Funke v. France
European Court of Human Rights
256-A Eur. Ct. H. R. (ser. A) (1993)

. . . .
FACTS:

THE CIRCUMSTANCES OF THE CASE

6. Mr Jean-Gustave Funke, a German national, was born in 1925 and died on 22 July 1987. He worked as a sales representative and lived in France, at Lingolsheim (Bas-Rhin). His widow, Mrs Ruth Funke, nee Monney, is French and lives in Strasbourg.

The house search and the seizures

7. On 14 January 1980 three Strasbourg customs officers, accompanied by a senior police officer (*officier de police judiciaire*), went to the house of the applicant and his wife to obtain 'particulars of their assets abroad'; they were acting on information received from the tax authorities in Metz.

Mr Funke admitted having, or having had, several bank accounts abroad for professional and family reasons and said that he did not have any bank statements at his home.

The customs officers searched the premises from 10.30 am to 3.00 pm, and discovered statements and cheque-books from foreign banks, together with a German car-repair bill and two cameras. They seized all these items and on the same day drew up a report.

8. The customs officers' search and the seizures did not lead to any criminal proceedings for offences against the regulations governing financial dealings with foreign countries. They did, however, give rise to parallel proceedings for disclosure of documents and for interim orders.

The proceedings for disclosure of documents (14 January 1980-18 December 1990)

The main proceedings

9. During their search on 14 January 1980 the customs officers asked the applicant to produce the statements for the previous three years — that is to say 1977, 1978 and 1979 — of his accounts at the Postsparkasse in Munich, the PKO in Warsaw, the Societe de Banque Suisse in Basle and the Deutsche Bank in Kehl and of his house-purchase savings plan at the Wurttembergische Bausparkasse in Leonberg and, lastly, his share portfolio at the Deutsche Bank in Kehl.

10. Mr Funke undertook to do so but later changed his mind.

(i) In the Strasbourg police court

11. On 3 May 1982 the customs authorities summoned him before the Strasbourg police court seeking to have him sentenced to a fine (*amende*) and a further penalty (*astreinte*) of 50 FF a day until such [ ] time as he produced the bank statements; they also made an application to have him committed to prison.

12. On 27 September 1982 the court imposed a fine of 1,200 FF on the applicant and ordered him to produce to the customs authorities the bank statements of his accounts at the Societe de Banque Suisse in Basle, the PKO in Warsaw and the Deutsche Bank in Kehl and of his savings account at the Wurttembergische Bausparkasse in Leonberg and all documents concerning the financing of the flat he had bought at Schonach (Federal Republic of Germany), on penalty of 20 FF per day's delay.

The reasons given for its judgment were the following:

> . . .
>
> On 12 February 1980 Mr Funke told the Customs Service that he was unable to make available the documents that he had undertaken to produce.
>
> He has provided no reason for this and has submitted no correspondence that would show he took the necessary steps to obtain the required documents or would prove that the foreign banks refused to supply him with any such document.
>
> Mr Funke acknowledged that, together with his brother, he bought a bedsitter at Schonach (Federal Republic of Germany) and produced photocopies of the contract of sale and of the entry in the land register; but he refused to produce documents concerning the financing of the purchase.

Section 65 of the Customs Code provides: 'Customs officers with the rank of at least inspector . . . may require production of papers and documents of any kind relating to operations of interest to their department.'

It appears from the present proceedings taken by the customs authorities that the prosecuting officer has the rank of inspector.

The documents sought, namely the bank statements and the documents relating to the financing of the purchase of the flat, can be brought within the category of documents covered by section 65 of the Customs Code.

The same section 65 provides in paragraph 1(i) that such requests for production may be made 'on the premises of (*chez*) any natural or legal person directly or indirectly concerned in lawful or unlawful operations falling within the jurisdiction of the Customs Service.'

In this context the term '*chez*' must not be restricted to 'at the home of' (*au domicile de*) but must be construed as meaning 'wherever . . . may be' (*auprès de*).

Any other construction would enable the person concerned to evade the Customs Service's investigations by keeping any compromising papers elsewhere than at his home.

The house search and Mr Funke's own statements provided sufficient evidence that there were bank accounts and financing operations concerning the defendant to enable the Customs Service to exercise their right of inspection in relation to the relevant documents notwithstanding that these were not at Mr Funke's home.

As the holder of an account used abroad, Mr Funke, like any account-holder, must receive statements following any transaction on the account. A statement is an extension, a reflection of the situation, of an account at a given time. The holder of the account is the owner of his statements and may at any time ask for them from his bank, which cannot refuse them.

(ii) In the Colmar Court of Appeal

13. Appeals were brought by Mr Funke, the public prosecutor and the customs authorities. On 14 March 1983 the Colmar Court of Appeal upheld the judgment of the court below other than as regards the inspection of documents relating to the flat at Schonach, and increased the pecuniary penalty to 50 FF per day's delay.

It dealt with Mr Funke's argument based on the Convention as follows:

> Section 413 *bis* of the Customs Code, which applies to financial dealings with foreign countries by virtue of section 451 of the same code, makes any refusal to produce documents and any concealment of documents in the cases provided for, *inter alia*, in section 65 of the aforementioned code punishable by imprisonment for a period ranging from ten days to one month and a fine of 400 to 2,000 FF.
>
> Under section 65, customs officers may require production of documents of any kind relating to operations of interest to their department, in general, on the premises of any natural or legal person directly or indirectly concerned in lawful or unlawful operations falling within the jurisdiction of the Customs Service.
>
> In the instant case Funke is liable only to a fiscal penalty: to a fine, therefore.
>
> It does not appear that the power conferred by the aforementioned provisions on a revenue authority conflicts with the protection of human rights and fundamental freedoms which it is the purpose of the instrument of international law relied on to guarantee.
>
> The defendant had a fair hearing.
>
> Obviously, no offences which performance of the duty to produce documents may disclose are yet before the courts; that being so, Funke's objections of principle are premature.
>
> Moreover, while everyone charged with a criminal offence is to be presumed innocent until proved guilty according to law, Article 6(2) of the Convention does not otherwise restrict the type of evidence which the *lex fori* places at the disposal of the prosecuting party in order to satisfy the court.
>
> Lastly, the obligation on a defendant to produce in proceedings evidence likely to be used against him by the opposing side is not a special feature of customs or tax proceedings since it is enacted in Article 11 of the New Code of Civil Procedure likewise.
>
> On the other hand, while Article 8 of the Convention provides that everyone has the right to respect for his private life and his correspondence, there may be interference by a public authority with the exercise of this right so long as it is in accordance with the law and amounts to a measure which is necessary in a

democratic society, *inter alia* in the interests of the economic well-being of the country or for the prevention of disorder or crime.

In most of the countries signatories to the Convention, moreover, the customs and revenue authorities have a right of direct investigation in banks.

(iii) In the Court of Cassation

14. On 21 November 1983 the Court of Cassation (Criminal Division) dismissed an appeal on points of law by Mr Funke. The third and final ground, in which Articles 6 and 8 of the Convention were prayed in aid, was rejected in the following terms:

> The Court of Appeal held that, while everyone charged with a criminal offence was to be presumed innocent until proved guilty according to law, Article 6 of the Convention . . . did not otherwise restrict the types of evidence that the '*lex fori*' placed at the disposal of the prosecuting party in order to satisfy the court; and that while it was true that Article 8 of the Convention provided that everyone has the right to respect for his private life and his correspondence, there might . . . be interference by a public authority with the exercise of this right so long as the interference was in accordance with the law and amounted to a measure which was necessary in a democratic society, *inter alia*, in the interests of the economic well-being of the country or for the prevention of disorder or crime.
>
> In so stating, and irrespective of any superfluous reasoning, the Court of Appeal justified its decision and the ground therefore cannot be upheld.

. . . .

RELEVANT CUSTOMS LAW

26. The criminal provisions of customs law in France are treated as a special body of criminal law.

. . . .

30. Section 65-1 of the Customs Code gives the customs authorities a special right of inspection:

> Customs officers with the rank of at least inspector (*inspecteur or officier*) and those performing the duties of collector may require production of papers and documents of any kind relating to operations of interest to their department;
>
> . . .
> (i) in general, on the premises of any natural or legal person directly or indirectly concerned in lawful or unlawful operations falling within the jurisdiction of the Customs Service.

The Sanction

31. Anyone refusing to produce documents is liable to imprisonment for a period ranging from 10 days to one month and to a fine of 600 to 3,000 FF (section 413 bis-1) of the Customs Code.

Furthermore, a pecuniary penalty of not less than 10 FF per day's delay may be imposed on him (section 431) and he may be committed to prison for non-payment (section 382).

. . . .

[Funke applied to the European Commission of Human Rights which found that his criminal conviction for refusal to produce the documents requested by the customs had violated his right to a fair trial under Article 6(1).]

DECISION [OF THE EUROPEAN COURT OF HUMAN RIGHTS]:

I. ALLEGED VIOLATION OF ARTICLE 6(1) AND (2)

Mr Funke claimed to be the victim of breaches of Articles 6(1) and (2) . . . .

A. Fairness of the proceedings and presumption of innocence

. . . .

2. Merits of the complaint

(a) Article 6(1)

In the applicant's submission, his conviction for refusing to disclose the documents asked for by the customs (*see* §§ 9 to 14 above) had infringed his right to a fair trial as secured in Article 6(1). He claimed that the authorities had violated the right not to give evidence against oneself, a general principle enshrined both in the legal orders of the Contracting States and in the European Convention and the International Covenant on Civil and Political Rights, as although they had not lodged a complaint alleging an offence against the regulations governing financial dealings with foreign countries, they had brought criminal proceedings calculated to compel Mr Funke to co-operate in a prosecution mounted against him. Such a method of proceeding was, he said, all the more unacceptable as nothing prevented the French authorities from seeking international assistance and themselves obtaining the necessary evidence from the foreign States.

The Government emphasised the declaratory nature of the French customs and exchange-control regime, which saved taxpayers having their affairs systematically investigated but imposed duties in return, such as the duty to keep papers concerning their income and property for a certain length of time and to make them available to the authorities on request. This right of the State to inspect certain documents, which was strictly supervised by the Court of Cassation, did not mean that those concerned were obliged to incriminate themselves, a requirement that was prohibited by the United Nations Covenant (Article 14) and had been condemned by the Court of Justice of the European Communities (*Orkem* judgment)'; it was not contrary to the guidelines laid down in the Convention institutions' case law on what constituted a fair trial.

In the instant case the customs had not required Mr Funke to confess to an offence or to provide evidence of one himself; they had merely asked him to give particulars of evidence found by their officers and which he had admitted, namely the bank statements and cheque-books discovered during the house search. As to the courts, they had assessed, after adversarial proceedings, whether the customs' application was justified in law and in fact.

The Commission reached the same conclusion, mainly on the basis of the special features of investigation procedures in business and financial matters. It considered that neither the obligation to produce bank statements nor the imposition of pecuniary penalties offended the principle of a fair trial; the former was a reflection of the State's confidence in all its citizens in that no use was made of stricter supervisory measures, while responsibility for the detriment caused by the latter lay entirely with the person affected where he refused to co-operate with the authorities.

The Court notes that the customs secured Mr Funke's conviction in order to obtain certain documents which they believed must exist, although they were not certain of the fact. Being unable or unwilling to procure them by some other means, they attempted to compel the applicant himself to provide the evidence of offences he had allegedly committed. The special features of customs law (*see* §§ 30 to 31 above) cannot justify such an infringement of the right of anyone 'charged with a criminal offence,' within the autonomous meaning of this expression in Article 6, to remain silent and not to contribute to incriminating himself.

There has accordingly been a breach of Article 6(1).

. . . .   ❖ ❖ ❖

Questions & Comments

(1) The European Court has allowed the drawing of adverse inferences from a criminal defendant's silence under strict conditions. In *Murray v. United Kingdom*, Case No. 41/1994/488/570, -- Eur. Ct. H.R. (ser. A) (1996), the applicant, an alleged IRA member, was arrested in a house where an informer had been held captive. The informer testified that he had been forced to make a tape-recorded confession and that he later saw the applicant pulling a tape out of cassette recorder at the house after his release by the police.

After his arrest, the applicant declined to answer police questions eight times during his interrogation. Police warned him each time that adverse inferences could be drawn from his silence. This police practice was based on a new and controversial statute that had superceded the commonlaw, which held the opposite. The new statute had been enacted for security reasons, *viz.*, to suppress illegal IRA operations.

For the first forty-eight hours, the police denied the applicant access to his lawyer, and even after the applicant was given access, his solicitor was not allowed to attend the interrogation. During his trial, the applicant continued to remain silent. In finding the applicant guilty for aiding and abetting false imprisonment, the judge relied upon the applicant's refusal to answer questions both during this police interrogation and trial.

The European Court held that there was no Article 6 violation for the judge's drawing of adverse inferences. While noting that silence in itself cannot be regarded as an indication of guilt, there were conditions in which adverse inferences could be drawn lawfully under Article 6. First, the Court noted that the judge was experienced. Second, warnings were given to the applicant. Third, the evidence was sufficiently strong against the applicant to call for an explanation that the applicant could give.

[However, the Court found an Article 6 violation for the police's refusal to allow the applicant access to his lawyer for forty-eight hours.] Francisco Forrest Martin, *et al.*, 1

INTERNATIONAL HUMAN RIGHTS LAW & PRACTICE: CASES, TREATIES AND MATERIALS 598 (1997).

(2)   Unlike Article 14(3)(g) of the ICCPR, the European Convention has no express right to silence. Furthermore, the European Commission of Human Rights has found such a right under Article 10's freedom of expression. In *K. v. Austria*, Report of 13 October 193, Ser. B, No. 236-B, the applicant was forced to testify against his will by being fined and detained for five days in a heroin case. Finding a violation of Article 10, the Commission held that Article 10 "by implication also guarantees a 'negative right' not to be compelled to express oneself, *i.e.* to remain silent." *Id.* at § 45.

(3)   Compare the ICT-Y's ruling that a defendant need not provide a handwriting sample to the Prosecution because it would violate his right against self-incrimination. *The Prosecutor v. Mucic*, Case No. IT-96-21,Int'l Crim. Trib.-Yugo., Trial Chamber, Decision on the Prosecution's Oral Requests for the Admission of Exhibit 155 into Evidence and for an Order to Compel the Accused, Zdravko Mucic, to Provide a Handwriting Sample (19 January 1998).

(4)   Under the Fifth Amendment to the U.S. Constitution, individuals have the right to remain silent in criminal proceedings. Furthermore, a prosecutor or judge cannot make an adverse comment on a defendant's exercise of this right. *Griffin v. California*, 380 U.S. 609 (1965).   However, the right against self-incrimination does not extend to evidence obtained in violation of this right in foreign prosecutions. *United States v. Balsys*, 118 S.Ct. 2218 (1998). How would you argue a customary international law claim challenging the Court's ruling in *Balsys*?

E. Right to Speedy Trial

Firmenich v. Argentina
Inter-American Commission on Human Rights
Resolution 17/89, Report Case 10037 (13 April 1989)
ANNUAL REPORT OF THE INTER-AMERICAN COMMISSION ON HUMAN RIGHTS
OEA/Ser.L/V/II. 76 (10 Sept. 1989)

BACKGROUND

1.   Case 10,037 refers to an alleged violation of the right of personal freedom stipulated in Article 7 of the American Convention on Human Rights (thereinafter the Convention) and, particularly, to the guarantees set out in subsection 5 of the aforesaid provision. According to the complaint, Argentine citizen Mario Eduardo Firmenich, being tried in two proceedings in the regular Argentine courts and currently imprisoned, has been denied the benefit of release requested under Article 379 (title 18)(6), of the Code of Criminal Procedure of the Argentine Republic which, in essence, corresponds to the guarantee established under Article 7(5) of the Convention [guaranteeing the right to a prompt trial].
        . . . .

. . . . The guarantee mentioned in the referenced article of the Convention would have been infringed because of "judicial procrastination" during proceedings against Firmenich, since the above-mentioned term has been exceeded.

In summary, the petitioner states that since more than three and a half years have elapsed since the arrest of Mario Eduardo Firmenich, the period mentioned in Article 379(6) of the Code of Criminal Procedure as well as the one mentioned in Article 701 of the same Code has been exceeded by far, said periods consecrating in internal law the "reasonable length of time" mentioned in the Convention within which a person is entitled to be tried or "to be set free, without prejudice to continuing trial." The claimant states, in keeping with the above, that Article 379(6) is the instrument ("inclusion") of Article 7(7) of the Convention in the Argentine legal system, since if this were not the case, the foregoing would represent a void that prevents the application of the guarantee in Article 7(5) and would also be a violation of the Convention by Argentina in view of provisions in Article 1 and 2 thereof.

The Argentine Government, also in summary, rejects the criterion of the complainant, commenting that "Argentine law must be construed as having adopted the two year term, mentioned in Article 379(6) in connection with Article 380, as one of the foundations of a "reasonable length of time" and that, therefore, two years could be considered a reasonable period, after which the judge can consider a request for release but which is not, at all, imposed on the judge without consideration for the personal characteristics of the accused, nor should said period be computed as if it consisted of calendar days, overlooking the behavior of the parties and its effect on the greater or lesser speed of the proceedings."

. . . .

The Commission believes that Article 379(6) is supplemented and "moderated" by Article 380 of the said Code, so that the definition of a "reasonable length of time" in Argentina's internal law is the result in each case of the harmonious consideration of these two provisions, leaving said consideration to the judge's criterion, since he must decide based on the parameters specifically determined by law for their joint weighing. As the Argentine Government states: ". . . the norm indicates the channels to be followed by the judge's criterion, that is: the objective assessment of the characteristics of the event and the personal characteristics of the accused." The judge fulfills a natural role entrusted to him: administering justice with the means expressly provided thereto by law.

Two important concepts are derived from the above in connection with the problem of a "reasonable length of time": first, that it is not possible to define this period *in abstracto* but, instead, that it shall be defined in each case after the circumstances mentioned in Article 380 have been considered and weighed. The Commission, in connection with these comments, agrees with the opinion that the referenced State party is "not bound (by the Convention) to fix a valid period for all cases, independently from the circumstances." This viewpoint is also shared by the European Court; second, releasing prisoners under conditions such as those in which Mario Eduardo Firmenich finds himself cannot be done based on a simple chronological consideration of years, months, and days. This has also been made explicit by the European Court . . . since the concept of "reasonable period" is left to the consideration of "the seriousness of the violation," when determining whether the detention has ceased to be reasonable.

The pronouncement of the European Court coincides, in this case, with what has been stated by the Court in San Martin, when deciding on the remedies submitted by counsel for Mr. Firmenich and stating:

> Said norm only requires that the person charged be tried within a reasonable period and, if not, be released on bail. The "amount" of reasonable length of time does not have to be set as being two years, as is claimed without additional basis, since if that period is appropriate for a simple and easily investigated case it might not be, when related to another, such as this one, whose complexity, scope and difficulties impose a longer period for it to expire. This last reasoning has been reflected by legislation in the very Article 701 of the ritual order, when it includes the caveat that a trial can take longer than two years when, as in this case, the delays cannot be attributed to the Judge's activity.

In view of the above, it must be concluded that the reasonableness of the period is set by the extremes of Article 380 of the Argentine Code of Criminal Procedure, together with the assessment thereof by the trial judge. This conclusion coincides with what has been stated by the European Court, when it states:

> The Court also believes that to decide whether, in a given case, the detention of the accused does not exceed the limits of what is reasonable, it behooves the national judicial authorities to investigate all circumstances which, because of their nature, lead to acknowledge or reject the existence of true public interest which justifies the repeal of the rule of respect for individual liberty (Neumeister case, sentence dated 27 June 1968, TEDH-5.p.83, Legal Consideration #5).

[ ] It does seem necessary, for brevity's sake, to engage in a detailed analysis of the criteria or factors which the European Commission of Human Rights examined in connection with the problem of a "reasonable period" in order to define an old and vague concept of international law. Both the interested petitioner and Government have made their views known at length.

Nevertheless, the Commission wishes to refer to three factors or features: a) the actual duration of imprisonment; b) the nature of the acts which led to proceedings against Firmenich; and c) the difficulties or judicial problems encountered when conducting said trials.

a. The duration of imprisonment

The claimant holds that the term indicated in Article 379(6) as related to Article 701 of the Code of Criminal Procedure must be computed starting on 13 February 1984, when he was arrested in Rio de Janeiro (Brazil).

The Government holds that the accused was turned over to Argentine authorities on 20 October 1984, and that, therefore, the "reasonable period" mentioned in Article 7(5) of the Convention must be computed as of that date, ". . . without prejudice to the time between both dates which must be credited to the sentence."

The Commission believes that the opinion of the claimant cannot be entertained since between the date of arrest in Rio and the delivery of the prisoner to the Argentine authorities, extradition proceedings were conducted and that they and the pertinent decision are subject (except insofar as the filing of the petition by the requesting State is concerned) to the authorities with jurisdiction in the State to whom the request for extradition is submitted, according to the latter's internal law and terms of the treaty applicable between both States, if any, or in the absence thereof, international practice.

The foregoing is also valid when applied to the petitioner's claim that the procedural responsibility of the accused cannot be taken into consideration during the extradition proceedings since the latter takes place without the participation of the accused. Firmenich's extradition followed provisions set out in the treaty applicable between Argentina and Brazil (1961), whose Article V indicates that the individual whose extradition is requested must be granted "the opportunity to exercise all the remedies and appeal to all instances foreseen by the legislation of the State receiving the request," remedies and instances which were actually employed by Mr. Firmenich to prevent or delay his extradition.

b. The nature of the crimes

The claimant was extradited for trial in connection with two different crimes (*non bis in idem*): one by the Federal courts (in Buenos Aires) for charges of double aggravated homicide in connection with attempted homicide, also with doubly aggravating circumstances and a request for life imprisonment; the other (Federal Court in San Martin), for twofold homicide with aggravating circumstances and kidnapping or ransom and a request for life and additional imprisonment.

In conclusion and in the light of the provisions in Article 380 of the Argentine Code of Criminal Procedure, the Commission is of the opinion that the characteristics of the (punishable) actions as described in the initial briefs of these proceedings and the penalties which could be imposed in the accused make it possible to assume, on a solid basis, that measures must be taken to forestall an avoidance of justice and that, hence, a request for release must be turned down.

c. Difficulties encountered during the trials

In the two trials against the claimant as is evidenced by the record, an intense investigation was conducted with the active participation of the accused, so that:

i. Case tried in San Martin (Province of Buenos Aires) wherein charges were filed in November of 1985, and the defense requested several extensions to answer the charges. Testimony was frequently waived, or offered extemporaneously on other occasions, "new facts" were introduced and international letters rogatory were dispatched to elicit depositions and during which the judge declared the defense negligent in submitting evidence or portions thereof. Summary investigations lasted one year, trial starting in approximately November 1986, as far as the Commission is able to deduce from the evidence submitted to it. Approximately 90 witnesses and an indeterminate number of accused, but not tried, and linked in one way or another to the case testified during the trial. It must be pointed out that, according to the record, some testimony was given after difficult proceedings and international letters rogatory requested by the defense. The trial phase, as such, was completed in 1987 and sentence passed in May of that year. The sentence of the first instance has been appealed by the defense, and the appeal is still pending. The sentence is prior to submission of the case to the IACHR.

ii. The case before the federal courts (Federal Capital) as evidenced by the record, the investigation was interrupted from February 1982 until February 1984. The accused was charged in October 1986. Ninety witnesses testified, three ballistic tests were conducted, two tests were conducted on explosives, two expert witnesses testified in connection with scopametorics, two handwriting experts testified, one expert witness testified on mechanics and another on typewriters during the investigation. Thirty Official Letters were sent, many through Interpol and others through the Ministry of Foreign Affairs, requesting evidence which would serve information purposes. Charges were made on 2 October 1986, but the defense made an appearance only on 16 March 1987, because of a request for release it had submitted and three requests for extension which were granted by the judge. On 15 May 1987, the defense suggested taking depositions from several witnesses outside the country, that a mechanical expert be called and 40 letter be sent, all of which was done in addition to granting a 90 day (extraordinary) term for submission of evidence, which had twice to be extended. On 14 June 1988, sentence was passed in the first instance.

The foregoing makes it possible to draw the conclusion that although four years is not a reasonable period, in this case because of its unique features and the complexity of the reasons affecting its progress such a period is not an unjustified delay in the administration of justice.

. . . .

❖ ❖ ❖

Questions & Comments

(1) Although the Inter-American Commission "for brevity's sake" refers to only three considerations in determining whether Firmenich's proceedings were unreasonably long, it earlier made note of nine more specific considerations. The Argentine government suggested the first seven, the Inter-American Commission added the final two:

(i) actual duration of imprisonment,
(ii) duration of preventive detention in relation to the nature of the acts which gave rise to the trial,
(iii) 'the material, moral or other effects of detention when normal consequences are exceeded,"
(iv) defendant's behavior and failure to cooperate,
(v) investigatory difficulties resulting from the nature of the alleged crimes,
(vi) conduct of investigation,
(vii) conduct of judicial authorities,
(viii) judicial opinions regarding release of the defendant, and
(ix) the undisputed facts mentioned by the petitioner in his appeal.

Firmenich v. Argentina at § 12.

(2) Article 6(1), ECHR, recognizes the right to a fair and public hearing within a reasonable time by an independent and impartial tribunal. Furthermore, the reasonableness of the length of detention and the reasonableness of the length of time until final judgment are assessed independently. *Maznetter v. Austria*, 10 Eur. Ct. H.R. (ser. A) (1969). In *Vendittelli v. Italy*, the European Court addressed a criminal prosecution lasting over four years. The European Court analyzed the circumstances surrounding the case and determined this period of time was not unreasonable. The European Court undertook the following analysis for determining Article 6(1) violations on the basis of length. Once the Court determines how long the proceedings have lasted, the Court determines whether the case is sufficiently complex to merit the delays. If the case is not justifiably complex, the Court will look to both the applicant's conduct and that of the relevant authorities. It is important to note that an applicant is under no duty to take steps in shorten the proceedings. *Moreira de Acevedo v. Portugal*, 13 E.H.R.R. 721, §72 (1991). Moreover the applicant's full use of available domestic remedies cannot be used against him/her in establishing unreasonable length of proceedings. *Eckle v. Fed. Rep. of Germany*, 51 Eur. Ct. H.R. (ser. A) (1982). Finally, in cases where the applicant has a significant stake in the case's outcome, the Court will hold State Parties to a higher standard. Francisco Forrest Martin, *et al.*, 1 INTERNATIONAL HUMAN RIGHTS LAW & PRACTICE: CASES, TREATIES AND MATERIALS 603-604 (1997).

(3) Are the Inter-American Commission and the European Court using substantially the same test?

(4) Consider *Suárez Rosero v. Ecuador*, Inter-Am. Ct. H.R., Judgment of 12 November 1997 (reproduced above in Chapter 11(C)):

> 70. . . . In the instant case, the first act of the proceeding was Mr. Suárez-Rosero's arrest on June 23, 1992, and, therefore, the time must be calculated from that moment.
> 71. The Court considers the proceeding to be at an end when a final and firm judgment is delivered and the jurisdiction thereby ceases (cf. *Cour eur. D.H., arrêt Guincho du 10 juillet 1984, Serie A n° 81*, para. 29) and that, particularly in criminal matters, that time must cover the entire proceeding, including any appeals that may be filed. On the basis of the evidence contained in the Case before it, the Court considers that the proceeding against Mr. Suárez-Rosero ended in the Ecuadorian jurisdiction on September 9, 1996, the date on which he was convicted by the President of the Superior Court of Justice of Quito. Although at the public hearing Mr. Suárez-Rosero referred to an appeal of that conviction, his statement was not substantiated.
> 72. This Court shares the view of the European Court of Human Rights, which in a number of decisions analyzed the concept of reasonable time and decided that three points should be taken into account in determining the reasonableness of the time in which a proceeding takes place: a) the complexity of the case, b) the procedural activity of the interested party, and c) the conduct of the judicial authorities (cf. *Genie Lacayo Case*, Judgment of January 29, 1997. Series C No. 30, para. 77; and cf. *Eur. Court* H.R., *Motta judgment of 19*

February 1991, Series A No. 195-A, para. No. 30; *Eur. Court H.R., Ruiz-Mateos case v. Spain judgment of 23 June 1993, Series A No. 262*, para. 30).

73. On the basis of the above considerations, after comprehensive analysis of the proceeding against Mr. Suárez-Rosero in the domestic courts, the Court observes that that proceeding lasted more than 50 months. In the Court's view, this period far exceeds the *"reasonable time"* contemplated in the American Convention.

74. Likewise, the Court considers that the fact that an Ecuadorian tribunal has found Mr. Suárez-Rosero guilty of complicity in a crime does not justify his being deprived of his liberty for more than three years and ten months, when two years is the maximum in Ecuadorian law for that offense.

75. In view of the foregoing, the Court finds that the State of Ecuador violated, to the detriment of Mr. Rafael Iván Suárez-Rosero, the right to be tried within a reasonable time or be released, as established in Articles 7(5) and 8(1) of the American Convention.

(5) Compare *The Prosecutor v. Aleksovski*, Case No. IT-95-14/1, Int'l Crim. Trib.-Yugo, Trial Chamber (23 January 1998), in which the Trial Chamber rejected the defense's claim that 577 days of preventive detention was excessive. The Trial Chamber was not convinced (i) that the 577 days he had spent in preventive detention was excessive in view of the crimes alleged, (ii) that the condition of defendant's physical health justified his release, (iii) that the effects on his family were unusual, or (iv) that his behavior in prison needed to be taken into account.

(6) Compare U.S. law governing length of proceedings. In *Barker v. Wingo*, 407 U.S. 514 (1972), the U.S. Supreme Court adopted a balancing test. The Court identified four factors in the balancing test: "[l]ength of delay, the reason for the delay, the defendant's assertion of his right, and prejudice to the defendant." *Id.* at 530.

F. *Ex Post Facto* or Retrospective Criminal Laws

Welch v. United Kingdom
European Court of Human Rights
307 Eur. Ct. H.R. (ser. A) (1995)
20 E.H.R.R. 247 (1995)

. . . .

FACTS:

I. The circumstances of the case

7. On 3 November 1986 Mr Welch was arrested for suspected drug offences. On 4 November he was charged in respect of offences concerning the importation of large quantities of cannabis. Prosecuting Counsel advised, prior to February 1987, that there was insufficient evidence to charge Mr Welch with possession of cocaine with intent to supply.

8. After further investigations, including forensic examinations, further evidence came to light and on 24 February 1987, the applicant was charged with the offence of possession with intent to supply cocaine, alleged to have been committed on 3 November 1986. Subsequently, on 5 May 1987, he was charged with conspiracy to obtain cocaine with intent to supply in respect of activities which occurred between 1 January 1986 and 3 November.

9. On 24 August 1988, Mr Welch was found guilty on five counts and was given an overall sentence of 22 years' imprisonment. In addition, the trial judge imposed a confiscation order pursuant to the Drug Trafficking Offences Act 1986 ("the 1986 Act") in the amount of £66,914. In default of the payment of this sum he would be liable to serve a consecutive two years' prison sentence. The operative provisions of the 1986 Act had come into force on 12 January 1987. The Act applies only to offences, proceedings for which were instituted after this date.

10. On 11 June 1990 the Court of Appeal reduced Mr Welch's overall sentence by two years. In addition it reduced the confiscation order by £7,000 to £59,914.

II. Relevant domestic law

11. The intended purpose of the 1986 Act was to extend existing confiscation powers to enable the court to follow drug trafficking money which had been "laundered" into legitimate property. In the words of the Secretary of State who introduced the Bill in the House of Commons:

> By attacking the profits made from drug trafficking, we intend to make it much less attractive to enter the trade. We intend to help guard against the possibility that the profits from one trafficking operation will be used to finance others, and, not least, to remove the sense of injury which ordinary people are bound to feel at the idea of traffickers, who may have ruined the lives of children, having the benefit of the profits that they have made from doing so.
>
> . . .
> We need the legislation because the forfeiture powers in existing law have proved inadequate. The Courts cannot order the forfeiture of the proceeds of an offence once they have been converted into another asset — a house, stocks and shares, or valuables of any sort. The Operation Julie case was the most notorious example of the courts being unable to deprive convicted traffickers, as they wished, of the proceeds of their offences . . . the Bill is designed to remedy those defects. It will provide powers for courts to confiscate proceeds even after they have been converted into some other type of asset. (Hansard of 21 January 1986, cols 242 and 243).

Chapter 12. Trial Due Process Protections

A. Drug Trafficking Offences Act 1986

12. The relevant parts of the 1986 Act provide as follows:

1. Confiscation orders

(1) . . . where a person appears before the Crown Court to be sentenced in respect of one or more drug trafficking offences (and has not previously been sentenced or otherwise dealt with in respect of his conviction for the offence or, as the case may be, any of the offences concerned), the court shall act as follows:

(2) the court shall first determine whether he has benefitted from drug trafficking.

(3) For the purposes of this Act, a person who has at any time (whether before or after the commencement of this section) received any payment or other reward in connection with drug trafficking carried on by him or another has benefitted from drug trafficking.

(4) If the court determines that he has so benefitted, the court shall, before sentencing . . . determine . . . the amount to be recovered in his case by virtue of this section.

(5) The court shall then in respect of the offence or offences concerned —

(a) order him to pay that amount . . .

2. Assessing the proceeds of drug trafficking

(1) For the purposes of this Act —

(a) any payments or other rewards received by a person at any time (whether before or after the commencement of section 1 of this Act) in connection with drug trafficking carried on by him or another are his proceeds of drug trafficking, and

(b) the value of his proceeds of drug trafficking is the aggregate of the values of the payments or other rewards.

(2) The court may, for the purpose of determining whether the defendant has benefitted from drug trafficking and, if he has, of assessing the value of his proceeds of drug trafficking, make the following assumptions, except to the extent that any of the assumptions are shown to be incorrect in the defendant's case.

(3) Those assumptions are —

(a) that any property appearing to the court —

(i) to have been held by him at any time since his conviction, or

(ii) to have been transferred to him at any time since the beginning of the period of six years ending when the proceedings were instituted against him, was received by him, at the earliest time at which he appears to the court to have held it, as a payment or reward in connection with drug trafficking carried on by him,

(b) that any expenditure of his since the beginning of that period was met out of payments received by him in connection with drug trafficking carried on by him, and

(c) that, for the purpose of valuing any property received or assumed to have been received by him at any time as such a reward, he received the property free of any other interests in it . . .

. . .

4. Amount to be recovered under confiscation order

(1) Subject to subsection (3) below, the amount to be recovered in the defendant's case shall be the amount the Crown Court assesses to be the value of the defendant's proceeds of drug trafficking.

(2) If the court is satisfied as to any matter relevant for determining the amount that might be realised at the time the confiscation order is made . . . the court may issue a certificate giving the court's opinion as to the matters concerned and shall do so if satisfied as mentioned in sub-section (3) below.

(3) If the court is satisfied that the amount that may be realised at the time of the confiscation order is made is less than the amount the court assesses to be the value of his proceeds of drug trafficking, the amount to be recovered in the defendant's case under the confiscation order shall be the amount appearing to the court to be the amount that might, be so realised.

B. Discretion of the trial judge

13. In determining the amount of the confiscation order, the trial judge may take into consideration the degree of culpability of the offender. For example, in *R. v. Porter* [12 Crim. App. 377 (1990)] the Court of Appeal held that where more than one conspirator was before the Court the total proceeds of a drug trafficking conspiracy could be unequally allocated as their respective share of the proceeds if there was evidence that the defendants had played unequal roles and had profited to a different extent. Similarly, in the present case, the trial judge made a much smaller order in respect of the applicant's co-defendant in recognition of his lesser involvement in the offences.

C. Imprisonment in default of payment

14. After a confiscation order has been made, the Crown Court decides upon the period of imprisonment which the offender has to serve if he fails to pay. The maximum

periods of imprisonment are provided for in section 31 of the Powers of Criminal Courts Act 1973. The maximum period for an order between the sums of £50,000 and £100,000 is two years.

D. Statements by domestic courts concerning the nature of forfeiture and confiscation provisions

15. Prior to the passing of the 1986 Act, Lord Salmon expressed the view that forfeitures of money had both a punitive and deterrent purpose. (House of Lords decision in *R. v. Menocal* [2 W.L.R. 876 (1979)].

16. The domestic courts have commented in various cases on the draconian nature of the confiscation provisions in the 1986 Act and have occasionally referred to the orders, expressly or impliedly, as constituting penalties. (*R. v. Dickens* [91 Crim. App 164 (1990)]; *R. v. Porter*, 12 Crim. App. 377 (1990); *In re Lorenzo Baretto*, High Court decision of 30 November 1992 and Court of Appeal decision of 19 October 1993).

In the Court of Appeal decision in the last mentioned case, which concerned the question whether a power to vary confiscation orders introduced by the Criminal Justice (International Co-operation) Act 1990 could be applied retrospectively, the Master of the Rolls (Sir Thomas Bingham) stated as follows:

> While it is true that a confiscation order is made before sentence is passed for the substantive offence, and the term of imprisonment in default is passed to procure compliance and not by way of punishment, these are in a broad sense penal provisions, inflicting the vengeance of society on those who have transgressed in this field.

17. However, the domestic courts have also referred to the confiscation provisions as not being punitive but reparative in purpose. (Re T (Restraint Order; Disclosure of Assets) [1 W.L.R. 949 (1992)]).

. . . .

[Welch filed an application with the European Commission alleging that the confiscation order imposed upon him constituted the imposition of a retrospective criminal penalty in violation of Article 7. The Commission found no Article 7 violation.]

. . . .

DECISION [OF THE EUROPEAN COURT OF HUMAN RIGHTS]:

I. Alleged Violation of Article 7(1) of the Convention

22. The applicant complained that the confiscation order that was made against him amounted to the imposition of a retrospective criminal penalty, contrary to Article 7 . . . .

. . . .

He emphasised that his complaint was limited to the retrospective application of the confiscation provisions of the 1986 Act and not the provisions themselves.

23. He submitted that in determining whether a confiscation order was punitive the Court should look beyond its stated purpose and examine its real effects. The severity and extent of such an order identified it as a penalty for the purposes of the Convention.

In the first place, under section 2(3) of the 1986 Act the national court was entitled to assume that any property which the offender currently held or which had been transferred to him in the preceding six years, or any gift which he had made during the same period, were the proceeds of drug trafficking. In addition, by seeking to confiscate the proceeds, as opposed to the profits, of drug dealing, irrespective of whether there had in fact been any personal enrichment, the order went beyond the notions of reparation and prevention into the realm of punishment.

Moreover, the fact that an order could not be made unless there had been a criminal conviction and that the degree of culpability of an accused was taken into consideration by the court in fixing the amount of the order also pointed in the direction of a penalty. Indeed, prior to the passing of the 1986 Act, the courts had regarded forfeiture orders as having the dual purpose of punishment and deterrence. Finally, confiscation orders had been recognised as having a punitive character in various domestic court decisions and in several decisions of the Supreme Court of the United States concerning similar legislation. *See Austin v. United States*, 509 U.S. 602 (1993) and *Alexander v. United States*, 509 U.S. 544 (1993).

24. The Government contended that the true purpose of the order was two-fold: first, to deprive a person of the profits which he had received from drug trafficking and secondly, to remove the value of the proceeds from possible future use in the drugs trade. It thus did not seek to impose a penalty or punishment for a criminal offence but was essentially a confiscatory and preventive measure. This could be seen from the order in the present case, which had been made for the purpose of depriving the defendant of illegal gains. Had no order been made, the money would have remained within the system for use in further drug dealing enterprises.

It was stressed that a criminal conviction for drug trafficking was no more than a "trigger" for the operation of the statutory provisions. Once the triggering event had occurred, there was no further link with any conviction. Thus, the court could consider whether a person had benefitted from drug-trafficking at any time and not merely in respect of the offence with which he had been charged. Moreover, an order could be made in relation to property which did not form part of the subject matter of the charge against the defendant or which had been received by him in a period to which no drug dealing conviction related.

Furthermore, the fact that a period of imprisonment could be imposed in default of payment could be of no assistance in characterising the nature of the confiscation order since there were many non-penal court orders which attracted such a penalty in the event of non-compliance. Similarly, the harsh effect of the order was of no assistance, since the effectiveness of a preventive measure required that a drug trafficker be deprived not only of net profits but of money which would otherwise remain available for use in the drug trade.

25. For the Commission, the order in the present case was not punitive in nature but reparative and preventive and, consequently, did not constitute a penalty within the meaning of Article 7(1) of the Convention.

26. The Court first observes that the retrospective imposition of the confiscation order is not in dispute in the present case. The order was made following a conviction in respect of drugs offences which had been committed before the 1986 Act came into force. The

only question to be determined therefore is whether the order constitutes a penalty within the meaning of Article 7(1), second sentence.

27. The concept of a "penalty" in this provision is, like the notions of "civil rights and obligations" and "criminal charge" in Article 6(1), an autonomous Convention concept. (*See inter alia* — as regards "civil rights" — *X. v. France* [234 Eur. Ct. H.R. (ser. A) at 90 (1992)], and — as regards "criminal charge" — *Demicoli v. Malta* [210 Eur. Ct. H.R. (ser. A) at 15-16 (1992)]. To render the protection offered by Article 7 effective, the Court must remain free to go behind appearances and assess for itself whether a particular measure amounts in substance to a "penalty" within the meaning of this provision. (*See, mutatis mutandis, Van Droogenbroeck v. Belgium* [50 Eur. Ct. H.R. (ser. A) at 20-21 (1982)], and *Duinhof v. The Netherlands* [79 Eur. Ct. H.R. (ser. A) at 15-16 (1984)]).

28. The wording of Article 7(1), second sentence, indicates that the starting point in any assessment of the existence of a penalty is whether the measure in question is imposed following conviction for a "criminal offence". Other factors that may be taken into account as relevant in this connection are the nature and purpose of the measure in question; its characterisation under national law; the procedures involved in the making and implementation of the measure; and its severity.

29. As regards the connection with a criminal offence, it is to be observed that before an order can be made under the 1986 Act the accused must have been convicted of one or more drug trafficking offences. (*See* § 1(1) of the 1986 Act at § 12 above). This link is in no way diminished by the fact that, due to the operation of the statutory presumptions concerning the extent to which the applicant has benefitted from trafficking, the court order may affect proceeds or property which are not directly related to the facts underlying the criminal conviction. While the reach of the measure may be necessary to the attainment of the aims of the 1986 Act, this does not alter the fact that its imposition is dependent on there having been a criminal conviction.

30. In assessing the nature and purpose of the measure, the Court has had regard to the background of the 1986 Act, which was introduced to overcome the inadequacy of the existing powers of forfeiture and to confer on the courts the power to confiscate proceeds after they had been converted into other forms of assets. The preventive purpose of confiscating property that might be available for use in future drug trafficking operations as well as the purpose of ensuring that crime does not pay are evident from the ministerial statements that were made to Parliament at the time of the introduction of the legislation. However, it cannot be excluded that legislation which confers such broad powers of confiscation on the courts also pursues the aim of punishing the offender. Indeed, the aims of prevention and reparation are consistent with a punitive purpose and may be seen as constituent elements of the very notion of punishment.

31. In this connection, confiscation orders have been characterised in some United Kingdom court decisions as constituting "penalties", and, in others, as pursuing the aim of reparation as opposed to punishment. Although on balance these statements point more in the direction of a confiscation order being a punitive measure, the Court does not consider them to be of much assistance since they were not directed at the point at issue under Article 7 but rather made in the course of examination of associated questions of domestic law and procedure.

32. The Court agrees with the Government and the Commission that the severity of the order is not in itself decisive, since many non-penal measures of a preventive nature may have a substantial impact on the person concerned.

33. However, there are several aspects of the making of an order under the 1986 Act which are in keeping with the idea of a penalty as it is commonly understood even though they may also be considered as essential to the preventive scheme inherent in the 1986 Act. The sweeping statutory assumptions in section 2(3) of the 1986 Act that all property passing through the offender's hands over a six-year period is the fruit of drug trafficking unless he can prove otherwise; the fact that the confiscation order is directed to the proceeds involved in drug dealing and is not limited to actual enrichment or profit (*See* §§ 1 and 2 of the 1986 Act in § 12 above); the discretion of the trial judge, in fixing the amount of the order, to take into consideration the degree of culpability of the accused; and the possibility of imprisonment in default of payment by the offender — are all elements which, when considered together, provide a strong indication of *inter alia* a regime of punishment.

34. Finally, looking behind appearances at the realities of the situation, whatever the characterisation of the measure of confiscation, the fact remains that the applicant faced more far-reaching detriment as a result of the order than that to which he was exposed at the time of the commission of the offences for which he was convicted. (*See, mutatis mutandis, Campbell and Fell v. United Kingdom*, [80 Eur. Ct. H.R. (ser. A) at 37-38 (1985)]).

35. Taking into consideration the combination of punitive elements outlined above, the confiscation order amounted, in the circumstances of the present case, to a penalty. Accordingly, there has been a breach of Article 7(1).

36. The Court would stress, however, that this conclusion concerns only the retrospective application of the relevant legislation and does not call into question in any respect the powers of confiscation conferred on the courts as a weapon in the fight against the scourge of drug trafficking.

. . . .

❖ ❖ ❖

Questions & Comments

(1) In *Jamil v. France*, 320 Eur.Ct.H.R. (ser. A) (1995), the applicant was convicted of smuggling and conspiracy to smuggle prohibited goods (cocaine). The French authorities imprisoned him and ordered him to pay a fine. Furthermore, if he did not pay the fine, he was subject to additional time in prison. The specific amount of time to be served in default of payment was established by a law enacted *after* his conviction. The European Court found a violation of Article 7.

(2) The *ex post facto* doctrine arguably can apply to civil proceedings; however, it has been recognized more generally as a criminal law rule. Related to the *ex post facto* prohibition are the legality doctrines of *nullum crimen sine lege* (which expressly addresses *criminal* liability) and *nulla poena sine lege* (which expressly addresses penalties).

Whether a proceeding is criminal or not, the European Court of Human Rights in *E.L., R.L. and J.O.-L v. Switzerland*, – Eur. Ct. H.R. (ser. A) (1997), ruled that three criteria must be considered for determining whether a person was being "charged with a criminal offence" for purposes of Article 6, ECHR: (i) classification of the offense under national law, (ii) the nature of the offense, and (iii) the nature and degree of severity of the penalty that the person risked incurring.

(3) The Nuremberg Tribunal did not feel that it violated *nullum crimen sine lege* doctrine even though the war crimes defendants were prosecuted under treaties which contained no language about individual criminal liability. The ICT-Y also has felt that it has not violated this doctrine even though prosecution of war crimes under common Article 3 of the Geneva Conventions is not mentioned in those treaties. Only until after the perpetration of those crimes was the ICT-Y Statute enacted that expressly allowed the prosecution of such crimes. The ICT-Y explained that the substantive prohibitions in the common Article 3 provisions were undoubtedly part of customary international law. *The Prosecutor v. Duško Tadić*, Decision on the Defence Motion on Jurisdiction (10 Aug. 1995) at 830.

Compare this approach to the U.S. Supreme Court's in *Cook v. United States*, 138 U.S. 157 (1891) in which the Court stated that as long as the crime was prohibited and there was no change in punishment, "[a]n *ex post facto* law does not involve, in any of its definitions, a change of the place of trial of an alleged offense after its commission." *Id.* at 183. For a fuller discussion of these issues, *see* Jordan J. Paust, *Nullum Crimen and Related Claims*, 25 DENVER J. IN'L L. & POL'Y 321 (1997).

G. Double Jeopardy or *Non Bis In Idem*

A. P. v. Italy
UN Human Rights Committee
Communication No. 204/1986
Inadmissibility Decision of 2 November 1987
2 SELECTED DECISIONS OF THE HUMAN RIGHTS COMMITTEE
UNDER THE OPTIONAL PROTOCOL
U.N. Doc. CCPR/C/OP/2 (1990) at 67

. . . .

1.   The author of the communication . . . is A. P., an Italian citizen . . . at present residing in France. He claims to be a victim of article 14, paragraph 7, of the Covenant by the Italian Government. . . .

2.1 The author states that he was convicted on 27 September 1979 by the Criminal Court of Lugano, Switzerland, for complicity in the crime of conspiring to exchange currency notes amounting to the sum of 297,650,000 lire, which was the ransom paid for the release of a person who had been kidnapped in Italy in 1978. He was sentenced to two years' imprisonment, which he duly served. He was subsequently expelled from Switzerland.

2.2 It is claimed that the Italian Government, in violation of the principle of *non bis in idem*, is now seeking to punish the author for the same offence as that for which he had already been convicted in Switzerland. He was thus indicted by an Italian court in 1981 (after which he apparently left Italy for France) and on 7 March 1983 the Milan Court of Appeal convicted him *in absentia*. On 11 January 1985, the Second Division of the Court of Cassation in Rome upheld the conviction and sentenced him to four years' imprisonment and a fine of 2 million lire.

2.3 The author invokes article 14, paragraph 17, of the Covenant, which provides:

No one shall be liable to be tried or punished again for an offence for which he has already been finally convicted or acquitted in accordance with the law and penal procedures of each country.

He further rejects the Italian Government's interpretation of this provision as being applicable only with regard to judicial decisions of the same State and not with regard to decisions of different States.

2.4 The author further indicates that in 1984 the Italian Government addressed an extradition request to the Government of France, but that the Paris Court of Appeal, by judgment of 13 November 1985, denied extradition because it would violate French *ordre public* to make the author suffer two terms of imprisonment on the same effects.

. . . .

5.1 In it submission . . . the State party . . . . argues that Mr. P. was tried for two different offences in Switzerland and in Italy.

. . . .

5.3 The State party . . . rejects the author's contention that article 14, paragraph 7, of the Covenant protects the principle of "international *non bis in idem*". In the opinion of the State party, article 14, paragraph 7, must be understood as referring exclusively to the relationships between judicial decisions of a single State and not between those of different States.

. . . .

7.3 With regard to the admissibility of the communication. . . the Committee has examined the State party's objection that the communication is incompatible with the provisions of the Covenant, since Article 14, paragraph 7, does not guarantee *non bis in idem* with regard to the national jurisdictions of two or more States. The Committee observes that this provision prohibits double jeopardy only with regard to an offence adjudicated in a given State.

8. In light of the above, the Human Rights Committee concludes that the communication is . . . inadmissible *ratione materiae* . . . .

❖ ❖ ❖

Questions & Comments

(1) Consider Article 10 of the Statute of the International Criminal Tribunal for the Former Yugoslavia:

1. No person shall be tried before a national court for acts constituting serious violations of international humanitarian law under the present Statute, for which he or she has already been tried by the International Tribunal.

2. A person who has been tried by a national court for acts constituting serious violations of international humanitarian law may be subsequently tried by the International Tribunal only if:

(a) the act for which he or she was convicted was characterized as an ordinary crime; or

(b) the national court proceedings were not impartial or independent, were designed to shield the accused from international criminal responsibility, or the case was not diligently prosecuted.

3. In considering the penalty to be imposed on a person convicted of a crime under the present Statute, the International Tribunal shall take into account the extent to which any penalty imposed by a national court on the same person for the same act has already been served.

Report of the Secretary-General Pursuant to Paragraph 2 of Security Council Resolution 808 (1993), U.N. Doc. S/25704 (3 May 1993) at 39-40.

(2) Is the UN Human Rights Committee's decision in *A. P. v. Italy* incongruous with the ICT-Y Statute?

PART FIVE: PUNISHMENT

Chapter 13.   Principles

Charter of the International Military Tribunal

Article 27.

The Tribunal shall have the right to impose upon a Defendant, on conviction, death or such other punishment as shall be determined by it to be just.

Article 28.

In addition to any punishment imposed by it, the Tribunal shall have the right to deprive the convicted person of any stolen property and order its delivery to the Control Council for Germany.

Article 29.

In case of guilt, sentences shall be carried out in accordance with the orders of the Control Council for Germany, which may at any time reduce or otherwise alter the sentences, but may not increase the severity thereof. If the Control Council for Germany, after any Defendant has been convicted and sentenced, discovers fresh evidence which, in its opinion, would found a fresh charge against him, the Council shall report accordingly to the Committee established under Article 14 hereof, for such action as they may consider proper, having regard to the interests of justice.

Statutes

Statute of the International Criminal Tribunal (for the Fmr. Yugoslavia)

Article 24

1. The penalty imposed by the Trial Chamber shall be limited to imprisonment. In determining the terms of imprisonment, the Trial Chambers shall have recourse to the general practice regarding prison sentences in the courts of the former Yugoslavia.
2. In imposing the sentences, the Trial Chambers should take into account such factors as the gravity of the offence and the individual circumstances of the convicted person.
3. In addition to imprisonment, the Trial Chambers may order the return of any property and proceeds acquired by criminal conduct, including by means of duress, to their rightful owners.

Chapter 13. Principles

Statute of the International Criminal Tribunal for Rwanda

Article 23

1.The penalty imposed by the Trial Chamber shall be limited to imprisonment. In determining the terms of imprisonment, the Trial Chambers shall have recourse to the general practice regarding prison sentences in the courts of Rwanda.

2. In imposing the sentences, the Trial Chambers should take into account such factors as the gravity of the offence and the individual circumstances of the convicted person.

3. In addition to imprisonment, the Trial Chambers may order the return of any property and proceeds acquired by criminal conduct, including by means of duress, to their rightful owners.

Statute of the International Criminal Court

Article 77 Applicable penalties

1. Subject to article 110, the Court may impose one of the following penalties on a person convicted of a crime under article 5 of this Statute:

(a) Imprisonment for a specified number of years, which may not exceed a maximum of 30 years; or

(b) A term of life imprisonment when justified by the extreme gravity of the crime and the individual circumstances of the convicted person.

2. In addition to imprisonment, the Court may order:

(a) A fine under the criteria provided for in the Rules of Procedure and Evidence;

(b) A forfeiture of proceeds, property and assets derived directly or indirectly from that crime, without prejudice to the rights of bona fide third parties.

Article 78 Determination of the sentence

1. In determining the sentence, the Court shall, in accordance with the Rules of Procedure and Evidence, take into account such factors as the gravity of the crime and the individual circumstances of the convicted person.

2. In imposing a sentence of imprisonment, the Court shall deduct the time, if any, previously spent in detention in accordance with an order of the Court. The Court may deduct any time otherwise spent in detention in connection with conduct underlying the crime.

3. When a person has been convicted of more than one crime, the Court shall pronounce a sentence for each crime and a joint sentence specifying the total period of imprisonment. This period shall be no less than the highest individual sentence pronounced and shall not exceed 30 years' imprisonment or a sentence of life imprisonment in conformity with article 77, paragraph 1 (b).

Article 110   Review by the Court concerning reduction of sentence

1. The State of enforcement shall not release the person before expiry of the sentence pronounced by the Court.

2. The Court alone shall have the right to decide any reduction of sentence, and shall rule on the matter after having heard the person.

3. When the person has served two thirds of the sentence, or 25 years in the case of life imprisonment, the Court shall review the sentence to determine whether it should be reduced. Such a review shall not be conducted before that time.

4. In its review under paragraph 3, the Court may reduce the sentence if it finds that one or more of the following factors are present:

(a) The early and continuing willingness of the person to cooperate with the Court in its investigations and prosecutions;

(b) The voluntary assistance of the person in enabling the enforcement of the judgements and orders of the Court in other cases, and in particular providing assistance in locating assets subject to orders of fine, forfeiture or reparation which may be used for the benefit of victims; or

(c) Other factors establishing a clear and significant change of circumstances sufficient to justify the reduction of sentence, as provided in the Rules of Procedure and Evidence.

5. If the Court determines in its initial review under paragraph 3 that it is not appropriate to reduce the sentence, it shall thereafter review the question of reduction of sentence at such intervals and applying such criteria as provided for in the Rules of Procedure and Evidence.

❖　❖　❖

Questions & Comments

(1) Principles governing the international law of punishment are codified in international instruments, such as the Statutes of the ICT-Y, ICT-R, and ICC. But, there are other international law principles which can be gleaned by discovering which social, moral, and political interests are served by international criminal law sanctions but not sanctions from domestic criminal law traditions that do not incorporate international law. Assuming that the imposition of the death penalty is no longer a viable sentence under international criminal law,[1] let us list existing and potential measures for imposing punishment under both domestic and international criminal law:

1.　Imprisonment for varying lengths of time
2.　Restriction to "half-way house," probation, and/or parole

---

[1] In recent years, the death penalty has become less an option with the adoption of several abolitionist protocols to human rights treaties (see Chapter 14 below) and the disallowance of the death penalty by the Statutes of the ICT-Y, ICT-R, and ICC.

3. Monetary penalties (both compensatory and punitive)
4. Return of property, assets, and proceeds
5. Ineligibility to participate in activities of government, political party, military, firm, or enterprise
6. Public censure
7. Public statement of contrition and full disclosure of crimes and assets
8. Community service (in and/or outside prison)

What are the interests served by these measures, respectively? They include:

1. Restriction of liberty to protect the public from further harm
2. Compensating the victim and the public for the crime
3. Deterring offenders and others from committing similar crimes in the future[2]
4. Eliminating head of state and other official immunities for crimes
5. Preventing peculiarly systemic or widespread criminal acts
6. Punishing the offenders through the restriction of his/her liberty, comfort, and forced labor
7. Shaming the offender
8. Disclosure of other criminals and criminal acts
9. Public education
10. Societal reconciliation[3]
11. Rehabilitation of the offender[4] and reintegration into society
12. Safeguard offenders against excessive, disproportionate or arbitrary punishment
13. Define, coordinate, and harmonize powers, duties, and functions of courts and administrative agencies responsible for dealing with offenders[5]
14. Differentiation among offenders with a view to just individuation in their treatment[6]

Of the above interests that are not generally considered shared with domestic criminal justice systems that do not incorporate international law are (i) the elimination of official immunities, (ii) the prevention of systemic or widespread crimes, and (iii) societal reconciliation. Accordingly, these three goals are particularly associated with *international* criminal law and serve to formulate distinctive principles of the international criminal law of punishment.

---

[2] MODEL PENAL CODE §1.02(2) (1985).

[3] One commentator has noted that the ICC "will help end cycles of violence by offering justice as an alternative to revenge, and it will contribute to the process of reconciliation by replacing the stigma of collective guilt with the catharsis of individual responsibility." Norman Dorsen, "The U.S. and the War Crimes Court: A Glass Half Full," 2 *Lawyers Committee for Human Rights Advisor* 1 (Fall 1998).

[4] MODEL PENAL CODE §1.02(2) (1985).

[5] *Id.*

[6] MODEL PENAL CODE §1.02(2) (1985).

Can these interests be used to justify deviation from domestic criminal law sanctions? Recall that in determining the terms of imprisonment, the Trial Chambers of the ICT-Y and ICT-R have recourse to the general practice regarding prison sentences in the courts of Rwanda and the former Yugoslavia, respectively. However, the ICC does not make mention of using domestic law to determine terms of imprisonment.

Can these interests be used both to determine the particular sanction employed as well as the severity of sanction? For example, if the offender was a military commander, an appropriate sanction would be ineligibility to continue military service. This sanction serves to prevent the perpetration of future systemic or widespread crimes whose perpetration is facilitated by the military command structure.[7] However, if a offender committed a single crime while acting in a private capacity, probably none of the goals would come into play, and no deviation from domestic criminal justice sanctions should take place.[8]

In summary, aside from the codification of principles governing punishment contained in the Statutes of the ICT-Y, ICT-R, and ICC, there appear to be three additional principles that can be extracted from international criminal law:

> In imposing sanctions, deviation from domestic law practice is allowed only to achieve any of the following goals:
>
> 1. eliminating official immunities
> 2. preventing systemic or widespread crimes
> 3. societal reconciliation

(2) What other methods can be used to glean international law principles of punishment?

(3) Why do you think the ICC Statute only authorizes imprisonment of up to thirty years or life imprisonment?

(4) The ICT-Y in *The Prosecutor v. Drazen Erdemovic*, Int'l Crim. Trib.-Yugo, Trial Chamber, Sentencing Decision (5 March 1998), examined the following mitigating factors in sentencing: (i) personal circumstances (*e.g.,* age, family situation, background, character), (ii) admission of guilt, (iii) remorse, and (iv) duress. Int'l Crim. Trib.-Yugo, 20 *Bulletin* 2 (20 March 1998).

(5) The sentences imposed so far by the ICT-Y have been comparatively lenient. For example, Tadic received only twenty years for committing both crimes against humanity

---

[7] The Inter-American Commission has held that the prohibition of the presidential candidacy of a former chief of state who had been put in power by a military coup d'etat is compatible with the ACHR. *Ríos Montt v. Guatemala*, Report 30/93, Case 10,804, ANNUAL REPORT OF THE INTER-AMERICAN COMMISSION ON HUMAN RIGHTS 1993 206 (1994).

[8] Indeed, it is doubtful that an international criminal tribunal would prosecute such a person, unless the domestic courts failed to do so. *See* Art. 17(1)(a)-(b), ICC Statute.

and war crimes. Erdemovic received only five years for committing a war crime. Compare these sentences to U.S. sentences of life-imprisonment for non-violent drug trafficking.

Chapter 14. Death Penalty: Its Applications and Death Row Phenomenon

Treaties

International Covenant on Civil and Political Rights

Article 6

1. Every human being has the inherent right to life. This right shall be protected by law. No one shall be arbitrarily deprived of his life.

2. In countries which have not abolished the death penalty, sentence of death may be imposed only for the most serious crimes in accordance with the law in force at the time of the commission of the crime and not contrary to the provisions of the present Covenant and to the Convention on the Prevention and Punishment of the Crime of Genocide. This penalty can only be carried out pursuant to a final judgement rendered by a competent court.

3. When deprivation of life constitutes the crime of genocide, it is understood that nothing in this article shall authorize any State Party to the present Covenant to derogate in any way from any obligation assumed under the provisions of the Convention on the Prevention and Punishment of the Crime of Genocide.

4. Anyone sentenced to death shall have the right to seek pardon or commutation of the sentence. Amnesty, pardon or commutation of the sentence of death may be granted in all cases.

5. Sentence of death shall not be imposed for crimes committed by persons below eighteen years of age and shall not be carried out on pregnant women.

6. Nothing in this article shall be invoked to delay or to prevent the abolition of capital punishment by any State Party to the present Covenant.

Second Optional Protocol to the
International Covenant on Civil and Political Rights
Aiming at the Abolition of the Death Penalty[1]

Article 1

1. No one within the jurisdiction of a State Party to the present Protocol shall be executed.

---

[1] G.A. res. 44/128, annex, 44 U.N. GAOR Supp. (No. 49) at 207, U.N. Doc. A/44/49 (1989), *entered into force* July 11, 1991.

2. Each State Party shall take all necessary measures to abolish the death penalty within its jurisdiction.

European Convention on Human Rights, Protocol No. 6

Article 1

The death penalty shall be abolished. No one shall be condemned to such penalty or executed.

American Convention on Human Rights

Article 4. RIGHT TO LIFE.

1. Every person has the right to have his life respected. This right shall be protected by law and, in general, from the moment of conception. No one shall be arbitrarily deprived of his life.

2. In countries that have not abolished the death penalty, it may be imposed only for the most serious crimes and pursuant to a final judgment rendered by a competent court and in accordance with a law establishing such punishment, enacted prior to the commission of the crime. The application of such punishment shall not be extended to crimes to which it does not presently apply.

3. The death penalty shall not be reestablished in states that have abolished it.

4. In no case shall capital punishment be inflicted for political offenses or related common crimes.

5. Capital punishment shall not be imposed upon persons who, at the time the crime was committed, were under 18 years of age or over 70 years of age; nor shall it be applied to pregnant women.

6. Every person condemned to death shall have the right to apply for amnesty, pardon, or commutation of sentence, which may be granted in all cases. Capital punishment shall not be imposed while such a petition is pending decision by the competent authority.

Article 5(3) and (6)

3. Punishment shall not be extended to any person other than the criminal.
. . . .
6. Punishments consisting of deprivation of liberty shall have as an essential aim the reform and social readaptation of the prisoners.

Protocol to the
American Convention on Human Rights to Abolish the Death Penalty

ARTICLE 1

The States Parties to this Protocol shall not apply the death penalty in their territory to any person subject to their jurisdiction.

Convention on Human Rights and Fundamental Freedoms
of the Commonwealth of Independent States

Article 2

1. Everyone's right to life shall be protected by law. No one shall be deprived of his life intentionally. Until abolished, the death penalty may be applied only in pursuance of a judicial sentence for particularly grave offences.

2. As a rule, women may not be sentenced to the death penalty. The death penalty may not be imposed on women who are pregnant at the time of sentencing, nor may it be executed in the case of women who are pregnant when the sentence is to be carried out.

3. The death penalty may not be imposed on persons for crimes committed by them before they attained the age of eighteen years.

4. Deprivation of life shall not be regarded as inflicted in contravention of the provisions of this Article when it results from the use of force solely in such cases of extreme necessity and necessary defenses are provided for in national legislation.

Arab Charter on Human Rights

Article 10

Sentence of death will be imposed only for the most serious crimes; every individual sentenced to death has the right to seek pardon or commutation of the sentence.

Article 11

Under no circumstances may the death penalty be imposed for a political offense.

Article 12

Sentences of death shall not be carried-out on persons below eighteen years of age, or a pregnant woman, until she gives birth, or a nursing mother, until two years have passed from the date of [her child's] birth.

Pinkerton and Roach v. United States
Resolution No. 3/87, Case 9647
Inter-American Commission on Human Rights
ANNUAL REPORT OF THE
1986-1987 INTER-AMERICAN COMMISSION ON HUMAN RIGHTS 147
OEA/Ser.L/V/II/71, doc. 9 rev. 1 (1987)

. . . . .

A. *Summary of the facts and Petitioners' complaint*

1. The Petitioners are James Terry Roach and Jay Pinkerton who were sentenced to death and executed in the United States for crimes which they were adjudged to have committed, and which they perpetrated before their eighteenth birthdays.

. . . .

3. James Terry Roach was convicted of the rape and murder of a fourteen year old girl and the murder of her seventeen year old boyfriend. Roach committed these crimes at the age of seventeen and was sentenced to death in the General Session Court, Richland County, South Carolina on 16 December 1977. Roach petitioned the United States Supreme Court for a writ of certiorari on three separate occasions. All petitions were denied. Roach also exhausted all appeals to the state and federal courts, and on 10 January 1986 was executed.

4. Jay Pinkerton was convicted of murder and attempted rape which he committed at the age of seventeen. The death [sentence] was appealed to the Texas Supreme Court which affirmed the trial court's decision. The United States Supreme Court denied Pinkerton's writ of certiorari on 7 October 1985. Pinkerton was executed on 15 May 1986.

. . . .

6. In their complaint to the Commission, the petitioners allege that the United States has violated Article I (right to life), Article VII (special protection of children), and Article XXVI (prohibition against cruel, infamous or unusual punishment) of the American Declaration of the Rights and Duties of Man by executing persons for crimes committed before their eighteenth birthday. The Petitioners allege a violation of their right to life guaranteed under the American Declaration, as informed by customary international law, which prohibits the execution of persons who committed crimes under the age of eighteen.

. . . .

V. OPINION OF THE COMMISSION

A. *Point at issue*

43. The question presented by the petitioners in the present case is whether the absence of a federal prohibition within U.S. domestic law on the execution of persons who committed serious crimes under the age of 18 is inconsistent with human rights standards applicable to the United States under the Inter-American system.

Crimes in the United States fall under either state or federal jurisdiction. A defendant may be tried in federal court if he is charged with the commission of a crime under federal law, or he may appeal to a federal court from a state court under certain circumstances. A great deal of autonomy has been left to the states in prescribing the appropriate

323

punishment for criminal conduct. However, all punishment must be in conformity with the United States Constitution as interpreted by the Supreme Court.

B. *The international obligation of the United States under the American Declaration*

44. The American Declaration is silent on the issue of capital punishment. Article I of the American Declaration reads as follows:

> Every human being has the right to life, liberty and the security of his person.

45. The American Convention on Human Rights, on the other hand, refers specifically to capital punishment in five of its provisions. Article 4 of the American Convention . . . protects the right to life . . . .
. . . .

46. The international obligation of the United States of America, as a member of the Organization of American States (OAS), under the jurisdiction of the Inter-American Commission on Human Rights is governed by the Charter of the OAS (Bogotá, 1948), as amended by the Protocol of Buenos Aires on 27 February 1967, ratified by the United States on 23 April 1968.

47. The United States is a member State of the Organization of American States, but is not a State party to the American Convention on Human Rights, and, therefore, cannot be found to be in violation of Article 4(5) of the Convention, since as the Commission stated in *Case 2141* (United States), para. 31: "it would be impossible to impose upon the United States Government or that of any other State member of the OAS, by means of 'interpretation,' an international obligation based upon a treaty that such State has not duly accepted or ratified."[2]

48. As a consequence of articles 3 *j*, 16, 51 *e*, 112 and 150 of the Charter, the provisions of other instruments of the OAS on human rights acquired binding force. Those instruments, approved with the vote of the U.S. Government, are the following:

- American Declaration of the Rights and Duties of Man (Bogotá, 1948)
- Statute and Regulations of the IACHR [Inter-American Commission on Human Rights]

49. The Statute provides that, for the purposes of such instruments, the IACHR is the organ of the OAS entrusted with the competence to promote the observance of and respect for human rights. For the purpose of the Statute, human rights are understood to be the

---

[2] Case 2141 (United States) Res. 23/81 of 6 March 1981 OAS/Ser.L/V/II.52, doc. 48, para. 16 (1981) in 1980-1981 Annual Report of the Inter-American Commission on Human Rights OEA/Ser.L/V/II.54, doc. 9, rev. 1 (16 October 1981) at 25 *et seq.*, and also in OAS, Inter-American Commission on Human Rights, Ten Years of Activities, 1971-1981 (1982) at 186 *et seq.*

rights set forth in the American Declaration in relation to States not parties to the American Convention on Human Rights (San José, 1969).

. . . .

D. *General principles applicable to the present case*

55. The concept of *jus cogens* is derived from ancient law concepts of a "superior order" of legal norms, which the laws of man or nations may not contravene. The norms of *jus cogens* have been described by publicists as comprising "international public policy." They are "rules which have been accepted, either expressly by treaty or tacitly by custom, as being necessary to protect the public interest of the society of States or to maintain the standards of public morality recognized by them."

According to Ian Brownlie, the major distinguishing feature of rules of *jus cogens* is their "relative indelibility." Brownlie suggests certain examples of *jus cogens* such as: "the prohibition of aggressive war, the law of genocide, the principle of racial non-discrimination, crimes against humanity, and the rules prohibiting trade in slaves and policy."[3]

Since the acceptance of norms of *jus cogens* is still subject to some debate in some sectors, it might be argued that the International Court of Justice did not consider the prohibition against genocide, for example, to be a norm of *jus cogens*. It has been argued, however, that the World Court has made "indirect references" the concept of *jus cogens*, without actually calling it such by name, in the advisory opinion on the *Reservations to the Genocide Convention* case, in which the Court stated:

> . . . that the principles underlying the Convention are principles which are recognized by civilized nations as binding on States, even without any conventional obligation.

The rule prohibiting genocide would be binding on States not parties to the Genocide Convention, even if derived only from customary international law, without having acquired the status of *jus cogens*, but it achieves the status of *jus cogens* precisely because it is the kind of rule that it would shock the conscience of mankind and the standards of public morality for a State to protest.

The International Court of Justice, in a later case, categorized the prohibition of genocide as an obligation *erga omnes*. Whereas the ICJ does not make reference to the concept *jus cogens*, it has been suggested that the examples given of obligations *erga omnes* are examples of what the ICJ would consider to be norms of *jus cogens*. The following distinction between obligations of a State vis-à-vis the international community (*erga omnes*) and vis-a-vis another State is taken from the judgment in the *Barcelona Traction* Case:

> In these circumstances it is logical that the Court should first address itself to what was originally presented as the subject-matter of the this preliminary

---

[3] *See*, Ian Brownlie: PRINCIPLES OF PUBLIC INTERNATIONAL LAW, Clarendon Press, Oxford (1979) at 513.

objection: namely the question of the right of Belgium to exercise diplomatic protection of Belgian shareholders in a company which is a juristic entity incorporated in Canada, the measures complained of having been taken in relation not to any Belgian national but to the company itself.

When a State admits into its territory foreign investments of foreign nationals, whether natural or juristic persons, it is bound to extend to them the protection of the law and assumes obligations concerning the treatment to be afforded them. These obligations, however, are neither absolute nor unqualified. In particular, an essential distinction should be drawn between the obligations of a State towards the international community as a whole, and those arising vis-à-vis another State in the field of diplomatic protection. By their very nature the former are the concern of all States. In view of the importance of the rights involved, all States can be held to have a legal interest in their protection; they are obligations *erga omnes*.

Such obligations derive, for example, in contemporary international law, from the outlawing of acts of aggression, and of genocide, as also from the principles and rules concerning the basic rights of the human person, including protection from slavery and racial discrimination. Some of the corresponding rights of protection have entered into the body of general international law (*Reservations to the Convention on the Prevention and Punishment of the Crime of Genocide*, Advisory Opinion, I.C.J. Reports 1951, p. 23); others are conferred by international instruments of a universal or quasi-universal character.

Obligations the performance of which is the subject of diplomatic protection are not of the same category.

As to whether "the principles and rules concerning the basic rights of the human person" is intended to mean that all codified human rights provisions contained in international treaties are embraced by the concept of *jus cogens* is an issue that is both controversial and beyond the scope of the matter presented for the Commission to decide.

56. The Commission finds that in the members States of the OAS there is recognized a norm of *jus cogens* which prohibits the State execution of children. This norm is accepted by all the States of the inter-American system, including the United States. The response of the U.S. Government to the petition in this case affirms that "[A]ll states, moreover, have juvenile justice systems; none permits its juvenile courts to impose the death penalty."

57. The Commission finds that this case arises, not because of doubt concerning the existence of an international norm as to the prohibition of the execution of children but because the United States disputes the allegation that there exists consensus as regards the age of majority. Specifically, what needs to be examined is the United States law and practice, as adopted by different states, to transfer adolescents charged with heinous crimes to adult criminal courts where they are tried and may be sentenced as adults.

58. Since the federal Government of the United States has not preempted this issue, under the U.S. constitutional system the individual states are free to exercise their discretion as to whether or not to allow capital punishment in their states and to determine the minimum age at which a juvenile may be transferred to an adult criminal court where the death penalty may be imposed. Thirteen states and the U.S. capital have abolished the

death penalty entirely. As regards the other states which have enacted death penalty statutes since the *Furman* decision, these states have adopted death penalty statutes which either 1) prohibit the execution of persons who committed capital crimes under the age of eighteen, or 2) allow for juveniles to be transferred to adult criminal courts where they may be sentenced to the death penalty. It is the discretion and practice of this second group of states which has become the subject of our analysis. Whereas approximately ten retentionist states have now enacted legislation barring the execution of under-18 offenders, a hodge-podge of legislation characterizes the other states which allow transfer of juvenile offenders to adult courts from age 17 to as young as age 10, and some states have no specific minimum age. The Indiana state statute (*supra*) which allows a ten year old to be judged before an adult criminal court and potentially sentenced to death shocks this Commission.

59. The juvenile justice system was established in the United States at the turn of the century as a result of reformist efforts to mitigate the harshness of the adult criminal justice system. Under common law, children under the age of seven were conclusively presumed to have no criminal capacity and for children from age seven to fourteen, the presumption was rebuttable and the child could be convicted of a crime and executed. By a long series of statutory changes this age has been steadily increased, and the age of criminal incapacity is now set at 14 in most states. Consequently a child below the statutory age may be prosecuted by an adult criminal court but would nor be adjudged responsible for a crime, the child would be adjudged a juvenile delinquent.

60. The Commission is convinced by the U.S. Government's argument that there does not now exist a norm of customary international law establishing 18 to be the minimum age for imposition of the death penalty. Nonetheless, in light of the increasing numbers of States which are ratifying the American Convention on Human Rights and the United Nations Covenant on Civil and Political Rights, and modifying their domestic legislation in conformity with these instruments, the norm is emerging. As mentioned above, thirteen states and the U.S. capital have abolished the death penalty entirely and nine retentionist states have abolished it for offenders under the age of 18.

61. The Commission, however, does not find the age question dispositive of the issue before it, which is whether the absence of a federal prohibition within U.S. domestic law on the execution of juveniles, who committed serious crimes under the age of 18, is in violation of the American Declaration.

62. The Commission finds that the diversity of state practice in the U.S. — reflected in the fact that some states have abolished the death penalty, while others allow a potential threshold limit of applicability as low as 10 years of age — results in very different sentences for the commission of the same crime. The deprivation by the State of an offender's life should not be made subject to the fortuitous element of where the crime took place. Under the present system of laws in the United States, a hypothetical sixteen year old who commits a capital offense in Virginia may potentially be subject to the death penalty, whereas if the same individual commits the same offense on the other side of the Memorial Bridge, in Washington, D.C., where the death penalty has been abolished for adults as well as for juveniles, the sentence will not be death.

63. For the federal Government of the United States to leave the issue of the application of the death penalty to juveniles to the discretion of state officials results in a patchwork scheme of legislation which makes the severity of the punishment dependent,

not, primarily, on the nature of the crime committed, but on the location where it was committed. Ceding to state legislatures the determination of whether a juvenile may be executed is not of the same category as granting states the discretion to determine the age of majority for purposes of purchasing alcoholic beverages or consenting to matrimony. The failure of the federal government to preempt the states as regards this most fundamental right — the right to life — results in a pattern of legislative arbitrariness throughout the United States which results in the arbitrary deprivation of life and inequality before the law, contrary to Articles I and II of the American Declaration of the Rights and Duties of Man, respectively.

CONCLUSION

64. The Commission concludes, by 5 votes to 1, that the United States Government violated Article I (right to life) of the American Declaration of the Rights and Duties of Man in executing James Terry Roach and Jay Pinkerton.

65. The Commission concludes by 5 votes to 1, that the United States violated Article II (right to equality before the law) of the American Declaration of the Rights and Duties of Man in executing James Terry Roach and Jay Pinkerton.

❖ ❖ ❖

Questions & Comments

(1) The major contention of the Commission in *Pinkerton & Roach v. United States* turned on whether there the prohibition on capital punishment for crimes committed by minors could be considered a peremptory norm. How widespread must a norm be to achieve such a status? Recall that evidence of a peremptory norm can be established expressly by the adoption of a treaty or domestic statute, or implicitly through practice. Thus while only nineteen states have adopted the American Convention on Human Rights with its explicit prohibition on the execution of persons for acts committed before the age, the practice of OAS member states suggests that there is broad consensus on this norm.

In fact, the Commission ends up agreeing that even if there is a norm against executing children there is no consensus on what age marks the close of this protected status. While the American Convention specifies 18 (as well as over 70) there is no strong basis for finding that this precise age has been widely accepted in the practice of member states. Is there any better evidence of an enforceable norm against the execution of minors generally?

The Commission nonetheless holds the U.S. in violation because by permitting each state to establish its own rule (within broad constitutional limits) a degree of arbitrariness enters into the judgment so that where you commit a crime becomes determinative of life or death. Does this suggest that on matters of international normative importance, even which do not involve *jus cogens,* the nation-state has responsibility for bringing local diversity into conformity? Francisco Forrest Martin, *et al.*, 1 INTERNATIONAL HUMAN RIGHTS LAW & PRACTICE: CASES, TREATIES AND MATERIALS 449 (1997).

(2) How convincing do you find the Commission's inequality argument on the disparate state impact of the death penalty in juvenile cases?

328

(3) Can a *jus cogens* norm be only regional? If so, how small regionally can it be? Does the norm have to be linked with an international body, such as the Commission? Can there be conflicting *jus cogens* norms from different regions? Can or should there be conflicting *jus cogens* norms from different regions even though the texts of the regional treaties which reflect the norm are identical? In the case of executing persons under age eighteen, is it not sufficient to note that numerous widely accepted, global and regional human rights treaties prohibit such executions as a non-derogable right, and, therefore, the prohibition reflects a *jus cogens* norm?

Can *jus cogens* norms not be part of customary international law? How important is the customary international law requirement of "widely-accepted practice" compared with its other requirement of *opinio juris*?

(4) In *Thompson v. Oklahoma*, 487 U.S. 815 (1988) and *Stanford v. Kentucky*, 492 U.S. 361 (1989), the U.S. Supreme Court explored the 8th Amendment implications of executing juveniles. In *Thompson* the Court held that the execution of a 15-year-old would be "cruel and unusual" punishment". *Stanford*, however, upheld death sentences for a 16- and 17-year-old (in two cases combined by the Court for review). Both opinions placed heavy emphasis on the practice of states within the United States. In *Stanford*, Justice Scalia specifically rejected arguments that international precedents be considered. "We emphasize that it is American conceptions of a decency that are dispositive, rejecting the contention of petitioners and their various *amici* . . . . that the sentencing practices of other nations, particularly other democracies, can be relevant . . ." *Id.* at 370 n. 1. The dissent, however, cited a number of international law sources including Article 6(5) of the International Covenant on Civil and Political Rights as well as Article 4(5) of the American Convention on Human Rights. *Stanford v. Kentucky*, 492 U.S. 361, 390 (Brennan, J. dissenting). However, the Court did not address a customary international law claim. How would you argue a customary international law claim? How would you argue a claim under the ICCPR – not withstanding the fact that the Senate made a declaration indicating that the right to life is not self-executing?

Soering v. United Kingdom
European Court of Human Rights
161 Eur. Ct. H.R. (ser. A) (1989)
11 E.H.R.R. 439 (1989)

. . . .

FACTS:

I. Particular circumstances of the case

11. The applicant, Mr Jens Soering, was born on 1 August 1966 and is a German national. He is currently detained in prison in England pending extradition to the United States of America to face charges of murder in the Commonwealth of Virginia.

12. The homicides in question were committed in Bedford County, Virginia, in March 1985. The victims, William Reginald Haysom (aged 72) and Nancy Astor Haysom (aged 53), were the parents of the applicant's girlfriend, Elizabeth Haysom, who is a Canadian national. Death in each case was the result of multiple and massive stab and

slash wounds to the neck, throat and body. At the time the applicant and Elizabeth Haysom, aged 18 and 20 respectively, were students at the University of Virginia. They disappeared together from Virginia in October 1985, but were arrested in England in April 1986 in connection with cheque fraud.

. . . .

[Soering applied to the European Commission of Human Rights alleging an Article 3 right to humane treatment violation. The Commission held that there had been no violation.]

DECISION [OF THE EUROPEAN COURT OF HUMAN RIGHTS]:

I.   Alleged breach of Article 3

80. The applicant alleged that the decision by the Secretary of State for the Home Department to surrender him to the authorities of the United States of America would, if implemented, give rise to a breach by the United Kingdom of Article 3 of the Convention, which provides:

'No one shall be subjected to torture or to inhuman or degrading treatment or punishment.'

. . . .

B. Application of Article 3 in the particular circumstances of the present case

. . . .

2.   Whether in the circumstances the risk of exposure to the 'death row phenomenon' would make extradition a breach of Article 3

(a) General considerations

100. As is established in the court's case law, ill-treatment, including punishment, must attain a minimum level of severity if it is to fall within the scope of Article 3. The assessment of this minimum is, in the nature of things, relative; it depends on all the circumstances of the case, such as the nature and context of the treatment or punishment, the manner and method if its execution, its duration, its physical or mental effects and, in some instances, the sex, age and state of health of the victim. [*See Ireland v. United Kingdom*, 25 Eur. Ct. H.R. (ser. A) at § 162 (1978); and *Tyrer v. United Kingdom*, 26 Eur. Ct. H.R. (ser. A0 at §§ 29 and 80 (1978).]

Treatment has been held by the Court to be both 'inhuman' because it was premeditated, was applied for hours at a stretch and 'caused, if not actual bodily injury, at least intense physical and mental suffering.' and also 'degrading' because it was 'such as to arouse in [its] victims feelings of fear, anguish and inferiority capable of humiliating and debasing them and possibly breaking their physical or moral resistance'. (*See Ireland v. United Kingdom*, § 167.) In order for a punishment or treatment associated with it to be 'inhuman' or 'degrading,' the suffering or humiliation involved must in any event go beyond that inevitable element of suffering or humiliation connected with a given form of legitimate punishment. (*See Tyrer v. United Kingdom*, loc cit.) In this connection, account is to be taken not only of the physical pain experienced but also, where there is a considerable delay before execution of the punishment, of the sentenced person's mental anguish of anticipating the violence he is to have inflicted on him.

101. Capital punishment is permitted under certain conditions by Article 2(1) of the convention, which reads:

> 'Everyone's right to life shall be protected by law. No one shall be deprived of his life intentionally save in the execution of a sentence of a court following his conviction of a crime for which this penalty is provided by law.'

In view of this wording, the applicant did not suggest that the death penalty *per se* violated Article 3. He, like the two Government Parties, agreed with the Commission that the extradition of a person to a country where he risks the death penalty does not in itself raise an issue under either Article 2 or Article 3. On the other hand, Amnesty International in their written comments argued that the evolving standards in Western Europe regarding the existence and use of the death penalty required that the death penalty should now be considered as an inhuman and degrading punishment within the meaning of Article 3.

102. Certainly, 'the Convention is a living instrument which . . . must be interpreted in the light of present-day conditions'; and, in assessing whether a given treatment or punishment is to be regarded as inhuman or degrading for the purposes of Article 3, 'the Court cannot but be influenced by the developments and commonly accepted standards in the penal policy of the member States of the Council of Europe in this field. (*See Tyrer v. United Kingdom*, § 31.) *De facto* the death penalty no longer exists in time of peace in the contracting States to the Convention. In the few Contracting States which retain the death penalty in law for some peacetime offences, death sentences, if ever imposed, are nowadays not carried out. This 'virtual consensus in Western European legal systems that the death penalty is, under current circumstances, no longer consistent with regional standards of justice,' to use the words of Amnesty International, is reflected in Protocol No 6 to the Convention, which provides for the abolition of the death penalty in time of peace. Protocol No 6 was opened for signature in April 1983, which in the practice of the Council of Europe indicates the absence of objection on the part of any of the Member States of the Organisation; it came into force in March 1985 and to date has been ratified by 13 Contracting States to the Convention, not however including the United Kingdom.

Whether these marked changes have the effect of bringing the death penalty *per se* within the prohibition of ill-treatment under Article 3 must be determined on the principles governing the interpretation of the Convention.

103. The Convention is to be read as a whole and Article 3 should therefore be construed in harmony with the provisions of Article 2. (*See, mutatis mutandis, Klass v. Germany*, § 68.) On this basis Article 3 evidently cannot have been intended by the drafters of the Convention to include a general prohibition of the death penalty since that would nullify the clear wording of Article 2(1).

Subsequent practice in national penal policy, in the form of a generalised abolition of capital punishment, could be taken as establishing the agreement of the Contracting States to abrogate the exception provided for under Article 2(1) and hence to remove a textual limit on the scope for evolutive interpretation of Article 3. However, Protocol No 6, as a subsequent written agreement, shows that the intention of the Contracting Parties as recently as 1983 was to adopt the normal method of amendment of the text in order to introduce a new obligation to abolish capital punishment in time of peace and, what is more, to do so by an optional instrument allowing each State to choose the moment when to undertake such an engagement. In these conditions, notwithstanding the special character of the Convention, Article 3 cannot be interpreted as generally prohibiting the death penalty.

104. That does not mean however that circumstances relating to a death sentence can never give rise to an issue under Article 3. The manner in which it is imposed or executed, the personal circumstances of the condemned person and a disproportionality to the gravity of the crime committed, as well as the conditions of detention awaiting execution, are examples of factors capable of bringing the treatment or punishment received by the condemned person with the proscription under Article 3. Present-day attitudes in the contracting States to capital punishment are relevant for the assessment whether the acceptable threshold of suffering or degradation has been exceeded.

(b) The particular circumstances

105. The applicant submitted that the circumstances to which he would be exposed as a consequence of the implementation of the Secretary of State's decision to return him to the United States, namely the 'death row phenomenon,' cumulatively constitute such serious treatment that his extradition would be contrary to Article 3. He cited in particular the delays in the appeal and review procedures following a death sentence, during which time he would be subject to increasing tension and psychological trauma; the fact, so he said, that the judge or jury in determining sentence is not obliged to take into account the defendant's age and mental state at the time of the offence; the extreme conditions of his future detention in 'death row' in Mecklenburg Correctional Center, where he expects to be the victim of violence and sexual abuse because of his age, colour and nationality; and the constant spectre of the execution itself, including the ritual of execution. He also relied on the possibility of extradition or deportation, which he would not oppose, to the Federal Republic of Germany as accentuating the disproportionality of the Secretary of State's decision.

The Government of the Federal Republic of Germany took the view that, taking all the circumstances together, the treatment awaiting the applicant in Virginia would go so far beyond treatment inevitably connected with the imposition and execution of a death penalty as to be 'inhuman' within the meaning of Article 3.

On the other hand, the conclusion expressed by the Commission was that the degree of severity contemplated by Article 3 would not be attained.

The United Kingdom Government shared this opinion. In particular, it disputed many of the applicant's factual allegations as to the conditions on death row in Mecklenburg and his expected fate there.

(i) Length of detention prior to execution

106. The period that a condemned prisoner can expect to spend on death row in Virginia before being executed is on average six to eight years. This length of time awaiting death, is, as the commission and the United Kingdom Government noted, in a

sense largely of the prisoner's own making in that he takes advantage of all avenues of appeal which are offered to him by Virginia law. The automatic appeal to the Supreme Court of Virginia normally takes no more than six months. The remaining time is accounted for by collateral attacks mounted by the prisoner himself in habeas corpus proceedings before both the State and Federal courts and in applications to the Supreme Court of the United States for *certiorari* review, the prisoner at each stage being able to seek a stay of execution. The remedies available under Virginia law serve the purpose of ensuring that the ultimate sanction of death is not unlawfully or arbitrarily imposed.

Nevertheless, just as some lapse of time between sentence and execution is inevitable if appeal safeguards are to be provided to the condemned person, so it is equally part of human nature that the person will cling to life by exploiting those safeguards to the full. However well-intentioned and even potentially beneficial is the provision of the complex of post-sentence procedures in Virginia, the consequence is that the condemned prisoner has to endure for many years the conditions on death row and the anguish and mounting tension of living in the ever-present shadow of death.

(ii) Conditions on death row

107. As to conditions in Mecklenburg Correctional Center, where the applicant could expect to be held if sentenced to death, the court bases itself on the facts which were uncontested by the United Kingdom Government, without finding it necessary to determine the reliability of the additional evidence adduced by the applicant, notably as to the risk of homosexual abuse and physical attack undergone by prisoners on death row.

The stringency of the custodial regime in Mecklenburg, as well as the services (medical, legal and social) and the controls (legislative, judicial and administrative) provided for inmates, are described in some detail above. In this connection, the United Kingdom Government drew attention to the necessary requirement of extra security for the safe custody of prisoners condemned to death for murder. Whilst it might thus well be justifiable in principle, the severity of a special regime such as that operated on death row in Mecklenburg is compounded by the fact of inmates being subject to it for a protracted period lasting on average six to eight years.

(iii) The applicant's age and mental state

108. At the time of the killings, the applicant was only 18 years old and there is some psychiatric evidence, which was not contested as such, that he 'was suffering from [such] an abnormality of mind . . . as substantially impaired his mental responsibility for his acts'.

Unlike Article 2 of the Convention, Article 6 of the 1966 International Covenant on Civil and Political Rights and Article 4 of the 1969 American Convention on Human Rights expressly prohibit the death penalty from being imposed on persons aged less than 18 at the time of commission of the offence. Whether or not such a prohibition be inherent in the brief and general language of Article 2 of the European Convention, its explicit enunciation in other, later international instruments, the former of which has been ratified by a large number of States parties to the European Convention, at the very least indicates that as a general principle the youth of the person concerned is a circumstance which is liable, with others, to put in question the compatibility with Article 3 of measures connected with a death sentence.

It is in line with the Court's case law to treat disturbed mental health as having the same effect for the application of Article 3.

109. Virginia law, as the United Kingdom Government and the Commission emphasised, certainly does not ignore these two factors. Under the Virginia Code account has to be taken of mental disturbance in a defendant, either as an absolute bar to conviction it if is judged to be sufficient to amount to insanity or, like age, as a fact in mitigation at the sentencing stage. Additionally, indigent capital murder defendants are entitled to the appointment of a qualified mental health expert to assist in the preparation of their submissions at the separate sentencing proceedings. These provisions in the Virginia Code undoubtedly serve, as the American courts have stated, to prevent the arbitrary or capricious imposition of the death penalty and narrowly to channel the sentencer's discretion. They do not however remove the relevance of age and mental condition in relation to the acceptability, under Article 3, of the 'death row phenomenon' for a given individual once condemned to death.

Although it is not for this Court to prejudge issues of criminal responsibility and appropriate sentence, the applicant's youth at the time of the offence and his then mental state, on the psychiatric evidence as it stands, are therefore to be taken into consideration as contributory factors tending, in his case, to bring the treatment on death row within the terms of Article 3.

. . . .

(c) Conclusion

111. For any prisoner condemned to death, some element of delay, between imposition and execution of the sentence and the experience of severe stress in conditions necessary for strict incarceration are inevitable. The democratic character of the Virginia legal system in general and the positive features of Virginia trial, sentencing and appeal procedures in particular are beyond doubt. The Court agrees with the Commission that the machinery of justice to which the applicant would be subject in the United States is in itself neither arbitrary nor unreasonable, but, rather, respects the rule of law and affords not inconsiderable procedural safeguards to the defendant in a capital trial. Facilities are available on death row for the assistance of inmates, notably through provision of psychological and psychiatric services.

However, in the Court's view, having regard to the very long period of time spent on death row in such extreme conditions, with the ever-present and mounting anguish of awaiting execution of the death penalty, and to the personal circumstances of the applicant, especially his age and mental state at the time of the offence, the applicant's extradition to the United States would expose him to a real risk of treatment going beyond the threshold set by Article 3. A further consideration of relevance is that in the particular instance the legitimate purpose of extradition could be achieved by another means which would not involve suffering of such exceptional intensity or duration.

Accordingly, the Secretary of State's decision to extradite the applicant to the United States would, if implemented, give rise to a breach of Article 3.

. . . .

Concurring Opinion of Judge de Meyer

. . . .

The second sentence of Article 2(1) of the Convention, as it was drafted in 1950, states that 'no one shall be deprived of his life intentionally save in the execution of a sentence of a court following his conviction of a crime for which this penalty is provided by law.'

In the circumstances of the present case, the applicant's extradition to the United States would subject him to the risk of being sentenced to death, and executed, in Virginia for a crime for which that penalty is not provided by the law of the United Kingdom.

When a person's right to life is involved, no requested State can be entitled to allow a requesting State to do what the requested State is not itself allowed to do.

If, as in the present case, the domestic law of a State does not provide the death penalty for the crime concerned, that State is not permitted to put the person concerned in a position where he may be deprived of his life for that crime at the hands of another State.

That consideration may already suffice to preclude the United Kingdom from surrendering the applicant to the United States.

There is also something more fundamental.

The second sentence of Article 2(1) of the Convention was adopted, nearly forty years ago, in particular historical circumstances, shortly after the second World War. In so far as it still may seem to permit, under certain conditions, capital punishment in time of peace, it does not reflect the contemporary situation, and is now overridden by the development of legal conscience and practice. (*See also* Art 6(2) and (6) of the International Covenant on Civil and Political Rights and Article 4(2) and (3) of the American Convention on Human Rights. The very wording of each of these provisions, adopted respectively in 1966 and in 1969, clearly reflects the evolution of legal conscience and practice towards the universal abolition of the death penalty.)

Such punishment is not consistent with the present state of European civilisation.

De facto, it no longer exists in any State Party to the Convention.

Its unlawfulness was recognised by the Committee of Ministers of the Council of Europe when it adopted in December 1982, and opened for signature in April 1983, the Sixth Protocol to the Convention, which to date has been signed by 16, and ratified by 13, Contracting States.

No State party to the Convention can in that context, even if it has not yet ratified the Sixth Protocol, be allowed to extradite any person if that person thereby incurs the risk of being put to death in the requesting State.

Extraditing somebody in such circumstances would be repugnant to European standards of justice, and contrary to the public order of Europe. (*See, mutatis mutandis,* the judgment of 27 February 1987 by the French Conseil d'Etat in the FIDAN case, [1987] Recueil Dalloz Sirey, 305-310.)

The applicant's surrender by the United Kingdom to the United States could only be lawful if the United States were to give absolute assurances that he will not be put to death if convicted of the crime he is charged with. (*See* the French FIDAN judgment referred to above.)

No such assurances were, or can be, obtained.

The Federal Government of the United States is unable to give any undertaking as to what may or may not be decided, or done, by the judicial and other authorities of the Commonwealth of Virginia.

In fact, the Commonwealth's Attorney dealing with the case intends to seek the death penalty and the Commonwealth's Governor has never commuted a death sentence since the imposition of the death penalty was resumed in 1977.

. . . .

❖ ❖ ❖

Questions & Comments

(1) The Commonwealth of Virginia subsequently gave assurances that Soering would not be executed if returned to Virginia. Consequently, Soering was returned, tried, convicted, and sentenced to two terms of life-imprisonment.

(2) In *Soering v. United Kingdom*, the European Court expressly declined to find that the death penalty inherently violated Article 3, on the grounds that Article 2(1), ECHR, allowed the death penalty. Evidence abounds that the death penalty has ceased to be a relevant penal practice in the nations covered by the ECHR, including its Sixth Protocol, which came into force in 1985 and explicitly bound its contracting parties to the complete abolition of the death penalty in time of peace. Presently, thirty states have ratified the Sixth Protocol. The Court has found the Sixth Protocol reason to refrain from a judicial reinterpretation of Article 2(1). While acknowledging that the Convention was a living document that could develop in line with evolving principles of justice among ECHR state-parties, the Court took the Sixth Protocol as evidence of a consensus among state-parties to resolve the issue through explicit legislative action by member states. The Court's reading of the Sixth Protocol as evidence of the will among the convention members to resolve the matter directly given that it represented the fruit of a long term and hard fought effort to begin the institutionalization of abolitionism within the European convention. William A. Schabas, THE ABOLITION OF THE DEATH PENALTY IN INTERNATIONAL LAW 228-38 (1993); Francisco Forrest Martin, *et al.*, 1 INTERNATIONAL HUMAN RIGHTS LAW & PRACTICE: CASES, TREATIES AND MATERIALS 459-60 (1997).

Recently, the Human Rights Chamber for Bosnia and Herzegovina has been examining cases in which military courts have ordered executions. Under Annex 6 of the Dayton Agreement, the Republic of Bosnia and Herzegovina, the Federation of Bosnia and Herzegovina, and the Republika Srpska are bound by the Sixth Protocol. Under Article 2 of the Sixth Protocol, the death penalty can be imposed only "in respect of acts committed in time of war or of imminent threat of war." However, the Dayton Agreement ended the civil war in Bosnia-Herzegovina; therefore, the Chamber found that the military court could not sentence individuals to death.

(3) The UN Human Rights Committee has held that prolonged detention on death row did not *per se* constitute a violation of Article 7, ICCPR, which forbids torture and inhuman treatment. *Pratt and Morgan v. Jamaica*, Communication Nos. 210/1986 and 225/1987, views adopted U.N. Doc. A/44/40, at § 13.6. As with the ECHR, attacks on the death penalty itself as inhuman treatment under Article 7 have run into treaty provisions allowing the death penalty. In the case of the ICCPR, Article 6 allows the death penalty.

In particular cases the Committee has found Article 7 violations surrounding the use of the death penalty. However, in cases involving extradition to the United States from a nation obligated under the Covenant, the Committee has declined to find Article 7 violations on death-row phenomenon grounds. However, the Committee has held that there are specific limits to using the death penalty.

For example, in *Ng v. Canada*, Communication No. 469/1991, views adopted 5 November 1993, U.N. Doc. CCPR/C/40/D/469/1991 (1994), the author had been charged with twelve murders in California and had been arrested for theft in Canada. When he was extradited, Mr. Ng authored a complaint to the Committee raising the conditions on death row but also adding a detailed attack on the use of gas asphyxiation then practiced in California. The Committee found on the basis of detailed evidence presented about the operation of the gas chamber that its use would violate the Covenant. The Committee concluded that execution by gas asphyxiation, should the death penalty be imposed on the author, would not meet the test of "least possible physical and mental suffering", and constituted cruel and inhuman treatment in violation of article 7. *Id.* at § 16.4.

In *Kindler v. Canada*, Communication No. 470/1991, views adopted 30 July 1993, U.N. Doc. CCPR/C/48/D/470/1001 (1993), the Committee upheld an extradition by Canada of a convicted murderer to the United States. Joseph Kindler was convicted of murder and kidnaping in Pennsylvania. The same jury voted to recommend death, but before his formal sentencing hearing in front of the judge he escaped custody . Some months later he was arrested in Quebec. The United States sought extradition which was granted by a Canadian court. The Canadian/U.S. extradition treaty allowed a state which does not practice the death penalty for a particular offense, to decline extradition unless that penalty is waived. The Canadian government did not exercise this option and instead extradited Mr. Kindler to Pennsylvania. Kindler submitted a communication to the UN Human Rights Committee challenging Canada's actions under the Covenant on a variety of grounds including the fact that he would face the death row phenomena in Pennsylvania. The Committee reiterated its earlier view that prolonged detention is not a *per se* violation but citing *Soering* the Committee held the existence of a violation in a particular case would turn on "relevant personal factors regarding the author, the specific conditions of detention on death row, and whether the proposed method of execution is particularly abhorrent." *Id.* at § 15.3. With regard to Mr. Kindler's claim, however, the Committee pointed out that

> important facts leading to the judgement of the European court [in *Soering*] are distinguishable on material points from the facts in the present case. In particular, the facts differ as to the age and mental state of the offender, and the conditions on death row in the respective prison systems. The author's counsel made no specific submissions on prison conditions in Pennsylvania, or about the possibility or the effects of prolonged delay in the execution of a sentence; nor was any submission made about the specific method of execution.

Id. at § 15.3; *see also Cox v. Canada*, Communication No. 539/1993, U.N. Doc. CCPR/C/52/D/539/1993, at §17.2 (rejecting death row phenomenon challenge to extradition to Pennsylvania). Francisco Forrest Martin, *et al.*, 1 INTERNATIONAL HUMAN RIGHTS LAW & PRACTICE: CASES, TREATIES AND MATERIALS 460-61 (1997).

(4) *Soering* represents a path toward abolition that leads to heightening the pressure on retentionist states to resolve the contradictory values underlying delay in carrying out the death penalty. The European Court was unwilling to demand that state parties refuse to support the death penalty elsewhere with extradition powers, but it was willing to require members to get involved in policing the integrity of the death penalty in other states. The Inter-American Court of Human Rights has used its advisory jurisdiction to foster a similar transnational influence of abolitionist on retentionist states.

In *Restrictions to the Death Penalty (Arts. 4 Sect. 2 and Article 4 Sect. 4 American Convention on Human Rights)*, Advisory Opinion OC-3/83 of September 8, 1983 the Court opined that Guatemala violated Article 4(2) which provides:

> The application of such punishment [death penalty] shall not be extended to crimes which it does not presently apply.

Guatemala executed four men under emergency decree laws for crimes that were made capital long after Guatemala signed the Convention. Guatemala argued that it had preserved its sovereign right to use capital punishment in social defense. It also argued that its explicit reservation to Article 4(4) ("In no case shall capital punishment be inflicted for political offenses or related common crimes") implied a right to continue expanding the death penalty. The Court opined that the reservation to Article 4(4) could not bear on Guatemala's obligations under Article 4(2). By the time of the hearing, however, a new government in Guatemala had already withdrawn the contested capital crimes. In 1986, Guatemala withdrew its reservation to Article 4(4) altogether.

In *International Responsibility for the Promulgation and Enforcement of Laws in Violation of the Convention (Arts. 1 and 2 of the American Convention on Human Rights)*, Advisory Opinion OC-14/94 of December 9, 1994, Inter-Am. Ct. H.R. (Ser. A.) No. 14 (1994), the Inter-American Commission asked the Inter-American Court to consider the obligations of state parties and their agents in the face of actions by the state that "manifestly violate[ ] the obligations it assumed upon ratifying the Convention." *Id.* at §1. The circumstances giving rise to the Commission's request for an advisory opinion was the Peruvian government's decision to add an additional capital crime for terrorism, a decision taken after the arrest of Abimael Guzman, the leader of a revolutionary group, called "the Shining Path." Since Peru's Constitution provided for the death penalty only for treason in time of war, Article 4(2) of the American Convention appeared to bar Peru from subsequently adding the death penalty for terrorism. Without considering the merits of the violation, the Court opined that:

> The enforcement of a law manifestly in violation of the convention by agents or official of a state results in international responsibility for that state. If the enforcement in question constitutes an international crime, it will also subject the agents or officials who execute it to international responsibility.

Id. at § 57. Francisco Forrest Martin, *et al.*, 1 INTERNATIONAL HUMAN RIGHTS LAW & PRACTICE: CASES, TREATIES AND MATERIALS 461-62 (1997).

(5) After *Soering v. United Kingdom*, the Lords of the Judicial Commission of the Privy Council in the UK addressed the death row phenomenon. In *Earl Pratt and Ivan Morgan v. The Attorney General for Jamaica*, Privy Council Appeal 2, A.C.1, 4 All E.R. 769 (P.C. 1993) (*en banc*), the petitioners had served fourteen years on death row including three times on which they were moved to a special cell for the condemned. In each case new legal challenges by their attorney's resulted in stays of execution. While acknowledging that defendants naturally played a role in extending the delays, the Privy Council condemned the inherent cruelty of allowing the process to stretch on so long.

The Privy Council concluded that, in all Commonwealth countries, a delay of more than five years would constitute presumptive proof of death row phenomenon. In the wake of vacating scores of death sentences because of the *Pratt & Morgan* holding, several Caribbean countries have reacted by withdrawing from international human rights treaty mechanisms. Jamaica withdrew from the Optional Protocol to the ICCPR, and Trinidad and Tobago has announced its withdrawal from the ACHR. *See* Natalia Schiffrin, *Jamaica Withdraws the Right of Individual Petition under the International Covenant on Civil and Political Rights*, 92 AM. J. INT'L L. 563 (1998).

Although U.S. Supreme Court Justice Antonin Scalia rejected the authority of foreign cases in *Stanford v. Kentucky*, others of his colleagues on the Supreme Court continue to use such cases. Mr. Justice Stevens cited *Pratt and Morgan v. Attorney General* in his dissent to the denial of certiorari in a case involving a prisoner who had spent seventeen years on death row and raised the "death row phenomenon" issue under the 8th Amendment. *See Lackey v. Texas*, — U.S. —; 115 S.Ct. 1421 (1995) (Stevens, J. dissenting). Justice Breyer also joined that dissent. Stevens and Breyer also cited *Pratt and Morgan v. Attorney General* and *Makwanyane & Mchunu* in their dissents in *Gomez v. Fierro*, — U.S. —; 117 S.Ct. 285 (1996).

Several lower courts also have considered the death-row phenomenon, but thus far without reversing a death sentence. In *McKenzie v. Day*, 57 F.3d 1461, 1466 (9th Cir. 1995), Judge Alex Kozinski cited *Pratt & Morgan*, and *Soering* but rejected the factual analogy, finding that the evidence did not suggest that the fault for the long delay in executing McKenzie (he had been on death-row for 20 years at that point) was Montana's. Further, Judge Kozinski raised the concern that recognizing the death-row phenonemon as an 8th Amendment violation would undermine the administration of capital punishment.

> By and large, the delay in carrying out death sentences has been of benefit to death row inmates, allowing them to extend their lives, obtain commutation or reversal of their sentences, or in rare cases, secure complete exoneration. Sustaining a claim such as McKenzie's would, we fear, wreak havoc with the orderly administration of the death penalty in this country by placing a substantial premium on speed rather than accuracy.

McKenzie v. Day, 57 F.3d 1461, 1467. In a vigorous dissent, Judge William Norris, cited the international cases as powerful support for the substantiality of McKenzie's 8th Amendment claim and accused the majority of substituting a "policy lecture" for a serious analysis of the penalogical justifications for executing those who have been held on death-row for extremely long periods. *Id.* at 1488-89. Francisco Forrest Martin, *et al.*, 1

(6) Finally, note that the Statutes of the ICT-Y, ICT-R, and ICC do not allow the use of the death penalty. Given the fact that the crimes covered by the these statutes address violations of *jus cogens* (which is not subject to the persistent objector rule governing the rest of customary international law) and that these statutes have and/or shortly will be globally accepted by states, how would you argue that there now is a *jus cogens* prohibition against the death penalty for *all* crimes by virtue of the fact that the crimes covered by the statutes are considerably worse than other common capital crimes?

INDEX